Mary Grace

The Communion of Saints

Talking to God and Grandma

The Communion of Saints
Talking to God & Grandma
Mary Grace

Cover image: Shutterstock.com
Cover and book design: Tau Publishing Design Department

For information regarding permission, write to:
Tau Publishing, LLC
Attention: Permissions Dept.
4727 North 12th Street
Phoenix, AZ 85014

ISBN 978-1-61956-119-9

First Edition April 2013
10 9 8 7 6 5 4 3 2 1

Published and printed in the United States of America by Tau Publishing, LLC
For additional inspirational books visit us at TauPublishing.com

TauPublishing.com

Words of Inspiration

Dedication

This book is dedicated to all those who are struggling: To those who are struggling financially and to all who are hard pressed to find a job during our economic crisis. Moreover, this book is dedicated to those who are struggling with mental and physical illness, as well as to their families and caretakers. This book is devoted not only to the brave people who are in the midst of their battles, but to the courageous souls who have lost the fight, and are now living with the angels. For it is in our common pain that we have forged a community here on earth, with our loved ones in heaven. It is in our shared struggles that we have formed a communion of saints. May this story be a beacon of light and hope in a time of darkness and despair; for I'm here to remind you that "Everything is going to be all right."

A special dedication goes out to Mom and Dad, Millie and Harry Moran, for giving me my faith foundation and for teaching me to pray to the saints; which helped me through my own struggles.

In addition, this book is dedicated to my mentor, Father Alphonsus Trabold, OFM of St. Bonaventure University, for seeking truth in science and religion, and for answering my prayers.

Finally, this book is dedicated to my best friends, Mikey and Lucey, who were my constant writing companions, despite their own physical struggles in their final years.

Proceeds

Fifty percent of all profits from the sale of this book will go to various non-profit organizations, which include, but are not limited to, the following:

The American Cancer Society
Catholic Charities
Call To Action
The Lily Dale Assembly
The International Association of Near-Death Studies
Spiritus Christi Catholic Church of Rochester, NY
Chiapas, Mexico Outreach Program of Spiritus Christi
St. Bonaventure University in Olean, NY
National Resources Defense Council

The other fifty percent of profits will go to "Gifts of Grace" Ministry to help educate and counsel the church on earth regarding paranormal, supernatural, mystical, and near-death experiences.

Endorsements

"From near-death experience to that silent moment in nature, God speaks to us in mysterious ways. In this important book, Mary Grace engages the Catholic Faith in a long overdue dialogue about the many experiences of a living God that exists outside church doctrine. I highly recommend this book to anyone who would like to investigate the omni-presence of God and the many manifestations of Spirit as the Word."

Rene Jorgensen, Founder of NDE Light and author of The Light Behind God: What Religion Can Learn From Near Death Experiences

"*Communion of the Saints: Talking to God and Grandma* is a very powerful book. The author presents a compelling case for the Catholic Church and other institutions to accept the reality of after-death communication (ADC) experiences and their healing ability as a normal and natural part of human life."

Bill Guggenheim, Coauthor of the international bestseller,
Hello From Heaven!

"Mary Grace had a firsthand afterlife communication causing her to question her church and her place in society. After having a second spiritually transformative experience, her reality changed and so did the course of her life. In this book she tells of the disenfranchised people that are seeking a way to have a relationship with God and their deceased loved ones. Through her extensive research she displays in simple to understand terms the history, science and religious history of afterlife communication; thus, giving us a roadmap toward a more progressive church model."

David Bennett, Upstate New York IANDS Director and author of
Voyage of Purpose: Spiritual Wisdom from Near-Death Back to Life.

Many works of intuition are not based on scholarship. Academic books often lack the spirit of mysticism. Mary Grace has given us a lively tweener. While supplemented by the guidance of inspiration, her study of the supernatural and paranormal in Catholic tradition capably blends insights from important sources and gives something useful to readers of any perspective.

Mason Winfield, author of ten books on the paranormal, including A Ghosthunters Journal: Tales of the Supernatural *and* The Strange in Upstate New York.

Although I found the information to be fascinating, especially her response as to how she got involved with the spirit world in childhood, I was most impressed with Mary Grace's in-depth revealing of her journey and her soul. I appreciate the clarity, simplicity and honesty with which she shares her experiences in talking with God.

Dennis Cole, Transpersonal Astrologer and author of Metaphysics of Love: The Journey to Meet Self

Foreword

Every time I prepare my Sunday homily, I light a candle. Not just any candle. The one I light is a gift from a very spiritual woman in our parish, Kateri Flannery. Kateri always prayed for my homilies over the years. I felt confident knowing her prayers were connecting me to the Holy Spirit for inspiration. She also gave me numerous long-burning candles for Christmas and Father's Day. Her unexpected death from renal cancer at age 47 left me and many others deprived of her love and guidance. However, since I still have many of her candles in my cabinet, I bring one out and light it every time I prepare for preaching. I leave the candle burning from start to finish, usually most of Saturday. In addition, I call upon my deceased mother and father to guide my preparation. With the candle burning and all three interceding, I know God will give me the right words for the people to hear.

Mary Grace's book is about the Communion of Saints, the spiritual solidarity that binds together those on earth with those in heaven. We are all in union with one another. But Mary pushes beyond our ability to talk with those in heaven or to call on them for help, like my example above. She says the church needs to teach people how to SEE and HEAR them, as well as call upon them. When people move to another part of the country, we discover ways to communicate with them through email, phone, Facebook, etc. We can also have conversations with God—and Grandma—and Kateri—and Mom and Dad. If we quiet ourselves and listen, we can do it. The key is our sixth sense, extrasensory perception. It's a power that lies dormant in everyone, but it can be developed.

While Mary Grace desires to show people how to communicate with loved ones who have passed, she finds obstacles to this in her

Roman Catholic Church. When she tried to discuss a visitation and conversation she had with her mother shortly after her death, the priest she approached wouldn't hear it. He didn't want to have anything to do with after-death communication or near-death experience; he legally expelled her from her small-town church. Under orders from this priest, Mary Grace was threatened by police with being arrested for trespassing if she attended Sunday Mass; she was effectively excommunicated.

Despite the hurt of this rejection, Mary Grace did not brood over it and remain stuck in the past. Following Jesus' instruction, she shook the dust off and continued to abide by the truth inside her. She knew the Holy Spirit spoke to people like her as well as to the hierarchy. She wanted others to understand her valuable insights.

The book points out the church's inconsistency. On the one hand, church tradition reveres its mystics—people who have psychic abilities, who are centered on God, and who have two-way conversations through meditation. At the same time, the church condemns mediums—people who are go-betweens, between humans and non-physical beings like angels, saints, and Grandma. This practice is called "spiritualism." It includes prophesy, gifts of tongues, healing, and visions. People in heaven are accessible by both mystics and mediums. However, church leaders have labeled mystics good and mediums bad. Invoking the saints is good, they say, but conjuring up the dead is bad. "What's the difference?" she asks. Mary Grace herself practices spiritualism, and is therefore not in good standing with the hierarchy.

In the spirit of John the Baptist, Mary Grace boldly goes ahead of the institutional church and prepares the way for people to embrace a broader understanding of the Communion of Saints. She hopes that the reader will see that psychic abilities are good and trustworthy, not some evil force of the devil. They are gifts from God to be used. She explains how everyone vibrates at a certain frequency. Mystics and mediums vibrate at higher levels than the majority. However, we can all raise our levels through certain practices, as outlined by the author. In this way, we can have two-way conversations with our departed loved ones.

I am grateful for the years of extensive research Mary Grace put in to prepare this enlightening and encouraging book. I am glad she trusted God's guiding Spirit within her, despite external reprimands from the larger church. And what a bonus it is for me that she is part of our own faith community.

Father James B. Callan
Associate Pastor, Spiritus Christi Church
Rochester, NY

Preface

It all started when Mom died - and then I died. My psychic and spiritual gifts were awakened. It was like discovering that I had wings; I was learning how to fly. Because I was not able to share this discovery with anyone in my Roman Catholic community, I became very withdrawn and isolated. Every day I spent hours meditating, praying, and walking to the nearby lake so I could spend time with God and his holy spirits; I also enjoyed exploring my new-found abilities.

In addition, I began learning all that I could about my non-physical being by reading books. One of the many gifts I received from my trip into the The Light was an insatiable thirst for knowledge. As a result, reading every New Age topic, as well as books on the great saints and mystical teachers, became my obsession. After about a year of seclusion, I was compelled to spread my wings and started taking many metaphysical classes. Like a spiritual sponge, soaking up vast amounts of new information and experiences, I not only learned how to fly, but how to soar. In addition, meeting other like-minded people made me realize that I was not so strange; as a result, my self-confidence began to grow.

Subsequently, I wanted to share my knowledge and experiences with others. Armed with conviction, I started teaching my own spiritual workshops and began speaking in public about my supernatural encounters. By that time I had been excommunicated for over a year and was happy at my new parish community, Spiritus Christi. However, it has always been my dream to present my classes and talks in the faith community I was raised. I wanted to help other Catholics to better understand their spiritual gifts and paranormal experiences, without having to go through what I did. But how could I get my message to those within the walls of the Roman Empire, since I was not allowed inside?

One day, the answer to my question was revealed. It was the winter of 2003, during a meditation class, when I received an angelic message that started me on a new path. In a state of deep contemplation, I saw the image of a seagull. At the same time, I heard a clear voice in my head say the word, "JONATHAN." I was immediately reminded of a book I had read as a teenager entitled Jonathan Livingston Seagull, by Richard Bach. Intrigued by the message, I went home, found the original copy of the book in my office library, and read it. That's when my mission became clear. Jonathan's story is also my story, let me explain.

Banished Bird

Jonathan Livingston was a young seagull who wanted to learn how to fly as fast and as high as he could. Flying was all he cared about, more than eating or hanging out with the other gulls. His parents scolded him for his odd behavior and told him that he should be more like the rest of the flock. He tried for a while but was only frustrated. He could not see the point of scavenging for food when he could be soaring high above the clouds.

So Jonathan followed his passion and did just that. He learned to do fantastic tricks like the loop, the inverted spin, the gull bunt and the pinwheel. He flew to heights that no other gull had ever flown and was able to reach death-defying speeds of over one hundred miles an hour. But one evening, when Jonathan returned to the Flock, after a full day of spectacular flight, he was greeted by a Council Gathering and the Elder Gull:

> Jonathan Livingston Seagull," said the Elder, "Stand to Center for Shame in the sight of your fellow gulls!" "....for his reckless irresponsibility," the solemn voice intoned, "violating the dignity and tradition of the Gull Family..." (38-40)

Jonathan was devastated; to be centered for shame meant that he would be banished from gull society and would live in exile on the Far Cliffs. Moreover, Jonathan was confused; he could not understand what was so terrible about flying in new ways. Furthermore, he could not understand why others would not want the same wonderful experiences that he had.

Although he was saddened by his loss of community, Jonathan went on to enjoy living a life in which he was free to fly as fast and as high as he could. Eventually, the time came when his lessons on earth, as well as his exile, ended. The seagull died and went to heaven, where he learned how to fly even faster and higher, how to transcend time and space, and how to move from one place to another in an instant. In addition, he understood that his true nature was perfect and unlimited; most importantly, Jonathan learned about kindness and love.

But all the while, the banished bird never forgot about his Flock back on earth and never stopped wondering if there were one or two gulls who wanted to spread their wings and fly like him. And so Jonathan returned to the physical world, and to the flock he had been exiled from, to teach them everything he had learned.

After reading Jonathan Livingston Seagull, I cried. I identified with the title character and knew exactly how he felt. I was living as an outcast from the flock because of my newfound abilities; and like Jonathan, I died and went to heaven. In addition, I never forgot about the community I was banished from and often wondered if there were others who wanted to explore their spiritual gifts.

The message I received on the day I had the seagull vision was profound; my mission became crystal clear. Like Jonathan, I returned to earth and felt compelled to return to the Flock I was banned from, to teach others new ways to fly. Although I was living in exile, my lessons could be conveyed through the written word. My literary voice could pierce through even the thickest Roman Catholic walls. Perhaps someone would listen, and perhaps a shift would occur in the very foundation of the church.

Introduction

In 1898 the Roman Catholic Church made its first official proclamation against spiritualism. Pope Leo XIII condemned the practice and threatened to excommunicate anyone who participated in séances or acted as a medium. The decree was essentially a restraining order, which forbid church members from any contact with their deceased family and friends. Instilling great fear upon its people, the Vatican locked the door to our loved ones in heaven and hid the key. Over one-hundred and fifteen years later, the key has been found; you are holding it in your hands.

Cleverly concealed in plain sight, an obscure church doctrine, unbeknownst by most Catholics, reveals how spirit communication does not go against the official teachings of the church, and in fact was found to be a practice that can enrich the faith. These findings, in support of spiritualism, which have been hidden from the faithful in secret church investigations and classified documents, will be revealed to the reader. New light will be shed on the truth that the Vatican sought so hard to suppress for over one-hundred years. The door to the afterlife has been opened, the restraining order has been lifted, and Catholics can once again talk with their deceased loved ones without fear. Relief from our grief is at hand; the healing begins here, with the Communion of Saints.

What is the Communion of Saints?

The "communion of saints" is basically the cosmology of the church. This Roman Catholic doctrine acknowledges the eternal relationships existing between members of the church who live in three different states, or dimensions: heaven, earth, and purgatory. It is through this teaching that the church recognizes and encourages relationships between those in the physical and non-physical worlds, or between the living and the "dead." For example, the on-going interaction that many on earth share with St. Anthony (finder of lost articles) or Mary, the blessed Mother of Jesus.

The Issue

As long as there are people dying, there will be people left behind who long to maintain the connection with a loved one who has passed. For Roman Catholics, however, it is more difficult because the church prohibits the faithful from practicing spirit communication, also known as "spiritualism." At the same time, the church encourages its members to pray and talk to the saints for guidance, favors, and for intercessions. This comes under an obscure doctrine known as the "communion of saints." This contradiction in church teachings results in a huge dilemma for the average Catholic, resulting in fear and confusion. If we can talk to God and the saints in heaven, then why can't we talk to Grandma in heaven?

Due to this contradiction, there is discrepancy on how church authorities treat those who possess paranormal abilities. On the one hand they revere our Christian mystics, while on the other hand they condemn psychic mediums. This has led to the discrimination and humiliation of some our most gifted members of the church, who are often shunned and excluded from their own parish communities. In addition, because of the fear and stigma attached to spiritualism, Catholics are afraid to even talk about a "sign" received from a deceased loved one, an event that should be cherished and celebrated, not condemned and kept secret.

My Purpose

After finding myself the target of this discrimination from church authorities, which led to my excommunication, I felt the need to educate Roman Catholics about supernatural phenomena and the importance of maintaining relationships with loved ones in heaven. By integrating my knowledge and experience of Catholicism, with my knowledge and experience of the paranormal, I felt I could facilitate much needed changes in Roman Catholic policies regarding spiritualism. The educational vehicle I'm using is a rather ambiguous, but foundational church doctrine called the "communion of saints."

With education, fear of the supernatural will be eliminated. This will put an end to the ostracization and emotional abuse caused by excluding God's mystical and psychic children from the Roman Catholic Church. As a result, others who have been misunderstood or mistreated because of their paranormal abilities or experiences, will be recognized as valued members of the church and, therefore, welcomed into the community.

Looking at the communion of saints doctrine through the eyes of a parapsychologist will help reveal the role that spiritualism plays in the Catholic faith. Speaking in a language that Catholics understand, my explanations will illustrate how science can, and does, support our belief in life after death; it simply uses a different language. Although it may seem at times that I am stretching the boundaries for all who consider themselves "good Catholics," it is my intent to write nothing that goes against the teachings of the faith that I hold dear.

Overview

In Talking to God and Grandma, I invite the reader to join me on a spiritual journey to discover that supernatural experiences are not a thing of the past; they are alive and well in the twenty-first century. It is quite normal to have a paranormal encounter, especially when it comes to after-death communication.

Supernatural occurrences happen every day to people throughout the world. What are they to do, however, when such an event happens? Should they tell someone? Would they be believed or told that they are crazy? Is it a good thing to get a sign from Grandma, or is it evil? What does it mean and how does it fit in with our religion? Integrating a supernatural event into our belief system can be a formidable task.

The communion of saints is an intriguing doctrine of faith because it is a little understood church teaching that has enormous implications. From a parapsychological viewpoint, this new interpretation will encourage the reader, as well as church leaders, to reexamine their beliefs about life after death and to consider alternate levels of reality that are an integral part of the Catholic faith. More importantly, this modern-day view of an ancient church principle changes the entire concept of what it means to be "truly Catholic."

Through interviews with many priests, mediums, and mystics, this book takes an inside look at the taboos that prohibit people from participating in the spiritual realms, and reveals how these same taboos are practiced in the Catholic Mass. In addition, a secret church investigation, as well as a classified doctrine on mediumship, apparitions, and revelations, will be disclosed. These were suppressed due to their positive findings in support of spiritualism. In the end, there are three important elements to this book I can promise the reader will agree with--that it is educational, inspirational, and controversial.

The Format

Talking to God and Grandma is set up in three parts. In Part I, *My Story*, I share my paranormal experiences, along with the struggles and numerous questions I had regarding my faith. Throughout the book, you will come across these questions in the section that addresses them; the answers, however, are not always clear-cut.

Part II, *We Believe in the Communion of Saints*, is the history of the communion of saints, as well as its many interpretations. This section also describes how "spiritualism," "parapsychology," and "supernatural phenomena," are an integral part of Catholicism.

In Part III, *We Practice the Communion of Saints,* you will be guided through exercises to teach you how to contact loved ones who have crossed over, as well as other holy spirits, such as canonized saints. In addition, you will learn how to maintain relationships with your family and friends in heaven. In the end, you will not only believe in the communion of saints, you will have practiced the communion of saints.

The Mission

With the complete understanding of the communion of saints, the fear and stigma attached to psychic phenomena and the supernatural will be dispelled. Contacting our dearly departed and participating in the spiritual realms will no longer be taboo. First-century thinking about the paranormal will be forever changed in light of twenty-first century knowledge. By integrating the science of parapsychology with Christian Theology, mysticism and modern-day Spiritualism, we will come to truly comprehend what we mean when we profess, "I believe in the communion of saints." We will then realize what it means to be a truly universal and all-inclusive church; as a result, a new age of Catholicism will dawn.

Contents

Heaven

I saw The Light and The Light was me
The veil was lifted, my soul set free
No longer confined to this body I wear
My spirit released from all earthly cares

I shed all my doubts, worries and fears
I know that my real home is not here
This reality is no longer mine
This is just the illusion of time

Heaven is where I long to be
With those who can remember me
And the love of God that we all share
The kind that exists on earth, nowhere

Soul recognition comes not from the eyes
But from somewhere much deeper inside
And in my spirit, where His love is true
My heart and my soul remembers you

With Unconditional Love,
Mary Grace

Part I
My Story

Chapter 1
Death and Dreams

"In the depth of your hopes and desires lies your silent knowledge of the beyond;
And like seeds dreaming beneath the snow your heart dreams of spring.
Trust the dreams, for in them is hidden the gate to eternity."
(Kahlil Gibran, *The Prophet*)

A Visitation

Two months after my mom died - she came to visit me. Asleep in my cozy waterbed, I thought I was dreaming; it started out that way. In my dream-like state, I was packing up boxes of my mother's belongings; it was shortly after her funeral. Suddenly, there was Mom. She bent over one of the boxes and pulled out two lit candles, a white one and a blue one, and handed them to me. I thought to myself, "How odd to have lit candles packed in a box." I took the candles and turned around to set them on the dresser. As I set them down I had the sudden realization that Mom had died; it couldn't be her. Hoping to clear my head of the obvious illusion, when I turned around I expected her to be gone. To my surprise, her serene figure remained.

"Mom, you're dead!" I stated with amazement. Confused by this strange circumstance, I doubted my eyes. She appeared much different than I had remembered. Over the years I had watched leukemia shrink her face into a pale thin mask. Now, however, she looked so young and healthy and I somehow knew she could not possibly be dead. But still I questioned, "Oh Mom, is it really you?" As soon as I spoke, I knew it was actually her and that she was very much alive. With this sudden realization I scolded her for not coming sooner, "I've been waiting and waiting to get a sign from you. Where have you been?" With a familiar smile my mother simply stated, "I'm here for you now, Mary."

Mom had returned! I threw my arms around her with great joy. We held each other and I could feel the touch and warmth of her body. She was very solid and very real. I then realized that I was sitting on her lap and we were cuddled in a rocking chair. As we held each other she consoled me by stroking my hair and saying over and over, "Everything's going to be all right, everything's going to be all right." She was rocking me like I was four years old, except I was now a forty-year-old woman. At this time in my life however, I had been feeling like a lost little girl who needed her mother. Her words of comfort brought relief to the deep grief that had been in my heart. I felt wrapped in a blanket of calmness that settled within me and for the first time, in many worrisome years, my soul, along with hers, was at peace.

Although my body was sleeping, I was wide-awake, and profoundly aware that this was no dream. I was no longer in my bed, but in a place that was somewhere between my world and my mother's. Surrounded only by white light, the room we were in disappeared and we were suspended in some sort of empty space. The only solid object was the rocker we were snuggled in. I was not concerned about my location however, I was with Mom and nothing else mattered.

The next thing I knew, I awoke in bed. Still feeling the presence of my mother's arms around me, tears of joy streamed down my face. Tears turned into sobs and wakened my husband who was lying next to me. "What's Wrong!" he exclaimed. "It's Mom!" I cried. "She was just here; she was holding me. She's alive - she's really alive! Oh my God, Mom is *not* dead; her spirit still lives!"

This profound realization changed the entire course of my life. It was one thing to be raised learning about eternal life, it was quite another thing to encounter it. I experienced help and comfort first-hand from someone living on the other side. I had fallen down into a pit of despair and my mother helped me back up. Before I went to sleep that night, heaven and life-after-death were just a concept to me. When I awoke, it became my new reality.

With this new reality I knew that Mom was still alive and still very much a part of my life. She had gone away to be with the Lord, but came back, if but for a moment, to be with me. Mom somehow found a way to let me know that "everything would be alright." I knew deep in my heart that she was not dead and I would somehow find a way to get in touch with her again. Our relationship did not end when she left her physical body; I would be sure that it never did. I decided to do whatever it would take to learn how to maintain that relationship and how to communicate with her. I had no idea how, but I was determined to find out. This after-death connection, with my mother's living presence, was my first personal encounter with the communion of saints.

For my mother, everyone called Millie, was indeed a saint. A devout Catholic, she raised six children on the income she received from mopping floors and scrubbing toilets at the Conesus Lake Nursing Home for over twenty-five years. Her strong faith helped her survive not only us kids, but also the years of struggle in a difficult marriage. Despite her challenging life, she was the embodiment of a true Christian. Everyone loved her kind, compassionate personality and her quirky sense of humor. Our front porch was the neighborhood hangout and my mother was the neighborhood mom. We always seemed to have an extra person at the dinner table or living in one of the many rooms of our huge Victorian house. Millie never turned anyone away.

Now I was not about to turn Millie away, after she made the effort to reach out to me. I could no longer act as if she were dead and could not ignore her presence in my life. For days I remained on a spiritual high from the intense love and peace that I felt when I was reunited with her. That high however, turned into an emotional low as we were separated once again. It was like she died for a second time. The two months of grieving I had gotten through abruptly ended, and I now had to start all over again. I felt like I did on the day of the funeral. Even though I knew she was still alive and able to contact me, I still had to grieve the loss of her bodily presence.

This time however, was different.

This time I had a new awareness that even though mom had passed, she was not gone from my life. Although I still had to grieve the physical separation, I no longer had to grieve the emotional separation. We would never again be apart, no matter what anyone else thought or said to me. It was our secret; it was our shared moment in time. More importantly, it was an extremely personal event that no one could ever convince me was not real.

There were two things that made me believe in the reality of this event. First of all, two hours after I woke up, I was still shaking and crying from the experience; I was an emotional wreck. Furthermore, I called my best friend, Angie and in between sobs, I explained my angelic encounter to her. Dreams don't have that kind of effect on you. Dreams usually fade from your memory shortly after waking up. The second thing that made the visit authentic was that I had no memory of being held as a child. I do, on the other hand, have a very clear memory of my mother rocking me in her arms that May of 2000, two months after she died.

The Research Begins

This after-death encounter caused an intense desire to know all I could about Mom's new home; I also felt a longing to reconnect with her. So I went to Borders bookstore to find information about the afterlife and spirit communication. This was my introduction to metaphysics, what many call New Age thinking. I was exposed to a whole other world when my Mom came to visit me, and that exposed me to a whole other field of science and spirituality. Due to my religious beliefs, this section of the bookstore was always taboo to me; now it was my salvation. I needed to understand and learn all I could about what happened to me and how to get back in touch with Mom; I bought a stack of books.

After reading my many metaphysical books, I learned that my supernatural experience was commonly known as a "dream visit" or simply a "visitation." It was also called an "after-death communication" or ADC. An ADC occurs when departed family members or friends spontaneously and directly make themselves known. There is no medium or third party involved and no rituals or oracles are used to "summon" the deceased person (Guggenheim & Guggenheim).

Often this contact from our spiritual friends comes in the form of "signs" such as flickering lights, an identifiable odor or the movement of physical objects. Other times they may make actual appearances, called "apparitions." It is quite common for people to receive signs from a loved one who has passed; something that caused them to "just know" it was from that particular person. My mom simply chose to come in a dream. It is the easiest way for spirits to communicate because we are naturally in an altered state of consciousness. After-death communications will be discussed in depth in Chapter 11.

I also learned that when loved ones in heaven contact us they often employ the use of our sixth sense, which is also called our psychic ability or extrasensory perception (ESP). As a college student I had taken a class in parapsychology and even participated in some experiments involving ESP. I was very aware of psychic phenomena but never thought about it in relation to contacting spirits. The paranormal subjects I studied were relegated to matters that occurred within the physical world, for example remote-viewing and the ability to move objects with the mind. When we use our ESP to communicate with the non-physical world, it is called "mediumship;" I never learned that in college.

Experimenting

I read all I could about developing my ESP so I could once again make contact with Mom. I found that anyone could learn to communicate with souls in heaven, the key was meditation. So I started meditating every morning and night to learn how to quiet my mind to receive information from the spiritual realms. After a while things started happening. I found that I often "just knew" things; I was having psychic experiences. These things did not usually happen during meditation, but often when I was doing mundane things like washing dishes or taking a shower.

One of the first psychic experiences I had occurred on a Sunday morning, while getting ready for church. I was in the bathroom, putting on makeup while singing "How Great Though Art." To my surprise, the very same hymn was the opening tune for Mass that day. It became a game for me each week to see if I would "just know" one of the songs that the choir selected that morning. It was fun and cool when it worked. The more I practiced, the better I got at it. In retrospect, I believe meditation opened me up to paranormal experiences, in the same way that contemplative prayer did for our many saints and mystics.

One day I decided to try a meditation exercise that was in a book I was reading by James Van Praagh, *Talking to Heaven*. This exercise was different than the many relaxation methods I tried. The purpose of this meditation was to put me in touch with a loved one who had passed. I got into a comfortable lotus position, relaxed my mind and before long found myself in the most beautiful garden. Seated on a comfortable park bench, I was surrounded by the most brilliant wildflowers; their colors were incredibly vibrant. Above me was a sapphire blue sky and below my feet was the cool, emerald green grass.

As I surrendered to the peace and serenity of the sanctuary, I soon found my mother seated beside me. There she was, as real and alive as the last time we met. She gave me the warmest smile and we embraced with joy as we were reunited once again. Words were not spoken or needed, as our souls burst with elation upon the meeting. Although the encounter lasted but a few minutes, it was profound.

This was not my imagination- Mom was real and I could feel and touch her, just like in my dream visit. This time however, I was fully conscious. Once again tears of joy came streaming down my face, as I knew that I was actually able to make contact with my mother. I did it, and it was wonderful! It was the sweetest, most heart- touching experience, to know I could continue a relationship with someone I thought was forever gone from my life. Not only that, but it seemed incredibly easy. Through simple visualization, combined with mental messages, a strong intention and a hypnotic-like state, I was able to spend a precious moment with my departed mother.

This was something no one ever taught me in religious education. No one ever taught me that our loved ones in heaven could communicate with us or that we could hold and touch them. No one ever taught me that we can maintain that love-bond and relationship after we are separated by death. No one ever talked about these things in church on Sundays. Yet, for the second time in my life, I experienced communion with the saint who was my mother. It convinced me that something wonderful and exciting was happening; I could not keep such huge events to myself.

I finally got the nerve to share my spiritual encounters with my more open brothers and sisters. They were happy for me and were glad to hear about a sign from mom. They even shared with me their own signs and dreams they had had of her. I sensed, however, that my experiences were somehow profoundly different from theirs. They acted as if it were nice to talk about but no big deal. They were only dreams to them, not reality. I just wanted to shake them and scream, "Don't you understand, Mom is not dead!" They did not seem to "get it" and had no way of knowing to what extent this experience had changed me. At the time, I did not know myself the impact it would eventually have on my life.

That summer, while watching TV, I came across someone who did "get it." I happened upon a television show called *Crossing Over* with John Edward. John is a psychic medium and on his show he demonstrated how he communicated with spirits. He did this by giving validating messages to the family and friends of the living souls that "came through" to him. John often explained and taught that our love bonds continue after death. On a daily basis he demonstrated and confirmed exactly what had occurred to me, an "after-death communication."

I was enthralled with John (a devoted Catholic himself), and he strengthened the conviction of my own experience. He helped me feel somewhat normal about a very not-so-normal subject matter. He understood that we could maintain relationships with our loved ones who have "crossed over."

Losing My Religion

One night, when I was watching John Edward, my very devoutly Catholic, and not so open-minded, brother came to visit; he was shocked by what he saw. He explained that I was a heretic for watching such a sinful show and that it was against the Catholic faith to communicate with spirits. That's when I decided to tell my brother that Mom had visited me and that I was learning how to contact her. I asked him, "How can it be against our religion to talk to Mom?" He explained to me that it was called "spiritism" and that it was evil. He even went so far as to pull out *The Essential Catholic Handbook* and point out the citation stating that spiritism is against the first commandment.

If talking to Mom was against my religion, then I reasoned I would just have to find a new religion. I was not about to disown my mother by staying true to my faith. Mom was real and was alive. I could touch her and hold her and she consoled me after she died. My religion did none of that for me. I did not want any part of a religion that denied the existence of my mother and denied my communicating with her. If that made me evil then so be it.

Besides, it's not like I was, what you call, the "model Catholic." I had questioned many of the beliefs ever since I was a child. Later, as a rebellious teenager, I turned away from the faith, as I found drugs and alcohol more appealing. When I left home for college at seventeen and was no longer forced to attend Mass by my parents, that was the end of my church-going. It wasn't until my late twenties that I rediscovered my faith. I found it in a hospital room, watching a Billy Graham special late one night; I was recovering from one of my many surgeries. Although I had started to go to church again, on the whole I never considered myself a very religious person, and certainly wasn't on any kind of spiritual path. My path was paved with coke, crack and Coors light - survival was the only goal.

I could not, however, simply switch religions just because I did not agree with some of the rules. Being Catholic is not just a religious faith; it's a way of life. It is much like being Jewish. Many of us were raised in a Catholic community and even attended Catholic schools. This is all we know, and it is what shaped and formed the standards and values for our lives. Many of our family members and friends are Catholic as well. We go to church together and have great celebrations for every sacrament we receive. A parish community is like a family and we especially feel so when it comes to funerals. No, changing religions did not seem like an option to me.

I was confused and angry. I was born and raised a Catholic and I loved my faith. Now it wasn't making any sense to me. How could the church leaders preach about eternal life and heaven and at the same time ignore the very real existence and presence of the spirits living in our midst? Furthermore, how could they possibly condemn communicating with our loved ones in heaven? This was not only unchristian-like behavior but also seemed to be a huge contradiction. How can one profess to believe in the saints in heaven and at the same time forbid talking with them? Why and how could it be taboo to talk with my own mother, now that she was living with God?

Although it may be against the church rules to talk with someone from another dimension, apparently in heaven there are no such rules. It seems that our dearly departed are free to make contact with their fellow parish members on earth whenever they feel so inclined. For what happened next in my life was something that none of the books I was reading prepared me for. This was something I did not understand and totally did not expect.

Losing My Mind

One day, while I was in the shower, I was suddenly aware that there was someone in my head - and it was not me. It wasn't like I was hearing voices; it was more like telepathic thought. This presence, which I somehow knew was male, impressed thoughts and feelings on me regarding a friend he had left behind on earth. The friend was a priest who was in the hospital undergoing some very scary tests; I could actually feel his fear. The entity wanted me to tell the reverend that he was with him throughout the procedures; the spirit was holding his hand and comforting him. I had no idea who this person was but in my mind's eye he showed me his involvement in a motorcycle accident; I understood that this was how he died.

Thus began what I called "unsolicited spirit communication." To say it was disconcerting is putting it mildly. Now that my psychic ability had increased, spiritual beings other than my mom began contacting me. They wanted to pass on messages to their earthly family or friends. Often these messages were for people I didn't know very well; some of them were mere acquaintances.

These spirit messages came with incredible feelings of love that went to my very heart and soul, feelings that compelled me to pass the information on. I felt an intense level of compassion, not only for the souls who were sending the message, but also for the people who were to receive them. I often felt the recipient's grief and my heart went out to those I barely knew, as I was living and feeling their emotions. I also learned some valuable lessons in discernment. Not everyone is happy to receive a message from a loved one who has passed. Some people just aren't ready for that kind of knowledge.

It can be quite scary and confusing to suddenly realize that people not of this dimension are communicating with you, and that you sometimes "just know" things about people that you have no earthly business knowing. I reasoned that I would simply keep this part of my life a secret. Besides, how did I know that these are really spirits talking to me? Maybe some sort of psychotic breakthrough caused the thoughts in my head. Maybe I was going crazy after all. I was beginning to question my own sanity. Who would understand, and who could I talk to?

I had no one to talk to about my unique problem because I was pretty much a loner. For most of my adult life I had suffered from the effects of two chronic illnesses. At the age of twenty-three I had developed epilepsy and for seventeen years I had been experiencing six to ten seizures a day. For fourteen of those years I was also extremely sick with an autoimmune disease called "lupus." The effects of my lupus led to five different surgeries and a hole in my heart. My body was slowly killing itself from an over-active immune system.

Due to my health issues, I was on twenty-four different medications and saw five different medical specialists on a regular basis. Weakness, fatigue and the side effects of my prescription drugs caused me to sleep for fifteen-eighteen hours a day. I struggled to keep my twelve-hour a week job as a mental health counselor and activity coordinator. I spent the better part of those years in pain and in bed. For this reason my social life was limited.

Being a country girl and somewhat geographically isolated, only added to my solitary lifestyle. My backyard was a seven thousand-acre wildlife preserve. On my good days, time was spent alone in nature. The social highlight of my week was going to Mass on Sundays, when I was well enough; most of the time I had to stay home and watch it on television. I taught my dog Mikey how to shake his paw with me at the sign of peace. It was a pathetic life and I was spiraling down into a pit of depression from which I had no escape. Now, to top things off, I began to question my own mental health and my grip on reality. I learned to cope with it all by increasing my usage of alcohol and illegal, as well as prescribed drugs. I was lonely and disconnected.

I became very depressed and loathed living in such a cold, cruel world. Mentally I thought I was going crazy. Physically I was dying while emotionally and spiritually I was already dead. I had hit bottom and I just wanted the pain to stop. I was sick and tired of this life and just wanted to be in heaven with my mother; I was homesick. Mom knew how to fix things; she knew how to make everything all right. The one time I needed her most however, she was not there. I never felt so alone in my entire life; I had to do something.

There was only one thing I could think of to do. I went to the cemetery, to be near Mom, and to talk to God; I went to pray. I had much to discuss and many heavy thoughts weighed me down; I no longer had the will to live. From the books I was reading on the afterlife, memories of my life and home in heaven were returning to me. I somehow knew that suicide was not an option. I somehow knew that I had made a contract with God. If I broke that contract then I would just have to return to this world, until I accomplished the mission I came for. But I no longer cared about my purpose in life. However, since I never wanted to come back to this earthly hellhole, I was stuck here.

I felt trapped. For some reason I was not yet dead, and I could not kill myself because of some stupid contract I don't even remember signing. But then I reasoned that with every good contract there is an escape clause. That was it, a loophole! So on the darkest of nights, on my mother's chilly grave, I pleaded with God, "I want out; I want the escape clause. This is all a big mistake, a bad cosmic joke. Ha-ha God, the joke is over, I get it; you won. Now it has to end; I can take no more."

My depression and unanswered prayers soon led to anger-I was pissed. I was furious with God and I told Him so:

Why me Lord, why me? I'm dying here; why do I continue to live? Make up your mind, shit or get off the pot. Either take me home to heaven or heal me. I beg you, just put an end to my suffering. Have you no mercy? Why God, why? Why is all of this happening to me? And why have I been cursed with this ability to hear dead people? What is it all about? I want some answers, damn it.

I demanded that God give me a sign that He had not deserted me. I went so far as to make a deal with Him:

If you give me a sign that you have not abandoned me, and that I am not going crazy, then I will quit drinking. If however, I receive no sign, then - screw you God - all bets are off. I will just drink myself to death.

After what seemed like hours of talking to myself, I finally admitted defeat and went home, emotionally and spiritually bankrupt. It was November first, 2001, All Saints Day.

My Near-Death Experience

The next day, All Souls Day, I got what I prayed for. Popping a couple of ephedrine pills for energy, I went to Rochester to pick up a bag of cocaine, and stopped by the liquor store for a bottle of whiskey. After that I headed towards Borders Book Store to purchase *One Last Time* by John Edward. I was driving on interstate 390 when I got my sign from God. The years of drugs, alcohol and chronic disease had finally taken a toll on my body—I died. I had what is known as a near-death experience, or NDE for short.

What happened was a series of events that began while I was driving down the expressway and led up to my actual death. Most people are familiar with the feeling of hearing a song that seems to speak solely to them and strikes a chord with their very heart and soul-when the words are exactly what you needed to hear at that precise moment in your life. For me it was a song by the 80's rock group, "Styx." The tune that suddenly came pouring out of my car radio was entitled "Why Me." It was a song I knew well but hadn't heard in probably twenty years. The lyrics summed up everything I experienced in the cemetery the night before, along with the very same question I demanded of God, "Why me?" The words that spoke to my broken spirit were the following:

Hard times come and hard times go
And in between you hope and pray the scars don't show.
Life is strange, but so unsure
And days you hardly make it through
You swear that there's a curse on you
And nothing seems to fit. Things don't go your way
You know you've had enough
You have the right to say, "Why me?"

When I heard this song I "just knew" this was my sign and I started sobbing with joy and relief, "My God, My God, you have not abandoned me; thank you, thank you!"

At that very same moment, I was aware that something else was happening to me; I felt an electrical shock surge through my body. It was as if the proverbial lightening bolt of God had struck me. I realized that I was most likely experiencing cardiac arrest, caused in part by the cocaine I had just put up my nose, the amphetamines I had taken a few hours earlier, and the hole in my already weakened and racing heart. But the most amazing thing was the absence of any pain in my chest.

By this time I was near my intended exit and managed to drive the car safely off the expressway. I pulled into the parking lot of Borders and turned off the ignition. For some reason, I noticed the time on the clock; it was 5:15 pm. All I could do was lay my head back against the seat and amid tears of gratefulness and emotional release, I repeated, "Thank you God, thank you. Thank you for not abandoning me."

The next thing I knew, I felt myself floating up towards the brightest, most beautiful light I had ever seen. Upon reaching the brilliant site I had the most incredible experience. I was immersed in a tremendous force of Love that permeated every cell in my body. The Light and Love not only enveloped me but also became me as we merged into one. This level of devotion was not of the world I had come from; it was a million times more intense. Any earthly notion of love was miniscule in comparison.

While in this light, a sense of peace and tranquility settled within my mind and I realized that I was completely free; all bodily cares seemed to vanish. I felt wrapped in a down-filled comforter that engulfed me with a warm sense of security and tenderness. It was like being tucked into bed by a doting grandmother; I relaxed into a total state of surrender. I was being taken care of now and assured once again, that everything was going to be all right. Now was the time for me to rest and to heal in the light and love that saturated my soul. Feeling cradled in the arms of this most magnificent Being, I recognized my long forgotten Creator, my Father in heaven - I was home.

Within this light was a great intelligence and power that caused my consciousness to expand into a knowingness I could not explain. At the same time I felt a gentleness and compassion beyond anything I had ever experienced. The Light made me feel like I was the most important person in the whole universe and nothing that I ever said or did would ever change that. This Being simply reminded me that I was His most precious child and that I was loved no matter what. There were no conditions, ifs, ands or buts. There was simply the purity of unconditional love, a love that was inseparable from me.

I was struck with a profound sense of reverence and awe for the Greatness in which I was not only in, but also a part of. We were two souls sharing an extremely personal and intimate encounter; it was a remarkably humbling and sacred event. It's almost like the feeling you get when you walk into an empty church. You know that you are in the presence of holiness and the only two beings that exist in that moment are you and God; it brings you to your knees.

Condemnation and punishment were concepts that did not exist within the realm and capability of this all-loving presence. I was not there to be judged; I was there to be comforted and held. Nothing else mattered when I was in The Light, not my earthly life or the physical body that I left behind. That world and person became a distant dream and was not the real world or who I really was. Any sins, which I had committed in that previous life, had already been forgiven.

But still, I was curious about the messages that I was receiving from discarnate beings. I wondered if they were real; I wanted proof that I was not a complete lunatic. With that request, I was shown scenes from my past in what could be described as a type of "life review." To explain all that I witnessed and the knowledge I gained is a whole other book. I will say, nevertheless, what I saw and experienced was the proof I needed. Along with that verification, I had a total comprehension of why everything had happened in my life and the role that other people played. People who I thought were unkind to me were only fulfilling their part to help me on my earthly mission and spiritual progression. All the suffering and insanity of my life on earth had a purpose, and therefore made sense; I was not crazy after all.

With this comprehension, the life review was over and I was back in The Light. Without any spoken words, God explained to me,

> *I did all that you asked of me. I gave you proof that you are not going crazy, I gave you a sign that I had not abandoned you, and I brought you back home. You cannot stay however, you must return. Your work is not yet finished.*

I understood completely and felt totally at peace with this decision. I knew I had to go back; I knew it was the right thing to do. In wordless response, I expressed to God that I would do anything He asked of me. How could I refuse anyone who loved me that much? In a complete state of ecstasy and in all that light and love, I would have promised anything, there was nothing I wouldn't do for Him. With that thought, The Light slowly pulled away from me; at the same time, I felt like I was being pulled backwards.

The next thing I knew, I was sitting in my Saturn car in a state of euphoria that was light years beyond any drug high I had ever experienced. I felt fantastic, as if I could conquer the world. As I slowly started to come back to my senses, I tried to process what had just transpired. Although I no longer questioned my sanity, the most incredible and unbelievable event of my life had just taken place. I noticed on my dashboard clock that forty-five minutes had passed since I parked the car; it was now 6:00 pm. "Wow, what the hell just happened?" I ironically said aloud. I was ecstatic over the fact that I had gotten a sign from God. I really wasn't crazy - now I had proof!

It wasn't long however, before reality started to sink in. From the console, I pulled out the bag of cocaine I had just purchased, along with the bottle of whisky that was stashed under my seat. I quickly did the math and realized at this point in time I had been drinking and doing drugs for over 27 years; this was not going to be easy. But a promise was a promise and I knew that I could no longer continue down the road of self-destruction. At the same, I no longer had the desire to drink or do drugs; they meant nothing in light of where I had just been.

When I returned from that most unusual trip I tried to gather my thoughts. Feeling like I was on cloud nine, I floated into the bookstore to make my purchase. I knew right away that something big had happened to me. Although I looked and acted like any other customer, I felt like I was a stranger in another world. It was like seeing life through rose-colored glasses. Everything seemed weird but wonderful to me; I was on a natural high. It was only with time however, that I realized the full extent of what occurred to me the day I saw The Light.

The After-Effects

For months I did not tell anyone what happened, not even my own husband. Everything had changed for me. I saw and experienced things differently. I wasn't sure what to make of it because everything was wonderful, and at the same time, extremely unsettling. Through my new awareness, I could see the light and love of God in all people. An overwhelming sense of connection to everything in the universe became a part of my new consciousness. In addition, I felt tremendous, unconditional love for all living creatures. My heart overflowed with an intense feeling of devotion and joy that was not human.

I became like a lovesick schoolgirl with a crush on some handsome young beau, only my crush was on all of humanity and all living things. I fell in love with everyone. I loved the homeless person on the street as much as I loved my husband. I loved the trees and animals as much as I loved my own family and friends. I loved so much it physically hurt; I felt a constant pain in my chest. I thought my heart would explode and it became clear to me that the physical body was not meant to contain such a force. I had to make up words to express what I was feeling.

I made up the term "passion attacks" to describe the sudden onset of total bliss. These bouts were much like "grief attacks" only for joy instead. They were overwhelming rushes of intense emotion that caused me to cry for no apparent reason. I would cry in sheer exultation at the pure beauty of a single daffodil or a butterfly warming its wings in the sunshine. Whole fields of flowers brought on a total ecstasy as I felt the overwhelming presence of God; it seemed to spew from the meadow like a fountain of love.

Every situation became a new way to experience God. I could feel Him on my face in the warmth of the autumn sunshine. I could feel His presence in each drop of rain that landed on my skin; I called it "liquid love." Walking in the rain was always an exhilarating communion I looked forward to. With the onset of winter, I experienced God in each snowflake that fell from the sky; snowstorms became opportunities for heavenly rapture.

The more extreme Mother Nature was, the better I could feel God's presence; each season brought a new adventure. I could feel Him in the bitter cold wind during a January freeze and in the searing heat of an August sun. I could also hear his voice. I heard it in the soft cooing of the mourning doves and in the excited chatter of the red squirrels in my back yard. I was acutely aware that God was in everything and there was nothing that was not of God.

Feeling His presence gave me more energy and the weakness seemed to be dissipating from my diseased body. I spent hours each day walking Mikey and Lucey, my black Labrador retrievers, through the woods and fields to Hemlock Lake. In addition, my vision became fourth-dimensional, everything stood out like I was seeing the world through a View Master. Colors became extraordinarily vibrant and beautiful. In many ways it was similar to the LSD trips I had taken in the 70's. What struck me the most, however, was the profound sense of love that emanated from all living things. It was this love and new awareness that was quickly healing me.

I was also aware that I was at one with God and all of His creations, including the trees, the plants, the animals, the birds and even the insects. I soon discovered that I could merge with all this life and love that surrounded me. This meant that many of the physical laws no longer applied to me. For example, I discovered that I could leave my body at will to feel what it was like to soar with the bald eagles over Hemlock Lake, or to bob up and down with the Canadian geese surfing on the waves. I could become one with a ripple of water and feel what it was like to drift down a stream.

I liked to merge with milkweed plants and then scatter the seeds to the wind; I could feel what it was like to be as light as a feather and to float on a warm summer breeze. In the winter months I could become one with a snow flake and gently fall from the sky in a profound sense of peace and joy. My favorite past time was "just being." I spent hours and hours "just being" with God's creations and exploring a whole new world that opened up to me.

The more time I spent with God in nature, the stronger our relationship became. The Holy Spirit was a living presence that I could feel in the deepest part of my soul. I was not only obsessed but also possessed by God. For the first time, I truly comprehended the meaning behind Saint Paul's claim, "It is no longer I who live, but Christ who lives in me" (Galatians 2:20).

With this realization, I had an epiphany; I thought to myself, "If God is inside of me, then He must be inside of everyone else too." They didn't teach me this in catechism class either. Furthermore, because I could actually feel this powerful force within me, I fully understood what Jesus meant when he said, "The kingdom of heaven is within you" (Luke 17:21). The mysterious allegories in the Bible were all making sense to me now; I was actually living and experiencing the scriptures.

Although I had heard these words many times before, I was also taught that God was someone who lived outside of me, in heaven. Death was the only way to be with Him, and only if I obeyed all the church rules. As a child, I learned that we are all brothers and sisters in Christ, although I never really understood this either. With full comprehension, I now knew that this was not a Biblical metaphor; this was real. The same life-giving energy that flowed through me also flowed through all people and all living things. This energy was the light and love of our Father in heaven. We truly are all his children; we truly are brothers and sisters. Feeling the presence of

God within me opened my mind to grasp completely the teachings of Christ and where he was coming from. Jesus and God really are one, just as we are all one with the Almighty.

It was clear to me that I was experiencing something most extraordinary. I could not feel the presence of God prior to my near-death experience. I could not feel my connection to everything in the universe before that day; I was like everyone else. Now, however my entire view of the world had changed. For this reason, I could no longer intentionally hurt another creation. I can't even kill an ant because I know that it too has a reason and purpose in life and that God loves that ant just as much as he loves me. I know in reality that the ant and I are connected by the life and love of God.

I also now know that what I do to another, I also do to God because He feels what we feel. For that reason, when I hurt another person, I not only hurt Jesus and God, but most of all I hurt myself, since we are all one consciousness. I now totally understand the meaning behind the words Christ spoke when he said, "Whatsoever you do to the least of my brothers, that you do unto me" (Matthew 25:40). These words will become eminently clear to you during your life review when you get to see, feel and experience the effect you've had on others, including ants.

Through my research I learned that this sense of connectedness to all things is called a "unitive experience." To give an example, I had a most unusual occurrence one day when I was getting out of bed. Suddenly, I felt a stab of pain in my right hand. I swiftly discovered a honeybee squirming and buzzing in my palm, his stinger firmly entrenched in my skin. Apparently he had been on the comforter of my bed and I had the misfortune of finding him.

My first instinct was to save the bee, as I knew he would lose his stinger and probably die. I quickly found a box to put him in so I could carry him outside. As I pulled the stinger out and examined my hand, I knew that the same life-giving force that flowed through the bee was now flowing through me in the form of venom. At this moment in time, I was literally at one with this bee and with God.

With this realization, I was suddenly struck with an overwhelming sensation of love that brought emotional tears to my eyes; I had a "passion attack." With the awareness of my relationship with this bee, in my stinging pain I could feel God's loving presence. I was filled with a deep sense of harmony and exultation as I thought to myself, "How sweet the sting of a bee, when it feels like a kiss from God." With that thought, the pain immediately went away and did not return.

I took the bee outside and freed him to die a natural death. His mission was over and it was time for him to go home, to heaven. Due to the absence of pain and any redness or swelling, I almost thought that maybe the bee didn't really sting me. I was reminded of the reality of it however, a few days later when the bite started to itch incessantly.

Because I could not bear to harm any of God's creations, eating became an event I did not look forward to. I often cursed the body I was in and hated the fact that something had to die in order for me to live. It seemed like an unnecessary sacrifice on the part of many plants and animals that had just as much right to live as I did. It was also very difficult to consume anything I felt at one with, it felt like cannibalism. For this reason, I gave up eating meat. I was keenly aware however, that even the plants had to die in order for me to survive. I would have gladly traded places with the stalk of wheat that became my bread. Why couldn't my life be sacrificed instead?

I knew the importance however, of keeping myself physically, mentally and spiritually healthy. Because I could feel the presence of the Holy Spirit inside of me, I understood the true meaning behind the words "Your body is your temple" (1 Corinthians 6:19). I knew that if I didn't take care of my own body that I would be hurting God, for He dwells within me. I wouldn't think of smoking pot or drinking beer in church, yet this is exactly what I was doing when I put these poisons in my body. Each of us is God's church, His temple. I knew that I must show respect for my body for it truly is the house of God.

I learned that I could enter my Father's house whenever I wanted, simply by meditating. By going within, in my daily alpha state, I discovered that I could return to The Light and love that I came to know during my near-death experience. I also found that I could talk to God, as well as Jesus and anyone else I chose. I even met my own guardian angel as well as several guides. Of course, I still kept in touch with Mom and was quite surprised one day to meet my Grandma Rose, whom I don't remember; she died when I was only five years old. Spending time with God and my soul friends became my new addiction. I meditated and prayed for hours each day, as a result, I spent more time communing with the spiritual world than I did with people in the physical world. I became even more of a recluse.

I withdrew from my family and friends and what little social life I had. My heart and home was with God and I knew that I was in this world but not of it. I felt like a stranger here and the things that were once important to me no longer mattered; if it did not affect my eternal life then I had no interest in it. Things like cleaning the house, doing laundry and even opening the mail all seemed so trivial. I also no longer worried about unpaid bills or anything else involving the physical world. I knew this was all just a temporary situation. I also knew that somehow God would take care of everything and besides, why waste time doing something that won't matter when I'm dead and gone anyway? My time was better spent with God.

Since God became the priority in my life, I looked forward to going to Sunday Mass. This proved to be another new way to experience His presence, as I made an amazing discovery. First, I must explain that I had never believed the communion bread was the actual body of Christ. I figured it was just one more of those many symbolic practices our Catholic faith is well known for. After my NDE however, I could see a faint but distinct aura of white light around the Eucharist when the priest held it up for consecration. A halo, much like the ring around a harvest moon, completely surrounded the communion.

It was at that point in time that I truly realized and believed that

Jesus was in fact present in the Eucharist. I knew this circle of light was the Holy Spirit. It was the proof that sealed the conviction of my faith, since I knew that only life has an aura. It was one of the most humbling and enlightening experiences of my life, and continues to be each week at Mass.

It's a Miracle

In the weeks that followed my near-death experience, I noticed significant changes in my body. Within a month's time my energy had gone through the roof. I went from sleeping fifteen hours a night to only four or five. Before my NDE it was all I could do to walk a few hundred yards. Now I was walking my dogs to the lake everyday; it was a two-mile hike. I would also forget to eat, as I rarely got hungry. It wasn't unusual for me to go six or eight hours without even thinking about food. It was much like being on amphetamines. I called this state "spirit mode," as I knew I was simply in touch with my spiritual side, which never needs to eat or sleep.

In addition to the increased activity, I was no longer having seizures. I had a general physical and had all my blood work done, including my anti-nuclear antibody levels. I went to all five of my doctors and got checked-out completely. A stress test was done on my heart and a new EEG of my brain waves. My doctors were dumbfounded when all the tests came back normal; even the hole in my heart was gone. Within a few more months I tapered off all twenty-four medications prescribed for me. For the first time, in over twenty years, I was medication and disease-free. I had been completely healed of two incurable illnesses, lupus and epilepsy. Furthermore, I kept my bargain with God and was also free of alcohol and drug addiction.

Losing My Church
The Downside

On the downside, integration between the two worlds was a

difficult, lengthy and an often depressing process. I found myself on an emotional roller coaster, going between states of joy and anger. As long as I was with God, in meditation or in nature, my feeling was one of bliss. When I had to interact with others, and play the role of wife, sister or professional, I was often frustrated for being stuck in such an unrelenting existence. I was detached from my physical life, and my spiritual life was my new reality. As a result, I became a mental basket case and I knew I needed help.

I decided to go to the one person I thought was trustworthy and who would understand; I went to my priest. I tried to explain to him all that had happened to me. I tried to tell him about the visit from Mom. I tried to tell him how I died and went into The Light. I tried to tell him how I was able to talk with people who were no longer alive. I even had a message from a friend of his, who had passed away several months earlier; the one who died in a motorcycle accident. Still, he would not believe me and thought I was playing a cruel joke on him. Over time I tried to convince him by sending letters and information about after-death communications and near-death experiences. He wasn't buying it however, and was clearly perturbed by my outrageous stories.

At first, my pastor reasoned that it was probably all a hallucination brought on by drugs and alcohol. He then pointed out that I was obviously suffering from a mental illness and needed to see a psychiatrist. Clearly the metaphysical books I was reading brought on my delusional experiences. On the contrary, I was reading those books *because* of the supernatural events that had occurred in my life; they actually helped me. Furthermore, I was accused of dabbling in the occult and treading on dangerous territory.

In the end, I was told that I needed to find another church. I refused and continued to go to Mass on Sundays. One day a police officer showed up at my workplace and told me that I was forbidden to step foot on the grounds of that church. I would be arrested for trespassing if I did. Forever banned from my own parish community —I was devastated.

I could not blame my priest however; I probably would have done the same thing if I were in his shoes. I knew he acted out of fear and was only trying to protect the congregation and himself. We fear what we don't know and don't understand. It was clear to me that seminary school had not prepared him to deal with supernatural phenomena and paranormal parishioners. I simply prayed, "Forgive him Father, he knows not what he is doing." It was this lack of education and compassion however, that I would ultimately devote my life to correcting.

Just My Opinion

This book is about my spiritual journey to discover the truth and where I fit into that truth. I had many, many questions and I wanted answers. My search for the answers turned into a seven-year investigation; it unveiled some interesting discoveries. These findings helped me understand all the reasons behind much of the fear associated with the supernatural and those who participate in it. My purpose is to educate people by sharing my research, my heavenly encounters, and the knowledge I gained as a result.

Just as my mother did not actually die, neither did I. Although my body was dead, "I" was very much alive. For the second time, in a little over a year, I had an encounter with eternal life, this time it was my own. Something happened while I was gone from my body and in the presence of God. The world I returned to was entirely different; everything had changed. I soon realized that it was I, not the world that had been transformed. I was wide awake while the rest of the world was still sleeping. The physical realm became my waking dream and the real world was home, in heaven. But this was no dream, or was it?

Was this a dream or was this reality? My reality before my death was one of drugs, alcohol, and disease. I know now it was just a dream, more like a nightmare. Afterwards, my entire life had changed and I was no longer the person I thought I was. I was no longer that lonely, sick, lost soul who longed for the end of her miserable life. I became a healthy spiritual being who returned with a mission. I found myself, however, in a new nightmare, since I felt my religion had turned its back on me. Now that I finally found God, and was in tune with the heavens, I had become an outcast. I was deeply hurt and ashamed; this became my new reality.

The feeling of injustice never abated and I felt that I must do something. No one should be banned from their faith for continuing a relationship with a loved one who has passed. No one should be forced to choose between their religion and their spiritual gifts. No one should have to go through the hurt and humiliation of being exiled from their parish community. It is my mission to be sure that no one else does.

I have practiced communion with the saints by welcoming all people into my life. It matters not whether they live in heaven or on earth. When we truly connect with God then we can truly connect with each other. I found that through meditation and prayer, I could not only talk with God, but with Jesus, my angels, my guides, and my spiritual family as well. I cannot imagine living my life without all of their constant guidance, strength and inspiration. They are my team of consultants, my biggest motivators, and cheerleaders. They are my comfort and my joy, as well as my consolers and healers. Furthermore, I consider myself an advocate for these unsung heroes by helping people in this world connect with their cosmic cousins.

Through a complete understanding of the communion of saints, the fear and stigma attached to contacting our deceased loved ones, and participating in the spiritual realms, will change. By integrating the science of parapsychology with Christian Theology and modern day Spiritualism, first-century thinking about spirit communication and psychic phenomena will be dispelled. As a result, the alienation of some of the most gifted people in our parish communities will be eliminated. In addition, through the communion of saints, we will better realize what it means to be a truly Catholic, universal, and all-inclusive church.

In closing, the writing of this book, and all that transpired in order for you to be reading these words, was a divine collaboration. It was inspired and choreographed by not only my family and friends in heaven, but a multitude of earth angels as well. Literally hundreds of synchronicities and small miracles occurred throughout the research and writing process. The precise people and information came into my life at the exact moment I needed them. From the beginning, it was clear that this book was written not by me, for I am merely the messenger. It is *through* me, that the communion of saints speak.

Let Me Introduce Myself

I want to end this chapter by introducing myself. I want you to know who I am, who I really am. This is the most important part of my story, because by telling you who I am, I hope to reveal to you who you are too. In the end, we will all have a better understanding of each other. When you know and understand another person you cannot judge him, you can only forgive him. This is what my story is about. So let me introduce myself.

The name by which I am called is Mary Grace, but I am not my name. I am a forty-eight year old white female, but I am not my body. I am of German and Irish descent and I am an American, but I am not my culture. I was raised a Roman Catholic, but I am not my religion. I am heterosexual, but I am not my sexuality. I have been married to the same tolerant husband for over 30 years, but I am not my marital status.

By occupation I am a spiritual counselor and a parapsychologist, but I am not what I do for a living. I went to Geneseo State College and received a degree in psychology and sociology, but I am not what I know. I grew up in the small rural town of Livonia, New York, but I am not from there. I now live in Hemlock, New York, but it is not my home. My biological parents raised me, but they did not create me; I was an orphaned soul who was lovingly adopted.

Who I am, first and foremost and all that matters, is a child of God. I am a holy, divine creation and am perfect in the eyes of my Father. I am the light and the love of God. When he looked upon his creation He saw that it was good. I am worthy by birthright. I am not a sinner, but a child who came to the physical world to make mistakes so I could grow and learn from them. In so doing I will return home with a soul that is more compassionate, more tolerant, more understanding, and therefore closer to God.

My church is the Kingdom of Heaven and my religion is Unconditional Love. To put it in a common phrase, "I am a spiritual being having a human experience." You can't put earthly labels on a spiritual being. None of those labels matter in the presence of God. They mean nothing in the afterlife, or as I prefer to call it, the "beforelife." All aspects of my physical body are only temporal; I have had many human experiences with many labels. My soul, on the other hand, is eternal. I have only one life but have had many incarnations.

You can take all earthly labels away from me and it will not affect who I am. You cannot judge me, only the person you perceive me to be. My body with all the attached labels is all part of the role I am currently playing. They are only illusions of my real self. Any judgments you make about me, are merely judgments about the character I'm playing, in this charade called life. I can't even honestly judge myself because I have forgotten a great deal about my former lives.

The veil of forgetfulness was given to me to wear so that I could remember who I am. I am remembering by learning who I am not, and am recalling more and more each day. The reason I remember more than most is because when I died and went into God's light, He lifted the veil for me. It was not lifted totally, for that would have prevented me from discovering myself. It was lifted just enough so that I could see "The Light" in all people and in myself. I was given a glimpse of divinity and saw it in all of humanity. I was loved without conditions, without labels, and I returned loving others in the same way.

It is my hope that I can pass this knowledge and love onto you and that you in turn can pass it on to others. You are not your body, religion, culture or sexuality. You are not your marital status or what you know; and earth is not your home. Let us journey together, to the mystical world of the supernatural, to discover exactly who you are and where you fit in. Come find your place among the communion of saints and let the healing begin - mind, body and spirit.

The Prophet - On Death

Then Almitra spoke, saying, We would ask now of Death.
And he said:
You would know the secret of death.
But how shall you find it unless you seek it in the heart of life?
The owl whose night-bound eyes are blind unto the day cannot
unveil the mystery of light.
If you would indeed behold the spirit of death, open your heart
wide unto the body of life.
For life and death are one, even as the river and the sea are one.

In the depth of your hopes and desires lies your silent knowledge
of the beyond;
And like seeds dreaming beneath the snow your heart dreams of
spring.
Trust the dreams, for in them is hidden the gate to eternity.

Your fear of death is but the trembling of the shepherd when
he stands before the king whose hand is to be laid upon him in
honour.
Is the shepherd not joyful beneath his trembling, that he shall
wear the mark of the king?
Yet is he not more mindful of his trembling?

For what is it to die but to stand naked in the wind and to melt
into the sun?
And what is it to cease breathing, but to free the breath from
its restless tides, that it may rise and expand and seek God
unencumbered?

Only when you drink from the river of silence shall you indeed
sing.
And when you have reached the mountain top, then you shall
begin to climb.
And when the earth shall claim your limbs, then shall you truly
dance.

–Kahlil Gibran

Chapter 2
Life After Near-Death

A New Journey Begins

"A prophet is not without honor except in his own country,
and among his own kin, and in his own house."
(Mark 6:4)

This is what I call my hodge-podge, transitional chapter. Here you will be introduced to the communion of saints, Spiritualism, and parapsychology. Subsequent chapters will cover each of these topics in more detail. Most important, is the story of my spiritual journey and trying to integrate my paranormal experiences with my religious beliefs.

Supernatural occurrences happen every day to people throughout the world. They happen to Christians and non-Christians, to the educated and uneducated, to our holy men and women of the church, as well as to the laity. Many have heard a disembodied voice call out their name or had objects mysteriously appear or disappear. Some have witnessed an electrical appliance or light fixture come on or go off by itself. Sensing an out-of-place aroma, such as perfume or cigarette smoke, from an unknown source, is not unusual. Sightings of ghosts, angels, and saintly apparitions are well documented throughout the ages. Evidence of the dearly departed living in our midst is a common event. Interaction between the physical and non-physical world takes place all the time.

What are people to do, however, when such an occurrence happens? Should they tell someone? Would they be believed or told they were crazy? Is it a good thing to get a sign from Grandma, or is it evil? What does it mean and how does it fit in with the Catholic faith? Integrating a supernatural event into our belief system can be a formidable task.

Such was the case for me, when I discovered that my spiritual experiences contradicted and challenged the religious beliefs I grew up with. What was common and natural for me, having innocent conversations with "dead people," was really uncommon and even prohibited by rules of the faith. My understanding of Catholicism became uncertain; I had to make sense, not only of my newfound spirituality, but also of my own beliefs. I had to make sense of why I was no longer allowed in my hometown church.

Living in Exile

Getting kicked out of the parish community I had grown up in was one of the most traumatic experiences in my life. It's where I made my first communion, the sacrament of reconciliation and my confirmation. It's where I went to religious education for twelve years. It's where I went to light a candle for my mother every single Sunday for four years, when she was battling cancer. It's where hundreds of our family's closest friends gathered for Mom and Dad's funeral mass. It's where I could pray to God for guidance, it's where many of my prayers were answered. The place I called my spiritual home for over forty years was my refuge.

Under the threat of being arrested for trespassing, I was no longer welcome in my own Father's house; I no longer had refuge. I felt as if someone had plunged the proverbial knife in my heart. To make matters worse, it was as though I had a scarlet letter emblazoned on my chest, only my letter was "U" for "unacceptable. Apparently I wasn't good enough to be a Roman Catholic. The level of pain and humiliation left wounds so deep it took years to heal. I was an outcast and my religion had turned its back on me when I needed her most.

My spirit was broken and I could not understand why things happened the way they did. I could not understand what I did that was so sinful, so horrible, and so unforgivable. I could not understand why I was living in exile from my own parish community. I knew, however, that everything happens for a reason and therefore trusted in God that something good would come of this injustice.

That good showed up in the form of Father Tom Hoctor. It was synchronicity that brought this open-minded minister into my life. He was not only a Catholic priest, but the diocesan psychologist as well. Now retired, for many years Father Tom was chaplain at St. Jude's Chapel, located within Rochester Psychiatric Center. When I learned that this pastor was also experienced in the mental health field, I set up a meeting with him.

It turned out that Father Tom was not only familiar with near-death experiences, he had counseled two other people regarding the phenomenon. I asked the reverend to evaluate me in order to get his professional opinion about my sanity. After telling him my story, he declared me quite competent. More importantly however, he believed me. Thus began a close friendship that started that May of 2002 and continues until this day.

But, I still needed help; my pathetic but "normal" life had been turned upside down. I was literally living in two different worlds and was having a hard time coping with my dual citizenship. Being in the mental health field, I knew that a psychiatrist would put me on medication and probably suggest some hospitalization. This was a God issue, not a medical condition. God had taken over my life and His divine force possessed me. I have since realized that God was there all along; I just didn't feel his presence before because I was spiritually asleep. Now it seemed like everyone else was asleep while I was wide-awake; I was lost and even more confused.

Through my books and research I found that what I needed was a transpersonal psychologist; one who specializes in mystical and transformational experiences. Eventually I found such a person. Linda Heron Wind, Ph.D. was able to give me the assistance I needed. She helped me to integrate my spiritual life with my physical life, but her compassion and understanding was what I needed most.

Although I had spiritual and mental guidance, I was left with the dilemma of where to go to Mass on Sundays. I had been Catholic my whole life and did not want to change my religious faith. There were no alternatives; I lived in a small town with only one Catholic Church, the one in which I was not allowed.

Sure, I could go to another Catholic service in another town, in fact that's what I did at first. I started going to Father Tom's Mass at the Psychiatric Hospital. At least there, no one cared if you talked with dead people. In fact, hearing voices in your head wasn't at all unusual for the parishioners at St. Jude's. Simply going to another church however, did not change the fact that I was considered evil for talking to my deceased mother. Why should I belong to a religion that could not accept me for who I was?

Voicing my concerns to Father Tom, he suggested I try a different type of church. He told me about Father Jim Callan, another open-minded minister, who is part of an independent Catholic community. The two priests have been friends for over twenty years, ever since they met at St. Andrews Seminary School in Rochester, NY. Father Tom explained to me that Callan's parish was different because everyone was allowed to receive communion, regardless of their religious beliefs, marital status or sexual orientation; everyone was welcome there.

This sounded like the place for me, so one Sunday I drove forty-five miles to a church service held at the Hochstein School of Music in downtown Rochester. Let me tell you more about the church that lovingly pulled the knife from my chest and stopped the initial bleeding in my heart. It was, and still is, an integral part of my spiritual journey.

Spiritus Christi

Many know Spiritus Christi as the excommunicated Catholic Church. This is because in August of 1998 the parish priest, Father Jim Callan, was reprimanded for unorthodox practices in his former Roman Catholic community, Corpus Christi. This included blessing gay partnerships, allowing women on the altar, and offering communion to non-Catholics. When Callan was re-assigned to another church, after twenty-two years of service to his beloved parish, the close-knit community was left in shock and despair.

The congregation then turned to associate pastor, Mary Ramerman for direction. For the next two months the community protested Callan's removal and made repeated requests to dialogue with diocesan officials regarding the issues. In response, the diocese fired Mary, along with six other staff members. This negative reaction proved to be the fatal blow to the already disheartened parish.

Rather than continue its fight with the diocese, and bow to the discriminating practices of the Roman hierarchy, nearly half of the 2,700 members decided to leave Corpus Christi to start their own, independent Catholic church. Standing firm in their convictions, while being encouraged by their parishioners, both Callan and Ramerman eventually joined the alternative community in order to remain with their faithful parish family.

The new community renamed itself "Spiritus Christi" because it wanted to be a living testimony to the "Spirit of Christ" and his teachings. They sought to uphold the philosophy of an all-inclusive church and decided that Jesus Christ would be considered their head Pastor. Here Jesus led a flock of lost sheep, many of which had been deemed outcasts by most modern-day religious standards. However, Christ wasn't concerned with the color of his sheep, their marital status, sexual orientation or even their spiritual gifts. This Good Shepherd welcomed all people to his church and to His dinner table. (www.spirituschristi.org).

Ten days after having their first Mass, officials from Rome declared that those who attend a Spiritus Christi service could consider themselves excommunicated. Nonetheless, to this day, Father Jim and Reverend Mary do not regard themselves, or their parish, to be in a state of excommunication, because the penalty was never officially imposed. In an interview, Callan explained, "To excommunicate yourself is like giving yourself a traffic ticket for speeding; you simply don't have the authority to do so." (Grace).

Just a Fact

Excommunication is a penalty that church authorities impose on members whose actions jeopardize the integrity of the Church. It prohibits a person from receiving the sacraments, which includes Holy Communion. It is not meant as a punishment but as an opportunity for reconciliation and repentance. Officially, it does not mean expulsion from the church, but it usually has that effect.

Because I was, in effect, excommunicated from my former parish, I felt that I had nothing to lose by checking out this liberal Catholic community. I did so however, with much trepidation; the first time I attended Mass I was petrified. Being used to a quiet, small town church, I was way beyond my comfort zone. There I sat, a country girl in downtown Rochester, attending Mass in a huge auditorium with hundreds of city people; I knew not a soul. I felt so scared and alone that tears welled up in my eyes; surely this was a big mistake. I was terrified and thought, "What am I doing here?"

As people started filling the seats the place became quite noisy with everyone talking out loud and freely visiting with one another. Between the clamor and the lack of kneelers (due to the stadium seating), I wondered, "How do these people pray?" Despite my irritation, I was sure to get a seat close enough to the altar to get a good view. I wanted to see for myself if the now-familiar aura would be present around the Eucharist during the consecration.

I tried to shift my focus by watching all the activity on the massive stage that lay before me. Several people were busy setting up flowers, a lectern, a sound system and a table, complete with a white cloth, candles, a crucifix, and two glass bowls filled with communion wafers. The once barren platform was quickly transformed into an altar. It was interesting to watch and helped to ease my tension as I began to feel like I was in an actual church.

When the opening music and processional started, the enthusiasm that emanated from the hand-clapping, toe-tapping congregation immediately struck me. The parishioners seemed free to express themselves in whatever way they wanted; many were even dancing in their seats. The excitement was so contagious that I soon found myself clapping along with the crowd and my fear was suddenly replaced with joy.

As the altar servers, readers, sacristans, and priests gathered on the make-shift altar, I was struck by the sight of a female, dressed in a full robe and stole, standing among them; it was Reverend Mary Ramerman. The former associate pastor had been ordained in 2001 by Bishop Peter Hickman of St. Matthew Church in Orange, California. Although seeing a woman priest was strange for me, at the same time, it seemed refreshingly appropriate, as well as empowering; I was delighted.

After Father Jim opened Mass, Reverend Mary asked the congregation to introduce themselves to the people seated around them. This was most unusual indeed. People actually wanted to know my name as they gave me theirs. Obviously the new person in the section, I was given a warm "welcome to Spiritus" greeting by everyone around me. "Wow, what a friendly place," I thought.

After that, people seemed to settle down rather quickly. Most of the Mass was rather typically Catholic with a reading from the Old and New Testament, followed by the Gospel and homily. When it came time for the transubstantiation, however, something else occurred that was unusual. Everyone in the congregation participated in this process by saying the familiar words that are part of the consecration of Holy Communion; the same words that are reserved for the priest alone in my old church:

> Before he was given up to death, a death he freely accepted, he took the bread, gave God thanks and praise, he broke the bread, gave it to his disciples and said, "This is my body, which will be given up for you." When supper was ended, he took the cup, again he gave God thanks and praise, gave the cup to his disciples and said, "This is my blood; the

blood of the new and everlasting covenant. It will be shed for you and for all so that sins may be forgiven. Do this in memory of me."

As I listened to the entire congregation say these words in perfect unison, I felt like I was part of something special, something meaningful. More importantly, as the priest held up the Eucharist I could see the circle of glowing, white light surrounding it. Sighting the aura, I knew that this was, indeed, a divinely approved Mass, for the Holy Spirit was visibly present in the Eucharist; tears of recognition and joy streamed down my face.

Just a Fact
Transubstantiation is when the Eucharistic bread and wine are changed into the actual body and blood of Christ during consecration. Although their appearance remains unchanged, their true substances are transformed.

When it came time for *The Lord's Prayer* I was delighted to hear the musical accompaniment because I knew this meant we would be singing it, which is so much better than just reciting the words. As we joined hands and sang, I looked around me and above me to the balcony. I was awestruck at the sight of hundreds of people, forming a gigantic, bi-level circle around the altar.

While singing the *Our Father,* with all the other parishioners, the tremendous, melodious sound not only filled the rafters, but my heart as well. A holy force seemed to flow through the crowd linking each person to the next like beads on a rosary. It was so powerful that I was overcome with emotion as tears came to my eyes once more, for the peace and joy I felt at that sacred moment could only be described as the experience of God.

Shortly afterwards, Father asked us to offer each other the "sign of peace." It came as a surprise to me when I witnessed the entire parish break into a ten-minute hug-fest that had all the appearances of complete bedlam. People were freely walking up and down the aisles, criss-crossing the entire length of the auditorium, just to give each other a heart-felt hug. In addition, the level of noise grew to pre-mass levels as many seemed to use the opportunity as social time; friends greeted each other and had quick, catch-up conversations. Everyone was so laid back and comfortable with each other that I felt like I was at a family reunion.

It was certainly different for me to see such camaraderie and such genuine affection being openly expressed. I was used to seeing the obligatory handshake, followed by the staring at one's feet in order to avoid any further contact. To my surprise, many people gave me a hug as well, making me feel even more welcomed. Wow, these people were really friendly. Not only that, they appeared to be actually enjoying themselves; amazingly, so was I.

While everyone was milling about, the choir broke out into a familiar song, "Lamb of God, you take away the sins of the world, have mercy on us." This seemed to be the cue for people to return to their seats for the next part of the Mass. What appeared to be chaos just a few minutes earlier was transformed into a quiet, respectful crowd as Father Jim and Reverend Mary proceeded with the communion ritual.

At this point Father Jim announced that all were welcome to partake in communion. It did not matter what religious faith parishioners had or if they had not been to church in a long time. The priest explained, "This is not a Catholic table, it belongs to Jesus, and Jesus said, 'Anyone who comes to me I shall not reject.' "

After communion, and when Mass was over, I made it a point to meet this unusual priest who seemed to cause such a stir in the news. The short, Irish man with a jovial personality appeared pretty harmless and friendly to me; he was quite approachable. So with a trembling voice and tears in my eyes I explained to Father Jim how and why I was there, I had been kicked out my parish for communicating with my mom and others, who were deceased. Father Jim put his arm around me and with a gentle smile simply stated, "You have a new home now." I nearly burst into sobs at this simple statement of automatic acceptance into his community.

"But what about talking to dead people?" I questioned. Father Jim laughingly remarked, "What's the big deal? We believe in the communion of saints." My heart leaped with joy and almost disbelief on hearing these affirming words from a Catholic minister. There were no questions, no condemnations, and no judgments. Father Jim was not like any priest I knew, and Spiritus Christi was certainly not like any Catholic Church I had ever been to; they let anyone in, including me. Ever since, I have always lovingly called Spiritus the "misfit Mass."

But what was this "communion of saints" Father Jim talked about? I tucked the question into the back of my mind because at that moment, for the first time since my near-death experience, I felt a level of love and acceptance that my soul had been longing for; that was what mattered most. Despite my spiritual anomalies, I was able to continue practicing the faith I love so much. As a result, I found a new spiritual home and my wounds began to heal.

Just a Fact

Spiritus Christi is one of the few Catholic Churches in the country with a woman priest. *Pioneer Priest, the Story of Mary Ramerman and Spiritus Christi Church*, by James Callan, describes the life and ordination of a valiant female leader and role model for women on the altar.

For more information on the history and difficult birth of this awesome, all-inclusive Catholic community, read *Standing in the Light* by Chava Redonnet or go to www.spirituschristi.org

---

Although I found acceptance in another Catholic Church, I still wondered why I was not able to attend Mass with my own family and friends in the community I grew up in. I wondered how and if I would ever again fit into my former parish. I wondered where it all went so wrong and what I did that was considered so evil. I knew God still loved and accepted me - why couldn't my own religion do the same? Instead of believing everything I had ever been taught about the faith, I began to question it all.

The Confused Catholic

The nagging question I could not get out of my mind was, "What did Father Jim mean about the communion of saints?" I had heard of it, I guess I even stated my belief in it at every mass during the *Apostles' Creed*. This only led to more questions:

> What exactly is the communion of saints and how does it work?
> How do we know that there is a communion of saints?
> Who are these saints and doesn't communion with them imply communication?
> Isn't praying to the saints the same as talking to them?
> If we "believe" in the communion of saints, doesn't it follow that we should "practice" communion with the saints?
> If so, what is the proper procedure for this practice, and where are the instructions?

To my surprise, when I tried to research the subject, there was not much to be found on the communion of saints. Only two paragraphs are devoted to it in the *Catechism of the Catholic Church*; there is a bit more in the *Catholic Encyclopedia*. It's not even mentioned in *The Complete Idiot's Guide to Understanding Catholicism*, and only two pages on the subject are in the *Everything Catholicism* book. I searched the Internet, Catholic Resource Guides, and dug deep in the archives of St. Bonaventure University library, only to find small articles in various periodicals.

The little I did find talked about a relationship with the saints in heaven, however, there was no mention of how one participates in this relationship with spiritual beings; there was no methodology. At first, I came to the conclusion that the communion of saints wasn't that important; it seemed to be no more than a footnote in history.

I knew the saints were guiding me, however, when I attended a "Call to Action" conference in Milwaukee, with Spiritus Christi, and found an entire book on the topic. *Friends of God and Prophets, A Feminist Theological Reading of the Communion of Saints,* written by Sister Elizabeth Johnson, has been an invaluable resource. Along with Johnson's later book, *Truly Our Sister, A Theology of Mary in the Communion of Saints,* I was able to learn all about the history of the communion of saints and what it means today. I found out just how important this doctrine is to our faith and how little people knew about it, including myself.

Just a Fact

Call To Action is a national organization working for equality and justice in the Catholic Church. It advocates a vision that believes the Spirit of God is at work in the whole church, not just its appointed leaders. The group promotes issues such as the right for women to be ordained and the right for priests to marry.

The more I learned about the communion of saints the more baffled I became. A huge part of this confusion stemmed from the clear statements in the *Catechism of the Catholic Church* opposing the practice of "spiritism" (spiritualism) or spirit communication. There are also warnings against conjuring spirits and summoning the dead; this added to my list of questions:

How is the practice of spiritualism different from invoking saints?

What's the difference between asking for guidance from St. Theresa and asking for guidance from Grandma in heaven?

How can we have a relationship with people in heaven if we can't contact them?

When it comes to invoking and talking to spirits and saints, there seems to be another contradiction in the teachings of the church.

Insight

"Spiritism," according to *The Essential Catholic Handbook*, is the belief that the living can communicate with the deceased by way of a human medium or inanimate objects, such as a Ouija board. According to the Roman Catholic Church, participating in this practice is a violation of the first commandment and opposes the virtue of religion. This definition will be examined and challenged in chapter five, "Taboo."

Another discrepancy, which had me asking questions, was the church doctrine that forbids people to consult with mediums:

Are mediums bad people, if so, why?
Aren't angels, saints and priests mediums; don't we consult them?
What about Jesus; isn't he a medium?
What is the difference between a psychic medium and a Christian mystic?

It seemed to me that practicing mediumship is simply practicing communion with the saints; I couldn't see why it would be forbidden?

Yet another contradiction I found was the Roman Catholic doctrine denouncing the use of clairvoyance and psychic ability; the questions continued to mound:

How are clairvoyant visions different from mystical visions?
Hasn't the church always valued prophets and seers, who were also clairvoyant?
What is the difference between psychic gifts and spiritual gifts?

When it comes to clairvoyance and psychic gifts, the teachings of the church are vague and contradictory; there don't seem to be any clear guidelines.

These ambiguous policies left me questioning where I belonged in all of this:

> Is the ability to see and hear dead people considered supernatural or paranormal?
> Is it a spiritual gift from God or a psychic curse of the devil?
> Is psychic ability to be revered or feared?
> What does that make me, a mystic or a medium, holy or evil?

If I could find the answers to these questions then I could find out just where and if I fit into my religious faith. I wondered how I could integrate my knowledge and experience of Catholicism with my knowledge and experience of the supernatural.

Education is Key

Serious study can shed much light on supernatural events, thus, alleviating the fear associated with them. We fear what we don't know and don't understand. People who have had mystical experiences often don't understand what is happening to them; they too become afraid. Their fear escalates in a community setting with little tolerance and knowledge of occurrences that are out of the norm. Experiencers in turn become shunned and are too afraid to talk to anyone because they dread being ridiculed or told they are nuts. Education is the key to eliminating these fears and the stigma associated with any paranormal events or practices.

Finding the answers to all my questions regarding supernatural phenomena and the communion of saints, was the beginning of my spiritual journey. I felt that I need not give up my faith to grow and be enriched by other religious traditions and scientific explorations that would help me in my search for the truth.

Insight

A wonderful educational resource I've used extensively is the series of books known as *The Complete Idiots Guide*. They are simple to read and make complex subjects easy to understand. They are also written by some of the top professionals in their area of expertise. Check out *The Complete Idiots Guide To Understanding Catholicism, To Being Psychic, To Communicating With Spirits, To Near-Death Experiences, and To Awakening Your Spirituality*.

This quest for answers which bridge science and religion, turned into a seven-year research project that unveiled some interesting discoveries. These findings helped me to understand all the reasons behind much of the fear associated with the supernatural and those who participate in it. By sharing my research, my heavenly encounters, and the knowledge I gained as a result, I hope to help others understand more about the practice and science of communication with our loved ones in heaven.

Speaking in a language Catholics understand, my explanations will involve learning a new language as well, with many words, terms and ideas that may not be familiar. It may seem at times that I am stretching the boundaries of what we've always been taught growing up as "good Catholics." It is my intent however, to write nothing that goes against the teachings of the faith I hold dear. The educational vehicle I'm using is a rather ambiguous concept called "the communion of saints."

Looking at this doctrine of faith through the eyes of a parapsychologist will help everyone see the role spiritualism plays in our religion. We will begin our education by introducing some of the basic disciplines. This will lay the foundation essential for a clear understanding of a highly misunderstood doctrine, "the communion of saints."

Spiritualism and Parapsychology

Due to the stigma attached to anything labeled "supernatural" or "psychic," I was forced to look outside my religion for help in coping with the unusual phenomena occurring to me. I looked to the religion, science and philosophy of Spiritualism and to the science of parapsychology to find the answers to my myriad questions regarding the paranormal and communion with the saints. For those of you unfamiliar with Spiritualism and parapsychology, I will give a brief definition. Each of these subjects will be explored in greater detail in subsequent chapters.

"Spiritualism" is the practice of communicating with the deceased or other non-physical beings, such as angels or God. It has been part of the human experience throughout the ages because it is an integral part of most religions. Modern-day Spiritualism, which started in 1847, became an organized religion seeking to prove the continuity of life after death through the practice of mediumship. All the ministers and many of the parishioners are mediums. Spiritualists often gather in home circles, called sèances, to "speak" with the spirits.

"Parapsychology" is the study of psychic phenomena or things outside the normal paradigms of science. These phenomena, such as clairvoyance (the ability to see with the mind), are known as extrasensory perception (ESP) because information is received without the use of our five physical senses of hearing, seeing, tasting, smelling and touching. Parapsychology is the study of ESP, also known as our sixth or psychic sense. For example, when St. Therese Neumann had a "vision" of Jesus' ascension into heaven; she had a clairvoyant psychic experience. In his book *Parapsychology, Science or Magic*, James Alcock defines parapsychology as "the scientific study of spirituality" (Alcock).

Parapsychology is also the science of Spiritualism. It arose when well-educated men attempted to scientifically explain the unusual but common events that occurred during sèances and other spiritualist gatherings. One example of this is the phenomenon known as "table tipping," which occurs when the séance table levitates off the floor. At first, scientists got involved in the study of Spiritualism with the intent to expose the mediums as frauds, and in many cases they did. There were a few cases, however, which seemed genuine and could not be explained by any known scientific means. These unexplainable events were called "paranormal."

Just a Fact

In 1883 The Society for Psychical Research was founded in London. In 1885, its counterpart, the American Society for Psychical Research was formed. Located in New York City, it is America's oldest organization for research into psychic phenomena.

Spiritualism and parapsychology helped me understand my own paranormal experiences. In seeking answers to my many questions I went to a medium for help and guidance. She was able to explain what was happening to me regarding unsolicited spirit messages. She told me I was experiencing a "spiritual awakening" that came as a result of my near-death experience. The intuitive also explained that I needed to learn to control the psychic power and suggested I find a Spiritualist church. I found comfort in her wisdom and in knowing that this gifted woman did not think I was strange, nor did she judge me as being less-than-holy.

I started attending Plymouth Spiritualist Church in Rochester to partake in psychic development classes. It was with the Spiritualists that I found acceptance regarding my paranormal abilities. I also found that I was much at home with them and started spending a lot of time in Lily Dale, a Spiritualist community in upstate New York. When I was with these like-minded people, I did not feel abnormal or out of place. I was a newbie and had much to learn; everyone I talked to was eager to help me on my spiritual path.

However, the more I learned about Spiritualism, the more I clung to my Catholic roots. As outdated as the faith often seemed, I found I did not want to give up the ancient traditions or many of my Christian beliefs. I continued going to a Catholic Mass every Sunday morning at Spiritus Christi and found myself at Plymouth Spiritualist church every Sunday afternoon. Morning mass was for getting in touch with God and Jesus. My afternoon gatherings were for getting in touch with spirit guides as well as family and friends on the otherside. In addition, I was learning how to control and hone the gift I often thought of as a curse.

Through my dual existence, I learned that as a Roman Catholic my psychic abilities were considered a curse and as a spiritualist it was a gift. I found however, that I was too Catholic to be a Spiritualist and too much a Spiritualist to be a good Catholic. I did not fit in anywhere but at the same time I was able to fit in both places, as long as I kept that other part of me a secret. When I was with my Catholic friends I did not talk about my Spiritualist side and when with my Spiritualist friends I did not talk about my love for Catholicism. I found myself leading a double life.

From the earthly viewpoint, I was leading a double life, from the cosmic viewpoint, we are all one and it was all a part of my single, eternal life. I knew that God did not care what religion I practiced and that it was all for my spiritual growth. I knew God has no religion and loves each of us no matter what our beliefs. Nevertheless, I still lived in the physical world and had to try and make sense of it all in light of my new-found understanding; my research continued.

Know the Lingo

Q: *What is the difference between "supernatural" and "paranormal?"*
Q: *What is the difference between psychic gifts and spiritual gifts?*

One of the first questions I sought to answer was the difference between "supernatural" and "paranormal" events. Up until now I have been using the words interchangeably. After all, there are only so many ways you can describe unusual phenomena. There is, however, a clear distinction in the eyes of both theologians and parapsychologists.

"Supernatural" is a theological term that usually refers to something that comes directly from God. For example, St. Francis heard a voice from God tell him "Repair my house." "Paranormal" (beyond normal) is a scientific term that refers to psychic phenomena, a "natural" human ability. An example of this would be "clairaudience," or the ability to hear non-physical beings, without using one's ears. Therefore, what some Christians would call "supernatural," parapsychologists may call "paranormal" or "natural" psychic occurrences. Although St. Francis heard a "supernatural" voice from God, at the same time, he had a "paranormal" experience of clairaudience.

To further complicate things, another term used by theologians is "preternatural." Doctor of Theology, John Heaney, of the Institut of Catholique in Paris, defines this term in his book, *The Sacred & The Psychic*. He suggests that "preternatural" refers to things that are not "supernatural" and not "natural" in the ordinary sense (Heaney, 22). The late Reverend Alphonsus Trabold, a Franciscan Monk and noted parapsychologist from Saint Bonaventure University, gives a further explanation:

> There always has been a belief or long tradition in the beginning that we had besides our natural gifts, preternatural gifts, which could include the paranormal. And the idea was that those were lost, along with our sanctifying grace. I believe now, what we would be saying is that they were not lost. They are dormant, or maybe some have them, I tend to think we all have them, at least in a root fundamental way. I think some have them in a very special, gifted way. (Miller, 4)

Trabold agrees with Heaney that "preternatural" may be considered "paranormal." These spiritual gifts are also known as "gifts of grace." Thus "grace" can refer to psychic ability. Although we thought they were "lost," these gifts were merely lying asleep, just waiting to be awakened. This is apparent in the mystics and psychic mediums of the past and of today, who possess these abilities.

Insight

"Amazing grace how sweet the sound that saved a wretch like me. I once was lost but now am found, was blind but now I see." In this famous song "grace" could refer to the gift of clairvoyance or "second sight." A transformational experience, such as near-death, often leaves the person with increased psychic abilities or gifts of "grace."

Distinct disciplines have their own language and often use different words to say the same thing. Because I believe everything comes ultimately from God, I do not believe that there is a huge difference between, "supernatural," "paranormal," "natural," or "preternatural;" it's vernacular hair-splitting to me. For the purpose of this book, we will keep things simple and continue to use "supernatural" synonymously with "paranormal."

Furthermore, I will be using many theological and metaphysical terms interchangeably. The word "heaven" is used synonymously with "spirit world," "the afterlife" or "the otherside." The word "spirit" is often used in place of "soul," for example, the souls in heaven are also referred to as "spirits." (To theologians, the "spirit" is unlike the "soul" but we will not differentiate between the two). The word "saint" will also be used in conjunction with "spirit" and "soul." "Guides" refer to our personal spirit helpers and are most like "guardian angels."

It is important to stress however, that when I refer to the "spirit world" I am only speaking about good or holy spirits, those who live in the higher realms known as heaven and purgatory. Therefore, "spirits" are all those who are members of the communion of saints. I am not referring to souls in the lower or darker regions, what some may call "hell." The following table may help with the terminology:

Theological Terms	Parapsychological Terms
heaven	spirit-world, afterlife, the otherside
soul, saint	spirit, holy spirit
guardian angel	spirit guide, angel
gifts of grace, spiritual gifts	psychic gifts, ESP
supernatural, preternatural	paranormal

Now that we have some of the vocabulary out of the way, we will continue our educational journey by looking into the history of paranormal phenomena and how it became the basis of our faith. We will next address the question of how we know the communion of saints exists.

A Supernatural Faith

Q: *How do we know that there is a communion of saints?*

Although we may not be aware of our friends in spirit, we are aware there is a heaven. We know this because heavenly beings have been communicating with humans on earth from the beginning of time. Spirits have been in contact with the physical world from the time that life on earth began. We were not just placed on this planet to fend for ourselves without any directions.

We have been given divine guidance right from the beginning. God himself spoke to Adam and Eve to lay down some ground rules for our earthly journey. He said, "You are free to eat from any tree in the garden; but you must not eat from the tree of knowledge of good and evil" (Genesis 2:16). Later on a voice from heaven spoke to Moses providing us with a set of ten guidelines for how best to live our lives. An angel spoke to Mary explaining her role as mother of the Christ. In addition, we are all supplied with a personal guardian angel, as well as many other spiritual guides and teachers, to aid us in this physical expedition.

Furthermore, we have historical evidence of our connection to the afterlife from ancient civilizations that pre-date the Bible by thousands of years. We know that as early as 3000 BC the Egyptians buried their dead in a way that would prepare them for their next life. Food, gold, as well as servants were buried with the bodies for their journey into the afterlife.

Many people had the opportunity to view the contents of King Tut's tomb when the mobile museum of treasure toured throughout the world in the 1970's; I saw an astounding replica at the Luxor Hotel in Las Vegas. It's nothing short of amazing to see how much time, care and thought went into the elaborate preparations for a life after death. Similar evidence of a bond between heaven and earth has been found in the Mayan and Native American cultures, as well as ancient civilizations all over the world.

In his book, *Voices, Visions and Apparitions*, Reverend Michael Freze, SFO and member of the Anaconda Catholic Community in Montana writes:

> The course of human history-concerning religious traditions of ancient or modern societies-indicates that there is a universal experience when it comes to communication with the supernatural: voices, apparitions, locutions, miracles, signs and wonders. Although these experiences are admittedly rare, they exist in so many stories, legends and mythological accounts from the ancient world that they ought not to be denied outright. (14)

Throughout history there seems to be a general acceptance in every spiritual custom when it comes to communicating with the heavenly realms. These are all indications of the earliest forms of communion with the saints.

When it comes to mystical phenomena, Reverend Freze also observed that there are few, if any, other religions that have as much documentation, including "writings, teachings, and personal anecdotes" than dose the Catholic Church. This includes "miracles, voices, visions, apparitions, locutions, and extraordinary charisms" associated with the supernatural (Freze, 4-5).

After spending innumerable hours of research at St. Bonaventure University, in Olean, NY, I completely understand what Freze was talking about. There is an overwhelming archive of Catholic books and articles written by and about the many great Christian mystics and saints. An abundant collection of supernatural material can be found within our own faith. This collection has not ended; on the contrary, it continues to grow with new experiences from each generation.

Bridging the Past and Present

People have been experiencing and writing about their contacts with the spirit world for thousands of years. Just look in the "religion" section of any bookstore and you will find hundreds of books written by and about great mystics, saints and yogis of all spiritual traditions who have had paranormal experiences. You can also find books on apparitions, stigmata, miracles, visions and other supernatural events.

Look in the "bestseller" and "New Age" section and you will find dozens of books written by and about ordinary people who have had extraordinary experiences. There are books about ghosts, angelic visitations, spiritual healings, the afterlife, near-death experiences and after-death communications, to name a few. You will also find inspired writings that include conversations with archangels, saints, Jesus and even God himself.

In the "psychology" department of any bookstore you will find spiritual books on manifesting your destiny, your sacred self, your higher mind and finding spiritual solutions to your problems. Look in the "science" section and you will find books on the survival of consciousness after death, the quantum physics of non-local reality and the cosmic consciousness. All of these publications indicate an on-going presence of God within our lives.

God did not stop revealing Himself to us after the Bible was written.

He continues to announce his presence through many private revelations. Reverend Freze stresses this point by saying:

> Should we ignore this enormous body of evidence as untrustworthy of serious consideration? Do we attribute these experiences to mere superstition, fraud, hysteria, mass hypnotic delusion, or imagination? Although many in the Church today would like to do so, it seems reasonably clear that there must be something going on here that cannot be explained away as some product of the imagination. (14)

Freze goes on to describe the importance of bridging the past with the present and recognizing that God's presence is still felt in "supernatural experiences and interventions" today. He explains that "Without this sense of continuity and commonality, we lose our perception of the divine working in our midst" (12).

The Communion of Saints

Q: *What is the communion of saints?*

So what exactly is "the communion of saints" and what does it have to do with the supernatural, spiritualism, and parapsychology? The "communion of saints" is a beautiful, uniquely Catholic belief, which is little understood by many and highly under-utilized. It is through this idea that the church recognizes the interaction between the believers on earth and those in heaven. According to the on-line Catholic Encyclopedia:

> The Communion of Saints is the spiritual solidarity which binds together the faithful on earth, the souls in purgatory, and the saints in heaven in the organic unity of the same mystical body under Christ its head, and in a constant interchange of supernatural offices. ("The Communion of Saints", 2)

This "supernatural interchange" refers to communication between physical and non-physical beings. As mentioned earlier, these supernatural events have been documented throughout church history. Many occurred to ordinary people who were later revered for being mystical and therefore unusually holy. People like St. Joan of Arc who heard voices from heaven, or like the children of Fatima, who had visions of the Blessed Mother.

These voices and visions were received through extrasensory perception, or psychic senses. Not only is our sixth sense used to receive messages from the heavens but also to send messages; we commonly call this type of psychic communication "prayer." Therefore, in order to maintain our relationships with the saints in heaven it is necessary to communicate via paranormal (supernatural) means. That is why parapsychology (the study of psychic phenomena) and spiritualism (communication with the dead) are an integral part of communion with the saints.

In the chapters that follow we will take an in-depth look at the communion of saints and by doing so will answer many more of the questions I raised. It is my hope that as you journey with me, you too will find your place among the haloed heroes.

Just My Opinion

Supernatural experiences are not a thing of the past; they are alive and well in the twenty-first century. As we evolve spiritually, these phenomena will only continue to increase. It can already be seen with the new generation of psychically gifted kids known as "indigo" and "crystal" children. These youngsters will raise our consciousness to new heights and things seen as paranormal in the past or even currently, will become the norm in the future.

My near-death experience was an extraordinary event that left me with unusual abilities. When I died, I found myself in an amazing world where communication takes place telepathically (mind to mind); no voice is needed or used. When I returned to earth, I discovered that I had retained this natural ability to speak without words with non-physical beings. My conversations with God, Jesus, and my own mother in heaven seemed as normal to me as talking to someone in the grocery store. What I soon learned however, was that talking about the metaphysical world, or to the people who live in it, was somehow unacceptable to my fellow believers and to the faith I loved.

Publicly, I quickly learned to keep quiet regarding any mention of the supernatural. Privately however, I began asking many individuals if they had ever had an unexplainable event happen to them. That is when I learned that it was quite normal to have a paranormal experience. It seemed that everyone had a story to tell, a story that always started with the phrase, "You're going to think I'm crazy..." or "Don't tell Father, but..." and ended with an interesting tale. Most of the people I asked, at some point in their life, had an unusual occurrence they could not explain, they just didn't talk about it. They too, had learned to keep quiet on the subject to avoid any ridicule.

But why was it so horrible to talk about these fascinating, mystical events? How could I make the Church understand that people who had these psychic experiences were not evil? Doesn't anyone in the Vatican realize that science has dispelled these ancient superstitions? How could I possibly change a two thousand-year-old doctrine?

To make this happen, I looked to the life of Galileo for inspiration. In the sixteenth century, he knew that new scientific discoveries were disproving some of the ancient religious beliefs. He challenged the Church with his conviction that the earth moved around the sun. Consequently, people came to understand the truth. In the twenty-first century, with new scientific discoveries regarding supernatural phenomena, it's time for another paradigm shift, one that fits the modern times we live. The antiquated teachings of the church are once again in need of refurbishing.

I also looked to the life of Jesus for inspiration. Christ often challenged the authority of the religious institution, especially when hypocritical policies invoked inhumane treatment towards its people. For example, in defense of the unfaithful wife he dared, "Let he who is without sin throw the first stone" (John 8:7). Jesus demonstrated how the power of love and compassion can create great changes in fear-based doctrines; he often used his supernatural powers to prove his point.

Both Galileo and Jesus questioned authority and challenged the establishment of their day. Their heretical teachings became the foundation for new standards in science and religion. In the same way, I hope by raising questions, people will re-think their position on age-old, erroneous taboos regarding communication with our loved ones in heaven. It's time, once again, to challenge outdated, superstitious beliefs that are roadblocks on the communication highway to the saints.

Summary

God did not stop revealing himself after the Bible was written. Supernatural phenomena occur every day to believers in the Catholic faith. Many have been blessed with receiving a "sign" from a loved one in heaven, such as hearing their partner's voice or smelling their favorite perfume. What should people do, however, when an event of this nature happens to them? Most would agree that it should not even be discussed; everyone knows that it's taboo to talk about.

After talking about my paranormal experiences, I found myself looking for a new church. I found acceptance and healing in an all-inclusive Catholic community called Spiritus Christi. I also found acceptance at Plymouth Spiritualist Church, where I learned about mediumship and communication with non-physical beings. Although I loved the philosophy and people of these congregations, I never stopped questioning why I was living in exile of my hometown parish.

I had many other questions as well and found myself more confused than ever. When it comes to spirit communication and other forms of paranormal practices, there seems to be a contradiction in the teachings and beliefs of the Church. On the one hand we are taught to believe in the communion of saints, and on the other hand we're taught that "spiritism" is against the faith. There are also contradictions when it comes to the spiritually gifted members of the church. On the one hand we revere our Christian mystics, while on the other hand we condemn psychically gifted believers.

In addition, there seems to be confusion in the difference between using supernatural gifts of grace, such as "visions" and our natural paranormal gifts, such as "clairvoyance." There don't seem to be any clear-cut guidelines when it comes to determining what a "gift" is and who is acceptably gifted. Science and religion often use different words to say the same thing; there seems to be no real difference between supernatural and paranormal events.

The communion of saints is a Catholic teaching, which recognizes the solidarity and interaction between believers on earth, in purgatory, and in heaven. If we "believe" in the communion of saints, we should be able to "practice" communication with the saints.

This "constant interchange of supernatural offices" requires the participants to utilize their sixth sense or psychic ability. Therefore, parapsychology and Spiritualism is essential to understanding this important church doctrine.

One thing is clear from all this--with ignorance comes fear. With fear comes prejudice and discrimination. As a result, whole groups of people are excluded from the body of Christ. Education is the key to understanding communication with the saints. It will eliminate fear and put an end to the ostracization and emotional abuse caused by excluding some of God's most gifted children from the Church.

Part II
We Believe in the Communion of Saints

Chapter 3
A Fellowship of Souls

The History of the Communion of Saints

"Religion encourages you to explore the thoughts of others and accept them as your own. Spirituality invites you to toss away the thoughts of others and come up with your own."
(Walsh, *Conversations With God*)

This chapter is extremely interesting for those who like history; it is also pertinent for a greater understanding of the communion of saints. In addition, it sheds much light on the philosophy of Catholicism and our Christian roots. We will cover the definition of a "saint" and learn how that has changed dramatically over the years. You will learn how the faith shifted from a horizontal, fellowship of souls, in which all were equal and included, to a vertical, patriarchal society, in which some souls were deemed holier than others, which excluded many. If you are just not that into history, then skip to *Just My Opinion* and the *Summary* at the end of this chapter. For those who are passionate about the past, we will start with a fascinating story about the first saint.

The First Saint

It was a daunting, dangerous time for all who dared to live in the shadow of the Resurrection. For Christians in the first century, the risks were even greater. Those who believed that Jesus was the Christ, Son of the one and only God, were in the minority. Their failure to pay homage to the Roman gods and emperors was seen as heretical acts of civil disobedience that must be punished. The new cult was a threat to the establishment and therefore outlawed. The penalty for those who denied the power and authority of the Roman State was severe (O'Gorman & Faulkner).

Torture was appropriate for the heathens and came in a variety of creative forms. Many were branded with hot irons, run through a gauntlet of whips, brutally beaten while locked in a stockade, or had arms or legs amputated. One punishment was to throw the insurgents in the gladiator's arena with a lion. If the prisoner lived then he would be set free. Viewing this sentence became a popular spectator sport, as the Christian fed felines grew fat on the faithful. Those who refused to denounce the Jesus God were condemned to death by beheading, crucifixion or burning. Body parts were displayed to deter others from joining the new rebellious religion. It can safely be said that those who followed Christ were more than just courageous; they were willing to die for their faith (Johnson, Paul).

Such was the case with St. Stephen, a disciple considered to be the first Christian martyr. In 35 C.E., through the laying on of hands, the apostles appointed Stephen, along with six others, as deacons in the Church of Jerusalem, "...and they prayed and laid their hands upon them. So the word of God progressed and the number of disciples in Jerusalem was greatly increased "(Acts 6:6-7). The supernatural gifts of Jesus and the chosen twelve were thus bestowed upon Stephen; he was said to be "full of grace and power" (Barclay, 51).

Although no specifics are given in Acts, Stephen is described as performing "great wonders and miracles among the people" (Acts 6:8). We can assume he followed in the footsteps of his predecessors by healing the sick and performing other supernatural feats; but the deacon did not stop there. He was often found publicly ridiculing the Jewish Sanhedrin for restricting the worship of God to the temples. In addition, he criticized their unrelenting adherence to the Jewish laws, which were stuck in the past. Stephen wanted to spread the Gospel and make it more accessible for future generations (Barclay, 53).

Stephen felt that Christianity was for the entire world, not just Jews, and that it must be taken outside the temples and cities to where the common people lived. Jealous of his paranormal gifts and enraged by his challenging beliefs, priests of the synagogues plotted against Stephen. He was brought before the Sanhedrin where he was accused of blasphemy towards the Jewish holy places and holy laws (Acts 6:11-13).

Stephen defended himself by citing Abraham and Moses as examples of those who ventured wherever God led them, including into the wilderness. Scriptures tell us that God said, "Leave your country and your people and go to the land I will show you" (Acts 7:3). In his book, *The Acts of the Apostles*, William Barclay, professor of Divinity and Biblical Criticism at the University of Glasgow, Scotland, interprets St. Stephen's allegations against the Jewish authorities:

> He [Stephen] insists that they have wrongly limited God. The temple, which should have become their greatest blessing, was in fact their greatest curse; they had come to worship it instead of worshipping God. They had finished up with a Jewish God who lived in Jerusalem rather than a God of all men whose dwelling was the whole universe. (60)

For this Stephen was found guilty of heresy and sentenced to death by stoning. An enraged, relentless crowd hurled chunks of heavy rock at Stephen, driving him from the city. In the face of death and in the face of the angry mob, he knelt down before them and shouted, "Lord, lay not this sin to their charge." Stephen forgave the ruthless attackers just before they threw him over a cliff. After surviving the plummet, boulders were heaved upon the broken and bloodied disciple until he died (Acts 7:58-60).

Stephen's life ended in a similar way to that of Jesus, an agonizing death with words of forgiveness to his executioners. Because of this, he was called a "martyr," which is the Greek word for "witness." Those who died for their religious beliefs were considered the greatest witnesses to the faith. So like Jesus before him, Stephen's horrible death and absolution to his oppressors, would assure his place in heaven. St. Stephen is considered the first martyr (O'Gorman & Faulkner).

Just a Fact
The order to put St. Stephen to death came from Saul, who later became a saint himself. Saul was better known as St. Paul.

Memorialized Martyrs

The persecution of Christians continued for the next three-hundred years. Although it was meant as a deterrent, their torturous deaths had the opposite effect. The dramatic killings raised people's awareness of the new religion. Many became captivated by the stories of heroes who were willing to pay with their life rather than bow to the pagan gods, as a result, countless were attracted to Christianity (O'Gorman & Faulkner). The martyrs became a source of inspiration and hope for those who were seeking an alternative to the violence and hypocrisy of the established religions. As a result, many conversions took place and the faithful began to find ways to honor the memory of these Christ-like figures (Johnson).

In her book *Friends of God and Prophets* Professor of Theology, Elizabeth Johnson, C.S.J., of Fordham University, describes how these martyrs were honored. The community of believers considered the bodies of the holy people to be sacred, consequently, it was also believed that possessing a part of the body or clothing worn by the saint, was a good omen (which led to idea of relics). To honor them, a special burial place was selected and a shrine was erected on or near the grave. These shrines soon became places of prayer and the destination of pilgrimages for other early Christians.

The date of the martyr's death was also their birth into heaven. For this reason, the anniversary of that day was given special recognition. All night vigils were kept on these occasions and with the arrival of dawn, a Eucharistic celebration was held. Keeping with the traditional pagan funeral, a meal was then served at the graveside for those attending (Johnson, 77).

During these services the mourners called upon their dearly departed to pray for them. This seemed appropriate as it was thought that the disciples' incredible devotion assured them closeness to Christ. The family and friends often invoked the spirit of their deceased relative by writing graffiti, like "Pray for us" on the shrines. In doing so, a bond of solidarity was formed between those who were left on earth and those in heaven who were consecrated to the Son of God. It was important to receive prayers of support from these holy spirits because early Christians never knew if they would be the next witnesses to the faith (Johnson, 77-78).

As the number of Christian martyrs began to rise, each town kept track of those in their community who died for the faith. Some of these early saints included Polycarp, Vincent, Phoebe, Blandina, Januaria and eventually all of the apostles. On the anniversary of their death a celebration was held which included a recount of their heroic stories. This was followed by "lessons of encouragement" which was a discussion as to what was learned from their righteous death. As the practice spread throughout the various regions, other towns began celebrating the martyrs' anniversaries as well. A special day was set aside for each of the sacrificed and this is how the "liturgical calendar of the saints" was begun (Johnson, 77).

Just a Fact
The anniversary of St. Stephen's death is celebrated on December 26. This is known as his "feast day" because physical death marked the beginning of his spiritual life in heaven

So Who are the Saints?

Historically the word "holy" and the concept of the communion of saints pre-dates Christianity. It actually came from the Jewish tradition of remembering and venerating distinctive ancestors who had passed. The founding mothers and fathers of Israel were honored for being "kadosh," the Hebrew word for "holy" which means dedicated or set apart. It means that something is separate and pure, unmixed with evil. Kadosh referred to both holy people and holy things. Some of the holy people honored were David, Zechariah, Rachel, Abraham and Sarah to name a few. They are remembered for the role they played in the nation's history and religious development. They are those who are described as being righteous, just, blameless, blessed, finding favor with God, or filled with the Holy Spirit (Johnson).

"Kadosh" also referred to the Jewish people as a whole as they believed they were "the chosen ones." It referred to a group of holy people sharing a covenant relationship with the God who led them out of bondage. This holiness is what separated them from others. The idea of the communion of saints is, therefore, deeply rooted in the Jewish tradition. It started with the concept of a sacred nation of people belonging to God (Johnson).

The Greek word for "holy" is "hagios," which also means "sanctified." Sanctified was derived from the Latin word "sanctus," which is where the English word "saint" comes from. Like the Jewish interpretation, "hagios" means to be separated from sin and therefore consecrated to God. Just as the Jewish community was considered "kadosh" or "holy," in the Old Testament, the Christian community was considered "saints" or "holy" in the New Testament. The main difference being that the Jewish covenant was with God while the Christian covenant was with Jesus Christ, the Son of God; both were consecrated to our Father in heaven (Catholic Apologetics [1]).

We can see examples of how the word "saint" was used to refer to all Christians by looking at the writings of St. Paul. "Give my greetings to every holy one (hagion) in Christ Jesus (Phil 4:21). "So then you are no longer strangers and sojourners, but you are fellow citizens with the holy one (hagios) and members of the household of God" (Eph 2:19). In Paul's letters to the Romans he opens by directing his greetings, "To all God's beloved in Rome, who are called to be saints" (Romans 1:7). At this point in time "saints" referred to not only the "holy community," but to the individuals who belonged to that community. "Saints" were all the *living* followers of Jesus; it did not yet refer to the dead (Johnson).

Shared Goods and Good

An important ritual in this community of saints was the sharing of meals. Jesus shared his meals with the rich and the poor, the healthy and the sick, the sinners and the righteous; this is how he connected with them. In the same way, the early Christians connected with Jesus and each other by participating in a meal of bread and wine, which represented the body and blood of Christ. It was through this shared supper that the Spirit of Jesus was poured into them. This diverse, all-inclusive gathering of a holy community sharing holy things was the foundation of Christianity and the communion of saints (Johnson).

These early followers of Jesus did not just share a meal but shared their possessions as well. They even sold their homes and land so that all may have an equal portion; early Christians did not possess anything of their own (Heredia). The idea was that together they formed one body in Christ, and as an extension of that, their material belongings were also one. This concept in not unlike the many communes, which were popular in the 1960's. Perhaps the early Christians were ahead of their time.

This idea of communal living is further explained by St. Thomas Aquinas. As cited in the *Communio* article, *Catholicism and the Communion of Saints*, Aquinas observes that "Because all the faithful form one body, the good of one is shared with all others. We, thus, believe that there exists in the Church a communion of goods or of good." St. Thomas contends that the good is Jesus and is shared with all Christians through the sacraments of the Church (Balthasar, 161).

Equality is the most important factor in this concept of a shared community and shared goods. For the early Christians were not only equal with each other, but also equal in their relationship with Jesus. They learned through the practices and teachings of their mentor, who did not put himself above others, but was their equal partner. They mimicked Jesus by opening their table to all who sought salvation through him, no one was excluded, no matter what their social status, ethnicity, or background. They were all saints, equally.

Insight

Communal living, as practiced by the early Christians, has continued throughout history. The priests are called "monks" and they live in monasteries. Check out the Abbey of the Genesee in Piffard, NY where the Trappists make the famous Monk's Bread. You may also attend Mass there and participate in the chanting of Vespers.

The First-Family

To help explain the changing face of the saints, we will look at the relationship between St. Stephen and the rest of his family. Before his death, Stephen and his family were all considered saints. This would include his mother, father, brothers, sisters, aunts, uncles, nieces, nephews, cousins, along with his friends; they were all related through Christ. Stephen had no wife because he was a young man and in the religious order of deacons.

Literary license was taken to create a family for St. Stephen for the purpose of tracking how their relationships with each other changes throughout the history of the communion of saints. Stephen now has Grandma Naomi, Mother Sarah, Uncle Joshua, Brother Adam and Niece Rebecca. Because Stephen is the first martyr, I call this fictitiously named group our "first-family" of saints.

It is important to remember that "saints" were people in the community who personally knew each other. They knew each other's children and grandchildren and shared meals and special occasions together. They even bought birthday presents for each other and attended weddings, funerals and family reunions together. This was not a disconnected group of holier than thou people; these were the simple but faithful followers of Jesus Christ.

Upon the death of St. Stephen this relationship did not change. Just because he left his physical body did not mean that he was any holier than the rest of his family. Johnson points out that in the New Testament there is never any mention of "degrees of holiness." All Christians were equally saints. Although the living and the dead believers remained equal in Christ, it was believed that the martyrs were now closer to Jesus and therefore could be called upon for favors (Johnson, 63).

When it came to honoring or venerating the martyrs, in prayer and in acts of remembrance, a solidarity was formed between the saints on earth and the saints in heaven. It was believed that the dead were dependent on the living for prayers to get them to heaven. In exchange, those who were with the Lord could help the struggling faithful on earth and also serve as an inspiration to them; the martyrs became "companions in hope." This egalitarian dynamic, that helped to lay the foundation for the communion of saints, is what Elizabeth Johnson calls the "Companionship Model":

> The companionship model structures relations along the lines of mutuality. ...the saints are not situated between God and living disciples, but are with their sisters and brothers through the one Spirit poured out in the crucified and risen Jesus Christ. (81)

In this model we see a *horizontal* relationship between the saints in heaven and those on earth. The focus is "mutual companionship in Christ" which is evident through the common bond of struggle between the faithful. For early Christians this bond acted as a source of encouragement for those who were persecuted by the opposing Roman belief system (Johnson, 78-81).

To help trace how the communion of saints (COS) has changed throughout history, and to provide a visual aid, a series of five flow charts was created. The first one shows the horizontal relationship between Jesus and all his followers, both the living and dead; all were considered saints.

COS I - Companionship Model - St. Paul: c 35-312 C.E.

For our first-family, this meant that Stephen, as well as Grandma Naomi, Mother Sarah, Uncle Joshua, Brother Adam and Niece Rebecca, were saints. They were all equal companions with Christ.

Great Constantine & The Holy Dead

Q: *Aren't saints mediums; don't we consult them?*

In 312 C.E. the outlawed religion of Christianity was given a major break. Constantine the Great took over as the Roman Emperor and soon afterward had a supernatural experience, which he believed was a sign from the Jesus God. In a clairvoyant vision he saw the words "In boc signo vinces" which means "In this sign shalt thou conquer." The vision was so powerful that he converted to Christianity and put an end to the persecution of the saints. He proceeded to convert the entire town of Byzantium into Christianity and renamed the city after himself; he called it "Constantinople." This new metropolis became "the third most important city in Christendom" (Farrington, 115).

When the threat of persecution disappeared so did martyrdom. This did not end however, the growing list of devotees who suffered greatly for the faith. The list expanded to include those who were tortured, but did not die. Later the list expanded again to include the holy men and women of the church who devoted their lives to the poor, sick and the marginalized. Together this sacred group formed a "cloud of witness" and was the setting of the church doctrine that later came to be called "the communion of saints" (Johnson).

Around the time of Constantine there were major changes in the church resulting in major changes in the communion of saints. The church was the governing force and its politics became one of control, with many of the clerics leading the way; there was no separation of church and state. Debate and controversy arose between the ecclesiastical and the lay governors over the divine nature of Christ; the church authorities won. At the Council of Nicaea in 325 C.E. it became official; Jesus was declared equal to God and above his fellow human beings. Instead of seeing him as a Nazarene who died to save the sinners, he was given the power to judge them. Elizabeth Johnson observes:

> The net effect of these and other major changes was that the official presence of the Spirit moved out from the community as a whole to rest in more specifically holy hands and places, or, to put it another way, "the sacred" migrated from the nave to the sanctuary. (86)

From then on the saints were no longer a living community of people. The word "saints" referred only to the holy dead. As a result, the relationship between the living and the dead changed as well. Instead of the dearly departed being companions to their fellow believers, through their "lessons of encouragement" and shared bond in Christ, they now became intercessors. They were given supernatural powers over the living and could grant them favors. In effect, they became mediums between earth and the kingdom of heaven (Johnson, 86).

This reconfiguration of Christians is what Johnson calls the

"Patriarchal Model" of the communion of saints. The "privileged dead" were put into the position of patronage and became important for their paranormal powers, such as the ability to grant miracles to the living (Johnson, 78). Instead of being companions, now the believers on earth were dependent on the saints in heaven for help. This placed a great chasm between the two groups, which changed from an equal, horizontal relationship to a vertical, unequal relationship in which one is superior to the other. The superior members, the dead saints, were called patrons and the inferior members, the living believers, were called clients. Johnson asserts:

> In general, the patronage system arises when concentrations of wealth and political power in the hands of the few, coupled with neediness of the many and lack of democratic process, conspire to create permanent social stratifications (87).

The Catholic Church applied their patronage system of governing the people to extend to the dead. The martyrs and apostles were considered the most powerful. Sociologist, G.E.M. de Ste. Croix suggests, "Just as the terrestrial patron is asked to use his influence with the emperor, so the celestial patron, the saint, is asked to use his influence with the Almighty" (89). The patriarchal model led to the loss of "lessons of encouragement" and the loss of a mutual and equal relationship among the communion of saints. Furthermore, the definition of saints changed to refer only to those who were tortured and killed for the faith; it did not include the believers who died of natural causes (Johnson, 87-92).

This new, vertical relationship between the communion of saints is depicted in the second flow chart. Jesus is no longer equal with his followers as he has been elevated to the level of God; these two are the most powerful. Below them are the dead martyrs or saints, who act as patrons or intercessors. At the lowest level are the Christians on earth, who are now clients instead of saints.

COS II- Patriarchal Model -Constantine: 312 C.E.

```
                  ┌─────────────┐
                  │ God & Jesus │
                  └─────────────┘
                         │
              ┌────────────────────┐
              │  Church in Heaven  │
              │ Saints = Martyrs only │
              └────────────────────┘
                         │
              ┌────────────────────┐
              │  Church on Earth   │
              │   None are Saints  │
              └────────────────────┘
                         │
     ┌──────────────────────────────────────────┐
     │ Saints are only the martrys in heaven     │
     └──────────────────────────────────────────┘
```

Going back to our model of St. Stephen, we can see how the new interpretation of "saints" radically changed the dynamics of the martyr with his family. Now Stephen is a saint and Grandma, Mom, Uncle Joshua and Niece Rebecca, who have now joined him in heaven, are not. They were, in effect, de-haloed, along with the generations of people that followed.

Ancestors of the first-family, who were left on earth, which includes Stephen's Great-nephew Noah, were now less holy than their deceased uncle in heaven. They are no longer considered equal parts of the Body of Christ; however, the relatives now have a medium in the family and may pray to Stephen for favors from Jesus and God.

Let's Make It Official

Q: *Doesn't communion with the saints imply communication?*

Up until this point in history there was still no official doctrine on the communion of saints. In a book entitled *Communio Sanctorum;* written by Stephen Benko, professor at Comwell School of Theology in Philadelphia, we discover the origin of the concept. Benko explains that originally the communion of saints came from the Greek phrase "baptismum salutore." It expressed the belief that eternal salvation and the forgiveness of sins were dependent upon the sacraments of baptism and the Eucharist. Thus, one is Catholic through the universal bond of baptism and the Eucharist (Benko).

After 350 C.E. "baptismum salutore" was replaced with the Latin phrase "communio sanctorum", which means "participation in the sacraments." The essence of Christ is communicated to worshippers through participation (communio) in the sacrament (sanctorum) of the Eucharist. Partaking in this event is what forms a bond between Christians and Jesus Christ; it is what the fellowship of the church is fundamentally based on (Benko).

In the theology of Paul, in the New Testament, "communio sanctorum" referred to the mystical unity of Christians with Christ. This fellowship is what brings unity to the faith and makes it truly Catholic or universal. The concept was so important at the time that it was added to the Eastern version of the Apostles' Creed and utilized in the Church of Constantinople (Benko).

Insight

The word "communication" comes from "communion." Therefore communion with the saints also implies "communication" with them. The act involves "participation" in an exchange of ideas, which we call "conversation."

A Fellowship of Souls

Initially "communion" meant "participation." Sometime between 381-408 C.E. the meaning evolved with the interpretation by Nicetus, a bishop of Remesiana who was later canonized as a saint. In his *Treatise on the Trinity*, "communion" was used in a metaphorical sense to refer to "fellowship" of the church, through common sharing in the sacraments. Nicetus describes this fellowship by stating "What else is the church but the congregation of all saints." He goes on to establish this fraternity as the body of the church:

> From the beginning of the world, the patriarchs, Abraham, Isaac and Jacob, the prophets, the apostles, the martyrs; and the other just who are and will be, are one Church, because sanctified by one faith and conversation, signed by one Spirit, they are made into one body, the head of which is Christ, as it is written." (Benko, 99)

Nicetus goes even farther by including the angels, the virtues and the powers from above. He states that all saints are one, not only those on earth but also those in heaven, for in Christ all things were reconciled. "Therefore, in this Church believe yourself to be gathered into the communio sanctorum." (Benko, 100).

By the fifth century, communio sanctorum lost its sacramental character and was replaced with the idea of the church as a body of saints. It was around this time that it was added to the Western version of the Apostles' Creed in Rome, where it was eventually translated to the English form "communion of saints." Emphasis was placed on Nicetus' "fellowship" modality, which became the predominate view from the Middle Ages to the present (Benko).

Because of this change, the phrase "communion of saints" is a misnomer; it does not accurately describe the meaning of the concept today. It misleads and confuses the average parishioner into thinking of only the most holy dead when, in fact, it includes all of the faithful, both in heaven and on earth.

If the word "communion," is replaced with the word "fellowship" it would make more sense. In the same way, if the word "saint" is replaced with "soul" it would make more sense because it applies to all Christians, not just the martyrs. Everyone has a soul, but not all consider themselves a saint. For these reasons, "fellowship of souls" is less confusing and more easily understood by all. Furthermore, it more accurately describes the whole idea behind the communion of saints. Whatever way you say it, its inclusion in the Apostles' Creed tells us that not only is it important, but it is intrinsic to the faith.

The third change in the communion of saints is represented in the following chart. Once again all the people in both heaven and earth are considered saints. Furthermore the angels were added. Together they represent the body of Christ and are therefore fellow members of the church.

COS III - Fellowship Model - Nicetus: 381-394 C.E>

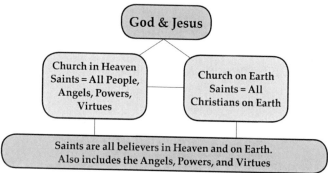

With this new interpretation of the communion of saints, another change in dynamics occurs for the first-family. St. Stephen's Grandma, Mom, Uncle Joshua, Brother Adam and Niece Rebecca have regained their halos. Furthermore, great-nephew, Noah (who married an Irish women and had six kids), and the rest of the family on earth are joined in sainthood with Uncle Stephen.

Also joining the clan is long lost cousin, Michael who had become an Archangel and warrior for the heavens. In addition, The Powers, the Virtues, and all other Angels were added to the community. This fellowship of souls had grown to include all those believers in heaven and on earth. Once again, the members of the first-family were equal companions with they're martyred brother in Christ.

Purify Me

In was in the fourth century when, yet another, change occurred in the communion of saints. At the Council of Carthage, in 394 C.E., the concept of purgatory and prayers for the dead was adopted. Another dimension was added to our belief system thus eliminating the idea of anyone going straight to heaven, except perhaps the martyrs. *The Catechism of the Catholic Church* declares:

> All who die in God's grace and friendship, but still imperfectly purified, are indeed assured of their salvation; but after death they undergo purification, so as to achieve the holiness necessary to enter the joy of heaven. (268)

The whole idea is that all souls have sinned and therefore must be subject to the consequences. For those who died in a "state of grace," the church offers absolution from sin thus sparing them from "eternal" consequences and hell. Although the confessor is forgiven, there are still "temporal" consequences that require payment before entering heaven.

This payment is made by passing through a state of purgation, thus cleansing the soul in preparation for heaven. It is important to note that the Eastern Churches, including Constantinople (now called the "Orthodox" Church), did not adopt the idea of purgatory, as did their Roman counterpart (Religious Tolerance.Org, 2).

With the addition of purgatory, the Christian church now existed on three levels. The first level was made up of the saints in heaven, called the "Church Triumphant." On the second level were the souls in purgatory, called the "Church Suffering," and thirdly, was the faithful on earth, called the "Church Militant" (Breton). In his book, *Purgatory*, Reverend F.X. Schouppe, S.J. describes the three levels as "sister churches" that form an eternal relationship through "continual communication" with each other. He claims that "the three churches assist in peopling heaven" (Schouppe, 1).

This change in the communion of saints can be seen in the fourth chart. Although there are now three levels to the church, all the members are still considered saints. Returning to our "first-family," we can see how the addition of purgatory changed their relationship to each other, again. Being a martyr, we can assume that St. Stephen remained safely in heaven. But instead of flying straight to paradise, as once believed, Grandma, Mom, Uncle Joshua and Niece Rebecca, had to make a layover in purgatory. Although Stephen and his deceased relatives have crossed over, they are in different levels of existence.

COS IV - Purgatory Model - Council of Carthage: 394 C.E.

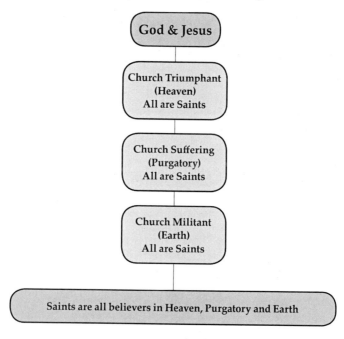

But how long must Stephen's departed family members remain in this state of limbo before they reach paradise? That answer depends on their descendants back on earth. Fortunately, they can rely on their trustworthy, devoutly Catholic great-grand nephew, Patrick (from the Irish side of the family), who is known by all in their tiny town as the infamous, Pat the Rat. It's up to him to obtain absolution to set them free from the horrific state they are stuck in. To accomplish this task, Patrick must say lots of prayers and have lots of money.

Indulge Me

Although the church never officially taught this, many believed that purgatory was like a little hell with great suffering and that one could spend hundreds of years in this state. To decrease the amount of time spent in the purification process, the Christians on earth could pay a penance. The penance could be either for themselves, before death, or on behalf of a loved one who had already passed.

Praying, fasting, reciting the rosary, and acts of kindness were all accepted forms of contrition. Once the penalty was paid, a dispensation or "indulgence" was granted. Indulgences released the confessors from temporal punishment due for their sins, thus reducing their time in purgation (Religious Tolerance.Org). As explained in *The Catechism of the Catholic Church*:

> Since the faithful departed now being purified are also members of the same communion of saints, one way we can help them is to obtain indulgences for them, so that the temporal punishments due for their sins may be remitted. (371)

Another accepted form of penance was called "alms giving." It was believed that money given to the church for indulgences was really payment to God. It could be used by God's servants to do good work and was, therefore, justifiable. The Church readily adopted "plenary indulgences" but because money was involved, greed and abuse soon followed.

Many avaricious clergymen saw an opportunity to fatten their parish purse by selling the indulgences (Catholic Encyclopedia [2]). The larger the sum of money paid, the shorter the time one had to spend in purgation. With enough money, one could go straight to heaven and bypass purgatory all together. Between the years 700-1500 C.E. the Church took advantage of this system transforming the "wealth of the sinful rich" into "ecclesiastical endowments" (Johnson, 232).

The incredible amount of currency amassed from indulgences was used to build many of the great Catholic Cathedrals and monasteries. The "Peter Indulgence" was a special fund that was set aside for the building of St. Peter's Basilica in Rome. The notorious monk, Father Johannes Tetzel (1465-1519), the most successful salesman of indulgences, declared, "A soul is released from purgatory and carried to heaven as soon as the money tinkles in the box" (Religious tolerance.Org, 4).

When the wealthy were tapped out, the monetary standards for indulgences were lowered. Eventually they became so cheap that even the poor could afford them; anyone with a few pennies could purchase their freedom from purgatory. Further abuses in the system occurred when people reasoned they could commit acts of adultery and other grave transgressions with the belief that atonement could be easily purchased.

The corruption and abuse that resulted from selling plenary indulgences was too much for a man named Martin Luther. On October 31, 1517, the Vigil of All Saints, he decided to protest the sale of passes to paradise. Luther made his objections public by nailing his 95 Theses to the front door of Castle Church on the campus of Wittenburg University. Thus, on a chilly day in Saxony, Germany, the Protestant Reformation was born (Johnson, 233). Forty-one years later, in 1567 St. Pius V put an end to the granting of indulgences for fees and the idea that people could purchase their way into heaven. (Catholic Encyclopedia [2]).

Returning to our first family, Pat the Rat and St. Stephen prayed their brains out to free the rest of the clan from purgatory. Just to be sure, Patrick laid down a chunk of his inheritance money to secure an indulgence for everyone's purification. Any sins they may have committed were atoned for and their souls were able to pass safely into heaven. St. Stephen and the rest of the first family were reunited at last.

Just a Fact
In 1521 C.E. Martin Luther (1483-156) was excommunicated and declared an outlaw by Pope Leo IX. After translating the Bible to German, he went on to organize the Lutheran Church.

Canonization of Saints

For the following several hundred years, as the popularity of Christianity grew, so did the popularity of saints. Feast day celebrations were plentiful, joyous occasions and a good excuse for a party. Honoring deceased Christians became huge and everyone wanted his or her dearly departed declared a saint. Because there was no official guideline to determine the exact qualifications of a saint, veneration for the dead became out-of- control.

One story tells us that a man, who had several miracles attributed to him, was intoxicated when he died. This drunkard of a soul was well-loved by many of the villagers who declared the man a saint. They bestowed great accolades upon his spirit and had huge memorials erected in his honor. The idea of an alcoholic martyr appalled Alexander III so he forbade people to venerate the miracle worker as a saint. This did not sit well with the townsfolk and created quite a conflict. Due to the vague doctrine, an atmosphere of confusion and controversy reigned in the communion of saints; it remained so until the seventeenth century (Catholic Encyclopedia [1]).

It wasn't until 1634 that the disputed matter over sainthood was settled. Pope Urban VII published a Bull, which gave the Holy See exclusive authority on deciding which deceased Christians could be revered. This was the official establishment of the canonization of saints. The Roman Catholic Church decreed "public ecclesiastical veneration" of certain individuals (Catholic Encyclopedia [1]).

Just a Fact

It is interesting to note that the Bull, which gave the Holy See authority on sainthood, was not accepted by Orthodoxy or other branches of the Catholic Church. These churches adopted a more democratic canonization process; sainthood is decided by a group of bishops or clergy. Therefore, the whose-who of saints differs between the various denominations.

Once again, as the definition of saints changed, so did the relationship between the living and the dead. The lowly believers on earth were becoming more and more remote from their fellow believers in heaven. Furthermore, the relationship between the faithful in heaven changed as well. Certain deceased individuals were now held in higher esteem than their Christian brothers and sisters in spirit. The once equal, horizontal relationship became an unequal, vertical pyramid of power with the canonized Christians at the apex, the uncanonized spirits below them, the souls in purgatory below that, and the faithful on earth at the bottom. The communion of saints had become a hierarchy of saints (Johnson).

As the years passed, so did many of our witnesses to the faith, and lost in the fog of a distant memory was the ideology of the communion of saints. The canonization decree hurt the once-sacred, unitive, collaboration in Christ, as the word "saint" was now only ascribed to the most holy deceased.

People could no longer identify with the martyrs and pious ancestors who were glorified for their unhumanly holiness; they just weren't normal. Many of the canonized saints were distinguished bishops, priests or nuns who had no intimate relationships and, therefore, no children. The faithful on earth often rejected any connection or identity with those who were deemed "holier-than-thou" and the phrase "I'm no saint" became colloquial. The saints lost their significance in the world and no longer played a role in contemporary society (Johnson).

In an interview with the late Father Thomas Hoctor, retired priest and psychologist of the Diocese of Rochester, he adequately summed up the history of sainthood by commenting:

> In the early days, the church called everyone saints. Later-on the word became limited to those who passed away. Then there was the process to make them saints with a capital "S," to be canonized. The idea of saints was people who were saved. They made it through purgatory in order to get to heaven. (Grace)

Sadly, the communion of saints was no longer a fellowship of souls. It had become a bureaucracy of the sanctified, a hallowed hierarchy of the holiest. This fifth change in the doctrine is shown in the next chart. Saints only referred to the canonized souls in heaven; there was no longer equality within the Body of Christ.

COS V - Canonization Model - Pope Urban VII: 1634 C.E.

God & Jesus

Church in Heaven
Saints =
Canonized only

Church in Purgatory
None are Saints

Church on Earth
None are Saints

Saints are canonized people in Heaven only

For St. Stephen and our first-family the dynamics changed, once more, with canonization. The martyr was held in higher esteem than the rest of his clan, both living and dead; he was the only saint in the family. Furthermore, there were no relatives left on earth who could actually remember great-great, Uncle Stephen. He was no more than a distant relation whose name popped up occasionally at family reunions and made for great conversation starters at parties or the local pub. One can hear the pick-up line now of his great-great grand nephew, Pat the Rat III, "I see you're wearing a St. Christopher medal. You know I'm no saint, but my great Uncle Stephen really is one; would it be a sin to buy you a beer?"

Just a Fact
"Beatification" (to make blessed) is another title of holiness
given to those who have demonstrated an outstanding life of
sanctity. It is often bestowed on those who are being considered
for sainthood, much like a halfway-house to full canonization
(Hallam).

Forgotten Saints

When our connection with the saints disappeared, the feast days
and celebrations for them disappeared as well. Many Catholics
today do not even know who their patron saint is or when their
feast day is. Furthermore, we are slowly seeing the disappearance
of babies being named after saints. We now attend baptisms of
children with names like Sky, River, Harley and Misty. These
young Christians don't even have a patron saint and therefore no
feast day to celebrate.

For those who aren't familiar with the term "feast day," it's the
anniversary of the death of the saint you were named for. For
example, if your patron saint is Anthony, then your feast day is on
June 13, which is the day that saint died. If you don't know what
your feast day is, check out *Appendix A, Patron Saints and their Feast
Days*, in the back of the book.

If you were not named after a saint then adopt one of the saints with
whom you can most identify. There is a patron saint for almost
every occupation and situation in life. For example, if you're in
the military you may like St. George, the patron saint of soldiers;
your feast day would be April 23. Once you have a favorite saint be
sure to acknowledge him or her and celebrate your feast day with
a simple prayer or by making a charitable donation in memory of a
loved one.

An example of how feast days are celebrated can be given from my personal family history; let me share how this worked:

> Growing up, my mother acknowledged this day by giving us a small gift, such as a rosary or statue of a saint, to celebrate; one year I received a children's book of saints. Mom had one rule, however; you would not receive the gift unless you remembered it was your feast day and told her so. I saw it as a little birthday, one extra day a year when I would feel special. For that reason, I always remembered October 16, the feast of St. Margaret Mary of Alacoque.
>
> Feast days were never a big deal to celebrate with a huge meal; it was more of a private, quiet recognition of the day. This became a personal time between my mother and me and formed a bond of remembrance that lasts till this day. Of the six kids in our family, my brother, Pat (St. Patrick's Day) and I were the only feast days I could remember. Mom, on the other hand, never forgot each of our saintly holidays and always bestowed a present on us to mark the holy occasion.

Even for those who do remember their feast day, how many are familiar with the lives of their patron saint and what remarkable acts led to their canonization? Stories of the saints are no longer a source of inspiration for most Catholics today, as they were for the early Christians. There are no "lessons of encouragement" taught in Sunday school, in fact, not much at all is taught about the saints. Sure, most people are familiar with the big names like St. Joseph, St. Mary, St. Patrick, St Michael, St. Anthony and of course St. Nicholas, but what did we really know about their personal lives and the lives of the hundreds of other saints?

Although the church still honors the liturgical calendar of the saints, it does not seem to publicize them very well and has reduced the major celebration of the saints to one day a year, "All Saints Day." Here-in lies another division in the body of Christ as we honor the rest of the less-than-holy deceased on a separate day called "All Soul's Day." Is the head more important than the feet, are we not many parts of the same body?

No Relationship with the Dead

Throughout the years, the changes in our relationship and attitude towards the saints led to an overall change with our relationship and attitude toward the dead. For the early Christians, family and friends who had passed remained a part of their lives. Their constant veneration and request for intercessions kept the connection firmly rooted in their consciousness. In turn, the prayers of the faithful enabled the spirits of loved ones to move safely into heaven. Communication between heaven and earth was a normal and essential part of daily life. When that connection deteriorated, so did the strength of our spiritual bond with the deceased.

In today's world of science and technology, we no longer have a relationship with the dead. Most people seem to believe that when one enters the change called death they cease to exist. Continuity in relationships with loved ones in heaven is a by-gone practice; as a result, the dead are no longer a part of our earthly experience.

Elizabeth Johnson observes, "Imaginatively, the clear and easy trafficking between heaven and earth enjoyed by early Christians and medieval ancestors in the faith has broken down." She goes on to contend that if we don't feel a kinship to our own family and friends in spirit then how can we possibly feel connected to the canonized saints, who are even more remote. "Why venerate saints when we don't even venerate our own family?" (Johnson, 19-20).

As cited in Johnson's book, Karl Rahner comments on this subject in his article, *Why and How Can We Venerate the Saints?*:

If people think of their own nearest and dearest as disappearing at death into that darkness which surrounds the meager light of our existence with its silent infinitude, how can they find it in themselves to take up an attitude of veneration towards other dead persons merely on the grounds that they were holier? (20)

The sad fact is that many people don't have a strong relationship with any of the canonized saints; most Catholics feel more connected with their deceased loved ones. However, with the suppression of spiritualism in the church, if the faithful fear talking to their dearly departed than why would they feel comfortable talking with a five-hundred-year-old dead martyr?

Dead Still Honored

Fortunately, Catholics from other countries and cultural backgrounds have a different attitude towards death and communication with the saints. For example, in Mexico and other Latin American countries, the Day of the Dead is a big celebration. On November first, All Saints Day, Hispanics all over the globe may be found in cemeteries visiting with their loved ones. Gravesites are decorated with flowers, candles and other memorabilia while prayers and offerings of food are made to their family in heaven (Johnson).

An example of how another culture differs in their view on death can be given from another personal experience:

> On a missionary trip to Chiapas, Mexico I witnessed the incredible devotion to one saint in particular, The Lady of Guadeloupe. The Blessed Mother became the national saint after she appeared to a peasant man in the year 1531. Most every home has a place of honor for the Mother of Jesus. The Spiritus Christi Church group I traveled with noticed the sacred shrines everywhere we went.
>
> Guadeloupe shrines were often tucked into corners or

subtly placed among shelves of books, baked goods, or boxes of produce. We spotted the altars in coffee shops, convenience stores, restaurants, souvenir shops, bars, cyber cafes, hotels, and even in the schools and orphanages. Shrines could be found in remote jungles and canyons, as well as busy street markets. The powerful presence of faith wafted in the air like a freshly fried tortilla. It permeated every nook and cranny of our trip and nourished my soul in a way as foreign to me as the country I was visiting.

I was struck by the fact that displaying one's spiritual beliefs, whether at the workplace or a public park, was not seen as offensive to anyone. It was liberating to think Catholics did not have to hide or be ashamed of their religious beliefs. Due to a devout belief in the communion of saints, Chiapas seemed spared of political correctness and spiritual sterility. It warmed my heart to see that the saints were still alive and well in Mexico. Death and the deceased are very much a part of their culture and something to be revered, not feared.

There is another group of people who have a positive attitude towards the dead and death in general. Just like the early Christians, they still practice and maintain a relationship with their dearly departed. They hold weekly gatherings, not only to acknowledge the spirits in heaven, but to invite them into their living rooms and churches as well. They firmly believe in the continuity of life and that it can be demonstrated through their communications with the martyrs and saints who have gone before them. Furthermore, unlike most Catholics, these faithful servants of God are more than willing to talk about the deceased because they have no fear of them. These enlightened people are called "Spiritualists."

Spiritualists carry on the tradition of the early Christians by maintaining a conscious relationship with their deceased family and friends. As part of their religion, they ask for favors from "spirit" and often receive those favors in the form of guidance and consolation for their loss. In return, the souls are able to progress in their spiritual growth in heaven by helping their earth-bound relatives. In the same way, cub scouts receive merit badges by helping others, in order to progress to boy scouts. A mutual, equal relationship is formed between the saints in heaven and the saints on earth; both benefit. Spiritualists don't just "believe" in the communion of saints, they "*practice*" communion with the saints.

In an article in *Communio* Magazine, Christoph Schonborn points out that many people have been led to spiritualism because the church has failed to maintain a "genuine communion with the departed." He feels that due to the "loss of the liturgical and spiritual memory of the dead," Catholics have been forced to go outside the Church to find comfort and reunion with their family and friends who have passed (Schonborn, 179). This certainly seems to be the case, since many Spiritualists are former Catholics.

Just a Fact

Due to their strong connection with the saints, many Catholics are drawn to Spiritualism; some have converted. The mediums who were interviewed for this book all have Catholic backgrounds; two are former nuns, one is a married priest, and one is currently a Bishop in the Orthodox Catholic Church.

Just my Opinion

I think that the loss of our connection with the dead, led to the loss of our innocence. We ceased believing in the saints in the same way we ceased believing in fairies, gnomes and Santa Claus (St. Nicholas). A void was left in our spiritual lives that hung like an empty stocking on Christmas morning. Gone are the feast day celebrations, gone are the lessons of encouragement, gone are the graveside vigils, gone are the candles, gone are the venerations, and gone is the constant awareness of our family and friends in spirit.

Our daily dialog with the dead has been muffled along with our imaginations; the phone lines went dead and the conversations ended. And where we once enjoyed an abundant exchange of spiritual gifts, all we have left now are a few wrinkled wrappings and a barren box of faith in a world beyond our own. When we lost our belief that the dead are really present in our lives, we also lost our ability to see and hear our loved ones in spirit; the once faithful fans of the saints became faithless.

We can see how great this loss is when we compare the youth of early Christians with the not-so-innocent youth of today. Where first-century children dreamed of becoming like Jesus Christ Superstar; twenty-first century children dream of becoming like Michael Jordan super-sports-star. Where yesterday's believers were inspired to be the next witnesses to the faith; fame and fortune inspire youngsters today. Little girls want to be more like Miley Cyrus than Mother Theresa while little boys would rather be a super-hero than a Christian-hero.

Our loss of touch with the spiritual world has shifted our focus to the material world. Instead of aiming for the heavens, teenagers aim for the nearest shopping centers to buy the latest designer name. Kids today don't care if they get stuck in purgatory; they just don't want to be stuck in the mall after closing.

The followers of Jesus taught us that we are a holy people sharing holy things and all are equal. Our material possessions are to be equally shared, as well as our spiritual gifts. But with our loss of sense of community, came a loss of the sense of responsibility to each other. The concept of shared goods and good has been traded for an all-for-one and one-for-all mentality, and you had better keep up with the Jones's while you're at it. When it comes to spiritual gifts, like the ability to talk with the deceased, they are not to be shared at all. The idea of a holy people sharing holy things has been replaced with holier-than-thou people who control things.

St. Stephen accused the Jewish Sanhedrin of creating a limited God who only resided in their temples and only for the people they chose. In the same way, Rome has created a limited God who only resides in their cathedrals and only for the people they choose. They finished with a Catholic God who solely accepts heterosexual, single celibates, and never-divorced married couples, rather than a God who accepts all His own children. Furthermore, what was once an all-inclusive meetinghouse of saints has been exchanged for an all-exclusive, boys only clubhouse. Equality in the church has been traded in for discrimination.

The concept of all Christians being equally bonded to Christ through a shared meal is no longer practiced either, as not everyone is welcome at the Lord's Table. Communion means participation but how can one participate in the mystical body of Christ if he or she can't receive communion? It seems the hand was cut off to spite the face, and the disembodied parts got tossed away like a dead nun's habit. As a result, the dismembered remains succumbed to disease, depression, addiction and despair. The body of Christ is broken and many of His limbs have been lost. Those who were once dinner companions of Jesus are now outsiders who are fed on scraps from the table.

The bottom line is that all relationships are a relationship with Christ, "Whatsoever you do to the least of my brothers that you do unto me." When we fail in our relationships with each other, we fail in our relationship with Jesus. Therefore, we need to stop excluding whole groups of people from our faith communities, whether it's the outcast saints in heaven or the outcast saints on earth. So let us welcome all of God's children to the Table of the Lord. Let us celebrate the bond between St. Stephen, the first-family, and all believers in the universe in one great communion of saints; a fellowship of souls.

Summary

Although the communion of saints may have been rooted in the Jewish tradition, it was the early Christians' devotion to martyrs that solidified the concept. They revered these "holy" people and called them "saints." It was from these martyrs, like St. Stephen, that we received lessons of encouragement, guidance and courage in the face of brutal punishment for defending the faith. In return these heroes were honored with great celebrations on the anniversary of their birth into heaven.

In the first century all Christians were called saints, as seen in the writings of Saint Paul. Through communion or participation in shared meals they formed a common bond with Jesus. By partaking in the sacraments of the body and blood of Christ, they also formed a community. In this community they shared all things equally, material, as well as spiritual possessions. It was a cooperative of shared goods and good.

The companionship model of the communion of saints demonstrated a horizontal relationship in which all were equal. This meant not only the saints on earth, but also those in heaven. When the divine nature of Jesus was established, this balance was shifted to a patriarchal, vertical relationship. Only the dead were called saints and they gained the ability to grant favors for those on earth.

Over time "communio" changed from "participation" in the sacraments to "fellowship" of the church. With the advent of purgatory, the fellowship of souls now existed on three levels—heaven, earth and purgatory. In order to go directly from earth to heaven, one could skip purgatory altogether by purchasing an indulgence.

With canonization the saints lost their popularity and the faithful lost their identity with the saints; this led to a loss of relationships with the dead. When communication with loved ones in heaven was condemned by the church, fear of the dead and death in general set in. The tie to the world of the saints was severed; the silver cord was cut.

We have seen how the communion of saints has changed over the years, especially for our first family. In the first century all followers of Jesus were called saints. The whole family shared in an equal partnership with Christ. After Stephen died and was later canonized, he was considered a saint but the rest of the family was not. Stephen became a patron and helped his relatives on earth by granting them favors and even facilitating miracles.

Unfortunately, many of the family members no longer felt they could relate to Uncle Stephen; he was a pious, holier-than-thou man whom no one even remembered. Eventually his descendants lost touch with him, consequently the anniversary celebrations ended, along with the need for his heavenly help. Finally, the conversations and invocations ended, along with the exchange of spiritual gifts.

Sadly we leave our brothers and sisters in sainthood, but with hope, not discouragement. We look to our fellow believers in the Hispanic and Spiritualist populations for an optimistic future for us all. We can revive an age-old tradition by removing an age-old taboo. We can take back our sainthood and reestablish equality with all people in the body of Christ.

Chapter 4
The Communion of Saints Today

The Apostles' Creed

I believe in God, the Father almighty,
Creator of heaven and earth;
and in Jesus Christ, His only Son, our Lord;
Who was conceived by the Holy Spirit;
born of the Virgin Mary;
suffered under Pontius Pilate,
was crucified, died and was buried.
He descended into hell;
the third day he rose again from the dead
He ascended into heaven;
is seated at the right hand of God the Father Almighty;
from thence He shall come to judge the living and the dead.

I believe in the Holy Spirit,
the Holy Catholic Church,
the communion of saints,
the forgiveness of sins,
the resurrection of the body,
and the life everlasting.
Amen.

Every time we profess the Apostles' Creed, we pray "I believe in the communion of saints," but do we really grasp its meaning? In this chapter we will explore what the communion of saints means in the twenty-first century. We will first examine the official definition and see how we incorporate the belief into our church practices today. We will then look through the eyes of several theologians and scholars to gain a more contemporary perspective. This will set the stage for understanding what it means to be a truly Catholic, all-inclusive church. As this doctrine continues to evolve, the assertion, "I believe in the communion of saints" may not mean the same for everyone.

The Church and the Communion of Saints

Q: *How does the communion of saints work?*

Although we have gotten away from the great feast day celebrations, and there is an overall decline in popularity of sainthood for the younger generations, many Catholics still have a love affair with the popular canonized saints. We may have a statue of the Virgin Mother in our homes and St. Francis can often be found in our gardens. A St. Christopher medal in our car or around our neck protects us in our travels, and many of us have a dashboard Jesus for good measure.

Nearly all Catholics have a favorite saint, the person we can most readily identify with. There are saints to guide us in every conceivable aspect of life. There is a saint for bakers, barbers and beggars, as well as a saint for carpenters, cooks and cripples. There is a saint for hunters, housewives and hopeless causes, as well as for innkeepers and invalids. There is even a saint who helps us find lost articles. We are able to embrace and employ the aid of these saints on a daily basis. We owe this dedication to a belief that has become an integral part of our faith, "the communion of saints."

As discussed in the last two chapters, there are three levels or dimensions in which the members of the church reside. The first level is made up of the saints in heaven, which is called the "Church Triumphant." On the second level are the souls who live in purgatory, also known as the "Church Suffering." The third level is the faithful on earth; they are members of the "Church Militant." Together they form the communion of saints (Breton).

This fellowship of souls is basically the cosmology of the church, which explains its three-dimensional nature. The whole concept is tied to the relationship between the members who live in these various planes of existence. It is both a vertical relationship, between the levels, and also a horizontal relationship within each level. *The Catechism of the Catholic Church* (C.C.C.) puts it more succinctly by stating, "What is the Church if not the assembly of all the saints?" Or even more simply put, "The communion of saints is the Church" (823). The following chart from the *True Catholic* website provides a wonderful visual-aid and graphic explanation:

Interrelationship of Church Members

As you can see, the communion of saints is an intricate network involving prayer and help, between and across the church levels. The way it works is that the people on earth (Church Militant) can pray or ask the saints in heaven (Church Triumphant) for help, not only for themselves but also for those in purgatory (Church Suffering). In addition, members on earth can pray for each other. In return, the saints in heaven can provide the help needed for people on earth and in purgatory. Therefore, the souls in purgatory benefit from prayers received from both heaven and earth (True Catholic.Org).

This continual communication and assistance is what the *Catholic Encyclopedia* calls "a constant interchange of supernatural offices."

The ongoing interaction establishes and maintains both the vertical and horizontal relationships among members. Thus, we are united not only with each other, but also with Jesus, "the head" of the communion of saints. This is the foundation of our church.

In the Vatican II document, *Lumen Gentium, The Dogmatic Constitution On The Church* we find further clarification regarding the communion of saints. This doctrine explains that the saints in heaven help in many ways to build a broader church because they are closer to Christ. They fix the whole church more firmly in holiness and add to the nobility of worship in the church here on earth (7:49). Through this relationship with Christ, the church unites God with humankind (1:1). The Vatican recognizes that our church and the way in which we worship God on earth are greatly enhanced by the saints in heaven (Paul VI, Pope).

Reverend Sebastian Falcone, professor of Biblical Studies and former president of St. Bernard's School of Theology and Ministry in Rochester, New York supports the Vatican interpretation. When asked what the communion of saints means to him, in an interview, Falcone replied, "It is the establishment of a relationship with the broader dimensions of the church." The well-respected scholar went on to provide a beautiful description of this often misunderstood, doctrine:

> My understanding of the communion of saints is that it is an attempt to put together in one cohesive pattern the full range of everybody who has effectively come to understand life in all its aspects as one of the blessings of God. It encompasses everybody else who has ever been in existence, whoever is not only still living but has moved into the next life, and within that whole context, the understanding of how we are part of this bigger, broader, fuller picture.

Falcone added that it included everyone, living or dead, "who in some way, has been a part in the search for a concept bigger than the church, the kingdom of heaven." He believes the communion of saints represents much more than our usual concept of "church." It includes everyone in the universe, past and present, who has come to know God. This cosmic group gives us the "broader dimensions" or the bigger picture of the church (Grace).

Just a Fact

Founded by Bishop Bernard McQuaid, St. Bernard opened as a Roman Catholic Seminary in 1893. Under Vatican II it was restructured into an institute for theological and ministerial studies. It became one of the first seminaries in the United States to open its doors to laity.

In his article "The Communion of Saints as Three States of the Church," published in *Communio: International Catholic Review,* Christopher Schonborn adds further light to the communion of saints. He believes that our understanding of the church takes on a deeper meaning when we embrace both the members on earth and in heaven "whose numbers are impossible to count." Schonborn insists, "It is of vital importance for the consciousness of the Church to live in the 'space' of this invisible, but wholly real community" (179). He agrees we must believe in the cosmic nature of the church, even though most can't see it.

"We walk by faith and not by sight," according to the Scriptures (2 Corinthians 5:7). Jesus put it another way, "Blessed are those who do not see and yet believe"(John 20:29). Faith, in itself, is invisible. We cannot physically see our prayers floating up to heaven. People, for the most part, cannot see angels, the saints, Jesus, God or anyone else in heaven, and yet we call on them for help and we believe. We even believe we can have a relationship and share spiritual gifts with heavenly beings we can only imagine. We will now take a closer look at this sharing of invisible goods among the communion of saints.

Just a Fact

Lumen Gentium, which is Latin for "Light of the Nations," was publicized by Pope Paul VI in 1964. One of the principal documents of Vatican II, it describes the unity of the "pilgrim church" (church on earth) with the church in heaven.

Spiritual Gifts

Q: *What exactly is meant by 'spiritual gifts' and how do we share them with someone who lives in another dimension?*

So far we have established that the communion of saints is defined by the relationship of its members with each other and with Christ. It is important to note that just as with the early Christians, the communion of saints still maintains the idea of shared goods and shared good. Carlos Heredia, S.J, from the College of Francis Xavier, agrees with this theology in his book *True Spiritualism.* He suggests, however, that when sharing possessions between two planes of existence, we are not concerned with "earthly goods" but with "spiritual goods" (10). We receive these spiritual goods, also called "spiritual gifts" or "special graces," through participation in the Eucharistic sacrament. *The Catechism of the Catholic Church* states that these spiritual goods are the "Church's treasury" (1476, 371).

Thomas Aquinas addressed this notion of shared goods in an essay on the *Apostles' Creed.* He wrote, "Because all the faithful form one body, the benefits belonging to one are communicated to the others. There is thus a sharing of benefits in the church and this is what we mean by communio sanctorum" (Johnson, 1998, 96). The Vatican II document, *Lumen Gentium,* reinforces this point:

So it is that the union of the wayfarers with the brethren who sleep in the peace of Christ is in no way interrupted, but on the contrary, according to the constant faith of the Church, this union is reinforced by an exchange of spiritual goods." (409)

From these various descriptions of "shared spiritual goods," from prominent Catholic sources, we see its central importance to the faith. It is even described as the "Church treasury." But what exactly is meant by these "spiritual gifts" and how do we share them with someone who lives in another dimension?

In his article, *Three States of The Church*, Schonborn reports, "The exchange of spiritual goods and gifts is both ascending and descending, from the saints in heaven to us through their intercessions, and from us to them through veneration." He believes this trafficking of goods and gifts is the greatest way in which we show our concern for each other, a concern which continues beyond death (173). Essentially, spiritual gifts are prayers, which establish a two-way communication system between the people on earth and in heaven for the purpose of providing comfort, support, and guidance.

As we saw in our flow chart of the "Interrelationship of Church Members" these shared spiritual goods were characterized by the terms "pray for," "help" and "helped by." It is through these intercessions and venerations that we call on one another for assistance. Even though we may live in two different worlds, we believe that we can communicate across time and space in order to provide whatever help is necessary. In the next section we will see examples of this two-way relationship between heaven and earth and how we share these spiritual goods.

Insight

Prayer is a form of telepathic communication, which requires the use of our sixth sense. Therefore, when we pray to the saints for intercessions, we are utilizing our psychic or spiritual gifts.

Relationship with the Dead
Church Teachings & Practices

In his article, "How Catholics Keep Alive Their Connection With The Dead" in *U.S. Catholic* magazine, Lawrence Cunningham, Theology professor at Notre Dame University, makes an argument for communication with people in heaven. He points out that, despite the Christian condemnation of the practice of conjuring spirits, the church has claimed from the beginning that the relationship between the living and the dead has not been severed; moreover, it maintains this position through its "teachings, liturgy, and piety" (10-11).

When it comes to associating with the deceased, Cunningham contends, "Indeed, it [the church] teaches quite the opposite through its emphasis on what we call, in a shorthand phrase, the 'communion of saints.'" The priest also believes that connecting with our siblings, babies and parents who have passed is a "deeply human thing to do" and "for Christians the gulf between those who have died and those alive is not unbridgeable." We owe this all to a profound faith in the communion of saints (Cunningham, 10-11).

In the remainder of this section we will examine some of the sources that teach us about this bond between the church on earth and the church in heaven and ways in which we practice communication with the saints. One such source is the *Catholic Apologetics* (CA), a theological science whose purpose is to explain and defend the faith. This school of thought explains the importance of understanding that the communion of saints refers to the bond of unity among all believers in Jesus Christ, both the living and the dead.

In the eyes of God, the distinction between His people who are "living" or who are "dead" is not at all important. We find the foundation of this doctrine in the New Testament:

> As for the dead being raised, have you not read in the Book of Moses, in the passage about the bush, how God told him "I am the God of Abraham, the God of Isaac, and God of Jacob?" He is the God of the living not of the dead." (Mark 12:26-27).

The key word in the above passage is "living." We are all "living" spirits, whether we reside in the physical or non-physical world. We are eternal beings and therefore will live forever. The human body is just the vessel for our soul or spirit, which will one day find its home in an eternal spiritual body. Death is but a transition from the physical to the non-physical.

We are all "living" children of God, no matter what form we happen to be in. This belief is supported in Romans 14:7-9, "Whether we live or whether we die, we are the Lord's. For to this end Christ died and rose again, that he might be Lord of both the living and the dead." *The Catholic Apologetics* explains that through baptism we pass from death to life. As Christians, death no longer has dominion over us. "If we can pray for and with saints in this life, we can pray for and with saints after human life" (CA, [2]).

A second source of Catholic teaching about the bond between heaven and earth is the *Sacramentary*, the official book of liturgy used by priests when presiding over Mass. This is where the many familiar prayers come from that we recite or hear on a weekly basis. These prayers of intercessions and veneration are the spiritual gifts we exchange when practicing communion or communication with the members of the church in heaven.

The Eucharistic Prayer

We practice praying for and with the saints in a variety of ways during Mass. One demonstration of this connection with the dead takes place during the Eucharistic prayer. This Liturgy is recited at each Catholic Mass to give thanks and to signify our offering to God so that we too can one day join the saints in heaven. The following are several excerpts of this prayer from the Sacramentary, which was written by the National Conference of Catholic Bishops:

Eucharistic Prayer I
...Remember, Lord, those who have died and have gone before us marked with the sign of faith, especially those for whom we now pray, (parishioners inject out loud or silently the names of loved ones who have died). May these, and all who sleep in Christ, find in your presence light, happiness,

and peace. For ourselves, too, we ask some share in the fellowship of your apostles and martyrs, with John the Baptist, Stephen, Mathias, Barnabas [Ignatius, Alexander, Marcellinus, Peter, Felicity, Perpetua, Agatha, Lucy , Agnes, Cecilia, Anastasia] and all the saints. (542)

Eucharistic Prayer II

...Remember our brothers and sisters who have gone to their rest in the hope of rising again; bring them and all the departed into the light of your presence. Have mercy on us all; make us worthy to share eternal life with Mary, the virgin Mother of God, with the apostles, and with all the saints who have done your will throughout the ages. (551)

Eucharistic Prayer III

...May He make us an everlasting gift to you and enable us to share in the inheritance of your saints, with Mary, the virgin Mother of God; with the apostles, the martyrs [the saint of the day] and all your saints, on whose constant intercessions we rely for help. (554)

Recalling our "Interrelationship" flow chart, we can see that the Eucharistic prayers demonstrate how we practice sharing spiritual goods among the communion of saints. In this particular prayer the members on earth (the Church Militant) pray for the souls in purgatory (the Church Suffering) that they may find "light, happiness, and peace." At the same time, we pray to the saints in heaven (Church Triumphant) "on whose constant intercessions we rely for help." In this invocation we recognize and affirm our bond with the saints in heaven, and with Christ.

Just a Fact

The *Sacramentary* and *Lectionary* or *Missal* is the official book used by priests, which contain the prayers and readings read or sung during Mass. These prayers are arranged in a three-year cycle making up the liturgical calendar. Parishioners may follow along with the prayers by using the condensed, monthly version called the *Missalette*.

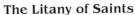

The Litany of Saints

Another place in the liturgy where we proclaim our connection with the dead is during the custom known as the Litany of Saints. Usually performed in song and only on special occasions, the canonized saints are invoked by the priest, choir, and congregants by singing out their individual names. There are so many saints mentioned that it forms a long list or "litany" of names. Acknowledging their role as mediators, the church community then petitions each saint by asking for help or to intercede for them. In this form of prayer the parishioners respond with a fixed phrase such as "Pray for us" (Whelen, 216 & 219). The following example is also taken from the *Sacramentary*:

The Litany of Saints Prayer:
Lord have mercy, Christ have mercy
>Holy Mary, Mother of God - pray for us
>Saint Michael - pray for us
>Holy angels of God - pray for us
>Saint John the Baptist - pray for us
>Saint Joseph - pray for us
>Saint Peter and Saint Paul - pray for us
>Saint Andrew - pray for us
>Saint John - pray for us
>Saint Mary Magdalene- pray for us
>Saint Stephen- pray for us
>Saint Ignatius- pray for us

Lawrence, Perpetua, and Felicity, Agnes, Gregory, Augustine, Athanasius, Badil, Martin, Benedict, Dominic, Xavier, John Vianney, Catherine, Teresa, All holy men and women - pray for us.

Lord be merciful, Lord, save your people. By your coming as man, Lord save your people. Be merciful to us sinners. Lord hear our prayer. (598)

As part of the liturgy of baptism, The Litany of Saints is performed on Holy Saturday (Easter Vigil) or on the vigil of Pentecost. It may also be used in the ordination of priests and deacons, dedication of churches, in the consecration of virgins, and in exorcisms. Summoning this extensive list of martyrs and asking for their intercessions is an age-old tradition that establishes and reinforces a relationship between the people on earth and the saints in heaven. Singing this incantation to myriad souls in the afterlife is an eloquent demonstration of how we practice communion with the saints.

Funerals

Perhaps the place we find the strongest support for our continued relationships with those in heaven is in the funeral rite. There are two sources of Catholic teaching which provide guidance during this time of bereavement, the *Catechism of the Catholic Church* (CCC) and the *Order of Christian Funerals* (OCF).

According to the *Catechism of the Catholic Church*, the Christian funeral is a liturgical celebration of the church, the purpose of which is to express effective communion with the deceased. This is accomplished by participation with all who have gathered at the burial ceremony for the proclamation of eternal life to the community (CCC, 1684).

The *Order of Christian Funerals* explains that the funeral rite, especially at the celebration of the Eucharistic sacrifice, is where the community expresses the union of the church on earth (Church Militant) with the church in heaven (Church Triumphant) in the one great communion of saints. At the death of a Christian, the church intercedes on behalf of the deceased and teaches us that death is not the end nor does it break the bonds forged in life. Some passages from the actual funeral rite, as written after the Second Vatican Council, describe this lesson:

"My brothers and sisters, we believe that all the ties of friendship and affection which knit us as one throughout our lives do not unravel with death."

"Lord our God...for those who believe in your love, death is not the end, nor does it destroy the bonds that you forge in our lives." (3)

Even though the dead are separated from the living, they are still one with the community of believers on earth and benefit from our prayers and intercessions. At the final tribute the mourners acknowledge the reality of separation and commend the deceased to God. The community recognizes the continuity of the spiritual bond between the living and the dead and the belief that one day its members will be reunited (OCF).

Furthermore, the *Catechism of the Catholic Church* teaches us the following: "The death of a member of the community, is an event that should lead beyond the perspectives of 'this world' and should draw the faithful into the true perspective of faith in the risen Christ." (1687, 419) Most of us don't spend a lot of time thinking about the afterlife until we find ourselves dealing with the loss of a loved one. It is in the funeral ritual that we are invited to go "beyond this world." In addition, the funeral rite states that "by the Eucharist the family of the deceased learns to live in communion with the one who has fallen asleep in the Lord." (1371, 420). It is through our common bond with Christ that we maintain a relationship with our loved ones who have passed.

In an article from U.S. Catholic magazine, Lawrence Cunningham (cited earlier) explains that the funeral liturgy is celebrated in white in order to emphasize the resurrection and to help us think of death as a beginning to a new life, not an end. Cunningham believes that death does not end our relationships and points out, "At funerals we affirm the dead are not beyond our caring or so separated that we cannot speak for them or *with* them." He argues that solidarity with the saints in heaven "enlarges our horizon." The Funeral Mass is where we are reminded of the connection with our loved ones in spirit and our eternal nature (11).

All Saints & All Souls Day

Another way in which Catholic ritual helps us to maintain our connection with the dead is by having special celebrations to honor them. One such commemoration is "All Saints Day." This day is set aside to venerate all the saints in heaven who have not yet been canonized, and therefore do not have a feast day.

Originally All Saints Day was held during Eastertide because the martyr's death was symbolically connected to the death of Christ. Sometimes it was also held on the feast of the Holy Trinity, the Sunday following Pentecost (the Orthodox Catholic Church continues this springtime custom today). In the Western Church, All Saints Day was moved to November 1 to coincide with "Samhain," the druid festival of the dead, thus, making it easier to convert the pagans (Johnson, 1998).

Just a Fact

"*Samhain*," Gaelic for "summers end," marks the end of the summer and harvest season and the beginning of the Celtic calendar; it is commonly called "The Celtic New Year." To help convert pagans to Christianity, the Catholic Church declared the day "Hallowmas" or All Saints' Day. This eventually led to the popular holiday we call "Halloween."

Besides the canonized saints, on All Saints Day we also honor our loved ones who made it safely to heaven. In an interview with Father Patrick Mulligan (a pseudonym used to keep his anonymity) of St. Mary's Catholic Church in Upstate, NY I asked, "How can we possibly know who is a saint?" He replied:

> We know there are many, many, many people, who are not canonized, who otherwise led good Christian lives, who are with God in heaven, who are saints; that's why we have

the feast of all saints. (Grace)

We can then assume that our good-hearted and virtuous family and friends, who have left the earth, are indeed among those souls in paradise.

In addition to all the known saints, All Saints Day eventually expanded to include the unknown or anonymous people who had died. According to Karl Rahner, this would be "those who lived quietly in the land, the poor, and the little ones who were great only in God's eyes, those who go unclaimed." (Johnson, 1998, 251). Examples of these anonymous saints would be the homeless people with no known family, the forgotten elderly who were left to die alone, the missing and abused children, and the unborn babies. For this reason, Elizabeth Johnson so aptly calls this November day "the feast of splendid nobodies." (Johnson, 1998, 8).

The second occasion on which we honor those who have departed is called "All Souls Day." On November second, we remember all who have died in an impure state. This would include those who had not been cleansed of sin or had not fully repented for past transgressions. It is believed that these souls are in purgatory and that the faithful on earth can help them by prayers, good works, or sacrifices; having a Mass said for the deceased is another common practice.

On both All Saints Day and All Souls Day, the church acknowledges and honors our connection with those who have died. Furthermore, the entire month of November is dedicated to these faithful, thus, helping us to maintain our relationships with all members of the communion of saints (Catholic Encyclopedia [1]).

We have learned how the church teaches us to maintain a relationship with the dead through Scripture, liturgy, doctrine and traditions. This gives us one view of the communion of saints. We will now take a look at a more contemporary perspective as seen through the eyes of several scholars and theologians. These viewpoints focus on the horizontal relationship among the members of the church on earth.

Relationship with the Living
World Views on the Communion of Saints

For many, "saints" has a much broader meaning than just referring to dead canonized Christians. It includes all people in heaven, earth, and purgatory no matter what their religious belief may be. This goes back to the Jewish concept of "holy" (kodash) meaning all people who believe in or have a covenant with God. This was also the predominate view of the communion of saints for the first sixteen-hundred years following the death of Christ. In this section, however, we will examine this "fellowship of souls" as it relates to "the living."

In an article found in *Catholic Megatrends* magazine, entitled "A Vision for the Unity of Mankind," professors of theology Michael and Kenneth Himes, O.F.M. defend this extended view of the communion of saints. They cite the questioning lawyer who asks Jesus, "And who is my neighbor?" (Luke 10:29). The response comes in the form of the parable of the Good Samaritan. Jesus expands the notion of neighbor to include not only strangers, but also enemies, those of different races and religions, and those with whom we have commonality of life. The article goes on to state how the apostle Paul insisted that through baptism in the spirit there is "neither Jew nor Greek, neither slave nor free, neither male nor female" (Galatians 3:28).

Jesus' and Paul's concept of neighbor is the whole idea behind the communion of saints. They both mean that race, nationality, class, gender, even distant dimensions pose no limitations within the shared life of people. Himes points out that these national, social and religious differences become insignificant in Christian communion. The source of all holiness is our oneness, which is universal and unbounded by time and space (Himes).

In *True Spiritualism*, cited earlier, Carlos Heredia describes the communion of saints as a "Divine Corporation, a great communism in which all the saints in heaven and all the souls in purgatory and all the children of the Church on earth form one vast family." Heredia declares that all races, people, nations, tribes and tongues, on both earth and in heaven, define the communion of saints. He also claims that although we may not be saints, in the ecclesiastical conception of the word, we are all in the communion of saints and it is well never to forget that (Heredia, 74).

In her book, *Truly Our Sister, A Theology of Mary in the Communion of Saints*, Elizabeth Johnson also emphasizes a broader view of this concept. She declares that the doctrine clearly includes relationships among all the holy people of God, Jewish and Christian alike. Johnson goes on to explain that although the communion of saints has become synonymous for Christians themselves, the Holy Spirit does not limit divine blessings to any one group:

> At its most elemental, then, the communion of saints does not refer to Christians alone but affirms a link between all women and men who have been brushed with the fire of divine love and who seek the living God in their lives. From this angle the symbol of the communion of saints shows itself to be a most inclusive belief. It crosses boundaries, breaking down social lines of division and building up a vastly diverse people by the play of the Spirit through the ages and across the wide world. (2003, 306-307)

Johnson believes that God calls all beings to His truth and love and emphasizes this point in her book, *Friends of God and Prophets*. She insists that God inspires all people to deeds of compassion and justice, bringing together the poor and socially marginalized with the rich and powerful. Johnson also contends that the gifts of the Holy Spirit are not dependent upon age, gender, class, race or sexual orientation. Citizens of all nations and cultures have responded to this call and happy are those who are doing His will. As diverse as this population may be, those "brushed with the fire of divine love" still form one church community (Johnson, 1998, 262).

The idea that the Holy Spirit is not confined to one group is also supported in a statement made in an interview by Michael Mahoney, D.Min., a spiritually gifted Deacon, from the Diocese of Raleigh, North Carolina (formerly of Rochester, NY Diocese). When asked, "What does the communion of saints means to you?" the Doctor of

Ministry explained:

> The communion of saints refers to all who are in Christ;
> whoever is unified in him. It is important to remember that
> Jesus is not confused about who belongs to him. We may be
> confused as to who belongs to Jesus, but he is not confused.
> So whoever belongs to Jesus, and only Jesus knows that,
> is in the communion of saints or what is also called the
> mystical body. (Grace)

In this statement it is important to note that we cannot judge or
pretend to know just who is or who isn't a disciple of Christ; we may
not even know ourselves. There are countless people who have led
what would be considered good Christian lives, even though they
may not be Christians. People from all other religions, whether it
be Buddhism, Judaism, Shamanism, or Spiritualism, often practice
the teachings of Christ because many of those same teachings have
been laid down by mystics and teachers who lived before Jesus.

The Golden Rule (Do unto others...) and communication with
heavenly beings (prayer) is the basis for most religions. Therefore,
no matter what your faith, if you practice these basic Christian
doctrines then you "belong to Jesus." As a result, you are a part
of his mystical body and a member of the communion of saints.
We will now take a closer look at how this communion of saints is
synonymous with the mystical body of Christ.

The Communion of Saints &
The Mystical Body of Christ

In the first century, the martyrs and saints were intimately connected
to Jesus by their willingness to suffer and even die for their faith.
These early Christians continued this connection by sharing a meal
of bread and wine, which became the body and blood of Christ.
Through this communal supper the spirit of Jesus was poured
into them. Throughout the ages this tradition has endured. To this
day, we maintain our connection to Jesus by partaking in Holy
Communion; for this reason, we are all parts of the mystical body
of Christ.

St. Paul describes this mystical body of Christ at great length in 1 Corinthians, Chapter 12. One could argue that he makes a great case for solidarity in spite of differences. He asserts that, although we are all different in our gifts and "administrations," we are still of the same Spirit and Lord. Paul further claims:

> For as the body is one, and hath many members, and all the members of that one body, being many, are one body: so also is Christ. For by one spirit are we all baptized into one body, whether we be Jews or Gentiles, whether we be bond or free; and have been all made to drink one spirit. For the body is not one member, but many. (1 Corinthians 12:12-14)

> Now ye are the body of Christ, and members in particular (1 Corinthians 12:27).

St. Paul also insists that when we participate in Holy Communion we are participating in Christ. "The bread which we break, is it not the communion of the body of Christ? For we being many are one bread, and one body: for we are all partakers of that one bread." (1 Corinthians 10:16-17). Because of the teachings of Paul, the idea of the church being the mystical body of Christ was made doctrine. *The Catechism of the Catholic Church* tells us:

> The Church is both visible and spiritual, a hierarchical society and the Mystical Body of Christ. She is one, yet formed of two components, human and divine. That is her mystery, which only faith can accept (779).

The belief that the Catholic Church is the mystical body of Christ is the foundation of our faith. At the same time, as we have learned, "the communion of saints is the church" (823). Consequently, logic would tell us that the communion of saints is synonymous with the mystical body of Christ:

> If A: The entire church is the communion of saints.
> And B: The entire church is the mystical body of Christ.
> Therefore C: The communion of saints is also the mystical

body of Christ, as well as the entire church.

This is an important point to make, as we shall see throughout the rest of this book. The mystical and spiritual gifts Jesus possessed are passed on to the members of the communion of saints. Each member is a unique part of Christ and together they make up his entire body. As individuals with very different backgrounds and gifts, we each struggle in our various roles to be more like the whole, to be like Christ. Yet, as individuals we only know the small piece, which is us. And because we don't know the other pieces, we don't always understand or appreciate where our gifts fit into the bigger picture. It is this unknowing and lack of understanding, in the very mystery that is Christ, that often becomes our greatest fear.

This fear goes unfounded, however, when we put our complete faith in God, and most of all, trust that He knows what He's doing with every single child in His kingdom. For it is our unique talents and individual personalities that create the communion of saints; it is the many parts that form the one mystical body of Christ.

Insight

A popular Catholic song celebrates the mystical body of Christ
and the idea of sharing our spiritual gifts
among the communion of saints:
"We are many parts, we are all one body,
and the gifts we have, we are given to share.
May the spirit of love, make us one in deed;
one, the love that we share, one, our hope in despair, one, the
cross that we bear." (Haugen)

Solidarity in Differences

From this diversity among members of the communion of saints, we might speculate that the teachings of Christ were rooted in the solidarity of our differences. By his actions, Jesus made it quite clear that faith was the common bond and that people's disparities had no bearing on their true convictions. He often praised those who demonstrated their unwavering belief in him, no matter what their religion, social status, or gender. We see this demonstrated in the story of the faithful, bleeding woman in need of healing. Despite her poverty and unclean body, she was convinced that if she could only touch Jesus' cloak she would be healed. Her faith was what Christ noticed, not her disability; as a result, the woman's health was restored.

The importance of fostering a sense of solidarity through faith is emphasized in the Vatican II document, *Gaudium et Spes, Pastoral Constitution on the Church in the Modern World*. This article insists that the communion of saints must be an all-inclusive, united community in which all members share in the responsibility of promoting the spiritual and material well being of others. By serving the common good, we should treat one another as family and act in a "spirit of brotherhood" (2:24). The inclusion of all persons and groups is a moral imperative and we should have respect and charity towards those who "act differently from us in social, political, and religious matters (Paul, Pope VI, 2:28).

Just a Fact

Guadium et Spes is Latin for "Hope and Joy." The title describes the spirit of the document, which embraces the idea that people are the heart of the church. It also addresses social responsibility, peace, war and the plight of the poor. It was promulgated by Pope Paul VI in 1965.

The *Gaudium et Spes* points out that solidarity in differences is all about respect for the human person because this is what Jesus was all about:

Today there is an inescapable duty to make ourselves the neighbor of every man, no matter who he is, and if we meet him, to come to his aid in a positive way, whether he is an aged person abandoned by all, a foreign worker despised without reason, a refugee, an illegitimate child wrongly suffering for a sin he did not commit, or a starving human being who awakens our conscience by calling to mind the words of Christ: 'As you did it to one of the least of these my brethren, you did it to me' "(Mt. 25:40). (Paul, Pope VI, 2:27)

This quote is commented on in the Himes' article cited earlier, *A Vision for the Unity of Mankind*. The authors observe that Catholic social teaching arises from the belief that we are united in one human family. The Catholic vision of a just society is one that shows people living "in right relationship to one another" (207). Through mutual respect, forgiveness, honor, and love, a genuine community is created. True dignity, as well as belonging and friendship, are imperative to the welfare of each individual. Therefore, it is the social and moral obligation of Catholics to welcome all people into community in order to avoid exclusivity.

For this reason, those living on the margins teach us that we have not achieved full participation in the body of Christ. From *Gaudium et Spes*, and other Catholic teachings, we learn that defending human rights is important to solidarity and that "building a truly inclusive social and global order is the hope held by those who believe in the communion of saints" (Himes, 209).

Church without walls

Solidarity in our differences, through a shared bond with Jesus Christ, is what the Catholic faith is all about. In his unique series of books, Paul Ferrini, a modern-day mystic and prophet, brings us the teachings of Christ through his own personal communion with Him. Ferrini's revelations remind us about the fundamental importance of an all-inclusive community. In *The Silence of the Heart*, we see Jesus' view of what a church community should be:

The community I am calling you to is a church without walls, a place where people of all faiths come together to love, support, and honor each other. My church has nothing to do with Christianity, or with any dogma that separates people. It has nothing to do with any religious hierarchy or elaborate organizational structure.

All are welcome in my church. Both the poor and the rich, the sick and the healthy. Those who call my name and those who call the name of any of my brothers or sisters. I do not stand against any man or woman, but for every man and woman, for each is God's child. I stand for the sanctity of all beings who in their innocence bless creation with their presence. I celebrate life in all its forms and in its quintessential formlessness. (151)

This universal church, where all are welcome, is the one around which we have built our faith. It reflects the teachings of Christ and is based on first-century Christianity, which was a church without walls. It substantiates the notion that a church made up of people from all walks of life is a truly "catholic" church.

On the subject of diversity, Elizabeth Johnson believes that our differences should be celebrated and honored as God's extraordinary display of the rich, divergent combinations comprising each person created in His image. Community should develop around our uniqueness and not as a result of "suppressing differences and homogenizing everyone into sameness" (Johnson, 2003, 107).

Holy Divisions

Unfortunately, suppressing differences is exactly what happened in the church. As "saints" we are united as a "holy" people belonging to God. However, what was meant to unite the people of God was often used as power to control and rule individuals or groups over one another. "Holy" eventually meant "holier-than-thou." It placed some people or groups in higher esteem than others. It took the meaning and ministry of Jesus and turned it upside-down. Instead of a tie to bind brothers and sisters in Christ, it was used as a sword to sever our relationships. It was used to pit brother against brother and "holy wars" were the result. Never is this more prevalent than in our own Catholic history. Never is this more apparent than in the present state of the Roman Catholic Church.

During the 2007-2008 presidential campaign, controversy arose when several Roman Catholic priests withheld communion from individuals who were either running for the Democratic Party or in favor of certain democratic candidates. This is just one example of how "holy" people used the Eucharist to divide the Body of Christ. This practice contradicts the teachings of Christ and is most likely not what Jesus had envisioned.

Repair My Church

Divisions in the church led to a broken body of Christ. St. Francis recognized this problem eight-hundred years ago when he received the message "Repair my church." He eventually understood that it was the *body* of the church that needed repair, not the *buildings* themselves. This still holds true, the church is still in need of restoration, and never is it in more imminent danger of falling apart than it is today.

In his book, *Conjectures of a Guilty Bystander*, Thomas Merton addresses this division in the church, which resulted in the exclusion of many people from the communion of saints:

> If I affirm myself as a Catholic, merely by denying all that is Muslim, Jewish, Protestant, Hindu, Buddhist, etc., in the end, I will find that there is not much left for me to affirm as a Catholic; and certainly no breath of the Spirit with which to affirm it." (18)

Merton goes on to say that we cannot reunite the church by eliminating groups of people or forcing one group upon another. If we take these actions then not only is the church not Christian, but "it is political and doomed to further conflict." Merton believes that any divisions we have must be contained within ourselves and can be transcended through Christ (21).

Hans Balthasar helps to make this point regarding a broken

church. In his article "Catholicism and the Communion of Saints, in *Communio* magazine, he observes:

> The Catholic Church has lost her sense of the "body" and the truth of the Eucharist: a church sustained by ethics, good works, social consciousness, and the liberation of those who are politically and socially downtrodden-essentially a caricature of the communion of saints." (167)

The author speculates that, although there have been great efforts to restore the church, the problems will continue until "faith and order" are aligned with the communion of saints.

Just a Fact

Thomas Merton (1915-1968) was a Trappist Monk whose most notable work was his autobiography, *Seven Storey Mountain*. The book describes his spiritual journey from a modern, materialistic scholar searching for meaning in life, to a contemplative who found peace and fulfillment in the monastery. The bestselling book was translated into over twenty languages.

In the interview with Reverend Sebastian Falcone former president of St. Bernard's School of Theology, he also addressed the issue of a broken body of Christ and a church in need of repair. He explained that the Roman Catholic Church sees herself as the "kingdom of God" and excludes other churches; consequently it closed off all discussion with others. Falcone noted that Vatican II declared "People of God" to be the true definition of the church, in short, "this means everyone who is searching for the kingdom." The Reverend insists, "The problem is if it [the true church] gets so tightly identified with something being taught by a Roman Catholic, without reaching out to the broader situation, it gets to be packaged under a false perception." (Grace)

Returning to the interview with Deacon Mahoney, D.Min., we gain another perspective on the need to repair the church. This comes following an inner locution, which the deacon received. While in deep contemplative prayer, the cleric heard the words, "Build my church." Since then Mahoney started a ministry to counsel anyone in need of healing, no matter what their belief system or lifestyle. He feels that by dressing the wounds of all God's children, he is indeed "building the church." The clergyman reflected:

> The Christian church, I'm afraid, is in disrepair. A divided church is a wounded church; it needs healing. Jesus advocated for community, for oneness, for unity, and for an open table. He prayed that we as Christians will be one, as a sign that God sent him into the world. Our future work will be to find that unity within a diversity that has deepened throughout the centuries. This will require us to be bold, be generous with one another, and expect miracles. (Grace)

Mahoney continued by explaining that the love of God and Christ Jesus is essentially unitive. "Love is unitive; His love for us and our love for Him. Jesus calls us to the table with him as his family. Conversation begins at the family table, which leads to deepening unity. We must continue to talk." The deacon believes we should work hard to realize Pope John Paul II's vision of full Christian unity as expressed in *Ut Unum Sint* (That They May be One). The church would soon begin to heal if we "simply open the table." (Grace).

Jesus had an open table; he had a relationship with all people. It did not matter to him whether he dined with the poor, the rich, the gentile, or the Jews. He did not exclude anyone-not even prostitutes, tax collectors, or thieves. He did not care about people's marital status, sexual orientation, or whether they were prophets, seers, sinners, or saints; everyone was his neighbor. Jesus was truly catholic; he was the great universalist. His life was a testimony to our oneness with God and each other. Every time he sat down to eat he practiced communion with the saints.

It is through participation in Holy Communion, and through Baptism, that makes us all members of the communion of saints. We take communion in remembrance and celebration of Jesus, of his teachings, and as an expression of our relatedness in Christ; we are members of a new family. To "re-member" is to "re-unite." It is our differences and uniqueness as individuals Jesus celebrated. It is our belief in God that makes us all holy, and therefore united. We belong and are worthy as we are all parts of the same mystical body of Christ. As children of God, united by faith, our unique differences are not an issue. Together, our individual personalities make up the Church, the communion of saints.

Just My Opinion

The communion of saints is synonymous with the word "catholic." They both refer to an all-inclusive, universal church that transcends time and space. In early Christian churches no one was excluded from attending Mass or from receiving Holy Communion. For "communion" means "participation" and how can one participate in Mass if he or she cannot receive communion? The original Catholic Church followed the teachings of Christ by practicing tolerance, acceptability and inclusiveness. It emphasized Jesus' teaching that everyone is our neighbor and therefore all were welcomed at the Eucharistic celebration.

When we do not honor differences, we really miss the point of being Catholic. Solidarity within the church comes from our common bond in Jesus Christ and our ability to see everyone as our neighbor. It comes from our common faith and the ability to come together in community for the purpose of helping one another in a time of need. Solidarity comes from the ability and willingness to share our unique, God given talents in order to meet these needs. When we do not honor differences, then we miss the true meaning behind the mystical body of Christ. When we do not honor differences we miss the point of the communion of saints.

Unfortunately, there are many "Catholics" who have missed the point. These modern day Pharisees have made themselves God by becoming judge and jury in deciding who is or isn't worthy of receiving Jesus. Holy Communion is being used as a political reward given only to those who join their party. It is being used as a down payment for a ticket to heaven and it is being used to determine who is and who isn't on that flight. As a result, this misuse of the Eucharist is creating divisions within the church.

Holy Communion has become the twenty-first century weapon of *Mass* destruction. It has led to the alienation, humiliation and degradation of millions of people. The effect is not unlike the tragic ethnic cleansing that occurred in Kosovo and Darfur. And like the millions of people in China, who are denied basic human rights within their own country, millions of Catholics are denied their basic right to receive communion within their own church. The fall-out from the abusive exclusion of large populations of God's children has left in its wake the wounded, the broken, the outcast, the poor and the socially marginalized. The Eucharistic nuclear winter is upon us, with many left out in the cold.

There is however a ray of warmth and sunshine in this divided nuclear freeze. If someone is excluded from one church, they can always find another that is more welcoming. There are many Catholic churches, the world over, simply waiting in the wings with their doors wide open. Whenever anyone decides that the party system is not working, they are welcomed to eat at the true table of the Lord. For this table is big enough for everyone, including the divorced, the unwed mothers, the gays, the lesbians, the Greeks, the Jews, the homeless, the psychics, the mediums, the mystics, the outcasts and priests of all kinds, including those who are women, married and/or gay.

With so many divisions in the church, there are many misconceptions about what it means to be Catholic. For many people, when they state, "I am a Catholic." they think that it means "Roman Catholic"; not necessarily. Most people think that Catholic is a denomination of a religion called Christianity; not necessarily. If the Church truly is the communion of saints it is much bigger than Roman Catholicism and even bigger than all of Christianity throughout the world, for it encompasses not only the faithful on earth, but also those who have died, those not yet born and even the angels in heaven. Add to this over twenty variations of Catholicism and no wonder we're so confused.

We must understand that as believers of God, we are all Catholic in one way or another. We are all God's children, no matter our shape, size, gender, or religious faith. We are all worthy because we are all parts of the same mystical body of Christ. As children of God, united by faith, it's not our human qualities that matter, rather the quality of our souls. It is at this soul level that we are all brothers and sisters of Jesus and of each other. We are all equal; we are all one, we are all catholic; we are all members of the communion of saints.

Summary

Catholics, the world over, have a love affair with the saints. We owe this to the church's belief in the "communion of saints." Most do not correctly understand, however, exactly who the saints are. Many think that "saints" are only the most holy dead. Therefore, when proclaiming, "I believe in the communion of saints," countless fail to realize that they are describing their relationship with all people in heaven, on earth and in purgatory. For this reason, a belief in the communion of saints may not mean the same for everyone.

The communion of saints is basically the cosmology of the church, which explains its three dimensional nature. The whole concept is tied to the relationship between the members who live in three planes of existence. It is both a vertical relationship, between the levels, and also a horizontal relationship within each level.

Even though we may live in three different dimensions or states, we believe that we can communicate across time and space in order to give and receive assistance when necessary. This is accomplished through intercessions, prayer and veneration. Through this process we exchange spiritual goods, which may come in the form of special graces or spiritual gifts.

We practice this communication with the saints in heaven during Mass. It helps us to establish a relationship with the dead. Despite the church condemnations regarding contact with the deceased, we continue this age-old custom through Scripture, doctrine, liturgy and practiced traditions. Examples of our on-going fraternization with the dead are: the Eucharistic prayer, the Litany of Saints, the funeral Mass and celebrations of All Saints and All Souls Day.

For many, the communion of saints has a much broader meaning than just referring to dead Christians. It includes all people on earth, no matter what their religious belief may be. It stems from Jesus' and St. Paul's concept of neighbor. Members can also include people of all races, nationalities, genders and class; sexual orientation and marital status pose no boundaries, no one is excluded. The only requirement is a desire for divine relationship and divine love.

Unfortunately, differences between members of the church have created divisions in both the past and the present. Although the Eucharist is intended to unite us to each other and to Christ, it is often used as a weapon to control and rule individuals or groups over one another. Fortunately, there are rays of hope among the divisions as there are still some Catholic churches that actually practice what they preach. These are churches where all remain welcome at the Lord's Table and Holy Communion is reuniting what was once divided. These all-inclusive Catholic communities are where the lost can be found, and where all belong to the communion of saints.

Chapter 5
Taboo

"If you can interpret the signs of the earth and sky, why is it that you cannot interpret the signs of the present time?"
(Luke 12:56)

It wasn't until Mom died that I learned spirit communication was against the faith. It wasn't until I started talking about my supernatural experiences, that I learned it was "taboo." I could not understand how the beautiful people and places in the afterlife could be off-limits. I made it my mission to find out why. In this chapter we will explore the following questions: "Why is the practice of mediumship, and contacting our loved ones in heaven, against the Catholic faith?" "Why is there such stigma and fear associated with it?" "Where exactly is it written and who decided it was such a bad thing?" Although there may not be any clear-cut answers, looking at pre-Christian beliefs from a present-day viewpoint will shed much light on the subject.

Ancient Beliefs in a New Age

We live in the twenty-first century, yet many of our Catholic beliefs pre-date the first century and come directly from the Old Testament. Some of these ancient tenets, which became canon law, no longer apply or are not realistic in today's society. For this reason, countless Catholics have already turned from the antiquated thinking of the church authorities. This can be seen concerning matters such as premarital sex, birth control, divorce and same-sex relationships. There are many devout Catholics, including priests, who do not agree with these rules and choose to simply ignore them.

Another example of an outdated church law is the one regarding spirit communication. Contacting our friends and relatives in heaven is quickly becoming the norm in the twenty-first century. People will always experience loss and grief. They will always seek consolation for their bereavement and to somehow hold onto their loved ones who have passed. With the conviction that life is eternal, they will seek to maintain relationships with those they care about in heaven. No matter what the church rules say, people will not deny their undying love for a kindred spirit.

The death of my mom, and her visitation, triggered my own desire to keep our relationship alive. Prior to that, death was never a part of my life and communication with the dead was something I never thought about; I was simply not aware of the world of spirits. As a result of my mother's after-death visit, and my subsequent near-death experience, I was not only aware of this other world; it became an integral part of my life. I became a member of a much bigger community with a whole new set of family and friends. This extended fraternity just happened to be part of the communion of saints who reside on the otherside. Reconciling my new-age, spiritual experiences with old-age, Catholic teachings was a formidable undertaking.

Ancient Taboos

Q: *Why was spirit communication and consulting mediums banned in Biblical times?*

The main reason there is stigma and fear attached to communication with the dead is because of several scripture passages in the Old Testament. Let's take a closer look at these dark-age insights and examine them in the light of the twenty-first century. The following passages are from Deuteronomy and Leviticus:

> Let there not be found among you anyone who immolates his son or daughter in the fire, nor a fortune-teller, soothsayer, charmer, diviner, or caster of spells, nor one who consults ghosts and spirits or seeks oracles from the

dead. Anyone who does such things is an abomination to the Lord... (Deuteronomy 18:10-12)

Do not go to mediums or consult fortune-tellers, for you will be defiled by them. I, the Lord, am your God. (Leviticus 19:31).

Taking a look at the first passage, I think everyone would agree that to sacrifice (immolate) children by fire is unacceptable; it is also illegal in our current society. At the same time, this Biblical wisdom would imply that sacrificing children using a different method might be permissible. Today, however, most would concur that any form of child immolation would be an abomination to the Lord; it would also be considered murder. Therefore this scripture is no longer applicable to present day values. We will now examine the rest of the two passages by looking at the individual taboos more closely. We will define these ancient practices and see how they fit or don't fit into modern day society.

Fortune-tellers & Soothsayers

Fortune-telling is the practice of predicting the future by the use of various tools of divination. In Biblical times this included astrologers, palm readers, numerologists and diviners. Soothsayers were people who predicted the future without necessarily using any divination tools; their knowledge was direct. Examples of soothsayers are prophets, charmers, "casters of spells," seers, visionaries and mediums. The ancient Hebrew language grouped all these practices in one word, which translates into "necromancy"; they did not differentiate between the various professions (Ebon, 21).

For this reason these terms are used interchangeably today, even though their meaning has changed over time. Modern-day mediums and prophets are not the same as "soothsayers" or "fortune-tellers." At the same time, often these categories overlapped. For example, knowledge of the future is common for both mediums and prophets, but not the objective, as with fortune-telling. Unfortunately, this is why there is so much confusion over what is and what isn't acceptable today.

Consulting Ghosts & Spirits

It doesn't make sense to condemn consulting with the spirits of those who are in heaven because this would be a direct contradiction to our belief in the communion of saints. Although different words may be used, seeking advice and guidance from the deceased is commonly practiced in the Catholic faith. When we examine precisely what these individual words mean in the Deuteronomy passage, we can easily see how this is so.

Ghosts

What exactly is a "ghost" and what's wrong with consulting one? Ghosts are usually described as earth-bound spirits. They are people who are without physical form and yet have not moved on to their heavenly home. Essentially, ghosts are the homeless people of the universe, although they would still be members of the Church on earth.

It is not unusual for deceased people to hang around their surviving family due to some unfinished business or strong attachments to the people and places they love. Sometimes they remain to protect individual family members. These types of situations may keep the person stuck in this dimension. From time to time ghosts make themselves appear to their loved ones, hence the term "apparition." These see-through, eerie figures are usually what we think of when we speak of "ghosts."

The Scriptures do not exempt certain ghosts from being consulted; it implies that all of them are off-limits. Sometimes, however, ghosts come down from heaven to make themselves visible. For example, apparitions of the Blessed Mother are well-documented throughout Catholic history. Another spirit with divine status is the one we call "The Holy Ghost." There is even an entire Catholic hymn, which is sung for the purpose of conjuring this special entity, *Come Holy Ghost.* Whether it's the ghost of Grandma, the Virgin Mary or the Holy Ghost, they are still members of the church. What could be wrong with consulting them? How would this be considered an "abomination to the Lord?"

Insight
Do you believe in ghosts? Although some Catholics say they do not, they do believe in the Holy Ghost. If there is a "holy" ghost then it follows that there must be other ghosts who are less-than-holy. If there is one ghost, there must be more.

Spirits

The term "spirit" usually refers to the souls that have completed crossing over; they may be in one of three places, heaven, hell or purgatory. The Deuteronomy passage makes no distinction between evil spirits and holy spirits, all are off limits. However, holy spirits are the people living in heaven, consulting them cannot possibly be an abomination to the Lord. If it were, we would be guilty of offending God each time we asked for help from the saints.

When we say a rosary we may be asking the spirit of the Blessed Mother to help with for whatever it is we are praying. We may have an important decision to make and consult with the Holy Mother for guidance. In the same way, we may ask for guidance from the spirit of our deceased mother or other loved one. This does not seem to fit in with the warning from Deuteronomy and is not congruent with the communion of saints.

Oracles

In the same Deuteronomy passage, we are cautioned not to "seek oracles from the dead." What exactly is an "oracle?" Webster's dictionary describes an oracle as "a person through whom a deity is believed to speak." It is also "a person giving wise or authoritative decisions or opinions."

When the Scriptures were written, "seeking oracles" most likely referred to a common practice done by the ancient Greeks. When they needed spiritual guidance, they went to a shrine, which was also called an oracle. There they would ask questions of their god, Zeus through a human medium. The "Oracle of Delphi" was a famous shrine, which was considered one of the most sacred and respected sites in Greece. It drew noteworthy people, such as Alexander the Great, from all over the country (Time Life Book Editors).

In all probability, the reason the Bible forbids seeking oracles from the dead is because in ancient times it referred to a common pagan practice. While the Greeks consulted "oracles" for answers from God, the Jews consulted "prophets"; they were both mediums. A prophet is "one gifted with more than ordinary spiritual and moral insight" (Webster). Therefore, asking for guidance from a prophet could be considered consulting an oracle, both give heavenly advice.

Furthermore, the word "oracle" can not only mean a shrine or person who speaks to God, it can also refer to the message itself. An oracle is the answer or decision given by a deity, also known as a "revelation" (Webster). Today, when Catholics seek divine guidance, they often call on the saints. Saints act as mediums who give us messages by answering our prayers.

For example, we may pray to Saint Anthony, to help us find our lost keys. We ask the deceased friar to somehow tell us where the keys are located. Often, when we do this we are struck with a sudden "revelation" as to where we left them, as we may have telepathically received an "oracle" from the saint. In another example, when the children at Fatima were getting messages from the Blessed Mother, they were receiving oracles from the dead virgin.

Insight
The Ten Commandments would be considered an oracle because it was a "revelation" that came through a prophet (Moses), by a deity (God). As Catholics, we may use different words, but we still "seek oracles from the dead."

In an interview, one priest explained that it was all right to pray or talk to the saints in heaven, but we could not get "information" (oracles) from them. Yet, we often pray in order to seek answers to many or our life's problems. The answer may come in many forms, maybe advice given by a friend, maybe in a book we read, or in something that is said in the Sunday homily. The knowledge may even come directly in the form of a telepathic message or even an auditory one; such was the case with many of our canonized saints.

When praying for guidance, if we did not expect to receive any information, then what would be the point of the prayer? Anyway you look at it; clearly we consult spirits every time we pray to the saints. How could this possibly be considered an "abomination to the Lord?"

Mediums

The dictionary defines "medium" as "something in a middle position." Synonyms are "go-between" and "intermediary." "Medium" is also defined as an individual held to be a channel of communication between the earthly world and a world of spirits. Synonyms include "seer" and "prophet" (Webster). On the other hand, saints are also mediums as they act as intercessors for our prayers.

The definition of a priest is a "mediatory agent between man and God" (Webster). When he presides over the Eucharist (the Mass) he is the mediator between God and the faithful attending the service. When he hears confession he is the go-between for God and the confessor. He takes the place of Jesus and in His name absolves the person of all their sins. Therefore, it follows that a priest could be considered a medium.

In the Spiritualist religion healers are also considered mediums. This could be said of healers in the Catholic faith as well. Father Richard McAlear, of the Oblates of Mary Immaculate order, is known as "the healing priest." He is the mediator between God and the person receiving the healing. In fact, when he lays his hand on people they are often "slain in the Holy Spirit." Priests, prophets, seers and healers are all mediums. Most people would not agree that consulting them would be defiling the Lord. It is only the uneducated and fearful who would subscribe to this thinking.

The Leviticus passage indicates that one should not use a go-between or medium, but rather should go to God directly. It implies that one who consults a medium or fortune-teller is worshipping that person instead of God. Could it be, that they are merely looking for additional guidance in the same way we would consult a spiritual director or a priest? If God feels defiled by someone who consults a medium then it follows that one who consults a priest would defile him as well. I don't know of anyone who would agree with this line of thinking, yet this is what the scripture is implying. Consulting a priest or medium does not mean that we worship him or her. Nor does it have anything to do with one's faith, or lack of, in God.

Insight

One of the priests interviewed for this book warned that we shouldn't have to consult the dead-if we did it meant we had little faith. The pastor explained that if we need answers we should just pray to God more. If that were the case then why would Catholics go to the doctor if they were sick? Wouldn't it mean that by consulting a physician they do not have faith that God could heal them? Shouldn't the patient just pray more? Most people would not agree with this view, but this is the same logic we are told to accept when it comes to consulting mediums.

We've examined the passages from Deuteronomy 18:10 and Leviticus 19:31 that condemns not only mediums and fortune-tellers, but also those who seek their advice. Now let's investigate the reason why this outcast group was banned and looked down upon in the days of the Old Testament.

Competing Religions

In his book, *The Otherside*, The late, Reverend James Pike, a Bishop of the Episcopal Church, also critiques these same scriptures. He gives us further insight on the prejudice against some of the most mystical professions. Pike explains that denouncing mediums came about as the result of two conflicting and competing religious systems in Israel at the time, Judaism and Paganism.

The Egyptians, Canaanites and the Babylonians who practiced paganism and worshipped many gods lived side by side with the Jewish people. The priests and prophets were the professionals of the Jewish faith while their professional counterparts in the Pagan religion were the soothsayers, diviners, sorcerers, mediums, wizards and necromancers. Fortune-tellers were merely Pagan prophets in that they could foresee the future. Pike explains:

> The Jewish religious professionals—the priests and prophets-had to protect their own roles as those who could reveal and interpret the Word of God, so they were quick to denounce with vehemence any competitors, like mediums and foretellers of the future. (284)

The issue wasn't one of faith but rather of control. What better way to control the Word of God than by eliminating the competition? (Pike).

We read in the Bible that King Saul maintained control by banning all mediums and Pagan professionals from the city (1Samuel 28:3). For this reason strict punishment was placed on anyone who went against Jewish law. This might explain the two scriptures we just analyzed, as well as the following passages from Leviticus:

> Should anyone turn to mediums and fortune-tellers and follow their wanton ways, I will turn against such a one and cut him off from his people (20:6).

> A man or woman who acts as a medium or fortune-teller shall be put to death by stoning; they have no one but themselves to blame for their death (20:27).

These passages do not condemn the custom of communication between heaven and earth. They only forbid certain ones from practicing it, namely, those who were not Jewish. The Jewish mediators, who were the prophets and priests, wanted authority over the pagan mediators who were the mediums and fortune-tellers, as well as the seers and mystics. The monotheistic religion sought to dominate the polytheistic religion because it feared loss of control over the people (Pike).

Bishop Pike goes on to explain that the Scriptures often cited to condemn mediums have no basis in today's worldview. He states, "We no longer think in terms of competing gods. We seek to know instead the One-the all-encompassing, unifying reality" (284). What Pike observes goes along with the religious beliefs of most modern-day mediums. Many mediums belong to The National Spiritualist Association of Churches (NSAC). This faith has its own creed stating the belief in one God, Infinite Intelligence. Furthermore, there are many denominations within the Spiritualist religion, some of which are Christian. So to condemn all mediums based on the fact that they are Pagans is another outdated and incorrect viewpoint.

In an interview with parapsychologist, Father Alphonsus Trabold of St. Bonaventure University, he explained that condemnations in the Bible were not infallible. "The Bible says to test men according to the circumstances of their times." The Franciscan pointed out that the church enacted disciplinary legislation in order to protect the morals of its members at a particular time. In early Christian times mediumship was being used to attack God by showing Him as either incompetent or untrustworthy. As a result, the church reacted by condemning the practice. For Spiritualist mediums of today, who believe in one God, that is not the case (Grace).

Saul and the Witch of Endor

Going back to King Saul, there is an interesting story in the Bible concerning his own consultation with a medium. It is called *Saul and the Witch of Endor*. Faced with having to go up against the Philistine army, Saul became afraid and consulted the Lord for guidance. When he received no reply he decided to go to a medium to get advice from the deceased prophet, Samuel. Since Saul had expelled all the mediums and fortune-tellers, he ordered his servants to find him one and was led to a woman in Endor. When the woman made contact with Samuel, he said, "Why do you ask me, if the Lord has abandoned you and is with your neighbor?" (1 Samuel 28:3-16).

Many people often use the above story when they want to cite why one should not consult with mediums. They claim that God punished Saul for doing so. The Reverend Pike clarifies this passage in defense of mediums. He explains that most people overlook the reason he went to the woman in Endor in the first place. He asked the medium for help because when he sought guidance from God directly he was given none. "He therefore consulted the Lord; but gave no answer, whether in dreams or by the Urim [a divination tool], or through prophets" (Samuel 28:6). Pike points out that Saul was already estranged from God before he decided to go to Endor for help (Pike).

Saul went to the "witch" because he wanted advice from Samuel, not from the medium. He needed the clairvoyant, however, to get that information. Saul must have been disappointed, nonetheless, with what he was told. Samuel himself confirmed Saul's estrangement from God by pointing out that the Lord had turned from him. Pike explains that many critics use this story to imply that getting advice from a medium means that one is automatically turning from God. The author states, "It merely implies that once cut off from God, no amount of advice-even through a medium-could save him; it only confirmed his fate" (Pike, 282).

Furthermore, in this Samuel account, there is an assumption made that a medium is the same as a witch. Throughout 1 Samuel, Chapter 28, the gifted woman is referred to as a "medium," yet the subtitle calls her "the witch" of Endor. Perhaps in Biblical times the terms were used interchangeably to refer to anyone with second sight. In the twenty-first century however, mediums and witches are not the same at all.

Witches today are members of the Wicca faith, which is a nature based, polytheistic religion. On the other hand, most mediums generally belong to the well-organized religion of Spiritualism, a monotheistic faith. Comparing a medium to a witch is like comparing a Christian to a Hindu. Although individuals in both religions may be clairvoyant, there are vast, fundamental differences in the two belief systems. Witches and mediums are not the same by any means but neither are they necessarily evil or sinful. This is another example of how outdated material, ignorance and fear leads to false judgments, criticism and prejudice towards some of our fellow citizens in the communion of saints.

Insight

Thousands of years of ignorance and fear have been projected upon the woman of Endor. As a result, she has been vilified and unfairly portrayed as some sleazy charlatan. However, this may not necessarily be the case.

It does not seem likely that a king would go to just any medium with his entire kingdom on the line. Therefore, it would be reasonable to presume that the woman of Endor must have been a highly-regarded and well-respected priestess with extraordinary gifts. In addition, there is no indication that the clairvoyant was calling on evil spirits or practicing any kind of devil worship. She was simply practicing her religion, which was Pagan, and therefore, outlawed.

The persecution of the medium from Endor may have resulted from the simple fact that the she was a woman. In the same way, church authorities slandered Mary Magdalen by demoting her from a disciple of Jesus to a prostitute. After two-thousand years the light is once again shining on the truth of who Mary was. Could it be that a patriarchal religion has deliberately chosen to demean any powerful or significant women in order to suppress them?

We have closely scrutinized the biblical passages that condemned the practice of consulting with spirits directly or through the use of a medium. We will now see how these Old Testament beliefs were translated into present-day Catholic teachings. We will also see how much was lost in the interpretation.

Contemporary Taboos

Q: *Why is spirit communication and consulting with mediums against the Catholic faith today?*

It is because of these ancient views and incorrect assumptions from the Old Testament that the Catholic faith censures mediums and spirit communication today. This antiquated misinformation was written into law and can be found in the *Catechism of the Catholic Church* (C.C.C.). It's clear that the authorities were not educated on the religious beliefs and practices of the people they sought to criticize. Let's take a closer look at one of the articles from the Catechism:

> All forms of divination are to be rejected: recourse to Satan or demons, conjuring up the dead or other practices falsely supposed to "unveil" the future. Consulting horoscopes, astrology, palm reading, interpretation of omens and lots, the phenomena of clairvoyance, and recourse to mediums all conceal a desire for power over time, history, and, in the last analysis, other human beings, as well as a wish to conciliate hidden powers. They contradict the honor, respect, and loving fear that we owe to God alone (2116).

This single paragraph in the *Catholic Catechism* erroneously lumps together a disparity of belief systems, rituals and often-misunderstood disciplines into one group, which it considers "taboo." Furthermore, it inaccurately equates spiritualism, paganism, and the science of parapsychology, with Satanism. As a result, in one sweeping statement, millions of people, including many Christians, are condemned and judged for using their God-given gifts or practicing ancient sacred traditions. Some of these practices are the very ones used in today's Catholic Mass.

There are so many inaccuracies in the catechism paragraph that one need not be a Rhodes Scholar to understand the out-dated nature of the proclamation. It is because of illogical thinking and incorrect assumptions that people find it so difficult to sort out the truth from mere superstition. To help discern fact from fiction, we will take a closer look at each of the taboos mentioned in the *Catholic Catechism*.

Divination

Divination is the practice of predicting the future using supernatural means. Examples of some of the tools used in divination include pendulums, dowsing rods, crystal balls (scrying), Tarot, I Ching and Runes. The forbidden tools cited in the *Catechism of the Catholic Church* are Ouija boards, astrology, horoscope and the interpretation of omens and lots. Most of these traditions can be traced back to ancient history and were commonly used for holy guidance; this is evident throughout the Bible. Let's examine some of these forbidden customs, starting with one from the Old Testament.

Urim and Thummim

Urim and *Thummim* are two divination tools used by priests in the Old Testament. They were two stones that operated in conjunction with the "breastplate of decision," (also known as the "breastplate of judgment") for the purpose of communicating with the Lord. The instrument was used when consulting God in the Holy of Holies:

> Whenever Aaron enters the sanctuary, he will thus bear the names of the sons of Israel on the breastplate of decision over his heart as a constant reminder before the Lord. In this breastplate of decision you shall put the Urim and Thummim that they may be over Aaron's heart whenever he enters the presence of the Lord. Thus he shall always bear the decisions for the Israelites over his heart in the Lord's presence. (Exodus: 28: 29-30)

In her book, *Divination of God*, author and hypnotherapist Shelly Kaehr, Ph.D., explains this ancient method. The Urim was a black stone made of basalt and the Thummim was a white stone made of alabaster. The priest would ask a "yes" or "no" question of God and receive his answer through the stones. If the black Urim glowed the answer was "no" and if the white Thummim glowed the answer was "yes" (105). In the story of the Witch of Endor, King Saul used the Urim when he was up against the Philistine army. When he did not receive an answer from God, Saul went to a medium to get advice from the late prophet, Samuel.

The Old Testament describes the breastplate as containing four rows of three stones representing the twelve tribes of Israel. Each stone was engraved with a letter of the Hebrew alphabet that represented one of the twelve tribes. When a question was asked, various stones would illuminate in a sequential order. The order of the letters on each stone spelled out the answer. If a "yes" or "no" answer was asked then the Urim and Thummim were used (Kaehr).

The breastplate doubled as a table as it was hinged on the bottom and could be folded down so that it protruded in a right angle from the chest and laid flat. Whenever Aaron entered the sanctuary tent, he opened the breastplate in this way in order to expose the stones that were imbedded in gold on the inside. He used the divination device to receive oracles from God and His holy spirits.

When knowledge of how this device worked got into pagan hands, they made replicas of the breastplate and used it to communicate with the spirits of loved ones. It was banned, along with mediumship to cut down on the competition and because some used it with less-than-holy intentions.

Insight

Ironically, the Breastplate of God, combined with the Urim and Thummim, may have been the predecessors of the Ouija board. On the top corners of the board are the words "yes" and "no"; this corresponds directly with the Urim and Thummim stones. Furthermore the Ouija is like the breastplate in that it is inscribed with letters so messages from spirits can be spelled out.

Ouija Boards

Over the centuries there were many variations of the breastplate divination tool, which came to be known as the "talking table." In 1890 the first patent was placed on the talking table, which was renamed the "Ouija Board" after the mystical Moroccan city of Oujida. Eventually the Parker Brothers Toy Company purchased the patent and marketed the timeless game that continues to sell today (Museum of Talking Boards). Due to the long history of people misusing the board to contact evil spirits, it often seems to attract negative energies. For this reason, it is not recommended and is by no means a "toy" for amateurs to play with.

Consequently, many would agree with the *Catholic Catechism's* ban on the use of Ouija Boards, but not for the reason given. Most people use the Ouija for entertainment purposes or to try to contact a loved one; it does not mean that they disrespect God.

Astrology

Astrology is the study of how the stars and planets influence human affairs (Webster). In the New Testament, three very famous Kings, who were also astrologers, used the stars to guide them to the baby Jesus. The Star of Bethlehem led the magi to the holy sight. As a result, the wise men were able to warn the first family of the danger they were in. Through the use of "astrology," the Christ child was saved. According to the *Catholic Catechism*, astrologers, like the three wise men, have a desire to control time and other human beings, and therefore dishonor God. This idea is as erroneous today as it was in the first century.

Horoscopes

A horoscope is an astrological chart, based on a person's exact time of birth, which uses the patterns of the stars and planets to predict his or her future (Hathaway). Most people are familiar with the signs of the Zodiac and even know which one they were born under. According to the Catechism of the Catholic Church, Catholics who read their horoscope in the daily paper are dishonoring God and associating with Satan. However, most people, who use this tool, are often just looking for a little guidance in their life, along with some entertainment. They would find the allegations of consorting with the devil ridiculous.

Former President, Ronald Reagan is just one example of a well-respected Christian who used this divination tool for guidance. Under the advice of his wife, Nancy, the president consulted his horoscope daily for direction in his leadership. No one felt that he had a secret desire to control other human beings, as the *Catholic Catechism* would imply.

Lots

Another example of divination is the casting of lots. In the New Testament the disciples cast lots in order to decide who would replace Judas. They prayed, "O Lord, you read the hearts of men. Make known to us which of these two you choose for this apostolic ministry." They used this method of divination to receive divine guidance for such an important decision. "And they gave forth their lots and the lot fell upon Mathias; and he was numbered with the eleven apostles" (Acts 1:23-26).

The casting of lots was the predecessor of the "lottery"; from which the name was derived. Every state in our country has a lottery, indicating that our elected officials do not view it has an activity that goes against God. On the contrary, the money is used to help fund the education of our youth in America.

In addition, under this category, sweepstakes and raffles would be forbidden also. In contradiction to this taboo, many Catholic Church organizations hold raffles to help fund parish projects or assist a particular congregate in financial need. Most people play the lottery or participate in raffles for fun, to help out a charitable cause, or with the hope of winning a prize or some extra cash. They are not trying to be disrespectful to God.

Holy Water, Medals & Rosaries

In each of the examples given from the Bible, divination was used for guidance from God. In the same way, Catholics use holy water, rosaries and medallions as divination tools, as well as for protection and guidance. Are these devices not used in attempt to give us "power over time" by controlling or changing the future? When we want to change the future of someone who is sick, we use the rosary to pray for healing. Holy water is used to change the future of one possessed by the devil. Many believe in the power of the miraculous medal and therefore use it when a miracle is needed in their life.

In addition, many Catholics wear a guardian angel pin on their shirt, a crucifix around their neck or have a dashboard saint in their car. If we felt these religious amulets had no effect on our future, by keeping us safe, then why would we have them at all? Does it follow that by using these tools for guidance and protection that one dishonors God? Does this mean that we "wish to conciliate hidden powers?" Associating divination practices with recourse to Satan is a viewpoint that most people would not agree with. It is just another example of how lack of education causes fear and how that fear leads to incorrect judgments and criticism of our brothers and sisters in the communion of saints.

Insight

Karen Prioletti and Ann Trump have invented a unique divination tool called *The Saint Deck Book*. The Catholic mediums have written a book on fifty of the most popular saints, which includes a description of their patronage and attributes. A companion set of beautifully illustrated cards depicts the various saints and can be used much like the Tarot.

The Saint Deck can be used whenever one seeks guidance from the canonized saints. For example, St. John the Apostle, the patron saint of writers, was called upon to assist in the writing of this book. His saint card was kept next to the computer in order to make that connection. Using this particular divination tool seemed most appropriate for a book on the communion of saints.

Conjuring the Dead

In the paragraph cited from the *Catechism of the Catholic Church*, there is a discrepancy regarding the warning on "conjuring up the dead." Conjuring the dead is no different than invoking the saints. The definition of "conjure" is "to summon by invocation or incantation." It also means, "to charge or entreat earnestly or solemnly" (Webster). We do this every time we pray the rosary. We recite the incantation known as the *Hail Mary* to summon the spirit of the dead Blessed Mother to answer our requests. Conjuring saints and spirits is a common practice in both Christianity and Spiritualism. It has nothing to do with demonology unless one is practicing the religion known as Satanism and is summoning the devil.

The misinterpretation may come from the connotation of the word "conjuring." The negative tone associated with this word implies that one is calling on evil spirits. Thus one "conjures" evil spirits and "invokes" good spirits. However, the catechism forbids talking to any dead people; it does not make any distinction between good or bad ones. It's safe to assume that it is OK to call on holy spirits since this is how we practice communion with the saints. Herein lies another contradiction in church teachings.

Clairvoyance

The writers of the *Catechism of the Catholic Church* are clearly misinformed when it comes to the subject of clairvoyance. Clairvoyance is a natural ability as part of our sixth sense. It means simply "clear seeing" and is often described in the Bible as "visions." The Bible also refers to it as a "spiritual gift." People who possessed this gift were called "seers," "prophets" and "mediums." They were valued for their God-given talent and therefore given prestigious positions in the church or society in which they belonged. Jesus himself was a clairvoyant as he was able to see and predict his own arrest and death in great detail. Furthermore, most of our canonized saints exhibited the gift of clairvoyance; descriptions of their visionary experiences are well-documented.

Just because one is clairvoyant does not mean that he or she desires control over time and other humans. Being clairvoyant does not mean that person disrespects or dishonors God. On the contrary, using personal spiritual gifts is the greatest honor anyone can give to God. Clairvoyance is covered in greater detail in chapter six.

Mediums

By the same token, to infer that mediums, and those who consult them, do not honor or respect God is not a logical or correct assumption. People may consult a medium in the same way they consult a priest. Parishioners may ask their priest to pray for them regarding a future event, such as an upcoming surgery. In the same way they may ask a medium to pray for them or to give insight about an upcoming event. In both cases the individuals may simply be asking for all the help they can get.

Abraham Lincoln is an example of a well-respected man who consulted a medium. The president and his wife regularly held séances in the White House and were members of the Spiritual Frontiers Fellowship. *The Emancipation Proclamation* was issued on the advice of a medium. The President wisely sought help from the heavens and was never accused of practicing Satanism (Heron)

Just a Fact

Spiritualist medium, Nettie Colburn Maynard was a good friend of Mary Todd Lincoln's and a regular visitor at the White House. On one of the occasions in which President Lincoln consulted her, she went into trance and told him that the Emancipation Proclamation was to be the crowning achievement of his administration and of his life.

Abraham responded by confiding in Nettie that he was being pressured to suppress the proclamation. He proclaimed, "My child, you possess a wonderful gift, but that it is of God I have no doubt." (Maynard)

In the *Catechism of the Catholic Church*, it is clear that lack of knowledge on the overall subject of mediumship and psychic abilities has led to great misconceptions and illogical deductions. This is just one more example of how fear of the unknown can lead to false assumptions and unfair judgments. Consulting mediums does not mean disrespect towards God. Discrimination against mediums however, shows disrespect for our fellow members in the communion of saints.

Spiritism and Spiritualism

Now let's take a look at two more taboos, "spiritism" and "spiritualism." It is clear that the church has little understanding of these subjects because the definitions provided are incorrect. The following are statements that come from the *Catechism of the Catholic Church* (C.C.C.) and *The Essential Catholic Handbook* (E.C.H.).

Spiritism often implies divination or magical practices: the church for her part warns the faithful against it. (C.C.C. 2117).

Spiritism, also called spiritualism, it is the belief that the living can communicate with spirits and with the deceased by way of a human medium or inanimate objects, such as a Ouija board; practices derived therefrom are a violation of the first commandment of the Decalogue and opposed to the virtue of religion (E.C.H.).

The first statement says spiritism implies the practice of magic. This is not true. Spiritism is a popular philosophy, with the fundamental tenet being a belief in reincarnation. Allan Kardec founded Spiritism in the 1850's in France and today it is considered one of the major religions in Brazil. It came out of the then popular practices of spiritualism and mesmerism (hypnotism). Magic, on the other hand, is a common practice done in the Wicca faith, an entirely different religion.

The second citation from above equates "spiritism" with "spiritualism." This is also incorrect by today's definition. Spiritualism is a philosophy, science and an organized religion. Its basic tenet is to prove the continuity of life through the use of mediumship. Spiritualism is a member of the Parliament of World Religions and also acknowledged as a legitimate religion by our federal government. Spiritualism does not support a belief in reincarnation, like Spiritism, nor does it include the practice of magic, as done in the Wicca faith.

The word "spiritualism" also refers to the practice of communication with the heavens or people in the spirit world. Spiritualism is practiced in some form by most belief systems and is the basis of all major religions. Various forms of spirit communication include chanting, praying, dancing, singing, meditating and just plain talking. All Catholics are spiritualists because they believe in, and practice, interaction with non-physical beings. Although this can be done directly, many choose to contact the celestial realm indirectly by asking a priest, a canonized saint, fellow believer, or other medium to send or receive messages on their behalf.

Just a Fact

The African American Spiritual Churches of New Orleans practice a syncretistic religion that includes elements of Roman Catholicism, Protestantism and Voodooism. With Jesus Christ as their central figure, this belief system is complete with baptisms, Holy Communion, ordinations, prophecy, healing and a strong belief in the communion of saints. (Jacobs & Kaslow)

The Voodoo Queen, Marie Laveau was a devout Catholic; she went to Mass daily at St. Louis Cathedral in Jackson Square. As a result, Spiritualism and Roman Catholicism are mutually respected companions in New Orleans. For a psychic reading, after Mass, parishioners only need to walk a few steps from church doors, where a medium is always set up for business and ready to serve. (Tallant)

In an interview with medium Lynn Forget of Lily Dale, NY, she helps to further clarify the meaning of "spiritualism." The clairvoyant explains that if you call yourself a spiritualist and you're just looking at the science or philosophy aspect of it, then you are a spiritualist with a small "s." "But if you're a Spiritualist and you embrace it as a religion to the point where you don't need any other religion to bolster it up or support it, then you are a Spiritualist with a capital 'S' " (Grace). In other words, when referring to the religion of Spiritualism, it is considered a proper noun, and therefore capitalized. When referring to the practice of spirit communication alone, which is not a religion in itself, the word is an improper noun and not capitalized.

According to the *Essential Catholic Handbook*, when we do communicate with the souls in heaven (spiritualism), we are in violation of the first commandment, which states, "Thou shalt have no other Gods before me." How does talking with Grandma in heaven go against the first commandment? It would have to imply that by communicating with spirits, one is therefore worshipping them. When we pray to St. Anthony or the Blessed Mother for favors or guidance we are not worshipping them. In the same way, Spiritualists do not worship their deceased family and friends.

Catholics, Spiritists and Spiritualists reserve worship for God alone. To state that communicating with the souls in heaven goes against the first commandment is another false allegation.

In a similar allegation, Protestants believe the use of statuary in churches is idol worship, and therefore, goes against the first commandment. Catholics understand, however, that they do not worship statues. The effigies are merely visual aids, which are used to help us direct our prayer or remind us that we are not alone. For these reasons, people should not judge each other's religious practices if they do not fully understand them.

Magic

The *Catholic Catechism* also warns the faithful against "magical practices." However, some of the rituals in the Catholic Mass come under that definition. Magic is "the use of supernatural powers over natural forces" (Webster). To pagans, Catholic priests practice the magic of "alchemy" at every Mass. Alchemy is the "power or process of transforming something 'common' into something 'precious'." Another name for alchemy is "transubstantiation," which means "to change from one substance to another" (Webster). During Mass, the supernatural powers of the Holy Spirit are invoked to transform "common" bread and wine into the "precious" body and blood of Christ. This clearly is in line with the practice and definition of magic.

To non-Catholics the magic of a Mass and other Catholic practices can be interpreted as deviant and even morally wrong. One Spiritualist from Lily Dale describes the practice of taking communion as "ritualized cannibalism." Furthermore, to many people, the drinking of the blood of Christ is seen as the practice of vampirism or Satanism, as blood drinking is done in a black mass. Unless one is well-educated in a particular religion and its traditions, some of the customs of that faith may seem sinful and even sacrilegious. This is why people who are not knowledgeable about the Catholic faith should not judge its practices.

Spiritualism vs. Catholicism

For the same reason, those who are not well educated in the religion of Spiritualism should not judge its practices. For if they understood it they would realize that Catholics perform many of the same rituals, they just call it by a different name. For example, what spiritualists call "spirit communication," Catholics call "prayer." What Catholics call "conjuring spirits" is no different than "invoking the saints."   Spiritualist ministers and Catholic priests are both mediums, they act as mediators between heaven and earth. The unqualified cannot judge mediums or the practices found in the religion of Spiritualism. Ignorance however, does not justify oppression and condemnation of our fellow members in the communion of saints.

Let's look at other ways we use different words to describe the same thing. When Catholics sit in rows of pews before an altar and have a priest invoke the spirits of martyrs and all the saints, it is called a "Mass." When spiritualists sit in a circle and have a medium invoke the spirits of family or friends it is called a "séance" or "circle." Similarly, small Christian communities often have prayer "circles," a séance-like configuration, for the purpose of communicating to heavenly beings. We are simply using different words to describe the same situations. Why, however, is one practice considered a matter of faith while the other is said to go against the faith? Both are demonstrations of communion with the saints.

The Devil Made Me Do It!

In Biblical times there was a Hellenistic mentality that anything supernatural or unexplainable was the work of the devil. With modern science and medicine, many of these beliefs have been dispelled. When it comes to the psychic phenomena of Spiritualism, however, diabolic associations still persist. The following story is an all too common scenario:

I was participating in a volunteer fair at the University of Geneseo as a representative of an organization for which I was chairperson. This meant manning a booth that displayed information on many of the human service agencies in the county. In addition, I used the event to promote my spiritual counseling service and work as a parapsychologist.

When a colleague, who is Catholic, noticed my little "Gifts of Grace" sign, she questioned me about it. I explained my paranormal work, which is helping people to maintain relationships with loved ones in spirit. She responded with disapproval, suddenly becoming quite indignant and judgmental. My conversation, with her (I'll call her Jill) went something like this:

Jill: "When you receive messages from spirits, how do you know that it's not the devil?"

Mary Grace (MG): "Usually the messages I receive are ones of comfort and love."

Jill: "But it could be the devil disguising himself as a good spirit."

MG: "Well if the devil decides to bring a message to console someone, then what's wrong with that? Besides, how do I know that you are not really the devil in disguise?"

Jill: "That's ridiculous."

MG: "So is the statement you made. Besides, don't you pray?"

Jill: "Of course."

MG: "How do you know that when you pray that you are really not communicating with the devil? How do you know that you are in fact talking to God?"

Jill: "All I know is that spirit communication is against the Catholic faith."

MG: "When you pray you are communicating to spirits, therefore prayer is spirit communication."

Jill: "But we don't call it that."

MG: "Just because you don't call it that doesn't mean that isn't what you are, in fact, doing."

Jill walked away in frustration and with an attitude that made it clear I was not the model Catholic she had once thought. I was trying to explain to her that although we may use different words, we are not that different in our beliefs.

The Reverend Herbert Thurston, S.J. explains one of the reasons why the devil is so closely associated with spiritualism. In his book, *The Church and Spiritualism*, Thurston observes that in the early Christian church Satan was everywhere. Teachers of that day were not aware of psychic phenomena and "had inherited an almost exaggerated belief in the power of the devil..." (141). They had a firm conviction that Satan was involved in all things unexplainable, even in common everyday occurrences. For example, those who used herbs for healing, practiced mathematics, or invented mechanical devices were accused of sorcery and for seeking knowledge of hidden things. One of these people was the pontiff himself, Pope Sylvester II, one of the most educated people of his day (Thurston). The church taught people that Satan was plotting against man's spiritual and physical welfare. Furthermore, they believed mediums, also known as witches, were used as concubines by the devil to plant his seed for the purpose of procreating baby devils, called " incubi." This diabolic influence became so prevalent in church teachings that it created hysteria. The more it was talked about, the more people accused each other of consorting with the devil or being a witch.

In the Middle Ages two churchmen got together to write a guidebook on how to identify, prosecute, torture and kill witches. *Malleus Maleficarum* (The Witch's Hammer) became the official church manual on the persecution of witches, thus the Inquisition was born. Over the next two hundred years it is estimated that between six-hundred thousand, and one million people (mostly women), were put to death. They were not only mediums, but also midwives, poets, gypsies, Jews, scientists, astrologers, herbalists, astronomers, inventors and even mathematicians. This all took place throughout Europe and ended in the New World with the Salem witch trials (Lovelace).

The Inquisition was so far reaching and so profoundly influential that the effects can still be felt to this day. If the church sought to instill fear upon the masses, in order to quash the competition, then they have succeeded without question. The profound ignorance and superstitious convictions of the seventeenth-century Church is almost unbelievable. The only thing more amazing is that, when it comes to mediums, this same rationale is still taught in the twenty-first century.

Quote Me

"*The Malleus Maleficarum* is one of the most blood-soaked works in human history, in that its very existence reinforced and validated Catholic beliefs which led to the prosecution, torture, and murder of tens of thousands of innocent people." (Lovelace)

Excerpt from the *Malleus*: "Whether the Belief that there are such beings as Witches is so essential a part of the Catholic Faith that obstinacy to maintain the opposite opinion manifestly savours of Heresy." (Kramer and Sprenger)

In his book, *Parapsychology and the Christian Faith*, Charles Cluff makes an astute observation regarding this "devil-made-me-do-it" mentality:

> The Christian who is afraid of the power of evil does not understand the power of God. Persons who preach against occult have audiences terrified. Where the Spirit of the Lord is, there is love and peace, not fear. (65)

It is hard to believe that the church still treats mediumship and spirit communication with the same suspicion today that it did five-hundred years ago. We can only hope it won't be another half century before changes are made.

Intention

Although the terminology we use may differ, it does not take away from the intent. Whether we call it "prayer" or "spirit communication," whether we call on "God" or "Infinite Intelligence"; it all has to do with intention. If our objectives are positive, and we are merely asking for guidance or trying to help our neighbor, the words which are spoken do not make a difference.

If a medium's goal is to contact a deceased friend or relative, this is what usually happens. Their work is done with good intention and for the highest and greater good of all. It is often considered a work of healing. This thought is supported by medium Lynn Forget, who was cited earlier; she explains:

> I think mediumship is healing. It's like grief therapy in a lot of cases. People are coming for upliftment, they're coming for validation, they're coming for understanding; and you know everyone is coming for a different reason. I often think of it as grief therapy (Grace).

In the same way, the work that priests do is done out of good intentions. During the Mass he intends to bring in the Holy Spirit to consecrate the gifts. We trust in his ability and feel confidant that this is precisely what is occurring. A non-Catholic might ask, "How does a priest know that when consecrating the bread and wine that it's really not the devil coming into the gifts?" We know because of the good intention he has in calling on God, the Holy Spirit, and not on Satan.

If we disregard intention, how do we know that when we pray to the saints we are not really invoking the devil? We know because of our intention in calling on good spirits and not evil ones. One has a Catholic Mass in order to commune with God, likewise, one has a black mass in order to commune with Satan; it depends on our intention. Catholics, Spiritualists, priests and mediums all practice communion with God and the people in heaven, through the use of good intentions.

Insight

Wayne Dyer's bestselling book, *The Power of Intention*, describes "intention" as a force of energy in the universe. This force is used by us to co-create what we want out of life. We manifest our destiny out of intention.

But what if one's intentions are not good? In an interview with the late Father Jerome Schifferli, of St. Matthew Church in Livonia,

NY, he was asked, "Why were consulting mediums banned in the first place?" The reverend explained that the church put into effect the ban in order to protect their people from all the frauds who were taking advantage of vulnerable parishioners. Indeed, in the first century of Spiritualism, from c1850 – c1950, there were a lot of fraudulent mediums and it led to the religion's decline.

Now, however, with the advent of accredited schools for mediumship, and required certification to practice in Lily Dale and Spiritualist churches throughout the country, fraud has been almost eliminated. Spiritualism is once again on the rise. Police departments are now consulting mediums to help solve crimes and find missing children. Sure, there may still be some less-than-honest mediums, but to say that all mediums are fraudulent is like saying that all priests are pedophiles. There will always be those with less-than-positive intentions. This however, does not take away from all the wonderful things happening as a result of those with good intentions, no matter what their religious faith.

Old Testament vs. New Testament

Despite the good intentions of most mediums, there still exists a stigma to the profession due to ancient thinking and church laws that persist to this day. Many of these Biblical rules are not realistic in today's world and therefore have not been included in church doctrine. But how does it get decided which laws of the Bible to keep and which ones to delete? Why is it that some of the Old Testament codes of conduct made it into Canon law while many others did not? The following are examples of Jewish laws, described in Leviticus, Chapter 19, which were not included in the rules of the Catholic faith:

"Do not plant your fields with two kinds of seed" (19).
"Do not wear clothing woven of two kinds of material" (19).
"Do not eat any meat with the blood still in it" (26).
"Do not cut the hair at the sides of your head or clip off the edges of your beard" (27).
"Do not cut your bodies for the dead or put tattoo marks on

yourselves" (28).

Somewhere along the line, the thinking of the church authorities changed. Somehow it was decided that breaking these laws was okay and did not go against the Catholic faith.

In the very same paragraph, however, is the warning, "Do not go to mediums or consult fortune-tellers, for you will be defiled by them" (Leviticus 19:31). Somehow it was decided that the laws pertaining to mediums is *not* okay to break.

Furthermore, if we are going to hold to the Old Testament laws regarding mediums, then it should follow that all mediums should be "put to death by stoning," which was also the law. Sadly, as we have learned, up until the eighteenth-century this is exactly what took place. Often accused of witchcraft, mediums were killed in a variety of ways. They were not only stoned to death, but also tortured, drowned, beaten, branded and even burned at the stake, like Joan of Arc. In her infinite wisdom, the church eventually decided that killing mediums was a Biblical law they could do without.

There is another Jewish law in the Old Testament that Christians do not adhere to. In this case, however, an explanation is given in the New Testament. We find the following in Leviticus Chapter 11:

> And the pig, which does indeed have hoofs and is cloven-footed, but does not chew the cud, is therefore unclean for you. Their flesh you shall not eat, and their dead bodies you shall not touch; they are unclean for you. (Leviticus 11:7-8)

In Acts we discover that Peter has an issue with this prohibition, which stemmed from a clairvoyant experience. In a vision he also heard a voice tell him to kill and eat "unclean" meat. When Peter protested, the voice replied, "What God has purified you are not to call unclean" (Acts 11:9). This Divine amendment to Old Testament principle is further described in Acts, Chapter 15, which says in order not to "cause God's Gentile converts any difficulties" they do not have to refrain from eating unclean meat (Acts 15:19-21).

In an interview with Father Patrick Mulligan, he explained that this meant the converted Gentiles (early Christians) were no longer bound to the Jewish Law. This passage marks a turning point from Old Testament views to New Testament views. If prohibitions regarding the eating of unclean meat or cutting your beard don't apply to Christians, then why would the Jewish law prohibiting the practice of mediumship apply to Christians?

Mulligan asserts that if you are Jewish you go by Old Testament precepts and if you are Christian you go by New Testament precepts. Nowhere does the New Testament prohibit communication with spirits in heaven. On the contrary, in 1 Corinthians 12 we are told that each person will be given some sort of spiritual gift which is to be used for the common good. This would include the gift of second sight or clairvoyance, which is a trait found in both mediums and prophets.

The Same Difference

Although Catholics and Spiritualists differ on their viewpoints regarding mediumship and contacting the dead, and the language they use is different, there are many similarities. Why not focus more on the common views we have? For starters, both faiths believe in one God or Infinite Intelligence. Both Catholics and Spiritualists believe that the living can speak with the deceased and vice versa.

Both faiths are based on the Bible, which is full of stories about communication between the living and the dead. The most significant example is when Jesus appeared to the disciples and to Paul, after His resurrection. This became the foundation of the entire Christian religion and the Catholic faith.

Spiritualism supports the Catholic view of eternal life and seeks to scientifically prove it through the practice of mediumship. Noted scientists have joined in the search and have made great strides in this area. As a result, many remarkable findings have been published supporting the Catholic belief in life-after-death. Most notably are the studies involving mediumship in *The Afterlife*

Experiments by Gary Schwartz, Ph.D.

Just a Fact

The Afterlife Experiment was a project, designed to conduct scholarly, systematic, and scientific research on the possibility of the survival of consciousness after death. It was carried out at the University of Arizona under the direction of Gary Schwartz, Ph.D., a noted professor of psychiatry and medicine. His findings are published in the bestselling book, *The Afterlife Experiments*.

In addition, both Spiritualists and Catholics believe in the doctrine of "Love Thy Neighbor," as well as the Golden Rule, "Do unto others, what you would have them do to you" (Matthew 7:12). Perhaps the biggest similarity between Spiritualism and Catholicism is that both faiths have great respect and reverence for the man known as Jesus Christ. Both faiths look to him as a role model for living a spiritual life. We revere him for going against the intolerant establishment of his day by standing up for the poor, the outcast, the diseased and the marginalized. We teach our children that Jesus showed his love for all by befriending even those who were considered most lowly, including Samaritans, sinners, tax collectors, lepers and prostitutes. Both faiths follow Jesus by teaching compassion and tolerance for all, no matter what their religion. Sure there are differences between Spiritualism and Catholicism, but there are many more similarities.

Just My Opinion

Most Catholics are under the mistaken belief that communication with loved ones in Heaven is against the teachings of the church. It's the mixed-messages we receive as parishioners that confuse us. On the one hand our faith encourages us to maintain relationships with loved ones in spirit, via the communion of saints. On the other hand we are told that contacting the dead and consulting mediums is strictly forbidden. Christian mystics and the saints are honored for their spiritual gifts while psychic mediums are criticized for it. When it comes to the supernatural, many don't know what to believe.

When members of the church receive signs and messages from their dearly departed, their conviction and desire will only be strengthened. When they don't get support from their own church leaders, they will turn to those who are willing to help-- the intuitive counselors, the transpersonal psychologists, the Spiritualists, the mediums and the psychics. The outdated beliefs about consulting mediums will be ignored (as is already often the case) along with the other unrealistic church laws. If the teachings of our faith don't change with the times, more and more people will find other spiritual practices that are more tolerant and make much more sense in light of the century in which we now live.

As a society, I believe our views on spirit communication and psychic phenomena have already changed. This is reflected in the countless television shows and movies produced on the subject. Examples of popular TV shows are *Psychic Investigators, Ghost Hunters, A Haunting* and *Celebrity Ghost Story*. Movies like *Sixth Sense, Dragonfly* and *Paranormal Activity* (1-5) sold millions of tickets. *Poltergeist, Carrie* and *Amityville Horror* are now classics. Even soap operas are getting in on the spiritual bandwagon with story lines revolving around ghosts, angels and spirit guides (remember *Dark Shadows?*).

With programs like *Long Island Medium,* James Van Praagh's *Ghost Whisperer* and frequent appearances by Sylvia Brown on TV, the stigma surrounding mediums is quickly vanishing; many Catholics are ignoring the ancient taboo. In addition, countless Christians flock to Lily Dale every summer, seeking guidance from a medium. The town is even visited by Roman Catholic priests and nuns who come incognito. Most people no longer believe that communication with the dead or psychic practices are evil, or go against their faith in God.

Although we all believe in the same God, we put labels on each other and on ourselves to separate us from one other. Whether one consults ghosts or oracles, whether one is labeled as a fortune-teller, soothsayer, charmer or diviner, he or she is still a member of the universal church, still a child of God and still a part of the communion of saints. But we are not our labels; these are merely the roles we are playing.

To condemn a child of God because of the label he or she wears is to condemn God. Jesus could not tolerate hypocrisy in church leaders, who were often quick to denounce those who were different - the deprived, the sickly and the outcasts. It is just another example of how lack of education causes fear and how that fear leads to incorrect judgments and criticisms of our fellow companions in life. To treat others with disdain, disrespect and ridicule is most unchristian-like. Are the church leaders of today just as hypocritical, intolerant and as fearful? Jesus came to save the world, not to condemn it.

So let our human compassion and mutual love for Jesus replace our fear of each other. Let us learn by his example that it is not how many gods we worship or whether we call ourselves a sinner or a saint; what matters is how we treat each other. What matters is that we have respect, tolerance and compassion for those who are different from us. What matters is that we not judge each other, for until we walk in another person's shoes we can never truly know him or her. What matters is that we respect all people and their religious beliefs as well. For we have each chosen a different spiritual path in this life but every one ultimately leads back to the same place-our Father in heaven.

So whether you call yourself a mystic or a medium, Christian or Pagan, whether you're conjuring saints or invoking spirits, what matters is that we are all children of God. Whether you're a Catholic or Spiritualist, attending a mass or a séance, we are all still brothers and sisters, all parts of the same Mystical Body of Christ and all members of the communion of saints.

Summary

In this chapter we started by pointing out how many of our Catholic beliefs are outdated and therefore ignored. It was argued that such is the case when it comes to mediumship and communicating with our loved ones in heaven.

We then asked the question "Why is spirit communication and consulting mediums against the faith?" We examined several Old Testament passages and learned about fortune-tellers, soothsayers, mediums and those who consulted spirits, ghosts and oracles. We learned that the meaning of many of these practices and professions is much different today than it was in biblical times.

It was explained how the Old Testament ban on mediums was based on fear and control over competing gods and religions. We also looked at how these fears were carried over into the present day by examining articles from the *Catechism of the Catholic Church* and *Essential Catholic Handbook*. We briefly studied divination, clairvoyance, spiritism, and spiritualism. In addition, we questioned the difference between conjuring the dead and invoking the saints. It was discussed how many of the Old Testament fears and views have become outdated, misinterpreted, and in some cases no longer true today.

We learned how many of these taboos were practiced in Biblical times for the purpose of divine guidance. We also revealed how the Catholic faith practices many of these same rituals; they just use different words to describe it. Also in this chapter it was observed how the religion of Spiritualism has much in common with Catholicism. Although the fundamental tenets are different, many of the practices and beliefs, as well as the good intentions of its leaders, are the same.

The Catholic faith has seen a lot of changes over the years. When it comes to mediums and the practice of communing with our loved ones in heaven, another amendment is needed. The Church needs to keep up with the society we live in today.

Chapter 6
Communication with the Saints

"Have you have eyes but no sight? Ears but no hearing?"
(Mk 8:18)

In this chapter we will delve into the supernatural side of Catholicism by delving into the science of parapsychology.   Although the language may get technical at times, this is the fun stuff of our faith. Examining the psychic side of religion, we explore ESP, telepathy, clairvoyance and clairaudience; examples will be given in the lives of Biblical figures and the saints.   Learn how paranormal practices are an essential part of prayer life and for communication with the saints.

Can You Hear Me Now?

We have learned there are three levels to the communion of saints, the Church Triumphant (heaven), the Church Suffering (purgatory) and the Church Militant (earth).   Communication takes place not only within each level, but between levels also.   For example, through this book I am now communicating to others in the Church on earth.   At the same time, my inspiration comes from my writing angels and guides who are communicating ideas from the church in heaven to myself, in the Church on earth.   In addition, what I'm writing may be of interest to those in the Church Suffering and Church Triumphant who may be reading this book along with you.   Just by writing these words communication with the saints is occurring on all three levels.

Although communication is just one aspect of the communion of saints, it is essential and can take many forms, such as talking, writing, e-mailing, praying, singing, sign language, body language and even telepathic thought. It can involve signs, symbols, visual cues, touch, taste, music and even dreams. Communication can be verbal or non-verbal, physical or non-physical.

Often communication takes place indirectly. It may come through the medium of television, radio, telephone, newspaper, satellite, cell-phone or computer. The medium may also be a person, such as a friend, family member, priest, doctor, lawyer, saint, angel, spirit guide, Jesus or even a psychic medium.

The way in which we communicate varies depending on the situation. We communicate with infants and children differently than we communicate with adults, teenagers or elderly people. We communicate with animals differently than with people. We communicate with the "living" differently than with the "dead." As many ways as there are to communicate within our world, there are ways to communicate between worlds as well. Such is life in the communion of saints.

Reverend Gino Concetti, Chief Theological Commentator for the Vatican newspaper, *L'Osservatore Romano* provides insight on the interchange between the various levels of the Church. In an article on Concetti, written by John Hooper for the *London Observer* Service, it explains:

> One of the most authoritative spokesmen of the Roman Catholic Church has raised eyebrows among the faithful by declaring that the church believes in the feasibility of communication with the dead.

> ...Concetti said the Church remained opposed to the raising of spirits, but added, "Communication is possible between those who live on this earth and those who live in a state of eternal repose, in heaven or purgatory. It may even be that God lets our loved ones send us messages to guide us at certain moments in our life."

His comments were made in support of an American theologian, the Rev. John Neuhaus. Neuhaus had described how a friend had seen a ghost. He said there were various explanations but "the important thing is not to deny such things as *a priori*."

Concetti said the key to the Church's attitude was the Roman Catholic belief in a "Communion of Saints," which included Christians on earth as well as those in the afterlife. "Where there is communion, there is communication," he said.

According to the editorial, Reverend Concetti suggested that the deceased could be responsible for physical manifestations, inspirational thought and appearances in dreams. The priest quotes St. Dominic, who, on his deathbed, implored his brothers, "Do not weep, for I shall be more useful to you after my death and I shall help you then more effectively than during my life." Concetti also held that the new Catholic Catechism specifically endorsed the view that the dead could intercede on earth (Hooper).

In this article, Reverend Concetti declares that communion, or communication applies to the faithful on earth, in heaven and in purgatory. Concetti also acknowledges that our deceased loved ones may send messages to guide us at crucial times in our lives. The two-way system of communication is acceptable in the Roman Catholic Church based on the key belief in the communion of saints.

We will now leave theology for a time to take a more scientific look at communication between the various levels of the church. Through a brief study of parapsychology, we will better understand the "supernatural" interchange which takes place within the communion of saints. But first, to better understand the science of parapsychology, we will start with its history, which is rooted in the religion and practice of Spiritualism.

Modern-Day Spiritualism
The History of Parapsychology

The study of psychic phenomenon actually began over a century ago in response to the highly popular Spiritualist movement. *The History of Spiritualism* by Sir Arthur Conan Doyle is a fascinating book from which the following story is derived. For more complete and detailed information, including scientific accounts of levitations and spirit materializations, I highly suggest reading Doyle's work.

Modern-day Spiritualism got its start in the small town of Hydesville, New York, thirty miles west of Rochester. In December of 1847, John Fox, along with his wife, Margaret and their two young girls, fourteen-year-old Maggie and twelve-year-old Kate, moved to the little village. They purchased a modest home there that had been built some years earlier.

A year later, in March of 1848, the Fox family began hearing rapping noises coming from within the walls of their home. At times the knocking noises were extremely loud and forceful enough to shake the beds and chairs. Mrs. Fox and the two girls became so frightened that on several occasions they stayed with friends. In their absence, the noises continued, as John Fox and many neighbors witnessed. Upon learning that the previous homeowners also experienced the rappings, the family concluded that the house was haunted.

One afternoon, after returning to her home, the frustrated Kate decided to challenge the ghost. She snapped her fingers several times and dared the entity to repeat the number of snaps she made. She had an immediate reply; every snap was followed by a knock. Maggie soon joined in and the girls discovered they could communicate with the mysterious rapper through snaps and by clapping their hands. They set up a simple code that enabled them to receive answers to their questions about the invisible intruder. They learned that the sounds were coming from the spirit of a peddler, who had been killed in the home, long before they lived there. They also learned that he was buried in the cellar.

The story spread like wildfire and hundreds of people came to the

Fox house to investigate the matter. It became apparent that the rappings were associated with the girls so they were sent away to live with relatives in Rochester. Maggie stayed with her brother, David, and Kate stayed with her sister, Leah. Hoping to find peace in their new locations, what they found were more rapping noises. It seemed that the girls were the common denominator in the cause of the disturbance.

Apparently a door to the otherside had been opened and Kate and Maggie were the key. Using the code they had devised, the girls learned that other spirits were able to communicate with them. It wasn't long before the Fox sisters were demonstrating their newfound abilities to many others. They gathered friends, neighbors and relatives in a circle and started hosting séances.

As their notoriety increased they were asked to give a public demonstration of their unusual talent. In November of 1849 hundreds of people packed Corinthian Hall in downtown Rochester to witness the unexplainable phenomenon for themselves. In response to questions, rapping sounds came from all parts of the huge meetinghouse; they could be heard from the ceiling, the floor and the walls. The knocking noises were so powerful that the audience could feel the vibration in their seats. Managed by their older sister, Leah, the girls decided to take their show on the road and organized séances and public appearances around the globe; Albany, New York City, London and Russia were part of their tour (Doyle).

The Fox sisters' discovery started a new craze; people everywhere were gathering to hold their own séances. In a time without television, weekly circles became the social equivalent of gathering for a Monday night football game. The highly popular pastime took the country by storm and lasted for over twenty years. By the 1860's a full thirty-percent of the U.S. population was practicing spiritualism - over eleven million people (Robinson & Carlson-Finnerty).

During the spiritualist movement, hundreds of people began reporting a slew of supernatural events occurring during their séances. The phenomena included spirit-materializations, objects moving by themselves, people speaking in tongues, tables levitating, automatic writing, musical instruments being played by invisible entities and elaborate paintings created by people who had died hundreds of years earlier.

Just a Fact

Sir Arthur Conan Doyle, famous for his Sherlock Holmes books, was a Spiritualist and a physician. He also authored *The History of Spiritualism*, a fascinating account of paranormal phenomena that occurred during séances of the 1800's. Many scientific investigations by noteworthy scholars of the day are documented in this two-volume historical treasure.

Beginning around 1850, various scientists organized groups to investigate the unusual phenomena. Their purpose was to study the famous mediums of that era, and whenever possible, to expose them as frauds. In many cases they did find deceitful psychics, in a few cases, however, no scientific explanation for the paranormal events could be found.

To maintain their respect as professionals, the scientists set extremely high standards for their experimental research and kept well-documented records. In 1882 a number of scholars founded the Society for Psychical Research in London; Henry Sedgewick was the first president. In 1885 its sister organization, The American Society for Psychical Research, was formed; William James was chairperson. It is America's oldest organization for psychic research with an enormous library housing records of every experiment in every area of the paranormal (Robinson & Carlson-Finnerty, 48).

In 1927, with the publication of J.B. Rhine's report, *Extra Sensory Perception*, Parapsychology became a recognized science. In 1969 the Parapsychological Association was accepted into the American Association for the Advancement of Science. Psychical research and paranormal phenomena could no longer be dismissed (Neff).

During the height of Spiritualism, parapsychologists exposed a significant number of fraudulent mediums. This led to the Roman Catholic Church's eventual condemnation of the practice; Spiritualism lost its popularity. For the genuine mediums and their followers, the circles continued and schools were organized to teach and refine mediumship. In 1893 the National Spiritualist Association of Churches (NSAC) was established to set standards for the Spiritualist ministry and to investigate fraud.

Fifty-six years after those first Hydesville raps were heard, a skeleton, along with a tin peddler's box was found in the basement of the Fox home (Heaney). The box, along with many other Spiritualist artifacts, such as slate messages and spirit paintings, can be viewed in the Lily Dale Museum in western, NY. Despite all the evidence, to this day many do not believe that the story of the Fox sisters was genuine. Furthermore, most American history books do not even acknowledge the nationwide Spiritualist movement that took place in the middle to late 1800's. Perhaps it is fear of the unknown that causes people to deny or ignore paranormal phenomena.

Spiritualism and Parapsychology Today

The Rhine Research Center in Durham, North Carolina was the first American facility built solely for the purpose of studying psychic phenomenon. Founded in 1927 by noted psychologist, Joseph B. Rhine, Ph.D., this state-of-the-art center, which began at Duke University, set the standards for psychical research and is one of the most reputable labs in the field. There are now over a dozen such facilities across the globe (Robinson & Carlson-Finnerty). The Rhine Center is also the current home for the International Association of Near-Death Studies (IANDS).

With advances in science, there have been advances in Spiritualism. In the high-tech era of the twenty-first century, experiments and research became more sophisticated. There are highly reputable, world-renowned, mediums today, like John Edward, Sylvia Brown and James VanPraagh, who achieved their prominence because of their willingness to undergo scrutiny by parapsychologists. They have been put through dozens of scientific experiments in laboratory settings to prove their authenticity. *The Afterlife Experiments* by Gary Schwartz is a fascinating book that documents one such study. Science has raised the bar for those in the business of mediumship.

With the great reduction in fraud, and with the popularity of the New Age movement, Spiritualism is once again on the rise. At the same time, interest in the supernatural is at an all-time high. Paranormal investigations and psychic detective work, along with television shows and movies on the subject, have become big business. Evidence of extrasensory perception and life-after-death is mounting with each passing year.

Just a Fact
Ron Nagy, curator of the Lily Dale Museum, is the foremost expert on Spirit Art. His book, *Precipitated Spirit Paintings* is an historical account of portraits that materialized on canvas during séances in the 1800's. Spirit art was created without the use of human hands and without the use of brushes or paint. The portraits, along with the tin peddler's box from the Fox home, and many other interesting artifacts are on display at the museum; a visit is highly recommended.

Now that we've learned how parapsychology got started, let's take a closer look at the subject and see how it can help us to better understand communication with the saints. This is not intended to be an authoritative book on parapsychology; there are many better resources for those who would like to know more on the subject (see bibliography). I simply would like to show that when we use our sixth sense, we are merely practicing communion with the saints.

Parapsychology 101

So what exactly is parapsychology? "Para" is a Greek word meaning "beyond." Parapsychology is the study of phenomena that are outside or beyond the normal paradigms of science and critical reasoning. These phenomena are called "paranormal," which simply means beyond normal (Heaney).

Paranormal phenomena are also called "psychic" phenomena, or what is referred to in the field as simply "psi." Psi is the first letter of the Greek word "psych," which literally means "breath" and refers to the mind and human soul. It is the root word in "psychology," which is the science of the mind (Robinson, & Carlson-Finnerty).

Parapsychologists study and investigate anything labeled "paranormal" or "psychic." Your psychic or non-physical senses allow you to gather information that your physical senses alone cannot detect, which are the senses of "seeing," " hearing," " smelling," "touching" and" tasting." For this reason, psychic impressions are called "extrasensory perception" or "ESP"; it is often referred to as our "sixth sense" (Heaney).

We also refer to our psychic or sixth sense as "intuition." Intuition is defined as "immediate cognition" and when it occurs we suddenly "just know," without any doubt, and often act on the information received (Berkowitz and Romain). Sometimes it comes in the form of a "gut feeling." For example, the phone rings and you "just know" it's Aunt Joan calling you. Or you're lost in a big city and you "just know" that if you make a left- hand turn at the next corner it will get you where you're going. For this reason, a psychic or a medium is also referred to as an "intuitive."

Insight

Two books were invaluable in doing research for this chapter: *The Complete Idiots Guide to Psychic Awareness* by Lynn A. Robinson, M.Ed. and Lavonne Carlson-Finnerty, and *The Complete Idiots Guide to Communicating with Spirits* by Rita S. Berkowitz and Deborah S. Romain. They are excellent resources for the basics of Parapsychology and Spiritualism.

Even Catholics are Psychic

Q: *Is psychic ability a spiritual gift from God or a curse from the devil?*

When two people are in love, or have a close relationship, they often don't need words to communicate with each other. Finishing each other's sentences is not uncommon. It's what we often refer to as being on the "same wavelength" or "tuning in" to another person's vibration. The emotional bond also creates a psychic bond; this lays the foundation for telepathic communication.

Have you ever walked into a room and just knew, without anyone saying a word, that another person in that room was mad at you? Perhaps a friend said, "You could have cut the air with a knife." At the same moment you may have noticed a queasy feeling in the pit of your stomach. Intuitively you knew someone was upset with you.

Most moms have a psychic connection with their children. For example, a newborn cries and the mother somehow knows whether the baby is hungry, tired, sick or needs her diapers changed. Often a mother will "just know" when her child is in trouble, even if she is hundreds of miles away. We often call this a "woman's intuition."

Authors Robinson and Carlson-Finnerty insist, "Everyone is born with some degree of psychic ability. It's not a sacred gift intended only for a few select geniuses" (11). We all have the capability of picking up on another person's feelings and thoughts because we all have extrasensory perception (ESP). We use this paranormal ability constantly, often without realizing it, because it can take place subconsciously or at the spiritual level.

Our spiritual level is the invisible part of us that continues to live after our physical bodies are gone; it's where our mind and non-physical body, or spirit, are located. When we send thoughts to another person, our mind or spirit is sending telepathic messages to the mind or spirit of the other person.

In the same way, we can use our thoughts (ESP) to send and receive messages to and from the spirit of loved ones who have crossed over. As discussed in chapter four, through prayers, intercessions and veneration, we share spiritual "goods and good" between the saints in heaven and those on earth; "Eucharistic Prayers" and the "Litany of Saints" were two examples cited. It is through the use of our psychic or spiritual gifts that we are able to transcommunicate our thoughts and love to each other.

Utilizing one's psychic gifts does not mean that he or she is practicing the occult or any other diabolical connotations that have been attributed to it. Father John Heaney explains this by saying:

> Parapsychology is not a synonym for the occult movement. The word "occult" means hidden or mysterious. The occult movement is based on claims to knowledge about supernatural agencies or mysterious events, which are inscrutable to humans in general but which are available to the initiated. The basis of this claim tends to be "dogmatic." That is, it seems to the observer to be overly "a priori," esoteric, and not sufficiently related to critical study. (5)

Some Catholic authorities believe that psychic phenomena are associated with hidden, supernatural forces and therefore condemn the study of it as being part of the occult. Father Heaney points out that parapsychology is not a secret society that reserves information for a chosen few. It does not seek to hide knowledge of the paranormal from the general public, but to share it with whoever wants to learn about it.

One bit of knowledge we all share is the ability to tap into our non-physical senses. So, no matter what our religious faith, sex, race, or occupation, we all have psychic abilities; they are as natural to us as the ability to see and hear. Whether we call them supernatural or paranormal, it's a part of who we are as spiritual children of God. Yes, even Catholics are psychic.

Types of Psychic Phenomena

Now that you know you're psychic, let's learn a bit more about it. Psychic phenomena are divided into two primary areas, "mental" and "physical." Mental psychic ability is using one's sixth sense to obtain information or knowledge. Examples of this would be telepathy, clairvoyance, clairaudience, psychometry, precognition, apparitions, automatic writing and xenoglossy (speaking in a language unknown by the subject). People who are gifted in any of these areas are called "mental mediums."

Physical psychic ability is using one's sixth sense to influence physical objects or beings. Examples of this would be materialization, dematerialization, levitation, healing, and psychokinesis (also called telekinesis), which is the ability to move or create objects with the mind. People who are gifted in any of these areas are called "physical mediums" (Robinson and Carlson-Finnerty).

Some of the subjects studied in parapsychology don't fall neatly into either category and may be a combination of both mental and physical events; for example, glossolalia (speaking in tongues), miracles, stigmata and lucid dreaming (Daniels). No matter what form is used, authors Robinson and Carlson-Finnerty explain:

All of these areas call traditional knowledge and

assumptions into question. For physicists, these subjects indicate that people may lack a basic understanding about space and time, and about how energy and information travel. For biologists, these subjects raise questions about what possible senses people may have that they aren't even aware of yet. Psychologists may work to reexamine the ways that the mind, memory and perception work. (52)

The field of parapsychology also raises many questions for theologians and challenges much of our traditional religious teaching as well. When it comes to communication with the saints (spirits), science can shed some light on the subject, taking away the fear and stigma attached to it.

Know the Lingo

Q: *What is the difference between psychic gifts and spiritual gifts?*
Q: *Aren't prophets and seers also clairvoyant?*

Before we continue, we will translate some parapsychological jargon into Christian theological terms. This will make it easier for Catholic readers to understand and will help them to see that science and religion often use different words to say the same thing.

For example, "clairvoyance" is the same as "visions," and "clairaudience" can be translated as "locutions." "Precognition" is used synonymously with "prophecy" while "mediums" are similar to "prophets." Telepathy and transcommunication is another way to describe prayer. The following table may be of help:

Theological Terms	Parapsychological Terms
grace, spiritual gifts visions	psychic ability, ESP, sixth sense clairvoyance
locutions, voices	clairauduence
prophecy	precognition
speaking in tongues	glossolalia
prayer, spiritualism seer, prophet, visionary, soothsayer	telepathy, transcommunication psychic, clairvoyant, intuitive, medium

The theological terms listed are familiar because they are found throughout the Bible. In the Old and New Testament there are many examples of people practicing or experiencing these "supernatural" abilities. With the development of parapsychology, we now have a more scientific perspective. Robinson and Carlson-Finnerty support this idea in their book on *Psychic Awareness*:

> The best-selling book of all time, *The Bible*, is filled with stories of heroes with powerful psychic abilities. Often these people heard voices, saw images, or had dreams-all of which led to prophecies that were realized at a future date. In short, these heroes predicted the future. Of course, Biblical text itself never refers to these abilities as "psychic," but they do fit the description. (20)

We will be taking a look at examples of psychic phenomena in the Bible. Because there are so many to choose from, we will limit our examples to just two types, clairvoyance (visions) and clairaudience (locutions); they both fall under the umbrella of "telepathy."

Quote Me
"If you took all the supernatural material out of the Bible, you would have nothing left but the covers." (Sylvia Brown)

Telepathy

Telepathy is a form of psychic ability; it comes from the Greek words meaning "far feeling." It's the process of transmitting or receiving thoughts or feelings between minds. (Berkowitz). In other words, it is mind-to-mind communication (Van Praagh). It is not however, "mind reading," as many people mistakenly believe. Parapsychologists sometimes refer to telepathy as bio-communication or psycho-spiritual communication.

When telepathic communication takes place on the earth-plane, between two human beings, it is making use of their psychic ability; those who have this gift are called "psychics." Often the average person will experience psychic moments when they know what someone else is thinking. For example, just as you reach for the phone to call a friend, the phone rings and it's that same friend calling you. You received information from your non-physical sense (ESP) seconds before you received information from your physical sense (hearing the phone ring). You and your friend were communicating telepathically, without even realizing it.

In contrast, when telepathic communication takes place between humans on earth (physical beings) and spirits or saints in heaven (non-physical beings), this is considered making use of mediumistic abilities. People who have this gift are called "mediums" because they act as a go-between or medium between two different dimensions.

Just a Fact

A "psychic" is one who uses telepathy to communicate with other physical beings (including pets) while a "medium" is one who uses telepathy to communicate with non-physical beings.

When we pray for another person, perhaps for healing, *we* are acting as intercessors or mediums. When we pray to the canonized saints or Jesus, *they* are acting as intercessors or mediums. In both cases there is a "go-between" the person being prayed for, or doing the praying, and God.

All mediums are psychics, because they can use their telepathic abilities to talk with people on earth or in heaven. However, not all psychics are mediums because some are limited to using their telepathic gifts on the earth plane only (Berkowitz and Romain, 140). Extremely gifted people, like John Edward, James Van Praagh and Sylvia Brown, can communicate telepathically on both levels, either with other humans on earth or with loved ones in heaven; they are called "psychic mediums."

In her book, *The Afterlife Connection*, psychotherapist, Jane Greer, Ph.D., uses the scientific term, "transcommunication" to describe telepathic communication with spirits. The theological terms for telepathic spirit communication are "prayer" and "spiritualism." Since the focus of this book is on the scientific explanation of communication with the saints, "transcommunication" is the preferred word that will be used. We will now examine what these concepts have in common.

Prayer

Q: *Isn't praying to the saints the same as talking to them?*

One of the common ways in which we communicate with the saints in heaven is through what is known as "prayer." We don't question whether or not we are heard; we just assume that someone is listening to, or receiving, our prayers. This comes from an innate, intuitive knowing (ESP) that on the spiritual level we are in communication with the higher realms. It is our eternal connection to those in heaven and to the divine.

We pray to God, to Jesus and to anyone who will listen. But exactly what is prayer and how does it work? *Webster's Dictionary* defines the word "pray" as "entreat" or "implore," to "plea" or "request earnestly in a humble manner." To pray is to "address God or a god with adoration, confession, supplication, or thanksgiving."

(Webster).

The *Catholic Encyclopedia* states that the words used in scripture to define prayer are "to call up, to intercede; to mediate, to consult, to beseech, and to cry out to." It also describes prayer as "the elevation of the mind to God with a view to asking proper things from Him." In addition, prayer is "communing and conversing with God" and "talking to God." ([4]).

When describing to whom we can pray the *Catholic Encyclopedia* states that it is not out of place to address our prayers to other divine persons as well. We may pray to the blessed Virgin, the angels and the saints to ask God to grant us our petitions. Furthermore, our prayers may be expressed internally, through our thoughts (telepathically), or externally, as in a vocal manner. Although it is God alone who can give us what we ask for, this does not prevent us from praying to certain creatures of God ([4]).

When we pray to God, the angels, or saints we are making use of our telepathic abilities. We often call on the saints, or our loved ones who have passed away, for help and support during difficult times. We also like to acknowledge our deceased mother or dad during the most triumphant times of our lives. Using our minds to communicate to the minds of discarnate beings in another world is practicing telepathy for the purpose of transcommunication.

Prayer is not just a religious practice, it has been studied in great detail by the sciences that have a different take on it; it can also be referred to as "intention." Thoughts are a form of energy that exists in waves (sometimes as particles), much like radio waves; they can be transmitted from one person to another. Quantum physics teaches us that our thoughts can influence events in the universe via the power of "prayer" or "intention." Our thoughts create a field that is much like gravity; it's often referred to as the "field of consciousness" (Robinson and Carlson- Finnerty).

Research in the field of consciousness suggests that when many minds focus on a single topic, it can result in measurable effects. Experiments with the use of random-number generators have shown this to be true. Individuals or groups of people have been able to affect the generators merely by focusing intensely on specific numbers. By doing so, this changed the random patterns to a pattern producing higher ratios of a specific number (Robinson and Carlson-Finnerty).

In the same way, when many people pray for a specific result, such as rain, it often results in a measurable effect, such as raindrops. The concentrated effort of the group creates a field of consciousness that brings rain; the collective power of intention somehow taps into a greater power. Quantum physics uses the phrase "thoughts are things" to explain how we create or manifest with our mind. Jesus understood how prayer and the field of consciousness worked; he explained, "Where two or three are gathered in my name, there I am in their midst" (Matthew 18:20).

Although science may not take the mystery out of prayer, it provides support to our religious practices and beliefs. Never is the power of prayer more evident than when it comes to its effect on healing. Scientific studies have shown that patients who received prayer recovered more quickly and needed fewer medicines than those patients who were not prayed for (Robinson & Carlson-Finnerty).

Most of us already know about the power of prayer and don't need science to validate it for us. What science does, however, is help us understand communication with the saints. It also shows how the mind can reach beyond its physical boundaries to tap into a powerful source that can affect the lives of many.

In the remainder of this chapter we will take a closer look at two specific types of telepathy, "clairvoyance" (visions) and "clairaudience" (locutions). In these forms of ESP, information is exchanged from mind to mind through the use of pictures, thoughts, feelings, sounds, or by simply infusing pure knowledge (inspiration). To help us better understand how this fits in with the communion of saints, each section will be followed by examples from both the Old and New Testaments.

Clairvoyance

Q: *How is clairvoyance different from "visions."*

Clairvoyance comes from the French word meaning "clear seeing" or "clear vision." It is the paranormal ability to see things that cannot be seen with the physical eye; for this reason clairvoyance is often referred to as "second sight" (Robinson and Romain).

A clairvoyant is a type of medium that sees objects, colors, symbols, people, spirits, or scenes in her mind (Van Praagh). Often these images come from beyond the earth plane and are direct communications from spirit. In addition, it is not unusual for a medium to see images of a future event (precognition) or a past event (retrocognition). For this reason, a clairvoyant may also have prophet-like abilities.

Let's compare this description of clairvoyance to another definition given by Reverend Michael Freze in his book *Voices, Visions and Apparitions.* He describes a "visionary" as one who sees a supernatural being by means of an imaginary or corporeal vision; the person is also called a "seer." Freze defines a "seer" as "one who tells about or predicts a future event" (precognition). A seer may also experience the phenomena of "private revelations, external or internal voices (locutions), prophecies, or various extraordinary gifts of the Holy Spirit, such as wisdom, knowledge, or understanding" (Freze, 78).

Freze's definition of "visionary" and "seer" accurately describes a "clairvoyant." He also suggests that the person possessing this ability may have the gift of prophecy. To sum it up, a "clairvoyant" is the scientific term for a "visionary," "seer" or "prophet," while "clairvoyance" is the scientific term for "visions." You may want to refer to the "Know the Lingo" chart.

Theologians may quibble about the definition of "prophet," as being one who speaks for God; however, because prophets in the Bible made so many predictions, the word "prophecy" became analogous for predicting the future. For that reason, a clairvoyant or medium can also be called a prophet. To look at it another way, many of the prophets in the Bible were clairvoyant; therefore, they can be considered mediums.

Clairvoyant images may be subjective or objective. Subjective clairvoyance is when an image is seen in the person's mind or mind's eye, also known as the "third eye." The images may be of past or future events, symbols, or the likeness of a deceased individual. Objective clairvoyance is when images are seen with the person's physical eyes. He or she can see non-physical objects, events, or beings as clearly as you and I can see physical objects, events, or people (Robinson, 73).

An example of subjective clairvoyance can be given from personal experience. Sometimes, when I'm meditating, I will actually see the face of a person in spirit who is "coming through" to me and I can describe that person in great detail. Other times I may get a symbol, such is the case whenever I see a rose; I know that either my Grandmother, Rose or my Mother, Mildred Rose is trying to contact me. The pictures are imprinted or projected into my mind and are seen with my third eye. Spirits often use imagery to send messages; this is one way communication with the saints works.

Insight

The "third eye" is a type of psychic receiver for inner vision. It is located in the middle of each person's forehead and is associated with the sixth chakra or energy center. Psychic development classes and meditation are ways in which people can open up their third eye to become more clairvoyant.

An example of objective clairvoyance can be given by telling a story; it explains how I started receiving messages from my grandmother:

Mike Allen, of Mt. Morris, NY is a veteran mental health professional and a colleague of mine. When I confided in Mike about my supernatural experiences with spiritual beings, he suggested that I meet with his wife. "Why would I talk to her?" I asked. "She's into that kind of stuff," he explained; so I set up a meeting.

The first time I met Valerie Allen she caught me off-guard with her spiritual gift. Shortly after we sat down at her dining room table to visit, Valerie asked me, "Who is the woman standing behind you that keeps saying, "Tell her my name is Rose, Tell her my name is Rose." She went on to describe the plump, large-bosomed woman who always wore her gray hair in a bun. Valerie described my grandmother, Rose.

With her eyes wide open, and in the middle of a conversation, Valerie saw my deceased grandmother. This was not a vision seen in trance or meditation; Valerie was able to see, with her physical eyes, the actual spiritual form of my grandma. She went on to explain that Rose was a guide for me and was around me all the time.

I wasn't sure how to take this information, as my Grandmother died when I was eight years old and I barely remember her. Since Valerie reintroduced me, I have become quite close to my

Grandmother, who often sends me signs in the form of roses. I now have a relationship with Grandma that I never had when she lived in the physical world. I have Valerie to thank for that; her objective clairvoyance brought two people together who live on different planes of existence. Gifted with second sight since childhood, Valerie is a well-respected medium, a devout Catholic, and an active member of the communion of saints.

Throughout history people from the church on earth and the church in heaven have been brought together by the use of extrasensory perception. Clairvoyance has always played a role in communication between the saints. Let's consider some examples from the Bible.

Clairvoyance in the Bible

To give Catholic readers an idea of how important visionaries were to our faith, various Biblical passages from the Old and New Testaments will be cited. There are so many examples that another whole book could be written on the subject; we will list just a few. The following references were found in *The Bible: A Spiritualist's View* by psychic research consultants Marilyn Awtry and Paula Vogt. Each of these cases describes a clairvoyant, psychic experience. The theological indicators for clairvoyance are "visions" or "seer":

The Covenant with Abram:
Some time after these events, this word of the Lord came to Abram in a *vision*: "Fear not, Abram! I am your shield; I will make your reward very great." (Genesis 15:1)

Blinded Aramean Soldiers:
Then he prayed, "O Lord, open his eyes that he may *see*." And the Lord opened the eyes of the servant, so that he *saw* the mountainside filled with horses and fiery chariots around Elisha. (2 Kings 6:17)

Elijah and Elisha:
When Elisha requested a double portion of Elijah's spirit, Elijah answered, "You have asked something that is not easy. Still if you *see* me taken up from you, your wish will be granted; otherwise not." As they walked conversing, a flaming chariot and flaming

horses came between them, and Elijah went up to heaven in a whirlwind. When Elisha *saw* it happen he cried out, "My father! My father! Israel's chariots and drivers!" But when he could no longer *see* him, Elisha gripped his own garment and tore it in two. (2 Kings 2: 10-12)

Messianic Entry into Jerusalem:
"Go into the village straight ahead of you. Upon entering it you will find an ass tied there which no one has yet ridden. Untie it and lead it back. If anyone should ask you, "Why are you untying the beast?" say, "The Master has need of it." (Luke 19:30-31)

Peter's Denial Foretold:
Jesus answered, "I give you my assurance, this very night before the cock crows twice, you will deny me three times." (Mark 14:30)

Through Asia Minor (Paul's Vision of the Man of Macedonia):
There one night Paul had a *vision*. A man of Macedonia stood before him and invited him, "Come over to Macedonia and help us." After this *vision*, we immediately made efforts to get across to Macedonia, concluding that God had summoned us to proclaim the good news there. (Acts 16: 9-10)

In each of these cases, Abram, Elisha, Jesus and Paul showed signs of clairvoyance. They had visions beyond their normal sense of sight; sometimes they were images of future events. These are clear examples of their psychic ability. In terms of parapsychology, these prophets would be considered clairvoyants. Whenever transcommunication took place (visions shared between two dimensions), as in *The Call of Jeremiah*, it would be an example of mediumship. For more Biblical references to clairvoyance see 1 Samuel 9:19, Exodus 3:2, Jeremiah 1:11-14 and John 1:48-50 (Awtry and Vogt).

Clairaudience

Clairaudience comes from the French word meaning "clear hearing." It's the ability to hear something outside the normal capability of our physical ears. Like clairvoyance, clairaudience can be divided into two categories, subjective and objective (Robinson, 73). Subjective clairaudience makes use of the non-physical ear or the inner ear of the mind; only the person receiving the message can hear it. "Objective clairaudience" makes use of the physical ear. An audible voice or sound, that may seem to come from nowhere, may be heard by more than one person.

Let's compare this description of clairaudience to another definition given by Reverend Michael Freze. He defines "locutions" in the following way:

> Supernatural words received in a clear, distinctive manner and are often perceived in the depths of the heart. Although locutions are not subject to external stimulus or the use of the physical senses, nevertheless the words they convey are very real and convincing to the recipient of such divine favors. (310)

Locutions are also divided into two categories, inner and outer locutions. They are another way to describe subjective and objective clairaudience. When one receives clairaudient messages or locutions from a saint, Jesus, God, or a deceased relative, he or she is experiencing transcommunication. In such cases the person is acting as a medium, or being used as a medium, to convey a message from one dimension to another.

An example of subjective clairaudience is when someone clearly hears their name being called and the sound is received with their mind's ear; no one else hears it. It may even be recognized, as the voice of a deceased loved one. I will share a personal experience that will help to explain:

> One night while I was baby-sitting my two nieces, Andrea and Hanna, at approximately two in the morning I was suddenly awakened by a loud, clear, urgent voice shouting, "Mary Margaret!" I was immediately jolted into an upright position as my eyes darted toward the half-open bedroom doorway. I was fully expecting one of the girls to be

standing there; surely something was happening.

The doorway was empty however, and the house was immersed in complete silence. I got up, walked down the hallway and checked on the two little-ones; they were both sound asleep. That's when I realized what was going on-- it must be my mom calling. My nieces always refer to me as "Aunt Mary," most know me as "Mary Grace"; my deceased mother, however, always called me "Mary Margaret."

I'm not sure why Mom woke me up; perhaps she just used the opportunity to let me know that she was helping out. I took comfort in the fact that Mom still found a way to communicate with me; it gave me a sense of peace.

"Objective clairaudience" is when an audible voice or sound, from a non-physical source, is heard with the physical ear; more than one person may hear it. I will give another example from personal experience:

One evening I attended one of Fran Carn's psychic development circles at Plymouth Spiritualist Church. Fran is a noted medium, hypnotherapist and certified Naturopathic Health Practitioner in the Rochester, NY area. That night she decided to demonstrate clairaudience by opening up our spiritual ears. Fran stated that we would not be using music for this exercise, as was customary. I was disappointed as I often depend on music to raise my vibration to the level needed to receive information from spirits.

Fran proceeded to guide the group of over twenty people through a meditation that would enable us to hear with our mind's ear. Soon, the church was filled with the most beautiful, most melodious music that I have ever heard. It sounded like a symphony of angels playing a concerto in a soft, but quite audible sound that seemed to emanate from the rafters and echo throughout the church. After the meditation, the sanctuary returned to complete silence.

We all heard the music and many of us were convinced that someone must have been playing a meditation CD in the basement; because that was the only possible place it could have come from. To our disbelief, no one else was in the building; in fact the doors are locked during every circle to prevent latecomers from disturbing the spiritual energy. Much to our surprise, it was indeed heavenly music that we all heard clairaudiently; it truly was an angelic symphony!

Fran described the spiritual orchestra, which she saw clairvoyantly, in great detail. There were many angels playing various instruments solely for our enjoyment. She pointed to the area where they held their mini concert, just above our heads in the space near the beamed ceiling. Fran kindly thanked the celestial beings for participating in our learning experience.

Another interesting example of clairaudience is in regard to how ministers choose their profession. A Catholic priest might explain that he decided to spend his life serving the Lord because he was "called" to the priesthood. He may have enrolled in seminary school because he answered his "calling." In this case, the message could have been received either clairaudiently or clairvoyantly (through intuition) depending on which extra sensory sense was used.

A final example of clairaudience comes from one of the priests interviewed for this book. The late, Father Jerome Shifferli, Pastor Emeritus of St. Matthew Church in Livonia, NY, recounted the following story:

> I had a brain aneurism and after a couple of months I came back to the rectory. I was walking up the stairs and I said to myself,
>
> "Lord, I should have died; the doctors said I should have died, but I didn't. What do you want from me?"
>
> And just as much as I can hear your voice, I heard His, and the voice said,

"Become like my son."

By this time I'm up the stairs and walking into my bedroom, I 'm sitting in a chair at my desk and there's a wall and a crucifix is up there. I was looking at the crucifix and I shook my head and said,

"Oh no, I ain't no Jesus."

And the answer came back again,

"Nothing is impossible with God."

That's the only time in all my years as a priest that I had ever heard a voice from God. I couldn't believe it but from who else could I have gotten this message? I think the validity of the message was in the message itself. *"Become like my son."* Who else would say that? No one. (Grace)

What Father Shifferli experienced was a telepathic or psychic message from God that came in the form of a voice; it was also a transcommunication. The source of the message was apparent to the priest as he explained that no one besides God himself could possibly say, "Become like my son," especially since the voice was heard while gazing at a crucifix of Jesus.

On another subject of clairaudience, it is not unusual for someone to see a psychiatrist for help when they start hearing voices. Most doctors would automatically assume that the person suffers from schizophrenia and would treat the patient with medication. Some of these people may actually be receiving spirit communication without realizing it. Because most psychiatrists are not trained in psychic phenomena, in some cases the patients are misdiagnosed.

Unfortunately many doctors don't realize that it is very "normal" to have a paranormal experience, such as clairaudience. Whenever a person's mental health is in question, all psychological possibilities must first be explored. If the investigation shows no clear cause, then all parapsychological possibilities should be explored.

Many of our great Christian mystics and saints were accused of being crazy because they heard voices; Joan of Arc was one. When the church investigates a person who has exhibited supernatural abilities, a psychological test is given. In Biblical times there were no such tests. For some reason, when scriptures describe a clairaudient experience, the sanity of the persons involved is generally accepted without question.

Clairaudience in the Bible

Clairaudience is another paranormal phenomenon found throughout the Bible, the following are just a few examples; there are dozens more to be found in scriptures. Again, *The Bible: A Spiritualist's View* is the source of information. The theological terms for "clairaudience" are "locutions" or "voices."

Revelation to Samuel:

The lamp of God was not yet extinguished, and Samuel was sleeping in the temple of the Lord where the ark of God was. The Lord *called* to Samuel, who answered, "Here I am." He ran to Eli and said, "Here I am, you *called* me." "I did not call you," Eli said. "Go back to sleep." So he went back to sleep.

Again the Lord *called* Samuel, who rose and went to Eli, "Here I am," he said. "You *called* me. " But he answered, "I did not call you, my son. Go back to sleep." ...When Samuel went to sleep in his place, the Lord came and revealed his presence, *calling* out as before, "Samuel, Samuel!" Samuel answered, "Speak, for your servant is *listening*." (1 Samuel 3:3-10)

Flight to Horeb (The Lord appears to Elijah):

After the earthquake there was fire-but the Lord was not in the fire. After the fire there was a tiny *whispering* sound. When he heard this, Elijah hid his face in his cloak and went and stood at the entrance of the cave. A *voice* said to him, "Elijah, why are you here?" He replied, "I have been most zealous for the Lord, the God of hosts. ..." (1 Kings 19:12-14)

The Coming of Jesus' Hour:

Then a *voice* came from the sky: "I have glorified it, and will glorify it again." When the crowd of bystanders heard the voice, they said it was thunder. Others maintained, "An angel was speaking to him." Jesus answered, "That *voice* did not come for my sake, but for yours." (John 12: 28-30)

The Vocation of Saul:
As he traveled along and was approaching Damascus, a light from the sky suddenly flashed about him. He fell to the ground and at the same time heard a *voice* saying, "Saul, Saul, why do you persecute me?" "Who are you, sir?" he asked. The *voice* answered, "I am Jesus, the one you are persecuting. Get up and go into the city, where you will be told what to do." (Acts 9: 3-6)

Peter Explains His Actions:
I was at prayer in the city of Joppa when, in a trance, I saw a vision (clairvoyance). An object like a big canvas came down; it was lowered down to me from the sky by its four corners. ... I listened as a *voice* said to me, "Get up, Peter! Slaughter, then eat." I replied: "Not for a moment, sir! Nothing unclean or impure has ever entered my mouth!" A second time the *voice* from the heavens spoke out: "What God has purified you are not to call unclean." (Acts 11:5-9)

In each of these cases, Samuel, Elijah, Jesus, Saul and Peter showed signs of clairaudience. They heard voices that were received with their psychic ear. The messages, that the voices conveyed, were examples of transcommunications because they came from spiritual beings. And because these messages were then passed on to others, each of these Biblical figures acted as mediums.

It is quite clear, psychic ability was used throughout the Bible to practice communication with the saints. The following chart identifies additional scriptures that provide evidence of paranormal phenomena. The information, from *The Bible: A Spiritualist's View*, is only a small sample. The original chart has over 150 Biblical citations listed for thirty-five categories of psychic phenomena (Awtry and Vogt).

Psychic Phenomena in the Bible

Materializations:

Genesis 3:8, 18:1-10, 19:1, 32:34   Exodus 24:10-11
Judges 2:1-4, 13:3   Job 4:12
1 Samuel 28:12-16   1 Kings 19:5-7
Ezekiel 2:9-10, 11:9   Daniel 3:25, 5:5
Matthew 17:1-8, 28:9   John 20:12-17, 19-30
Acts 26:16
Luke 1:1-13, 2:9-11, 21: 4, 24:15, 24:30, 25-27

Speaking in Tongues:

1 Corinthians 14:18, 14-10, 14:5, 14:30   Acts 2:3

Trance:

Genesis 15:12-17   Numbers 24:4
1 Samuel 10:6-10   Job 42:3
Ezekiel 2:2   Daniel 8:18
Acts 10:10, 11:45, 22:17

Levitation:

1 Kings 18:12   2 Kings 2:11, 6:5
Ezekiel 3:12, 8:3, 11:1   Acts 8:39

Physical Phenomena:

Exodus 4:2-9, 14-31   Judges 6:36-38, 14-19
1 Kings 19:6, 7, 11   2 Kings 4:42-44
Ezekiel 8:3   Matthew 8:26, 28:2
John 20:30, 21:6-11   Acts 2:2, 5:19-20, 12:7-10

Just My Opinion

The physical body can be a barrier to God; many have eyes but cannot see and ears but cannot hear. Most can't see the Christ light that glows brightly within their neighbor and most people can't hear the voice of God crying out from those in need. For if they could see and hear the Lord in all of creation, never again would they judge, condemn, harm, or exclude another creature of God.

When we judge others based on our physical senses alone, we do not truly see them. We cannot see beyond the person's body to the Holy Spirit that lies within.

Seeing, hearing and speaking with the saints or loved ones in heaven is quite natural for many people, even though it may seem supernatural to others. However, we all have this telepathic ability; we call it prayer. Most people think it is quite natural to pray and think nothing of practicing this form of transcommunication.

Many believe that using psychic ability is socially and morally unacceptable because the Church bans it; it is considered taboo. If someone pointed out to a group of Catholics that they were using ESP whenever they prayed, the believers might scoff and take offense to it. If someone pointed out that prayer is a form of mediumship, they might become irate at the implication of heretical behavior. What many Catholics don't understand is that it is acceptable and necessary to use psychic ability to pray or talk with God and other souls in heaven, for that is how we practice communion with the saints.

People who are in touch with their psychic senses understand their cosmic connection. Those who use their sixth sense are using their higher mind to connect with a higher source, which in turn connects us with all others, both in heaven and on earth. Highly spiritual people understand we are all one and know that whatever they do to their brothers, they also do to themselves. To reach the level of spirituality that enables the faithful to connect with the saints in heaven, people need only to drop their judgments; it will help open up their psychic ability.

Often our psychic ability opens up at crucial times in our life, when we are most vulnerable, most confused and most afraid. It is in these difficult times, when we ponder life's deepest questions and allow ourselves to let go and let God, that mystical experiences take place. Maybe it's a voice telling us exactly what we needed to hear; maybe it's a vision making everything seem perfectly clear.

Perhaps our psychic ability helps us remember there is much more to this world beside what we see with our physical eyes or hear with our physical ears. Perhaps it is to remind us that we are connected to our loved ones in heaven. Maybe our ESP is telling us to have hope because there is something much better waiting for us on the otherside; and maybe it gives us a reason to believe in something greater than ourselves. Our sixth sense is a reminder that we are connected to something much bigger and we are not alone.

Our psychic ability is our connection to our Father in Heaven. It is the holiness in each of us manifested as spiritual gifts. It is our divinity coming through our humanity. These gifts are the part of us that remembers who we are as divine children of God. These gifts form the Christ-light shining in each of us.

Communion with the saints in heaven and with God can only be experienced with our psychic senses-- how else can we explain love? There is no physical body part that gives and receives love. We often speak of the heart as being the center for love, but we know that is not true. The heart controls the flow of blood throughout our body and nothing more. We maintain our ability to love after our heart stops pumping, after we leave our physical bodies. Our spiritual body enables us to experience the love of God and all the saints in heaven through our psychic senses.

It is my hope that the reader will begin to see how psychic ability is not some evil supernatural force of the devil, but a natural God-given gift. Perhaps this knowledge and understanding about ESP will help to quell the fears and lessen the stigma associated with the paranormal. We all have an intuitive side, a part of us that is connected to the divine; let us celebrate our gifts of grace in honor of the one who gave them to us.

Summary

As *human* beings it is natural and necessary for us to communicate with each other; we have found countless ways, despite barriers in distance and physical limitations. As *spiritual* beings it is also natural for us to communicate with each other; many have found ways, despite barriers between space and other dimensions. "Where there is communion there is communication," explains one Vatican spokesman. It is simply a part of life in the communion of saints.

Communication with the saints in heaven has been part of mankind's history since Adam met Eve; the Bible is full of examples. Many call this form of communication "spiritualism" or "prayer." Modern-day spiritualism gave rise to the study of psychical research, which came to be known as the science of parapsychology. Some parapsychologists use the word "transcommunication" to describe spiritualism or prayer; it is how communion with the saints takes place.

Parapsychology is the study of paranormal or psychic phenomena. It may include such subjects as telepathy, clairvoyance and clairaudience. It may also include the subjects of prayer, visions and locutions. Information concerning these matters comes from our extrasensory perception (ESP) or sixth sense.

In the Old and New Testament, many of the supernatural phenomena that occurred, such as visions and locutions, were the same types of events witnessed during the spiritualist movement in the late 1800's. In the twenty-first century, these phenomena continue to be demonstrated by psychic mediums and are now studied in laboratories by renowned physicists and parapsychologists. Today we call these supernatural occurrences "paranormal" or "psychic" phenomena.

Everyone has a psychic sense, even Catholics. Some people have heightened ESP and are said to possess psychic or spiritual gifts, sometimes called gifts of grace. These unusual people may be called psychics, mediums, intuitives, clairvoyants, seers, prophets, visionaries, or mystics. Whatever label you put on these special individuals, they are still children of God and have been given a unique talent to prove it.

Chapter 7
Science and Religion

"Blessed are those who have not seen and yet have believed."
(John 20:29)

In this chapter we will learn how science influences religion by exploring how parapsychology relates to Christianity. More specifically, we will examine how psychical research supports the Catholic faith through a better understanding of the person of Jesus. It will be revealed how the church has taken a serious interest in the study of spiritualism and the supernatural side of our faith. In addition, there is a discussion on the need for both *faith* and *reason* to fully understand religion. Lastly, we will look at the need to return to mystical experiences that formed the basis of Catholicism and the importance of feeding our spiritual appetites.

Transcommunication in 2020

Imagine it to be the year 2020, and the latest gadgets to hit the market have just been unveiled at the annual Consumer Electronics Show. Coming soon to a department store near you will be "spirit-specs" - special fourth-dimensional eyeglasses. The unique lenses give people the ability to detect the higher vibration of life forms on other planes of existence. Simply by wearing the 4-D glasses, buyers can see their departed family and friends, as well as, their guardian angels, spirit guides and patron saints.

To talk directly with these heavenly beings, people can purchase the "soul-phone," another new electronic toy. With this palm-sized phone one has the ability to easily communicate with those on the otherside. Now you can acknowledge your deceased loved ones on their birthdays and anniversaries simply by calling them. You may also phone to ask for advice on anything from how to make a carrot cake, to help with computer glitches. Oh, and those lost keys may be easily found by dialing St. Anthony directly. With your new "soul phone" there will be no need to waste time on endless searches.

This may seem like a far-fetched idea, but is it really? In her book, *The Afterlife Connection*, noted psychotherapist, Dr. Jane Greer explains that, prior to his death, Thomas Edison was working on a device enabling humans to communicate with those in the spirit world. As we have learned, Greer calls this cross-dimensional interchange "transcommunication." The details of Edison's device were published in *Scientific American* magazine in 1920. He was convinced that if life after death existed then it would be electrical in nature; unfortunately, he died before he finished the invention (Greer).

Science tells us that Edison was correct in his thinking. We are carbon-based electromagnetic beings. As such, many people know that images of the deceased can be captured on film using a basic point-and-shoot camera. "Orbs" of spirits are often recorded on videotape by paranormal investigators and displayed on television shows like *America's Most Haunted*. The voice of spirits can be imprinted on a simple tape recorder; this is known as electronic voice phenomena (EVP). Movement of ghosts can trigger even the cheapest motion detector. The presence of living souls can often cause a sudden drop in room temperature, triggering "cold spots" that can be detected with a basic thermometer. Spirit-specs and soul-phones are not a far-fetched idea; they are only an inspiration away.

What will happen when these high-tech glasses and phones become so commonplace that they can be purchased at any Sharper Image or the local Radio Shack? When these tools become just another office fixture, along with the fax machine and cell-phone, how will it affect our religious views? Will they be accepted as another great invention or will they be feared and condemned as evil devices?

Will you be afraid to buy the newest gadget or will you be the first in line to purchase the latest model? What will you tell your children when the hottest inter-dimensional toy appears on their Christmas list? Will it be a matter of science or a matter of faith?

History reveals that technology and scientific theory have often clashed with religious beliefs. Copernicus challenged the church with his theory that the earth was round and not flat. With the invention of the telescope, Galileo challenged church authority by stating that the earth was not the center of the universe, as the Church had taught. With the invention of the microscope we understood that microorganisms and not evil spirits caused disease, which contradicted what was believed in Biblical times.

In more recent times, Charles Darwin's theory on the evolution of species forced many believers to question the literal interpretation of the Bible and the story of creation. With the development of psychology we learned that mental illness was the cause of many cases previously diagnosed as demon possession. With each of these scientific inventions and theories, a new paradigm challenged the antiquated ideas and thinking of our religions. Slowly, the Catholic Church was forced to accept science over old religious beliefs.

Before modern-day science, people lived in fear about much of their world. People fear what they don't know, and in pre-industrial times there was much unknown about the planet; it seemed enormous. Prior to contemporary discoveries, communication across town was difficult, not to mention across nations and oceans. Entire countries were isolated from those in far-off lands, and therefore their citizens had little knowledge about foreigners. The strangers spoke a different language, had a different skin color, had unusual religious beliefs, and had odd cultural practices that they did not understand. For this reason, populations not only feared each other, but also felt threatened by each other. This led to wars as nations sought to conquer and exploit those who were different. In a world where many people were disconnected from each other, everything was scary.

With education and development in science and technology, many fears disappeared. People's beliefs, ideas and perception of their world constantly changed and were challenged with each new generation. With the invention of the radio, telegraph, telephone, television, cellular phones, and the Internet the planet became smaller. With mass communication came mass exposure and education about people who lived in distant lands.

Seeing images of other countries on television brought people of various races and creeds into living rooms across the world. Millions of viewers were able to see, first-hand, the effects of war, poverty, disease and natural disaster on entire nations of which they were unaware. Fear was often replaced with compassion and humanity as countries sought to help those who were less fortunate or in dire need. Christianity took up the cause to aid desperate people in far-off lands. Most of the support came from citizens whose only contact with third-world nations was through the media. With communication, education and understanding, judgments, and perceptions about the world changed and our old beliefs and fears were seen in a new light. Science affected our religion in many positive ways.

One day spirit-specs and soul-phones will make our universe seem as small as our planet. Our fear of communicating with the spiritual realm will be replaced with compassion, as Christians will seek to help the less fortunate who live in other dimensions. Just as television and computers changed our beliefs about the world, so will transcommunication. Once again, our religious beliefs may have to be reexamined. We will now take a look at how one man managed to combine science and religion through the study of the supernatural, the metaphysical doorway that will forever link the two disciplines.

Father Alphonsus Trabold
Theologian and Scientist

"There can never be any true contradiction between true belief and true science because God is the author of both," stated Father Alphonsus Trabold (Grace). He should know, because this

Franciscan parapsychologist was both a man of the cloth and a man of science. A Roman Catholic Priest, whose field of expertise was the paranormal, Trabold, not only devoted his life to God, but also to the study of supernatural phenomena. He even taught classes on the subject at his scholastic home in St. Bonaventure University in Olean, NY. It was at the Friary, located on this beautiful, peaceful campus, where Trabold was interviewed one sunny, August day in 2004, eight months before he passed away.

Father Al, as he liked to be called, looked like the typical friar, in his traditional brown, Franciscan robe, tied with a rope belt hanging to one side. He was tall, thin and wore only sandals on his feet year round, even in the snow. He seemed to fit the stereotype of a peacefully humble monastic priest.

Father Al was an informal man, with a friendly personality who was passionate about his unusual side profession as a parapsychologist. When talking about the paranormal, his favorite subject, he became quite animated and excited. He was like a kid in a candy store as he savored subjects like clairvoyance, exorcism, levitation and telekinesis. He seemed to relish each topic as he eagerly, but patiently, answered each of my questions with great enthusiasm and knowledge.

At the same time, Father Al was like an adventurous explorer of uncharted territory crossing the lines of both science and religion. Because of this, he was often the target of much criticism. For the most part he was able to sidestep the daggers of condemnation hurled in his direction. Sometimes, however, he took a direct hit when colleagues of the faith stabbed him in the back with accusations of heresy.

Despite these obstacles, Father Alphonsus was able to remain faithful to both his religion and to science because he understood the person of Jesus. He understood that Jesus' life was a demonstration of both the physical and metaphysical nature of man, "One who seeks the truth must understand both," Trabold insisted. In an interview done for *The Bona Venture* newspaper, the Franciscan further explained:

You have such things as prophesy in religion, and miracles, like healing miracles and raising people from the dead…. If these things can be verified as happening they should have a tremendous influence upon our life, upon our belief, upon what we accept and how we understand things-how we understand God and reality…showing that we're more than just the atoms that make us up." (Miller, 3)

Trabold believed the science of parapsychology could help support our belief in the spiritual side of us that that can never be separated from God or each other. He reasoned that this is what Christ taught us and showed us.

Friar Al understood that science and religion serve totally different functions and therefore are not in competition with one another. In his book, *Issues in Science and Religion*, Dr. Ian Barbour provided a helpful analogy on this subject:

A hammer will not be replaced by even the best of saws, since they are used to perform dissimilar tasks, when religion is doing its proper job it has nothing to fear from science, which does a different job. (247)

Reverend Trabold successfully juggled faith and science with a hammer in one hand and a saw in the other. Furthermore, he combined these two disciplines to contribute to the church by also serving as the diocesan exorcist and expert supernatural consultant. The Franciscan's conviction and passion for both religion and science was testimony to the harmonious nature of two seemingly different disciplines.

Through the mediumship of Father Patrick Mulligan and me, a posthumous interview was conducted with Father Al. In July of 2006, sixteen months after his death, Trabold revealed how he continues his work among the saints in heaven. He maintains his priestly duties by acting as an intercessory for prayers. When asked how this process works, he explained, "Intercessors act as an amplification system; I add my prayers to the prayers of others and it amplifies that request to God, which enables a prayer to get more attention."

To help us to better understand, Father Al projected a vision to Father Pat, who described what he saw through his clairvoyance:

> He's showing me a picture, a mental image. He obviously had a good sense of humor on the earth plane, that he has maintained very well, because he's showing me an image of kids standing around a mother's dress or robe, tugging on her sleeve and he says, "You know when one kid tugs, it's not as effective as when you have three or four kids tugging hard." It's a metaphor to help explain what happens. He keeps giving me that image of a mother and the kids tugging on her dress or robe.
>
> It's interesting that he uses the image of the mother's robe. And he feels clearly that he doesn't work alone either, he's showing me a large group; this is how he relates to us the concept of the communion of saints. (Grace)

What Father Al depicted was a visual aid for what happens when we practice transcommunication with the souls in heaven. If one of us prays for a fellow parishioner, who is sick, our prayer is amplified by the intercessor, in the same way a child gets her mother's attention by tugging on her clothes. If, however, an entire congregation prays for the sick person, then a great deal more attention is given to the prayer requests, in the same way a whole group of kids would better be able to get a mother's attention.

Even after his death, Father Alphonsus Trabold demonstrates how science (transcommunication) and religion (prayer) can unite to educate members of the communion of saints. Furthermore, through many of the books from his personal library, which is located at St. Bonaventure University, Father Trabold continues to teach us how the study of paranormal phenomena can add to our understanding of Christianity. The spirit of Father Al continues to be an active member of the communion of saints, not only as an intercessor, but as a parapsychological consultant and literary agent; he has aided in such things as the writing and publishing of this book.

Parapsychology - The Damn Facts

In his book, *Parapsychology: Science or Magic*, James Alcock, Ph.D., Professor of Psychology at York University in Toronto, describes "religion" as a belief in superhuman beings and the believers' social relationship with them. Parapsychology takes a closer look at this relationship by studying the spiritual side of humans, which includes psychic phenomena, extrasensory perception, spiritualism and the paranormal in general. Former Chief Psychologist of Trafalgar Hospital and Professor at Roosevelt University, clinical psychologist and cancer researcher, Lawrence LeShan, Ph.D. points out, however, that parapsychology is much more than that. He states, "In the most profound sense it is the study of the basic nature of man" (LeShan, 3).

And what is the basic nature of man? In his book, *The Medium, The Mystic and The Physicist*, LeShan observes that most of us believe we are made up of flesh and bone and are separated from each other by the confines of our physical body. He points out, however, if this were the case it would be impossible for people to do the things they sometimes do; things like telepathy, clairvoyance and precognition. For this reason, LeShan describes parapsychology as the study of the "damn facts"; the facts that do not fit in. These are the facts that say that there is far more to the nature of man than simply flesh and bone (11).

The "damn facts" scientifically demonstrate that our previous concepts of man are not adequate to explain all he is capable of. As is often the case with science, it is in the unexplainable incidents and unusual cases that we learn about the rest of what we are studying (LeShan). For example, when Charles Darwin discovered new and inexplicable species of birds and animals on the Galapagos Islands, he learned about all the other species as well. It was the "damn facts" that led him to his theory of evolution. In the same way, in the field of psychical research, "the facts that do not fit in" (extrasensory perception) forces us to redefine man. A new concept of what it means to be human emerges, and that is what makes parapsychology so important for our Christian faith.

Just a Fact
The Charles Darwin Foundation for the Galapagos Islands (CDF) is a non-profit organization, dedicated to providing scientific research to ensure the conservation of the treasured islands.

The year 2009 marked the 150th anniversary of Darwin's ground-breaking work, *On the Origin of Species* (CDF).

In his book, *The Sacred and the Psychic*, John Heaney, D.Min., Catholic Theologian of Fordham University, believes that "psychic phenomena may be seen as a kind of bridge between the secular and the sacred." He quotes theologian, Edward Schillebeeckx who contends that "theology finds its identity not alongside of or above sciences, but in and through them" (196). Heaney feels that in order to truly understand religion, we need to also understand where the "psychic and the sacred meet" (250). It is the contention of this author that transcommunication (spiritualism) is just that bridge, and the meeting place is the communion of saints.

Both science and religion are found in the communion of saints. It's where the physical world meets the non-physical world, where the body meets the soul, where the medium meets the mystic. The spirit depends on science to guide it in the world of reality and in turn, science depends on spirit to provide meaning to life (LeShan). For this reason, parapsychology and theology will always be connected.

Sylvia Brown put it best in her audio book, Phenomenon, where she stated, "Spirituality and the paranormal are handmaidens" (CD1).

Parapsychology and Christian Theology

Q: *What about Jesus, was he a medium?*

Although parapsychology cannot substitute for religion, we can make use of it to shed light on the life of Jesus Christ. It also makes the study of scriptures much more fascinating and, therefore, theology less boring (Heaney). Everyone is fascinated by the supernatural, which attracts people, especially children, to the stories of Christ. Why not utilize science to help us better understand Jesus, Christianity and the communion of saints? One way in which we can do this is by taking a closer look at the miracles Jesus performed.

In the context of parapsychology, Jesus was one of those "damn facts" that do not fit in. We know he performed many miracles but we don't know how. We do know he demonstrated both mental and physical psychic abilities, including clairvoyance, telepathy, psychokinesis and levitation to name a few. We now know that when he multiplied the loaves and fishes he was using his psychokinetic (telekinetic) powers to create physical matter. When he walked on water he was using his paranormal powers of levitation. He used telepathy (mediumship) to have conversations with God and clairvoyance to foretell the disciples of the details surrounding his own death.

In each of these cases, Christ was simply making use of his very human, extrasensory perception or psychic ability. The fact that these abilities were far superior to any other man in his time, or since then, is scientifically unexplainable; it does not fit in, but it does tell us something of the nature of man.

Furthermore, Jesus was special because his spiritual gifts seemed unbounded. His paranormal powers were not limited to one or two cases. Over and over again, Jesus demonstrated his supernatural talents in a variety of ways. He healed hundreds, if not thousands of people, and many more bore witness to his miracles. It was Jesus' mastery of these God-given gifts that placed him on a divine level. More importantly, he was unique because he used his highly developed ESP to bring people closer to God.

Despite his great works, we must remember that many people did not believe Jesus was on God's side. His paranormal feats were often condemned for being works of the devil because it was well-known that even evil people possess supernatural abilities. Those who knew him best could not believe that the local carpenter's son was of any divine importance; therefore, they took offense at his paranormal displays. Jesus responded, "No prophet is without honor except in his native place, indeed in his own house" (Matthew 13:54-58). He left his hometown without performing many miracles because of their lack of faith (Hull).

These paranormal events, although miraculous, were not unheard of. There were several before Jesus who had demonstrated similar feats of power. For example, Elijah and Elisha were described in the Old Testament multiplying matter and raising the dead (1 Kings 17:7-24, 2 Kings 4:8-44). Moses parted the Red Sea and turned the Nile River to blood (Freeze). In addition, there were many other prophets, mediums and priests who could foretell the future or communicate with heavenly beings. Jesus himself declared that we all have the ability to perform great acts, even the least among us. "I solemnly assure you, the man who has faith in me will do the works I do, and greater far than these" (John 14:12).

Quote Me

"To a Christian or a Jew, the study of psychical phenomena constitutes an additional aid to understanding his religion and its Scriptures; affords one more means of applying the teachings of Jesus and the prophets more confidently and more effectively."
(Heron)

The paranormal powers Christ demonstrated, although miraculous, were not totally unique to him. To prove his point, he passed his extra, extrasensory perception on to his disciples so they too could spread his divine message. The apostles themselves were able to heal the sick, raise the dead and perform many other psychic "Acts."

For this reason, the disciples did not realize the true divinity in Jesus while he was alive. During his life, Jesus was thought of as a great teacher (rabbi) and prophet, but not the Son of God. He often referred to himself as the "son of man." The disciples even debated about who exactly their mentor was (Luke 9:18-20). They all had doubts about him being the true Messiah (except Peter). This humble man, with incredible gifts, who hung with the poor and outcasts, puzzled many people.

Of course the true uniqueness of Jesus was not unveiled until after his resurrection. It wasn't until his after-death appearance to Mary Magdalen, the Disciples, Paul and countless others, that his message hit home. That is when all the pieces of his life fell into place and people were able to see the big picture. His teachings, his unconditional love for all, and his miraculous powers, painted an enormous, breathtakingly beautiful masterpiece that could not be seen until after his death. This is when thousands of people realized Jesus' sacred heritage; "Clearly this was the Son of God" (Matthew, 28:54).

John Heaney points out that just because Jesus' powers may have been an extension of his own psychic gifts, that it in no way takes away from his divine status as both man and God. He explains that miracles alone could not make men believe in Christ's divinity. They had to first accept Jesus' divinity before they could believe in the miracle stories.

The study of supernatural phenomena can bring credibility to the New Testament and strengthen our faith. It can help support our belief that Jesus really did perform miracles; the stories we were told as children were not just fairy tales. Devout believers don't require any proof, but for those who are questioning their faith, it might just be the evidence they need (Moore). It may be Jesus' humanity that brings them closer to understanding their own divinity. We were all created in the image of God; our model is Jesus Christ. When we understand we all possess some psychic ability, then we can better understand Jesus and, therefore, our Christian faith.

Many people have had a paranormal experience at some point in their lives, and when it happens, they wish to understand where it fits in their Christian belief system. They can ignore it, bury it, deny it or pretend it didn't happen, but they can't always explain it. It's one of those "damn facts" that don't quite fit into our religion. It helps to know, however, that average people have been having these experiences throughout history. The problem is that psychic phenomena have been recorded in the lives of the Christian saints and mystics, but not for the common believers (Ebon). In an interview, Father Patrick Mulligan explained:

> You're not even asking Roman Catholicism or organized Christianity to accept another religion, you're asking them to be open to something which occurs among all peoples in a very natural phenomena, even though it's called supernatural or preternatural by some. (Grace)

No matter what you call it--spiritualism, transcommunication, paranormal, supernatural, or preternatural phenomena--when we understand that Jesus and the saints had psychic experiences, then we know that it must fit into our faith somehow.

Quote Me
"Psychical Research is the ally of religion in that it corroborates religion's basic claim that the non-material is a reality." (Moore)

True Spiritualism

The idea of practicing spiritualism (transcommunication) in church sounds sacrilegious at first, but when we understand that we practice it every time we pray, we see it in a different light. In his book *True Spiritualism*, Father Carlos Heredia S.J., from the College of St. Francis in Xavier, NY, claims that Catholics are true spiritualists because they believe in God, angels, spirits and eternal life of the soul. He contends, "Catholics believe that these souls may appear to them on earth when God chooses. This is *true spiritualism*" (Heredia, 199).

Clergyman and professor at Notre Dame University, Morton Kelsey supports the idea that Catholics are spiritualists in his book *The Christian and the Supernatural*. He points out that Church Fathers such as Ambrose, Jerome, Augustine and Gregory the Great all had psychic abilities. They understood these abilities were natural to all people and could be embraced by God; this most likely stems from the Old Testament role of priests as "seers." In fact, the Hebrew word for "priest" is "kohen," which is similar to the Arabic word "kahin," meaning "soothsayer." Kelsey notes that people of these times were supposed to go to their priests and prophets for advice because they were also "seers." It is through openness to spiritualist practices that the Catholic faith became so rich in its history of gifted leaders, saints and mystics (Kelsey, 90).

For this reason, in the early church, paranormal phenomena were not looked at with disdain, the way it is today. Even as late as the 1860's, when modern-day spiritualism was at its height, the Catholic Church did not yet officially condemn the practice. During this time, séances became one of the most popular pastimes in the country. It was as common as gathering for a Saturday afternoon game of bridge. Many saw it as a harmless form of entertainment.

In her article, *Fighting for the Afterlife*, published in *Journal of Religious History*, Lynn Sharp reveals some interesting history on the church and spiritualism. She reports that church authorities did not want to quickly condemn the popular pastime of spiritualism because they did not want to alienate the many Catholics who were practicing it. In addition, some believed that condemning spiritualism would have the reverse effect by spreading the belief.

In an attempt to deal with the sticky situation, between 1830 and

1850, an effort was made to revive supernatural practices into the Catholic faith, expressing an era of "romantic Christianity." Sharp reports, "In the face of the mid-century emphasis on rationality and faith in positive science, many Catholics reasserted a faith in the supernatural" (288). She observes this was most apparent when it came to the many Marion visions (apparitions of the Blessed Mother) and pilgrimages to holy sites of healing taking place during that time.

Insight

Every year many people journey to Fatima, Italy for healing. In the same way, many believers make pilgrimages to the Healing Temple in Lily Dale, NY to experience the power of the Holy Spirit at work. The sacred site has been in existence since 1955 and offers healing services twice a day during the summer months. A trip to this tranquil shrine will bring peace of mind; it is highly recommended.

Church leaders thought that proof of life-after-death would help promote Catholic teachings and a belief in God. Therefore, it was permissible for members to participate in paranormal activities, but only if the church was in control of the situation. Much to their chagrin, however, spiritualism became out of their control; therefore, it needed to end. In 1898 the first official proclamation against spiritualism was made. Pope Leo XIII condemned the practice and threatened to excommunicate anyone who participated in séances or acted as a medium (Sharp). By then, however it was too late; millions of Catholics were already hooked on the worldwide-craze.

The result of this mass epidemic in communication with the spirit world led to an explosion of supernatural phenomena. Reports were coming into the church by the thousands. Ordinary citizens were experiencing things such as levitation, telekinesis, speaking in tongues, trance states, as well as, visions of saints, stigmata and miraculous healings. The paranormal accounts were so prevalent that the Church could not ignore it; they needed to study and investigate the matter. At the same time, scientists also felt the need to study the supernatural reports in order to expose the mediums they considered frauds. With spiritualism at its height, both science and religion had a stake in what was going on.

Let's Study the Matter

Beginning around 1850, scientific investigations into spiritualist séances unearthed a slew of phenomena that seemed supernatural to many people. This included the ability to hear and see spirits, to speak in tongues, to move physical objects with the mind, to heal, to have knowledge of future events, and even to levitate. These are the same types of paranormal events that have been reported throughout history. There is ample evidence in the Old and New Testaments, as well as in the lives of the Christian mystics and saints.

When science started to seriously study the possibility of an afterlife and things beyond the normal five senses, the spiritual implications could not be avoided. Many who set out to debunk the phenomenon of spiritualism and mediumship became believers themselves; as they often found that the most reasonable explanation was the simplest - the survival of consciousness after death and the ability to communicate intelligently with people in other dimensions. What arose was the science of parapsychology, which gave us evidential proof of what religions have been teaching us for thousands of years, that death is not the end of life, but the beginning of a new one.

Just a Fact

Ockham's razor, sometimes referred to as the "law of parsimony," states, "All things being equal, the simplest solution is the best." This principle was attributed to William of Ockham, a fourteenth-century logician and Franciscan friar; his law can be applied to spiritualism. (Wikipedia)

Our sciences, psychologies and philosophies have embraced life-after-death and spirituality in the hopes to better understand what it means to be human. They recognize the interconnectedness between the physical and spiritual body and the idea of the existence of another dimension we call "heaven;" there is too much evidence to ignore it. Ironically, the one institute seeming to lag behind in the serious study and acceptance of the supernatural in today's world is organized religion.

Although the Catholic faith may not be up-to-date on the subject of supernatural phenomena, historically it has promoted the study and investigation of the matter. In researching the communion of saints, I went to the nearby Abbey of the Genesee to ask about any books they had on the subject. After purchasing several loaves of their famous "Monks Bread," I spoke with a friendly and helpful Trappist monk, known simply as "Brother Louis." He told me that I might find the information I was looking for by studying the Mystical Body of Christ.

Brother Louis just happened to have an encyclical letter written in 1943 by Pope Pius XII on this subject. Entitled *Mystici Corporis*, this document proved to be a wealth of information. In several places, the letter describes how it is important to study and be open to supernatural or mystical occurrences.

> We know that from well-directed and earnest study of this doctrine, and from the clash of diverse opinions and the discussion thereof...much light will be gained, which, in its turn will help to progress in kindred sacred sciences. Hence we do not censure those who in various efforts to understand and to clarify the mystery of this our wonderful union with Christ. (34)

Pope Pius also acknowledges that as spiritual beings and people of faith it is only natural to seek truth and comfort from our heavenly connections, especially in times of great distress.

Furthermore, in *Mystici Corporis*, Pius states that with sorrow during the "calamities of stormy times" it is natural for the souls of grieving people to have a "certain secret thirst and intense desire for spiritual things." The encyclical explains that "Thus, urged by the Holy Spirit, men are moved, and, as it were, impelled to seek the Kingdom of God with greater diligence"(4). Parapsychology is the science seeking to understand the kingdom of God by examining the spiritual side of the universe.

Pope Pius goes on to teach the importance of studying the mysteries of God's kingdom and utilizing the knowledge gained by this study to add to the sacred development of the church:

> Mysteries revealed by God cannot be harmful to men, nor should they remain as treasures hidden in a field, useless. They have been given from on high precisely to help the spiritual progress of those who study them in a spirit of piety. (7)

The Pope is saying that only by careful and diligent study can the many mysteries of God be revealed. Once revealed, "reasons illumined by faith" may be utilized to add to the spiritual progression of the Church (7). When we refuse to study and open up to these mysteries, we fail to uncover some of God's greatest gifts to man and therefore to the Church. These gifts, which may come in the form of special graces, would thus "remain as treasures hidden in a field, useless." Indeed many of these mysteries were revealed through the prophetic visions, locutions and apparitions experienced by Christian mystics. Had the Church turned a blind-eye to those supernatural occurrences, then it would indeed have lost a precious store of treasures.

Taking a last look at the *Mystici Corporis*, we can apply the Pope's thoughts on studying the mystical Body of Christ to the study of the communion of saints. The Church is the Mystical Body of Christ and as individuals we are all parts of that same body. "Now you are the body of Christ, and each of you is a part of it" (1 Cor 12:28). In the same way we are all members of the communion of saints. We are the soul and life-force that make up the Body of Christ. By comparing the two, we can draw inferences from the Vatican letter:

We consider it part of Our pastoral duty to explain to the entire flock of Christ, ... to draw certain lessons that will make a deeper study of this mystery bear yet richer fruits of perfection and holiness. Our purpose is to throw an added ray of glory on the supreme beauty of the Church; to bring out into fuller light the exalted supernatural nobility of the faithful who in the Body of Christ are united with their Head; and finally, to exclude definitively the many errors current with regard to this matter. (7)

The Pope sees that by ignoring the supernatural occurrences in our lives, we are omitting an essential part of the beauty of Catholicism and all the fruit it has to offer. Also important, is that by serious study of the supernatural, we can eliminate apparent phenomenon that may not be truly authentic and may in fact be fraudulent.

Quote Me

"To ignore parapsychological phenomena, or let it bypass us is possibly to overlook what God may be revealing to us today. We may have to do some mental and spiritual adjusting." (Cluff)

Returning to the wisdom of parapsychologist and Franciscan, Alphonsus Trabold, we can understand the importance of examining all supernatural occurrences. In our interview he insisted, "It's God's will that we study 'it' [the supernatural] and open up the powers He gave us." He argued that, "It would be a sin not to study paranormal and psychic phenomenon" (Grace). It was his belief that studying the supernatural does not go against the teachings of the faith. To make his point, Father Trabold taught a theology class called *Religion and the Paranormal*; the students dubbed it Spooks. It was the most popular course at St. Bonaventure and was part of the college curriculum for over twenty years.

Another proponent of studying the supernatural was the noted Reverend and author, James Pike, Bishop of the Episcopal Church and former head of the Department of Religion at Columbia

University. He wrote an entire book about the numerous after-death communications he received from his deceased son. In his book, *The Otherside*, he commented about the serious study of spirit communication:

> I feel that the time is fully upon us, as is demonstrated by the work being done in this field by reputable scientists and psychologists, when we are ready to examine all extrasensory phenomena with the same objectivity with which thoughtful people have sought to examine other aspects of our universe. (287)

Following the death of his son, Pike had numerous paranormal experiences; for example, objects appeared out of nowhere or were moved from their original place. One time the Bishop's clothes closet was totally rearranged, and on several occasions displayed photographs were completely missing, only to be found in another room. He began to keep a log of all the strange events and after several months, with much trepidation, he confided in some trustworthy colleagues in his parish.

Pike was not alone in his paranormal encounters, however, because thousands of other Catholics throughout the world were reporting their own supernatural experiences to their local diocese. These testimonies became so commonplace that the church was forced to deal with it in a decisive way.

Revelation Investigation

In the wake of the spiritualist movement, extraordinary occurrences happened so often that the Vatican had to lay down a set of guidelines and rules for investigating such matters. Thus, on February 25, 1978 was born the *Norms of the Sacred Congregation for the Doctrine of the Faith about How to Proceed in Judging Alleged Apparitions and Revelations (Apparitions and Revelations Doctrine)*. Signed by Cardinal Franjo Seper, then head of the Sacred Congregation for the Doctrine of the Faith, this document details the policies and procedures for bishops to follow when presented with an alleged supernatural event. Part of its purpose is to determine the authenticity of such an occurrence (Freze).

In reference to this document, in his book, *Voices, Visions and Apparitions*, Reverend Freze explains:

> In order to assure the integrity of supernatural experiences, the magisterium of the Church has issued a secret four-page document dealing with alleged voices, visions and apparitions... Although this Latin document is little known among the faithful—indeed, it is considered "sub secreto" (secretive or classified)—nevertheless it is to be followed faithfully by the local ordinary of the diocese in which the alleged experiences are taking place (95).

Freze points out that the local bishop is obligated to thoroughly investigate any supernatural claims "under obedience to the supreme authority of the magisterium of the Church." The first and foremost stance that the Church takes is that it must, by faith assume that it is of God. Following an investigation, if a supernatural event is proven to be something else, then divine revelation can be ruled out (Freze, 95).

The investigation, according to the *Apparitions and Revelations Doctrine*, is to be carried out in three stages. First a preliminary judgment of authenticity, based on positive and negative criteria, must be made. Second, if the initial evaluation proves positive, then public devotions can be allowed (as in the Lourdes case) while the investigation continues. Third, "after a certain time, and in light of experience," an official statement on the genuineness of the supernatural character of the case is required (Sacred Congregation for the Doctrine of Faith, 2).

Freze argues that it is simply not an option for the local ordinary to ignore the issue, to remain silent about it or to prejudge it before a proper investigation is done. To do so would be to go against the teachings of the church. Furthermore, Reverend Freze contends:

> To prematurely disregard the authenticity of any

supernatural experience or the character of a visionary or seer without following these criteria is to show irrational judgment, narrow-mindedness, and perhaps even disobedience to the teachings of the Church. To prematurely dismiss divine origin would undermine the teaching authority and wisdom of the Church, and may destroy the credibility of those who really do receive authentic, supernatural phenomena. (97)

Doctor of Ministry, Charles Cluff, of San Francisco Theological Seminary, supports this observation in his book, *Parapsychology and the Christian Faith*. He insists that Christians should not ignore psychic phenomena because "if it is of God then we would be opposing him." Cluff sites Acts 5: 38-39, which refers to the question of whether or not the disciples were really preaching for God: "If their purpose or activity is human it its origin, it will destroy itself. If, on the other hand, it comes from God, you will not be able to destroy them without fighting God himself." In addition, Cluff advises the faithful to find ways in which paranormal manifestations can serve God and bring more meaning into their life (27).

Unfortunately, dismissing supernatural phenomena and destroying the credibility of the person reporting it, is all too often the case. One victim of this "narrow-minded" thinking was Bishop James Pike. In his book, *The Otherside*, Pike describes how he was the target of hostility from the Catholic community, after disclosing that he had received communications from his deceased son, Jim. Some of the messages came directly to him while others came through a medium.

One of these transcommunications was captured on a Canadian television show, on which the bishop appeared. During the broadcast Pike's son spoke to him via the noted medium, Arthur Ford. Shortly afterwards, the House of Bishops decided to charge the priest with heresy and went so far as to censure him without due process. In addition, he was accused of having a mental illness and consorting with the devil. The church authorities disgraced Pike and disregarded his claim without ever considering the possibility that the bishop was actually in contact with his son (Pike).

I use my own case as another example of someone who was dismissed and humiliated when trying to seek help for a supernatural experience. When I tried to discuss with my priest my near-death experience and after-death communications, he refused to believe me. There was no assumption made that it may have been a divine revelation and was indeed God's will that it occurred. On the contrary, the only assumption made was that I was a mentally imbalanced person who needed to see a psychiatrist. Furthermore, I was told that I was "dabbling in dangerous territory" and was therefore no longer allowed in the church community. I was rejected without any investigation, or so much as an inquiry, on the authenticity of my experience.

When people claim to have had an encounter with a person who is not of this world, what they experienced is communion with the saints. This is something that should be treasured as a gift to the church, not something to be disregarded as someone's delusional thinking. To do so is to go against the teachings of the Church. To make this point clear, Reverend Freze warns:

> Can we afford to ignore or turn our noses up at this divine illumination? If we do so without following the above criteria [Apparitions and Revelations Doctrine] or because we are prejudgmental in nature, then indeed our sin may be as great as those who have turned their backs on God. Let the reader beware! There is often a very fine line between divine faith and human faith that is illuminated by divine wisdom. The line may be so close that one had better be sure of one's convictions before dismissing all supernatural experiences as something that originates in the fantasies of the mind. (98)

The church has decided what "divine faith" is and what makes up the Sacred Deposit of Faith based on Scripture. Since the close of the Apostolic era all public and universal revelation was completed. When it comes to personal experience however, it can be believed based on "human faith." Therefore, when someone has a personal paranormal experience it is not against the Catholic Faith to believe the occurrence happened just because it is supernatural in character.

The Reverend Carlos de Heredia, agrees with this thought in his book *True Spiritualism*. He advises that when it comes to human testimony it is essential that the character of the witness is credible. If that is the case then "to deny knowledge through the testimony of another is, however you may put it, however you may quibble over it, simply and obviously 'knowledge by faith'" (43).

Just a Fact
The Lady of Fatima Shrine and Basilica in Lewiston, NY is an awesome place to visit. Built by the Barnabite Fathers in 1954, the devotional center honors the Blessed Mother and the Holy Site in Portugal, where three children witnessed an apparition of Our Lady in 1917. If you go, be sure to hike to the top of the basilica dome to see the thirteen foot statue of the Virgin Mary. The view overlooks the sixteen-acre, park-like sanctuary with over eighty statues of saints and a giant rosary pool. A trip during the Festival of Lights is highly recommended. (www.fatimashrine.com)

So what happens, if in good faith, a reported supernatural event is believed and later found, through investigation, to be erroneous? Reverend Freze wrote that Pope Urban VIII (1623-1644) addressed this matter and contended that "If you believe, and it should be proven false, you will receive all blessings as if it had been true, because you believed it to be true." Urban argues that our Holy Mother asks us to believe, therefore if an unexplainable occurrence is proven to be true then you would be glad that you believed (Freze, 3).

One could suggest that if you do not believe a supernatural occurrence has happened, and it is later to be proven that it is of the divine, then you will have shown your lack of faith. It is better to believe and be proven false, than not to believe and be proven faithless. It is important therefore to take all paranormal claims seriously, as laid out by the investigation guidelines of the church.

Concluding our examination of the *Apparitions and Revelations Doctrine*, we can see that the Catholic Church has acknowledged and taken seriously the issue of supernatural phenomena. They have laid down some ground-breaking rules to help protect the faithful in such circumstances. Unfortunately, it seems this doctrine was so secret that no one told the parish priests about the rules; either that or they were lost and forgotten.

Perhaps nobody thought this doctrine was of importance any longer in a day and age when everything has a scientific or medical explanation. Maybe it was thought that Christian Mysticism is a thing of the past. Nevertheless, the information did not trickle down to the average lay person who needed help in dealing with a disconcerting supernatural experience. One such paranormal experience, we will examine now, is mediumship, the ability of some parishioners to be able to see and/or hear fellow believers who have crossed over.

The Church and Spiritualism

Long before the Roman Catholic Church took action on apparitions and revelations, the Church of England decided to investigate the possibility of communication with the dead. In 1937, Archbishop of Canterbury, Lang and Archbishop of York, Temple, appointed a Majority Report committee to investigate the then popular phenomenon known as "spiritualism." They felt that before a judgment could be made on the subject, careful study of it was first warranted. After the committee spent two years studying "communicators" (mediums) and their messages, they wrote their findings in *The Church of England and Spiritualism*. Below are several of the over seventy conclusions found in the report:

> It is clearly true that the recognition of the nearness of our friends who have died, and of their progress in the spiritual life, and of their continuing concern for us, cannot do otherwise, for those who have experienced it, than add a new immediacy and richness to their belief in the Communion of Saints. (3)

There seems to be no reason at all why the Church should

regard this vital and personal enrichment of one of her central doctrines with disfavour, so long as it does not distract Christians from their fundamental gladness that they may come, when they will, into the presence of their Lord and Master, Jesus Christ Himself, or weaken their senses that their fellowship is fellowship with Him. (3)

It is necessary to keep clearly in mind that none of the fundamental Christian obligations or values is in any way changed by our acceptance of the possibility of communication with discarnate spirits. (5)

Where these essential principles are borne in mind, those who have the assurance that they have been in touch with their departed friends may rightly accept the sense of enlargement and of unbroken fellowship which it brings. (5)

There is no reason why we should not accept gladly the assurance that we are still in closest contact with those who have been dear to us in this life, who are going forward, as we seek to do ourselves, in the understanding and fulfillment of the purpose of God. (5)

If spiritualism, with all aberrations set aside and with every care taken to present it humbly and accurately, contains a truth, it is important to see that truth not as a new religion, but only as filling up certain gaps in our knowledge, so that where we already walked by faith, we may now have some measure of sight as well. (7)

The study finds that recognizing the presence of our dearly departed adds to our belief in the communion of saints, consequently, spiritualism only enriches this "central doctrine" of the faith. Communication with the souls in heaven does not change any of our basic Christian tenets. As long as it does not distract Christians from their relationship with Jesus Christ, and is not seen as a new religion, there is no reason to object to the practice of it. On the contrary, those who have been in touch with their deceased family and friends may more fully accept the "unbroken fellowship it brings." Furthermore, this fellowship can bolster our beliefs by providing "some measure of sight" to our faith.

Although the findings were favorable to the practice of Spiritualism, the Church wisely warns the faithful that it does not allow them to "escape from the responsibility of making their own decisions as Christians under the guidance of the Holy Spirit." In addition, the study advises that it is "unquestionably dangerous" to allow spiritualism to "replace that deeper religion which rests fundamentally upon the right relation of the soul to God Himself" (Majority Report of the Church of England, 5).

With these warnings in place, and after much discernment, the following noted scholars, who made up the Church of England Majority Report Committee, signed the conclusions of the study:

> Dr. Francis Underhill, Bishop of Bath
> Dr. W. R. Matthews, Dean of St. Paul's
> Canon Harold Anson, Master of the Temple
> Canon L.W. Grensted, Nolloth Professor of the Christian Religion at Oxford
> Dr. William Brown, Celebrated Harley Street Psychologist
> Mr. P. E. Sandlands, Q.C., Barrister-at-Law
> Lady (Gwendolen) Stephenson

For nine years however, the House of Bishops kept the findings secret. A.W. Austen, then Editor of *Psychic News* investigated the matter and found the committee decided to "pigeon-hole" the reports. After much inquiry, a copy of *The Church of England and Spiritualism* showed up on Austen's desk. The editor then contacted one of the members of the committee who wanted the document published. Under a vow not to disclose this person's name, the unedited version of the Majority Report was confirmed to be accurate and was retyped with corrections to grammar and missing lines (Austen, 1).

Quote Me
"Spiritualism is a great and mighty truth, and it came, I am convinced in the Providence of God to dispel the skepticism and materialism of this unbelieving age." (Sexton)

When this document was released, it was world-wide breaking news. A council of influential church authorities from England found spiritualism was true and could be a valuable addition to the Christian ministry. The Catholic Church in Rome, however, chose to silence the information rather than publicize it. One may only speculate as to why.

Faith and Reason

Religion has always felt threatened by science because history reveals that scientific knowledge has often prevailed over religious beliefs. In the words of Wayne Dyer, "Belief implies doubt, and when a belief is confronted with a knowing, the knowing will always win out"(Dyer, tape 1). We cannot, however, have faith without knowledge, for faith involves intelligence. According to John Heaney, faith is not "blind feeling" and traditional Catholic theology does not believe in "sweeping away knowledge to make room for faith" (Heaney, 224).

Heaney insists that faith and knowledge are not opponents because faith resides in our spirit while knowledge resides in our mind. Reason is never without some faith and therefore faith and reason, or religion and science, should be friends (Heaney). St. Augustine put it best in his work *Praedestinatione Sanctorum*, where he concluded, "But everybody who believes thinks - both thinks in believing and believes in thinking" (as cited in Heaney, 2).

Bishop Pike supports Augustine's concept with his own theory "facts + faith = theological truth." He states that if there are no facts to support a belief then you have nothing more than blind faith, which is of "little real significance" (Pike, 233). Without facts you have a conviction that draws not from evidence but from wishful thinking. Such a belief system is "the child of superficial aspiration rather than of intelligent conviction" (Heaney, 224). Therefore, faith without facts does not lead to theological truth but rather to delusional thoughts.

Charles Cluff, D.Min., cited earlier, observes that Christians want to honor God with conscientious thoughts and actions. Sometimes, however, we are not willing to accept "new things" that are different from what we were "taught" to believe in. New paradigms make us uncomfortable and force us to make decisions on something because we can no longer deny it. When we are ignorant of a situation we don't have to deal with it and can even pretend it does not exist; when we know about a problem we must face it. In *Parapsychology and the Christian Faith* the Reverend warns:

> Parapsychology is an empirical phenomenon today. It is relying on observation and experimentation. To ignore it or let it bypass us is possibly to overlook what God may be revealing to us today. (23)

We are not asked to change what the Christian faith means, but to consider new ways to express it and embrace it in our ever-expanding world (Cluff).

Often religious dogma dictates to us what we should think, without question. It is much easier for someone to tell us what to think, than to decide for ourselves. It is human nature, however, to question our world to find how we, as individuals, fit into it. No blanket-creed can explain our unique role in the universe; we must discover it for ourselves.

We explore our world by asking questions and drawing our own conclusions as to what to believe. Someone can *tell* us what to believe, but they can't *make* us believe it, for what is true for someone else may not be true for us. True belief comes from within, not from without. It can only be found by searching our own hearts and when our mind agrees with our soul then facts + faith = conviction.

However, no matter what we believe, or how strong our convictions, until we actually "experience" something, we cannot know for sure that it is true. For example we may believe we know how to swim, because we have studied and learned all about swimming and others told us we could do it. But until we actually get in the water, and "experience" what it is like to move our body in such a way as to not sink, we don't know for sure that we can swim. We may, in fact, find that we really can't and have to be rescued to escape from drowning. Our next segment explains how spiritual "experience" is a necessary part of faith and therefore must be added to the equation, hence, facts + faith + experience = divine truth.

Insight

Many near-death experiencers have a difficult time with organized religion. It's not unusual for spiritual experiences to contradict church teachings; religious convictions often require an adjustment. "Facts" + "faith" can never substitute for "experience."

Where's the Beef?

Many readers may remember the Wendy's commercial that ran in the 1980's featuring Clara, a short, pudgy, elderly woman who portrayed the stereotypical senior citizen. The scene is set in a competing fast food restaurant where Clara and two friends just received their order, which is a hamburger.

When the three old ladies inspect the sandwich, they find a half-dollar-sized piece of meat, which seems lost within the massive bun. Obviously upset with the minuscule meal, Clara angrily demands, "Where's the beef?" She was justifiably upset because she went to the restaurant with very clear expectations; what she received however, was much different. She knew the under-sized burger would not fill her empty, over-sized belly. She therefore, goes to the competition, Wendy's, for a fulfilling meal.

The advertisement made a point by saying, "What has happened to the American burger?" Somehow the traditional fast-food chains lost sight of their purpose and the whole reason people went to their restaurant in the first place, for nutritional satisfaction. When skimpy burgers were served, customers were left wondering, "Where's the beef?" Profits took priority and as a result people were left hungry for more, so they went elsewhere, to Wendy's. This scenario is an analogy for what has happened to the Catholic Church when it comes to satisfying people's spiritual appetites.

In his book, *The Christian and the Supernatural*, clergyman and professor, Morton Kelsey declares that people have the right to expect mystical experiences from their church. Believers are starving from spiritual malnourishment because "they are not satisfied by bread alone" (124). Christians long for more but look to the Church in vain, for she cannot fill their emptiness as long as she ignores and condemns psychic experiences. When these phenomena are not accepted, or given a legitimate place in the life of the church, then people will treat the church's message as irrelevant and look elsewhere to nourish their souls (142-3). They will walk away wondering, "Where's the beef?"

With the New Age movement Christians are re-discovering their spiritual side through other religions. The ancient art of meditation, as practiced in Spiritualism and Eastern belief systems, are helping people explore their inner life. Many are participating in classes, such as yoga, to help them experience mystical union with God and nature. It is through such a contemplative lifestyle, along with a deep faith, that extrasensory perception happens. Other religions understand that these paranormal occurrences provide enrichment to true believers and an opportunity to delve deeper into their faith.

Just a Fact

Research shows that there are many benefits to practicing meditation; the following are a few:

- It increases exercise tolerance in heart patients.
- Leads to deeper levels of relaxation.
- Reduces anxiety.
- Decreases muscle tension and headaches.
- Builds self-confidence.
- Enhances the immune system.
- Helps in post-operative healing.

(Health & Yoga)

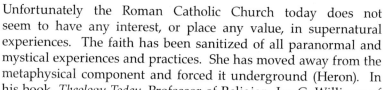

Unfortunately the Roman Catholic Church today does not seem to have any interest, or place any value, in supernatural experiences. The faith has been sanitized of all paranormal and mystical experiences and practices. She has moved away from the metaphysical component and forced it underground (Heron). In his book, *Theology Today*, Professor of Religion, Jay G. Williams of Hamilton College supports the idea that people will lose interest and find new avenues for spiritual growth if not provided with meaningful experiences. Williams argues:

> The prophets were not just political commentators who drew their inspiration from the ancient equivalent of the "New York Times" but visionaries who, in their flights of ecstasy, beheld a world not visible to the physical eye. Today, however many churchmen seem to want to engage in prophetic criticism without the benefit of motivating ecstasy. And because the churches have become this-worldly, more and more young people are turning to yoga, Indian rain dances, divination and drugs as a means of bridging the chasm which the church apparently doesn't even admit exists. (as cited in Heron, 19-20)

Father Alphonsus Trabold adds further insight to this problem. He suggests that religion can meet the New Age challenge by "reintroducing wonder and mystery into our faith." In his essay

Cult and the Occult, he argues that if the church doesn't meet the deep, spiritual needs of today's youth then she will miss a "golden opportunity" to reach them. Trabold warns that it would be a great tragedy to allow this to happen (Trabold, 1979a, 14). This is exactly why Father Al taught parapsychology to Catholic college students. He believed that the reason the paranormal is not widely embraced by the church is "not the fault of our faith, but the fault of our understanding" (Grace).

Just My Opinion

As the times change, so must our religious beliefs. With an increase in knowledge and understanding of the survival of consciousness, science will soon take away much of the fear, mystery and stigma associated with spirit communication. With advances in our technology, in the near future psychic mediums will be replaced with the medium of inner-dimensional phones and spectacles. Once more our world will become smaller as fellow believers in foreign galaxies and dimensions will be only a digital device away. We will be able to talk to them as easily as we talked with men on the moon over thirty years ago.

When this time comes, we will be able to learn about the lives and people who live in the cosmos as well as in the heavenly realms. Our fears will be replaced with compassion and the human desire to help others, no matter what plane of existence they live on. When this time comes, how can it be considered against the faith to call up Grandma in heaven to ask, "Exactly what did you put in that carrot cake to make it so good?" Our ancient opinions on communing with the dead will be as laughable and out-dated as the belief that mental illness and disease was caused by demon possession. Just as we had to stop drilling holes in people's heads, we will have to stop judging and denouncing those who communicate with spirits, without the use of technology. When this time comes, our religious views must change as well.

Through Christ, the Catholic faith recognizes the intricate connection between heaven and earth. Jesus came to show us, not that "he" was special and more divine than the rest of us, but that "we" are special and we too are divinely connected. It is in these supernatural glimpses of Jesus that we see ourselves; and this is what gives us hope. Hope that we too, can one day achieve the highly spiritual levels that often manifest themselves in the form of special graces or paranormal gifts from God.

The church acknowledges the importance of spiritual gifts and supernatural phenomena and has seriously studied certain aspects of it. Why, however, were both the *Apparitions and Revelations Doctrine* and *The Church of England and Spiritualism* study kept secret from the public and from parish priests? Moreover, based on the results of their own investigation, why were there no changes made in church doctrine regarding paranormal experiences and spiritualism? Did authorities fear what would happen if the masses knew that the church findings defended communication with the deceased? Perhaps by suppressing the information, they felt they could maintain control in deciding who has an authentic experience. Unfortunately, although the intent may have been to protect the people, by keeping the studies quiet, many were hurt by deceptive, discriminatory practices.

The church is sending mixed-messages to her members compelling them to question the wisdom of their leaders. On the one hand Catholicism teaches and promotes communion with the saints, while on the other hand it expresses disapproval of any active participation in the spirit world. Contradictions such as these make the faith less credible and force people to re-examine their beliefs. In the future, scientific advances may changes people's opinions about spiritualism (transcommunication), even if Rome refuses to change church doctrine.

There are entire populations of people who experience supernatural or paranormal phenomena on a daily basis, who have been dismissed, ridiculed and rejected by the Catholic Church without any type of investigation being done whatsoever. Many have been pre-judged as being frauds, mentally ill, or evil; consequently, destroying the credibility of the individuals in the process, not to mention their self-esteem. An innumerable amount of believers have been told that using the spiritual gifts they possess is against the teachings of the faith. More importantly, I ask, "What is more harmful, the practice of spiritualism, done with only the best of intentions, or the practice of abuse with the intent to oppress?"

It seems to me that it is simply a lack of understanding and general knowledge about paranormal phenomena that leads to fear and misunderstanding of those who are affected by it. The average priest seems to know very little about the supernatural and even less when it comes to knowing how to handle such cases. There are no seminary classes to instruct future ministers on how to deal with voices, visions, or apparitions. There is no training about near-death experience, the side effects of such an experience, and how to professionally counsel someone who is in such spiritual crisis. When it comes to the paranormal, education in the church is painfully lacking.

Where does this put the parish priests who are the front-line people when it comes to dealing with congregates who have had a supernatural encounter? From my own experience, I can tell you that it puts them at an extreme disadvantage. As a result, a profoundly sensitive and sacred situation can be turned into something hurtful and even diabolical. What may in fact be a gift from God goes unrecognized by the uneducated pastor who has lost an opportunity to know more fully the mystery of our Father's kingdom. Evidence of grace carelessly discarded is like tossing away an out-of-season oyster along with the precious pearl hidden inside. The trained person knows how to recognize the treasure within, while the untrained fail to see any value.

For example, if St. Paul lived today and told his priest that he just encountered Jesus on the road to Damascus, what kind of reaction do you think he would receive? Would he be considered a mystic and treated like a saint? On the contrary, he would most likely be called a lunatic and condemned for dabbling in spiritism? He may even be referred to a psychiatrist and told that he needed to find a new church. In any event, I highly doubt an investigation would be conducted to preclude the possibility that he actually may have had a mystical encounter with the Lord. Had the priests of St. Paul's day been as skeptical and ignorant of private revelations, as they are today, the religion of Christianity, and the mysteries it contains, may never have taken root.

It is participation in these mysteries that gives us the experience of God; we share in this divine encounter each time we attend Mass. By partaking in the Eucharist we participate in this interchange between heaven and earth; as a result, we are given spiritual graces. Why then, do we renounce our supernatural heritage and the paranormal gifts coming from this weekly encounter with Jesus?

We are called to be like Christ, this is what we strive for and what our religion teaches us. Jesus was one of the most psychically gifted children of God. Through his mediumship, the Catholic faith recognizes the intricate connection between the physical and non-physical worlds. Jesus demonstrated this divine connection through his supernatural abilities; furthermore, he taught us that we too have these gifts, even the least among us. If we are to be like Christ, we cannot disregard his paranormal powers and his role as a medium between heaven and earth. Furthermore, psychic phenomena can be used in the present-day the same way Jesus used it - to bring people closer to God.

The Catholic Church needs to become more open to exploring new ways to provide spiritual experiences for its people. One way is by opening the lines of communication between the saints in heaven and the saints on earth, via the practice of transcommunication, or what the church calls "spiritualism." Through the Christian tradition of meditation or contemplation, people can learn to "listen" to those they pray to and receive messages from them. The church needs to integrate these psychic practices into the religion by providing safe, spiritual settings for people to learn about the science of the supernatural without being afraid of it. Then when paranormal phenomena occur, like after-death communications, the faithful have a place to freely talk about these experiences without the fear of ridicule.

With spiritual practices, such as meditation, parishioners can learn a positive way to open to the non-physical world. With psychically trained spiritual directors and priests to lead them, Catholics can develop a closer relationship to the saints, to Jesus and, therefore, to God. At the same time, the church could learn to pay more attention to their parishioners in heaven and encourage those on earth to have a relationship with them. These relationships with heavenly beings could be with departed family and friends, or with angels and guides they had never met before. As a result, after-death communications from loved ones or saints would be taken more seriously, therefore allowing people to accept them as a "normal" part of spiritual life. In addition, when we focus on our spiritual gifts we place less emphasis on our material gifts.

In an age where people are driven to buy the latest car, clothes, computers and crazy electronic gadgets, it seems the church should be more instrumental in providing spiritual alternatives to bring people into the church. Perhaps if we had classes on how to communicate with Jesus and the saints, as well to develop our psychic ability, people may actually leave their televisions long enough to participate in church activities. Instead of watching reality shows of other people's adventures, the faithful could be having their own adventures in the reality of the spirit world. Wouldn't it be wonderful if people chose to spend more time with their Christian idols, rather than with *American Idol*? Wouldn't it be wonderful if Catholics learned to embrace the supernatural side of their heritage so they could one day proclaim, "Here's the beef!"

So what will we believe when technology creates another paradigm shift and digital devices replace psychic mediums? What will we believe when communicating with our loved ones in heaven is no big deal? Will we change our attitude towards those who have been doing it all along, the psychic mediums? Must we wait until that time comes before we change how we treat our spiritually gifted brothers and sisters in Christ? I hope not. When that day does come, however, I suggest you go to your local Radio Shack, pick up a pair of spirit-specs and a soul-phone, and reach out to those you love on the otherside.

Summary

Throughout history, science and religion have seldom seen eye-to-eye. Science has often dragged religion kicking and screaming into the present-day world. Much of that resistance has been due to fear. We fear what we don't know and many of our ancient beliefs were based on these fears. With new inventions, increased technology and education, gradually our fears were dispelled, as a result, our religious beliefs changed.

We have seen how science and religion can work together to help us strengthen our faith. Father Alphonsus Trabold is an example of how one can be a devoted Catholic while embracing the science of parapsychology to better understand the person of Jesus. With this comes a better understanding of the nature of man and who we are as divine children of God. When science and religion work together we can embrace the "damn facts" and use them to answer the question, "Where's the beef." We can restore our supernatural heritage and share our spiritual gifts and experiences so, like Jesus, they "fit in" to our religion.

Two thousand years ago religious views changed when a new paradigm arrived on the scene in the man called Jesus. His heretical views were radical and gave rise to much suspicion and doubt. His teachings could not be ignored, however, because they were accompanied by a multitude of unexplainable phenomena. Christ took command of the people's attention and they listened. Divine wisdom, along with his God-given gifts, forced people to question their previous beliefs.

By resurrecting and appearing to thousands, after he had been crucified, Jesus demonstrated that there is life-after-death. This event became the cornerstone of the Christian faith; because of this, Jesus Christ is the tie that binds science and religion. It is in the diversity and complexity of his life that we can see how parapsychology and Christian theology do not oppose, but compliment each other; they are two pieces of the same puzzle. When we put these two pieces together we get a bigger picture of the whole, thus giving us a better understanding of the one we call "God."

We covered how the Catholic Church recognizes the importance of the supernatural by seriously studying the subject. Consequently, it made a valiant attempt at addressing the issues by establishing some official procedures for analyzing apparitions, revelations and spiritualism. In contrast, although the Church may have this elaborate set of rules and regulations, they often ignore their own policies and even the results of their own investigations. Furthermore, we have also seen how, through their research, the Church concluded that the practice of "spiritualism" does *not* go against its teachings; on the contrary, it can help to enhance our faith. Instead of publicizing their findings however, the Church chose instead to suppress information that may be beneficial to those who have had a paranormal experience.

We discussed the importance of validating those who have had a supernatural occurrence and providing them with a safe haven to talk about it. We have also seen a need for re-introducing spiritual experiences back into the faith. It is important for believers to receive meaningful fulfillment; if they don't get it in the Catholic Church, then they will go elsewhere.

Chapter 8
Mystics, Mediums and Muggles

"Ask not the sparrow, how the eagle soars."
(A Course in Miracles)

What is the difference between a mystic and a medium? How are they similar? Why are mystics considered "good" and mediums considered "bad?" Where exactly do I fit into this picture? These are some of the questions I asked following my near-death experience. My investigation into the matter led to an even bigger question - "What is reality?" In this chapter all of these issues will be addressed in the context of the communion of saints. We will begin by setting the stage with an example of one man whose life was a paradox; he provided a supernatural service, to both God and the Roman Catholic Church.

St. Padre Pio

In August of 1918 a young, simple friar wrote an account of a supernatural experience he had:

> While I was hearing the boys' confessions on the evening of the 5th I was suddenly terrorized by the sight of a celestial person who presented himself to my mind's eye. He had in his hand a sort of weapon like a very long, sharp-pointed steel blade that seemed to emit fire. At the very instant that I saw all this, I saw that person hurl the weapon into my soul with all his might. I cried out with difficulty and felt I was dying. I asked the boy to leave because I felt ill and no longer had the strength to continue.

This agony lasted uninterruptedly until the morning of the 7th. I cannot tell you how much I suffered during this period of anguish. Even my entrails were torn and ruptured by the weapon, and nothing was spared. From that day on I have been mortally wounded. I feel in the depths of my soul a wound that is always open and which causes me continual agony.

One month later, while kneeling before a crucifix, this Capuchin Franciscan, Padre Pio, received the sacred wounds of Christ known as "stigmata"; it lasted until his death fifty years later. His visions, locutions, miraculous healings, bilocations, and devotion to the poor and Jesus, made him one of the most noted mystics of the twentieth century. He was canonized as a saint in the Roman Catholic Church on June 16, 2002 (St. Albans, 50).

Padre Pio, like Jesus and many prophets before him, was also a gifted medium. He demonstrated clairvoyance, telepathy, precognition and transcommunication with angels, as well as demons. He was able to "read the hearts of his penitents," which meant he was psychic. Padre Pio used his extrasensory perception to help the lost souls who came to him for confession. He often knew the sins of his parishioners before they even spoke to him.

In one case, famous Italian actress, Lea Padovani confessed to Padre that she had fallen in love with a man who was about to die of an incurable illness. She didn't know how she could live without him and so came to the priest for help. Pio admonished her for not telling him that her lover was married to another woman. The monk told the mistress that she must leave this man so that he could die without sin. When the adulteress refused to abandon her boyfriend, Pio would not grant her absolution; she left the church in tears. After reflecting on the intuitive priest's advice, the young woman returned to him with a repentant heart. She agreed to leave the married man; as a result, Pio pardoned her sins (Ignatius Press).

Padre Pio was gifted with mediumistic abilities from childhood; he had visions of Jesus and the Blessed Mother when he was just a boy. As a youngster Pio had a close relationship with many of the canonized saints; in fact, he often had two-way conversations with them. These spiritualist phenomena lasted until his death. For Padre, "supernatural" occurrences were a "natural" part of his daily life, because he practiced communion with the saints.

Psychic or spiritual gifts cannot be separated from the mystical experience; they are an inevitable byproduct of one who lives in union with God. In the same way, paranormal practices, such as telepathy, cannot be separated from communion or transcommunication with the saints; they are an integral part of the process. In his essay *Parapsychology and Religion*, psychologist Walter Houston Clark, claims "the same triggers that release mystical experiences often release paranormal experiences as well." The origin of both seems to come from deep within our personality (Wolman, 772).

It may be that the source of all psychic phenomena comes from the part of us that is deeply connected to God — our spirit or soul. For this reason, spiritual practices, which are found in religion, cannot be separated from mystical or paranormal experiences; they exist in the same level of reality. But what exactly is this level, and how do we access it? For that matter, what is reality?

Reality Check

Before my near-death experience (NDE) my reality was confined to the physical world. I believed I was separate from all other individuals and talking with the saints was not a part of my daily experience. After my NDE, however, the world of spirits, oneness with the universe, and communicating with non-physical beings became my new reality. What was "supernatural" before my heavenly encounter became quite "natural" for me afterwards; what was unreal became real.

Someone who is able to relate to my unusual perspective is Doctor of Ministry, Deacon Michael Mahoney. He, like Padre Pio, has the gift of "reading the hearts" of those to whom he gives spiritual counsel and has dedicated his life to God. In an interview about his own paranormal experiences, Mahoney shared that several years earlier he began to receive "words of knowledge" and to experience "spiritual insight" in both prayer and while working with his clients. From this perspective, the Catholic deacon explained, "What you describe as 'paranormal,' I have come to understand as 'reality.'" A feature of reality is that we are spiritual beings; that's how we're made" (Grace). If we are spiritual beings having a human experience, which is real - the body or the soul? Could there be more than one reality, or are we simply experiencing facets of the same reality?

In his book, *The Medium, the Mystic, and the Physicist*, Psychologist Lawrence LeShan, posits three levels of reality. These levels describe the differences in perception between mediums, mystics and those without any psychic ability (LeShan). After studying this fascinating theory, I translated LeShan's complex language of physics into simple theological and scientific terms to make it comprehensible to the average person. Furthermore, I developed my own principles and interpretation, based on research and personal paranormal experiences, and applied my findings to the communion of saints doctrine. As a result, I created what I call "The Transcendent Church Model" as a way of shedding new light on an age-old belief.

Just a Fact
It is not unusual for near-death experiencers to have a permanent change in their perception of reality. Furthermore, an alteration in the actual structure of their brain can be observed. This transformation is known as a "brain-shift" and often results in increased psychic ability.

The Transcendent Church Model

The Transcendent Church Model identifies parallels between the three levels of reality and the three states of the Catholic Church. As we progress from one level to the next, so does our level of consciousness and spirituality. With an increase in awareness of other dimensions, there is an increase in psychic abilities or gifts of grace. This elevated state of being can occur both within and without the physical body. Furthermore, the Transcendent Church Model proposes that there is scientific support for the ancient church doctrine on the communion of saints.

Before explaining this model further, let's review the structure of the communion of saints, which is depicted in the Chapter Four diagram, *Interrelationship of Church Members*. There are three levels or states of the church: the Church Militant (believers on earth), the Church Suffering (believers in purgatory) and the Church Triumphant (believers in heaven). Through the transcommunication of prayers and intercessions, the people on earth can help those in purgatory or heaven and vice versa.

In the Transcendent Church Model, the names of the three levels of reality are "physical," "metaphysical" and "mystical," each representing a different level of consciousness and a different state of the church. We all operate in the "physical reality," which represents the Church Militant (earth); this includes non-psychic people, as well as mediums and mystics. The mediums and mystics also share the second level or 'metaphysical reality," which includes the Church Suffering (purgatory) and/or Church Triumphant (heaven). The mystic alone can consciously function in the third level, "mystical reality," which represents the Church Triumphant (heaven). The following chart will help as a visual guide:

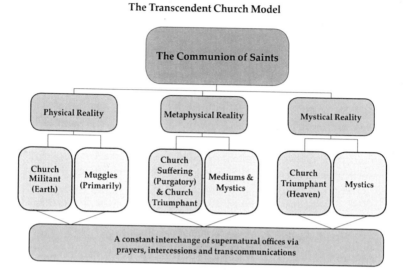

The Transcendent Church Model

In the remainder of this chapter we will delve deeper into the Transcendent Church Model. We will learn about levels of reality that exist beyond the physical realm and look at examples from the lives of the saints and modern-day mystics. We will learn about "muggles" and come to better understand the medium, the mystic, and the communion of saints. Let's start with some definitions.

Define Me

Q: What is the difference between a mystic and a medium?

The Muggle

Most people do not have the gift of vision and prophecy. Scientifically speaking, they do not have a well-developed sixth sense or psychic ability. I felt the need to come up with a term for "non-psychic" people that would accurately and objectively describe the members of this enormous segment of the earth's population. I also needed a simple word that I could use when referring to this group. After several frustrating hours consulting the thesaurus, I finally asked my husband, Bob, for suggestions. Without missing a beat, while watching an episode of CSI, and in between bites of his jelly sandwich, he simply responded, "Muggles."

"Muggles?," I questioned; "What is that?" Apparently, during the seven years I spent writing and doing research for this book, the rest of the world was reading *Harry Potter*. Sure, I had heard about the bestsellers; I even saw one of the movies, but I admit I was not knowledgeable about the lingo of the fantasy, and Hogwart School escaped me. My husband explained that "muggles" were people without wizard powers. "That's perfect!" I exclaimed, and went back to writing.

Just a Fact

The *Harry Potter* series of books has sold more than 450 million copies in 67 languages. Author, Joanne Rowling changed her first name to "J.K." at the urging of her publisher, *Bloomsbury*. It was thought that her target audience of young boys might not purchase a book written by a woman. As a renowned philanthropist, some of the causes Rowling supports is *Comic Relief, One Parent Families* and the *Multiple Sclerosis Society of Great Britain*. (Wikipedia)

Although most people can see with their physical eyes, they are blind to other dimensions because they lack second sight. Although many muggles believe in an afterlife, they are not sensitive to or aware of those in other realms. Being a "muggle" is not a bad thing, it's simply a common condition of life in a physical body; the sixth-sense is more limited.

Muggles are well-grounded people who are firmly rooted in the earth plane. Much like beavers, they are good at staying focused on the work that needs to be done in the physical world and are therefore very productive. Muggles make necessities and comforts for everyone on the planet; they create things such as homes, cars, computers, clothes and toys. In addition, most of our educators, leaders, farmers, blue and white collar workers and those from all walks of life, are muggles.

More importantly, muggles help keep the mystics and mediums grounded so they don't stray too far into other realities; balance is always a struggle for clairvoyants. Behind every great mystic and medium, is a muggle. So be proud if you fit the description of a muggle; you play an important role in the universe. Besides, you can always learn to activate or develop your sixth sense through classes and books on the subject. So from now on, the term "muggles" will be used to describe those in a dormant state of psychic awareness.

Insight

Because children are generally more psychic than adults, we can conclude that as we mature and progress in physical abilities, we tend to regress in spiritual abilities. We grow out of our psychic-state and into our muggle-state.

The Medium

In the chapter *Communication with the Saints* we defined "mediums" as "go-between" people who practice telepathic or transcommunication with non-physical beings, such as angels, spirit guides, the saints and even Grandma; we call this practice "spiritualism." According to the National Spiritualist Association of Churches (NSAC), a medium is defined as a person who is sensitive to vibrations from the Spirit World, and through them, non-physical beings are able to convey messages. In so doing, the individual produces the phenomena of Spiritualism, which includes the following:

> ...prophecy, clairvoyance, clairaudience, gift of tongues, laying on of hands, healing, visions, trance, apports, levitation, raps, automatic and independent writings and paintings, voice, materialization, spirit photography, psychometry and any other manifestation proving the continuity of life as demonstrated through the physical and spiritual senses and faculties of man." (NSAC)

Most think of a medium as a person who charges money to contact loved ones who have crossed over. The information that "comes through" to the medium is called a "reading" because the intuitive "reads" or interprets the messages from spirits. Readings can cost anywhere from thirty dollars up to hundreds, depending on the demand for a particular clairvoyant's services. As we see in the NSAC description, however, anyone who is "sensitive to the vibration of the spirit world" is considered a medium, whether they do it professionally or not. This means all those who are gifted with extrasensory perception and demonstrate "phenomena of Spiritualism." Padre Pio was one such person; he could "read" the hearts of his confessors.

Just a Fact

During Spiritualist church services, several mediums will stand before the congregants and take turns giving free readings to selected parishioners; this is their way of "serving spirit." Some call this practice "prophesying," which is an ancient Biblical tradition.

The Mystic

Although mystics often display paranormal abilities, they are not the same as mediums. However, it is not so easy to define a mystic. There are as many definitions as there are books on the subject; everyone has a little different perspective on it. The following description is compiled from many resources, which are cited throughout the rest of the chapter.

Mystics are people whose lives are first and foremost centered on and around God, or a God-like concept, such as "The One Source," "A Higher Power," or "Supreme Being." They have a deep devotion to the divine and spend much time in communion with "Him" through meditation and contemplation. Mystics are found in all religious traditions. "Christian mystics" are those who have developed a special connection with God through his son, Jesus Christ. The direct, intimate and personal relationship with holiness touches the hearts of the devotees and causes their minds to expand into another dimension. This unitive experience forever changes the person's perception of reality, as a result, the understanding of their own true identity. In the words of St.Paul, "It is not I who lives, but Christ who lives in me" (Galatians 2:20).

One of the first mystics known was a man by the name of Svetasvatara. He lived three-thousand years ago and was one of the authors of the Upanishads. Five-hundred years later lived a mystic by the name of Siddhartha, also known as the Buddha. After another five-hundred years, a Jewish mystic from the Middle East came into the world; he was known as Jesus of Nazareth. Later on there were such notables as Catherine of Genoa, Rumi, Jnaneshvar, Milarepa, Kabir, Basho, Eckhart, Boehme, and Emerson (Abhayananda). According to noted parapsychologist, William James, "The mother sea and fountain-head of all religions lie in the mystical experience of the individual" (as cited in Wolman, 769).

In his book, *When the Lion Roars*, Father Stephen Rosetti, Ph.D. suggests that Christianity could not survive in today's world without its mystical roots. He explains, "It is not so much that mystics have something that others do not. Rather, they are beacons pointing each of us to a divine intimacy that God offers all" (8). We see the holiness of Jesus Christ at work in the lives of the Christian mystics (Rossetti).

Indeed, Padre Pio was just this kind of man; a beacon of Christian light. During his life however, he was persecuted by his own church for being a charlatan, a fake, and even for practicing sorcery. While many believers thought he was a great mystic, church authorities thought he was a medium who consorted with the devil. In order to suppress his paranormal powers, the priest was banned from saying Mass, hearing confessions and was held prisoner in his own monastery for eleven years. It was his spiritual gifts, however that led millions to seek out Padre Pio, thereby furthering the cause for Christianity (St. Albans).

Now that we have defined the three types of church members, we will now define the three levels of reality and corresponding states of the church. There are five basic principles of perception discussed in each level that will aid in comparing the similarities and differences in mystics, mediums and muggles. These principles describe the way in which we receive "information" and the way in which we perceive "individuality," "time," "space" and "spiritual gifts." The Transcendent Church Model will explain these common principles in the various levels of the church; therefore, helping us to better understand the communion of saints. For reference, there are two tables provided later on in this chapter that will help guide you through the following sections; you may want to flip ahead to check them out.

Physical Reality
(Church Militant)

In physical reality, or in the church on earth, information comes to us by way of our five basic senses: seeing, hearing, tasting, smelling and touching. People who do not have a well developed sixth sense operate primarily in this level of reality; they are called "muggles." Although physical reality applies primarily to muggles, it also applies to mediums and mystics, who function in several levels of reality at once. All members of the Church Militant are subject to the same physical laws, mediums and mystics, however, can sometimes operate outside these laws.

In physical reality, members of the church on earth all perceive life the same way, based on the principle concepts of "individuality," "time," "space" and "spiritual gifts." The following descriptions of these concepts will help to clarify:

Individuality
Individuality, or individual identity, is a fundamental part of physical reality. We see ourselves as separate from one another and therefore our thoughts belong to us alone. Because we believe we're separate individuals we treat others differently than we treat ourselves. "I" is the foundation of our perception and existence.

Time

Time in physical reality is linear; it is made up of past, present and future. Events "occur" in sequential order. We think in terms of yesterday, today and tomorrow.

Space

Space, as seen in physical reality, is a barrier to the accessibility of information. Space is a boundary that separates people and prevents direct communication and the direct exchange of knowledge and ideas. In order to access information from a distance we need to use some type of intermediary device, such as a telephone, computer, or another person.

Spiritual Gifts

Spiritual Gifts or ESP are not a conscious part of one's life in physical reality. Psychic experiences may occur on occasion but are not the norm. Clairvoyance and telepathic communication are not natural and are often viewed as "paranormal" or "supernatural" phenomena.

In physical reality and the Church Militant, muggles base their perceptions and judgments about the world entirely on their ability to physically see, hear and feel it. If they cannot sense something in any of these ways, then for many muggles, it simply does not exist or is suspect.

Metaphysical Reality
(Church Suffering and Church Triumphant)

The second level of awareness is called "metaphysical reality" and includes all those in purgatory and heaven. It's also the level in which both the medium and the mystic share. In this reality information comes to us by way of our extrasensory perception, such as telepathy, clairaudience, clairsentience and clairvoyance. In theological terms this means, locutions, voices, visions and apparitions. In this dimension "individuality," "time," "space" and "spiritual gifts" are viewed much differently than in physical reality or in the church on earth.

Quote Me

"And the lives of the great mystics-of the Lord Buddha, of Jesus of Nazareth, of Meister Eckhardt, Jalal-ud-din Rumi, Jacob Boehme and the Baal Shem Tov-all bear testimony to the fact that they were basing their actions and lives on data that did not come to them through the narrow windows of their sensory channels."
(LeShan)

Individuality

In metaphysical reality individual identity is simply an illusion; our thoughts cannot be separated out from the cosmic consciousness. Family and friends, as well as those we do not even know, are viewed as one big celestial family; all thoughts and information are available to everyone. In metaphysical reality, "I" no longer exists, there is only "we."

For this reason, judgment does not occur in metaphysical reality. To judge others is to judge not only oneself, but the entire universe, including God. Therefore, the concepts of "good" and "evil" do not exist. Instead of judging people or situations, the clairvoyant simply observes. Things, like disease, pain, disabilities, poverty, hunger and suffering are not judged as evil but as opportunities for spiritual growth. One can never judge another child of God or His plan for each individual's soul.

Time

Time is another illusion in metaphysical reality. Past, present and future do not exist in a linear framework, as with physical reality. Events do not "happen," they simply "are." LeShan explains this concept by comparing time to movie film. The entire movie, beginning, middle and end, is already on the celluloid. But, as we view the motion picture frame by frame, we only see a small portion of the whole feature. The clairvoyant, on the other hand, may have access to all parts of the movie at any particular moment. Thus, she might see the end of the film before the middle (LeShan).

Voicing the end of a movie to a person locked in physical reality may be viewed as precognition or predicting the future. To the mystic or the medium the information was there to begin with. The concept of "future" being a separate state from "past," and "present," is an illusion to one who operates in the metaphysical reality (LeShan). Let's look at two examples of how time can be perceived in this dimension. The first example is from a mystic and the second from a medium.

Through her highly developed sixth sense, the mystic St. Bridget of Sweden (1303-1373), witnessed the crucifixion of Jesus. She saw the naked and brutally beaten body of Jesus as his wrists were tied to the cross and nails driven into his hands. St. Bridget's vision was so detailed and clear that she was able to see the nerves and veins of Christ's arms rip apart when they were severely stretched apart. The saint also had a profound vision of the nativity and one of the Lord's agony in the Garden of Gethsemane (Freze).

For St. Bridget, although thirteen-hundred years had passed in physical time, in metaphysical time she was able to experience the details of Christ's birth, passion and resurrection. This would be considered an example of retrocognition (knowledge of past events) by most people, but to the mystical saint it was simply a part of her present metaphysical reality.

In another example of metaphysical time, registered medium of Lily Dale, Shirley Smith, confided in me about a holy vision she had. During our interview Shirley related the story of her sacred experience:

> The first time I had a vision I was eighteen and married. My grandmother died and because I was the first grandchild I got to have anything I wanted of hers. I wanted the grandfather clock on the mantle because I always remember my grandmother with the long braid, and every night she would go to the clock and wind it; I loved the chime. Although it quit working years ago, I've carted that clock all over the countryside with me.

This one day I was crying because I was going to get a divorce, and I didn't believe in it. I was feeling so sorry for myself and I felt like I was on the verge of having a breakdown. I was so sad, and the clock, which was broken, started chiming. It just started chiming and I could feel this presence come over me and then I had my first vision.

The vision was like the picture you see in Sunday school of Jesus on this little hill with all the children around him. I can still see it as I tell you; it was the most beautiful colors and everything. Jesus was talking and he was so gentle and loving and the children were all around the base of this little hill and he was talking to them. Jesus looked like the pictures I had seen of him before. He just looked very gentle with the beard, the long, white hair, a white robe and sandals on his feet. Common sense would tell me that his hair might not have been white, but that's what I saw. The grass on the hill and everything was just really, really clear.

It was like a filmstrip in the air that I was seeing; I saw it right in the middle of the room. Between the clock chiming and that vision, I got this wonderful feeling, and I just got better. That was the very first vision I had, before I knew anything about this stuff (mediumship), but I don't remember ever telling anyone about it. Like I said, it was like a filmstrip in the air, it was bright, beautiful colors (Grace).

Shirley's ability to access metaphysical time transported her into the first century. Likening her description of the vision to a filmstrip supports LeShan's theory that clairvoyant reality is similar to a movie reel. Information about past, present and future events are already in existence; they are imprinted on the celluloid of the universe. Anyone can access this information at anytime; the mystic and the medium just seem to be better equipped for it, due to the grace of God and their spiritual gifts.

Quote Me
"Just as we know that gravity loses its pull once a space vehicle reaches a certain height, so should our concepts of the past, present and future remain open to examination." (Ebon)

Space

"Space" is the third concept that appears to be an illusion to the mystic and the medium. In metaphysical reality, information can be accessed directly from a distant source. Space poses no boundaries, because thoughts can flow freely anywhere within the one cosmic consciousness. No intermediary device, such as a phone or computer, is necessary to access information from a far-off location, which is unlike the case with physical reality.

An example of how space is perceived in the metaphysical reality can be seen from a reading given by Registered Medium and former nun, Reverend Mary Ockuly, M.Ed. Mary is "clairsentient," which is a form of clairvoyance that means "clear sensing." The intuitive is able to "sense" or pick-up on another person's emotions or feelings. Mary gives many long distance readings over the telephone from her home in Lily Dale. The following one took place in November of 2007:

> I was talking to a woman in California, I felt that she was definitely in a downward spin, she was very depressed, and I had never talked to her before. I said, "You're hitting a downward spiral that seems to be taking you away and you're having difficulty being in touch. And also there is karma around a relationship that you both have to work on." The woman then told me that she had just broken up with a boyfriend.

> I then said, "There aren't very many people you trust, there's only two." She said, "Yes," one was her sponsor (AA) and one was her psychologist. I said, "I feel you're getting information and help from your spirit guides, through

your sponsor, the spirit guides are working through her (the sponsor)." She was very touched by that. (Grace)

Through her clairsentience, Mary was able to know the emotional state and personal details about a person who lived three-thousand miles away. She was also able to bring messages through from the spirit of the woman's grandfather and beloved cat. Mary brought comfort and healing to someone in desperate need of help. Space posed no boundaries while she was working in the metaphysical reality.

In another example, the great Christian seer, Edgar Cayce was able to diagnose illnesses, and prescribe remedies for people all over the country, without ever leaving his office. By going into trance, he entered into the metaphysical reality where all the information he needed was available to him. Transcripts of over 30,000 readings done by Cayce are on record at the Association for Research and Enlightenment in Virginia Beach, Virginia (Sugrue).

In his book, *The Spontaneous Fulfillment of Desire*, Deepak Chopra, Ph.D. uses the term "nonlocal reality" to describe the level of consciousness where space and time do not exist. The noted physician and spiritual teacher explains that this domain, or "field of potential," is "where information and energy emerge from a sea of possibilities." It consists of pure intelligence. "We call it nonlocal because it cannot be confined by a location—it is not 'in' you or 'out there.' It simply is" (43). What Chopra calls "nonlocal reality," accurately describes "metaphysical reality."

Spiritual Gifts

In metaphysical reality, spiritual gifts, such as extrasensory perception, are a natural part of one's life. Many children who possess these gifts, often don't realize that not everyone else has the same abilities. Adults may devote much time and attention to developing and practicing their intuition. Psychic experiences are, therefore, "typical" in this level of reality. Spiritual gifts may be viewed as "paranormal" and not necessarily connected to a higher power.

Insight

"Indigo Children" is the name given to kids who seem to be more highly evolved than most. They have a well-developed sixth sense, are extremely empathetic and unusually selfless for their age. "Indigo" refers to the color of their aura. For more information read *Indigo Children*, by Lee & Tober, or see the wonderful movie, *Indigo* by Emissary Productions.

In metaphysical reality, mediums, mystics, and members of the Church Suffering and Triumphant, perceive their world through their sixth sense. For mediums and mystics this provides information in addition to that which is received through their physical senses. For this reason, their judgments about life in general are different than those who operate solely in the physical world. Things, such as ESP, exist for those in the metaphysical reality that simply do not exist for people in the physical reality. The table on the following page sums up and compares the principle concepts of physical and metaphysical reality through the "Transcendent Church Model."

Table 1
Comparison of the Principle Concepts of
Physical and Metaphysical Levels of Reality
In The Transcendent Church Model

Physical Reality (muggle level)	Metaphysical Reality (medium & mystic level)
Communion of Saints Level:	
All members of the Church Militant (souls on earth), specifically muggles (non-psychics) but includes mediums and mystics as well.	All members of the Church Suffering (souls in purgatory) & Church Triumphant (souls in heaven). Accessible by mediums and mystics of the Church Militant (earth).

Information:	
Comes through the physical senses of sight, sound, taste, smell and touch; these are the primary sources.	Comes from physical senses, as well as from extrasensory perception (spiritual gifts) such as clairaudience and clairvoyance (voices and visions). ESP provides more accurate information than physical senses, which are often illusory.
Individuality:	
Individual identity is a principal concept. Objects, events and people are primarily separate, although they may be related in groups or families. "I" is foundational.	Individual identity is an illusion. Objects, events, and people exist separately, but, their individuality is secondary to their part in the whole universe. "I" no longer exist, there is only "we."
Time:	
Is divided into past, present, and future. It is linear, moving in one direction from past to future. It is "sequential-time."	Has no division. Past, present, and future are illusions; they exist all at once. It is "singular- time."
Space:	
Can prevent an exchange of information or energy between two individual objects or people. Some sort of intermediary device must be utilized in order to transmit the information from one individual source to the other.	Cannot prevent an exchange of information or energy between two individual objects or people. Direct access is available through ESP or spiritual gifts; no intermediary device is needed. Separateness and space is an illusion; all is one.
Spiritual gifts (ESP, voices, visions, etc.):	
Are not a conscious part of one's life and are viewed as "unnatural;" often referred to as "paranormal" or "supernatural." Psychic experiences may occur but are "atypical."	Are natural and an integral part of one's life. Much time and attention may be devoted to developing and practicing them. Gifts may be viewed as "paranormal" and not necessarily connected to a higher power. Psychic experiences are "typical."

Both mystics and mediums consciously live in two worlds, two different realities. The ability to receive information outside the normal five senses is a trait common to both; they have a more highly developed sixth sense than most people. For some it is a natural gift with which they were born. For others, they learned to develop and hone the gift through spiritual instruction, meditation, and much disciplined practice. For still others, these special graces were the byproduct of an unexpected spiritual transformation, following a direct experience with the divine (such as a near-death experience). However they arrived, both mystics and mediums seem to be able to walk freely between two dimensions of reality. Some case histories will help to clarify this point.

Clairvoyance in Christian Mystics

Further examples of clairvoyance and metaphysical reality can be seen in the lives of many of our canonized saints and Christian mystics, who are members of the Church Triumphant. They provide us with yet another perspective on psychic phenomena because they lived in more recent times and were often subject to investigation by both church authorities and scientists. In the following cases, it would help to remember that "vision" is the theological term for "clairvoyance."

St. Hildegard of Bingen, Germany (1098-1179), abbess and founder of a Benedictine community, was noted for her *visions*, which started when she was three years old and continued until her death. These clairvoyant images concerned the relation between God, humanity, and the cosmos. She wrote extensively about her *visions*, which were presented and accepted by the archbishop of Mainz. She was then provided with a secretary who helped compile her works into what became known as *Scivias*, which means "Know the Ways" (Ellsberg, 406).

St. Margaret Mary (1647-1690) of Alacoque, France was a nun in the Order of the Visitation. She had four *visions* of Jesus in which he revealed his Sacred Heart to her. She saw flames coming out of the heart, which symbolized Christ's burning love for us. Around his heart was a crown of thorns symbolizing his sacrifice for our sins. In these clairvoyant encounters, Jesus made her twelve promises. She dedicated the rest of her life to promoting devotion to his Sacred Heart (Lovasik).

St. John Bosco (1815-1888) of Italy had a *vision* of St. Francis of Sales who revealed to him detailed instructions about a new religious order Bosco would establish. St. Francis showed Bosco a book that described rules and regulations regarding the behavior of the spiritual people who enrolled and how the foundation would be successful. Bosco trusted his clairvoyance and went on to establish the Salesian Order, with over sixty foundations in Europe and America (Freze).

Therese Neumann (1898-1962) of Germany, one of the greatest *visionaries* in the history of the church, saw images from the life of Mary, the Blessed Mother. On September 8, 1928 she clairvoyantly witnessed Mary's birth. She describes seeing Mary's mother, Anne, with several other women; one was a midwife. The infant, Mary was smiling and was visibly surrounded by a glowing light. Therese saw the midwife place the newborn Mary into her mother's arms and was able to see the baby's blue eyes and light blonde hair. Therese also had visions of the last supper and Jesus' ascension into heaven (Freze).

Insight

Many of our great Christian mystics were thought to have suffered from mental illness. A beautiful mural in St. Jude's Chapel, located in Rochester Psychiatric Center, depicts many of the saints who were suspected of being "crazy." The painting includes Joan of Arc, Teresa of Avila, Francis of Assisi, Simon the Stylite, John of the Cross and Francis of DeSales, to name a few. Diocesan psychologist, Father Thomas Hoctor, pastor of St. Jude's for 22 years, commissioned the mural to encourage those with mental illness to never give up hope.

Clairvoyance in Mediums

Father Daniel O'Rourke, former Franciscan Priest from St. Bonaventure, current newspaper columnist for the Dunkirk, NY Observer, and author of *The Spirit At Your Back*, is also a spiritual healer in Lily Dale, NY. Healers are considered mediums in the religion of Spiritualism, and therefore, have access to the metaphysical reality. During an interview, Father Dan shared this holy vision with me:

> I was at a funeral of a friend who was in a writer's guild with
> me. She lost a daughter in New York City who was killed
> when pushed in front of the train; she was decapitated. My
> friend had a big family; seven children. This girl was a
> beautiful girl. Anyway, I went to the funeral, the whole
> community went to the funeral; a Roman Catholic Mass.
> When it was over, after communion, a woman who was
> at my daughter's wedding sang Ave Maria; I was very
> peaceful. Then I looked up and I saw the Virgin Mother
> beside the altar. She had her arms outstretched, embracing
> the mother and the family of the girl who had died. (Grace)

Besides visions, it's also not unusual for O'Rourke to receive psychic
impressions from individuals when he is performing spiritual
healing on them. He often gets a sense of what the person's physical
ailment is or if they are in need of emotional or psychological
healing.

Insight

Spiritual healing, also known as "laying on of hands," was once
a common practice in early Christianity and is still practiced by
Charismatic Catholics, who also believe in the spiritual gifts of
prophesying and speaking in tongues. People like Father Richard
McAlear (the healing priest), of the Charismatic Renewal, have
helped revive the Biblical tradition of hands-on-healing in Roman
Catholicism.

In another example of clairvoyance in mediums, Ginger Smith,
resident medium of Lily Dale, recounted the following story during
my interview with her.

> I was going to the post office and I saw Bill Corbin. I came
> out of the post office and I saw him walking down Melrose
> Street, just in front of the big house. Now he's from Toronto
> and just comes for the summer. So I said, "Hi Bill." And he
> said "Hi Ginger." And I said, "Gee you're here awful early
> this year." He put his arms up in the air and he said, "I just

love this place."

He had on a greenish pair of pants and a long sleeved sweater with two deer on the front and he had red hair. And when I came home I was talking to my friend, Virginia and I said," Bill's here awful early this year." And she asked, "What are you talking about?" I said. "I saw him this morning when I went to the post office" (This was around Easter time). And she told me, "Ginger, Bill's been dead for three months." (Grace)

Bill passed away in his home in Toronto. When Bill's wife found out about Ginger's vision she called to tell her that his dying wish was to return to Lily Dale one more time. The wife was happy to know that Bill got his wish; it gave her a sense of peace.

A third example of clairvoyance in mediums can be seen in an account given by Ron Skowronski, pastor of the Church of Religious Science. He recalled a vivid vision he had in his apartment when he lived in Rochester, NY:

I can remember, it was when I was a teenager; I knew the difference between imagination and something I couldn't explain. I can remember looking up a flight of stairs and seeing a man at the foot of those stairs whom I could actually see and describe. He had brown boots up to his knees, had riding pants, he looked Amish or maybe a farmer, I don't really know. To make a long story short, at the same time I could see through him. That's what we refer to as an "etherealization" or an apparition. (Grace)

Ron went on to explain that as a medium he often gets impressions that do not originate in his own consciousness. One of things he has had to learn over the years is how to discern the objective visions, as in the case of the Amish man, from the subjective ones that occur in his mind. He insists, "Discernment is the hugest." (Grace)

In each of these cases, the mystics and mediums demonstrated the gift of clairvoyance. They were blessed with a well-developed sixth sense. They did not consider their psychic abilities as "supernatural" powers, but something that was quite "natural" to them.

The following quote is a brief reminder of what the *Catholic Catechism* teaches us about clairvoyance:

> Consulting horoscopes, astrology, palm reading, interpretation of omens and lots, the *phenomena of clairvoyance*, and recourse to mediums all conceal a desire for power over time, history, and, in the last analysis, other human beings, as well as a wish to conciliate hidden powers. They contradict the honor, respect, and loving fear that we owe to God alone (C.C. 2116).

This article was covered in detail in Chapter 5, *Taboo*, but it bears repeating. Just because one is in tune with his or her own sixth sense, does not mean that person conceals a desire for power over time, history and other human beings. It does not follow that utilizing your God-given spiritual gift of "seeing," disrespects or dishonors our Father in heaven in some way. On the contrary, in most cases the visions received were used to convey a message that helped people. With the Christian mystics, the clairvoyant information aided in spreading the Gospel to people throughout the world.

So far we have examined two levels of reality shared by the medium and the mystic, physical and metaphysical. We will now take a look at a third level of awareness that seems to be accessible by the mystics only, those we consider our most highly spiritual leaders. I call this simply the "mystical reality." It is this third domain of consciousness that seems to separate the mystic from the medium.

Mystical Reality
(Church Triumphant)

In the mystical reality, mystics and members of the church in heaven receive information directly from a Supreme Being or God; knowledge comes through being a part the whole. As described earlier, mystics spend much time in communion with this higher power through meditation and contemplation. A personal and intimate relationship with the divine seems to elevate or expand their level of consciousness, thus, making them aware of their oneness with God, the universe, and all of creation. This state of awareness is also called "Christ consciousness" because it describes the highly spiritual mind of Jesus. From this unitive position, all sense of "individuality," "time," and "space," as well as "spiritual gifts" is essentially unimportant.

Individuality
Individuality in the mystical reality does not exist; identification with religion, culture and language is lost. All beings are part of the whole. "We" no longer exists, there is only one, great "I AM." Jesus described this revelatory experience when he declared, "I and the Father are one." (John 10:30).

Time
Time is another concept that does not exist in the mystical reality. All sense of linear and sequential time order is lost. Only the present moment is real; it is "eternal-time."

Space
Space in the mystical reality is an illusion, but completely unimportant. Parts of the whole appear to be separated by space, but it does not matter because all are one with the Source or God.

Spiritual Gifts
Spiritual Gifts in the mystical reality are typical side-effects of a life that is totally centered around, and in close communion with, God or a higher power. Mystics seem to possess extraordinary supernatural powers; they can even perform "miracles." Examples can be seen in cases of bi-location, levitation, materializations, multiplication of food, healings and even stigmata. Also, mystics use their supernatural abilities sparingly and only to further the kingdom of God.

In the mystical reality less value is placed on spiritual gifts because people are easily seduced by the status and prestige they may bring. One of the dangers of mysticism is that more time may be spent on developing one's psychic ability than on developing a closer relationship with God. For this reason, mystical teachings constantly warn of the dangers of getting caught up in the *siddhis*, the miracles, the charisms and paranormal phenomena, which can prevent spiritual growth and progression to the mystical reality (LeShan).

In an interview with medium, Pastor Ron Skowronski, he commented on the difference between a Christian Mystic and a psychic medium regarding spiritual gifts. He eloquently explained:

> I think that the Christian Mystic can identify that Christ is not a human being but a state of consciousness and as a result of that state of consciousness, that nature, that divine nature, that is in every being on this planet, here and hereafter, will blossom forth normally and naturally; whereas the average medium or psychic is probably focused very heavily on the beginnings of that process. The beginnings of that process are spirit medium or psychic impressions. There is a big difference between psychism and mysticism in that psychism tends to focus on the individual soul, while mysticism focuses on the oversoul (Grace).

The meditative or contemplative life, which is so often found in monastic-type settings, fosters a person's psychic ability through altered states of consciousness. As one moves closer to unity with the Divine, a sixth sense develops naturally. For the mystic, however, paranormal gifts possessed by individuals are secondary to the spiritual welfare of the whole community of souls or "oversoul."

Quote Me

"Without spiritual maturity, absorption in psychic experiences can cause spiritual stagnation. In the last analysis, what really matters is faith and love." (Heaney)

In mystical reality, members of the Church Triumphant, as well as those who are mystics, perceive their world through a unitive consciousness. Their views on life in general are different from those who are limited to the physical or metaphysical world. For example, individuality and time simply do not exist for this unique group of people. The following table sums up and compares the principle concepts of metaphysical and mystical reality as understood in the Transcendent Church Model. Remember, mediums and mystics are able to operate in both the physical and metaphysical reality. The mystic, alone, is able to access the mystical reality.

Table 2
Comparison of the Principle Concepts of
Mystical and Metaphysical Levels of Reality
In The Transcendent Church Model

Metaphysical Reality (medium & mystic level)	Mystical Reality (mystical level)
Communion of Saints Level:	
All members of the Church Suffering (souls in purgatory) & Church Triumphant (souls in heaven). Accessible by mediums and mystics of the Church Militant (earth).	All members of the Church Triumphant (souls in heaven). Accessible by mystics of the Church Militant (earth).
Information:	
Comes from physical senses, as well as from extrasensory perception (spiritual gifts) such as clairaudience and clairvoyance (voices and visions). ESP provides more accurate information than physical senses, which are often illusory	Comes directly from God or a higher power. Knowledge comes through being a part of the whole and provides the most accurate picture of reality.

Individuality:	
Individual identity is an illusion. Objects, events, and people exist separately, but, their individuality is secondary to their part in the whole universe. "I" no longer exist, there is only "we."	All sense of an individual identity with religion, culture, and language is lost. All beings are part of the whole. "We" no longer exists, there is only one, great "I AM."
Time:	
Has no division. Past, present, and future are illusions; they exist all at once. It is "singular- time."	All sense of linear and sequential time order is lost; there is only the present moment. It is "eternal-time."
Space:	
Cannot prevent an exchange of information or energy between two individual objects or people. Direct access is available through ESP or spiritual gifts; no intermediary device is needed. Separateness and space is an illusion; all is one.	Parts of the whole appear separated by it, but being one with God and the universe, this does not matter. Space is an illusion, but completely unimportant.
Spiritual gifts (ESP, voices, visions, etc.):	
Are natural and an integral part of one's life. Much time and attention may be devoted to developing and practicing them. Gifts may be viewed as "paranormal" and not necessarily connected to a higher power. Psychic experiences are "typical."	Are side-effects of a life centered around and in close communion with God or a higher power. Gifts are unimportant; they can be a distraction and prevent a person from further spiritual growth. Gifts are viewed as "supernatural" as they come directly from a divine source; miracles occur. Psychic experiences are "typical" but utilized sparingly and only to further the kingdom for all.

In the mystical reality one becomes fully aware of the size and nature of his own true identity as a part of the vastness of God. It leads to an overwhelming feeling of humility and reverence that awakens a deep spiritual connection with the divine. The experience of pure knowledge and unconditional love that permeates every molecule within the body and soul brings clarity of the entire cosmos and one's role in it. The mystic knows he is not bound to a physical body and that he is truly an eternal being. Death is seen as an illusion; doubt, worry and fear do not exist at this level of consciousness.

The initial event leading to this change is often described as a "spiritual conversion," "transformation," "transcendence" or even "grace." It is also known as "samadhi" by the Hindus, "nirvana" by the Buddhist, "fana" by the Muslims and the "the mystic union" by Christians. The direct experience of God fills the person with such emotional love that it creates a state of euphoria or "ecstasy," as well as a great sense of peace and compassion. For these reasons, a "mystical" experience is closely associated with a "religious" experience (Abhayananda).

It is from these states of "ecstasy" that some of our greatest works of creativity have been born. Poetry, music, books, dramas, paintings and sculptures have all been outlets for attempts to express that which is inexpressible. They are attempts to transcribe mystical reality into physical reality by using the common language of "imagination," which is found in the arts. We call this process "inspiration" (in spirit) because it comes from the part of us that is connected to the spirit world.

Examples of mystically inspired works can be seen in Kahlil Gibran's *The Prophet*, St. Teresa's *The Interior Castle*, John of the Cross's *Dark Night of the Soul*, Thomas Merton's *Seeds of Contemplation* and in the writings of the anonymous author of the *Cloud of Unknowing*. Inspiration can also be seen in the art of DaVinci, the music of Mozart, and in the architecture of our great cathedrals, which were built by divinely inspired masons. In Evelyn Underhill's, *Mysticism*, the author explains how we need to have an open mind on the subject of reality and mysticism:

> We must come to this encounter with minds cleared of prejudice and convention, must deliberately break with our inveterate habit of taking the "visible world" for granted; our lazy assumption that somehow science is "real" and metaphysics is not. We must pull down our own card houses - descend, as the mystics say, "into our nothingness"- and examine for ourselves the foundations

of all possible human experience before we are in a position to criticize the buildings of the visionaries, the poets and the saints. We must not begin to talk of the unreal world of these dreamers until we have discovered - if we can - a real world with which it may be compared (5).

Underhill acknowledges that reality goes beyond the "visible world"; there is both a physical and metaphysical world. We cannot assume that one is more "real" than the other if we have nothing with which to compare it. Is a human being more real than an angel, is a heart more real than love, is science more real than religion, is physical reality more real than metaphysical or mystical reality? We cannot make judgments on that which we have not experienced, and therefore do not truly understand.

Quote Me

"The fact that one way of looking at reality is valid, however, does not mean that a different way may not be equally valid. There is an old poem about seven blind men and an elephant that has some relevance here." (LeShan)

Modern-Day Mystics

To help us better understand mystical reality, let's look at examples in the lives of two modern-day mystics. The first, Roman Catholic priest, Father Patrick Mulligan (mentioned earlier) was born with spiritual gifts of grace. Clairvoyant since childhood, perhaps it was a foreshadowing of his future service to God. In adulthood, like Jesus and Padre Pio before him, Mulligan devoted his life to teaching the Gospel. An example of the clergy's supernatural abilities was revealed to me on the day we met in his office. Let me first explain how this meeting came about.

A mutual friend had given my e-mail address to Father Patrick and suggested that we meet. We had a couple of correspondences to arrange a time and place to get together; we decided on Mulligan's office near Canandaigua, NY. Excited that the priest contacted me, I asked if he would be interested in being interviewed for the book I was writing; he agreed. I had two sets of questions, one for priests and one for mediums. Naturally, I was prepared to ask the first set. We had never met prior to the day of the interview and knew virtually nothing about each other, except that we had a mutual acquaintance. I was stunned when fifteen minutes into the interview Father Patrick let his extraordinary psychic ability slip out:

Father Patrick (FP): I want to interrupt you here because you mention Joan of Arc and there are two other people that I want to mention to you because I see them with you. Now that may sound strange coming from a Catholic priest but that's also because I recognize the possibility of mediumship.

Mary Grace (MG): Well, there is a very interesting connection between myself and Joan of Arc, now that you bring it up, so I find it fascinating that you see her around me. Who else do you see?

FP: A priest who is related to you a couple of generations ago. I'm trying to get if he is a member of a religious order or not but many times when I see people in holy orders in almost like a monastic type of appearance, it doesn't necessarily mean that but this is how I can identify this clerical garb. I'm getting Father A-N. He's related to you, a somewhat distant relative. He is working with you, very closely actually. When you were driving here today was there an instance when you felt like you were nodding off, because he's showing me how he nudged you? (Father Patrick demonstrates an elbow nudge).

MG: I was reading my directions to your office, while I was driving on the thruway, and I kept swerving into the other lane.

FP: He was trying to get your attention. There is also a Douglas, I can't get the relationship with Douglas but he also came in with you. Those are the three presences that came in with you.

MG: I do have a priest friend who has been helping me with this book.

FP: This person is dead though.

MG: So is the person I'm talking about (I laugh).

MG: A priest I interviewed two summers ago was Father Alphonsus Trabold.

FP: Oh the "A," I think this is the same person. Was he a Franciscan?

MG: (Gasping) Yes. Oh my God.

FP: That's why I'm seeing the robe and I'm getting the nudge that this is the same person. That is the "A." He is agreeing that this is who he is and he is glad that you recognize him. Apparently he was nudging you today to bring back your attention to your driving. Did he work as an exorcist?

MG: Phenomenal!

FP: He was quite active as an exorcist; he's telling me that he consulted on things that were of this nature too. He was actually quite active in it; he calls it "parapsychology study," is what he's telling me. He's very much, very much helping you on this aspect. Apparently he was active in the Southern Tier.

I see that he was active as an exorcist and that he is one of the people that would be called upon for this office within the local Roman Catholic diocese. He passed on a couple of years ago. You had a close relationship with him so I thought it was a family relationship. He's encouraging you with this work.

MG: Thank you Father Al (Trabold's nickname). I don't know how I could have written this book without his help.

FP: You have his help, certainly.

MG: I interviewed Father Al for three hours back in August of 2004. He was a parapsychologist and has been my mentor. (I tell the story about how Trabold left his library of books on the supernatural to St. Bonaventure. Two days later, at a midnight séance with Patricia Price, Father Al showed up to tell me that he left me everything and wanted me to carry on with his work).

FP: I will be very interested to know if you find this book among his collection. (Father Pat hands me a piece of paper on which he had written "The Church and Spiritualism" by Herbert Thurston).

MG: I can't believe it! I was led to this exact book and copied several chapters out of it when I was doing research in Father Trabold's library.

FP: He said that it would be very helpful to you.

MG: Thank you very much, incredible, just incredible.

FP: So naturally, I believe that the communication is two-way (Mulligan laughs heartily). And you're going to have to argue loud and long to convince me otherwise because I've been having those experiences since I can remember (Grace).

I soon realized that Father Patrick Mulligan is no ordinary priest; he is also a gifted medium. He could not have possibly guessed about a person who is a Franciscan, exorcist, parapsychologist, priest whose name begins with "A." He knew too many details, including the fact that Father Al was helping me with the book. Furthermore, Mulligan not only has a well developed sixth sense, he leads a virtuous life, devoted to Christ. Father Patrick clearly meets the criteria for a mystic.

Insight
Many Orthodox Catholics are similar to Charismatic Catholics in the Roman Church in that they believe in "spiritual gifts," as described in 1 Corinthians, chapter 12. Both denominations practice hands-on-healing, prophesying (mediumship), speaking in tongues and other psychic phenomena.

The second example of a modern-day mystic was already mentioned in Chapter Six, Taboo; he is Father Richard McAlear of the Oblates of Mary Immaculate order. When McAlear performs hands-on-healing, many people fall to the floor as they are "slain in the Holy Spirit." He travels the world serving God in this way and for that reason he is known as the *Healing Priest*.

I had the honor of working with this holy man during six or seven of his healing Masses over the course of four different years that he toured to Upstate, NY; my role was that of "consoler." The job consisted of comforting those who were overcome with emotion following the healing; often times they would break down in tears. Standing on the altar next to McAlear, while he is exuding this most phenomenal, divine energy is an incredibly humble and sacred experience.

On break during one of McAlear's seminars at Holy Spirit Church in Webster, NY, I had the opportunity to interview him about his extraordinary gift. The following is a segment from that conversation:

MG: When people come up to you for healing can you tell me how you know things about them, like their physical ailments or how they are feeling? Tell me what you see, hear, and feel.

FM: I call it compassion. When someone comes up depressed I can see the depression and feel the depression. I enter into like this force-field, I enter into the depression, so I'm sensing it and feeling it. Then the next person is despairing and going to commit suicide so I enter into that. And then the next one is grieving over a lost love one and I just keep entering into their space. I say that I touch the spirit within the person with the sense of what it is.

MG: Do you see the person's illness, like a vision or do you just know it?

FM: No, I do not have visual things, I'm just not visual, but it's a sense. Like I know the person has cancer, I just know it. And the strange thing is that I think the person who is standing beside me must see what I see because it's just there. You just know it's there and then you find out the other person didn't see anything, nothing. I don't understand that. To me it's like looking out the window at the trees; I just know the trees are there. I don't see it as anything unusual; it's just there. And then the surprise to me is that everybody else didn't know it too, because it's so obvious.

MG: You're clairsentient, you know that?

FM: Is that what it is?

MG: Clairsentient is a form of psychic ability in which you feel other people's feelings.

FM: Yes, I certainly do. But I'm not very visual at all, generally speaking.

MG: You said that you can see into a person's soul?

FM: If I look into their eyes it is like looking into the soul. I can see whether it's clear or foggy or confused or pained. Certain things that are very clear are pain, confusion, fear. Those are just clear looking at their eyes. You can see someone's fear just looking right back at you.

MG: Do you see it in your third eye or is it more of a feeling?

FM: It's interesting; I've accepted that I don't see anything. When I look at someone and they have fear I am looking at the fear in their soul. It's not like I see a little demon, they look frightened; I see fear. It's pretty obvious but again a priest up in Buffalo wanted me to show him and I was walking with the priest and I said, "Well, do you see the fear?" And he said, "no." "It's right there; you can't see fear in this person?" And he said "no."

I guess I'm seeing what other people don't but I certainly can see into someone's eyes, which is a different thing then entering into their space. I actually see fear looking at me, I see panic, or hate, or hurt, or pain looking out at me, does that make sense? I feel what they feel. (Grace)

Father McAlear also fits the description of a true mystic. Like Jesus and Padre Pio, he has devoted his life to Christ, and through his healing Masses, he continues to spread the Gospel and bring people closer to God. Due to his paranormal abilities, thousands of hurting souls are not only being healed, but are also listening to his message of hope and renewal.

No two people will ever agree on an exact definition of a mystic, which seems to be part of their mystery. And although the mystic may be more spiritually advanced than the medium, it does not make one better than the other. Likewise, a college student is not better than a high-schooler, any more than a doctor is better than a nurse. We are simply in different stages of development, whether physically, psychologically, intellectually, emotionally or spiritually. We are God's children, complete with flaws and faults. It matters not to Him what spiritual path we take, if any at all, or in what level of reality we operate. What does matter is how we treat each other in the time and in world we live.

Mystic Mode

The Christian mystics and our canonized saints led a life that exemplified Jesus; they were prayerful, generous, honest, kind and caring to all people. For them, the most important characteristics are love, faith and compassion for our fellow human beings. Although they possessed some form of psychic ability, more importantly, the mystics and saints led a God-centered, virtuous life that truly embodied their faith.

There are many mediums living today who also fit these saintly criteria. The fact that they are called "mediums" or "psychics," however, automatically disqualifies them from being taken seriously as true Christian mystics. This is because of the stigma attached to the labels and because of fear and general ignorance of the paranormal. Reverend Dan O'Rourke is one such person. Like Father McAlear; he is a gifted healer (healers are mediums), as well as a man of God. O'Rourke commented on just this subject:

> I think mystics are those who are aware of the pervasive influence of the mystery and presence we call God in human life. That He's all around us, in nature, in our relationships and in spirit. If we become more sensitive, then we become more mystical. I know mediums who are mystical and I know mediums who are more psychic than mystical and who are sometimes very unspiritual. But I know priests that way and I know bishops that way and sometimes I myself am that way, and sometimes I'm more mystical. (Grace)

Father Dan acknowledges there is much more to being a highly spiritual person than wearing priestly robes. To be a mystic is to experience and understand a divine presence in all things and all people and to treat them accordingly. Although many of us may have mystical moments, and may be very spiritual, the pressures of life in the physical world often drive us to behave in unspiritual ways.

Jesus tried to teach us how to act more spiritual when he said, "Whatsoever you do to the least of my brothers, that you do unto me" (Matthew 25:40). Because Christ lived in the mystical reality, he was fully aware that in the "real" world we are all one. We should therefore treat others the same way we want to be treated ourselves. To help a neighbor is to help Jesus, God and ourselves. To harm a neighbor is to harm Jesus, God and ourselves. For this reason, Christ taught that if someone strikes us we should turn the other cheek. On the physical level of reality this philosophy makes little sense, however, on the mystical level it makes perfect sense.

Insight

While dying on the cross, Jesus pleaded, "Father, forgive them, they know not what they do" (Luke 23:34). Christ knew that those locked in physical reality were unaware of how their actions affected those in all levels of reality. His muggle-executioners were not only hurting Jesus, but also themselves and everyone in the entire cosmos.

LeShan points out that our greatest spiritual teachers, for whom we reserve a special place of honor, have taught us a path which encompassed information from all levels of reality. He explains:

> And indeed does not everything we most highly regard - beauty, love, heroism, laughter, awe, religion - tell us that there is a buried part of us desperately demanding recognition and expression? In the world of Sensory Reality these things make no sense...They do not fit a human being seen only from the viewpoint of the Sensory Reality. Given a total human being, including both aspects, both realities, both ways of being, they do fit." (92)

The mystics, like Jesus, are teachers. They teach us about love, humility, compassion and spirituality. They are living examples of the potential that is in all of us. By their actions, they point the way to heaven and teach us how to be God-like. That is why a great sense of peace and compassion seems to be felt by all who come into the presence of the mystic. People resonate with the mystic because in him they recognize their true selves; their connection with God is awakened. "You shall know the truth and the truth shall set you free" (John 8:32).

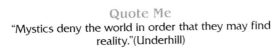

The Communion of Saints & The Transcendent Church Model

The Transcendent Church Model describes how there are three levels of reality making up the communion of saints. In this last section of the chapter we will discuss the practical application of this model. We will learn how we utilize these various levels of reality, which often co-mingle with each other, in our daily lives. Before we continue, however, a brief review of the communion of saints doctrine will be helpful. As cited in Chapter 4, the following definition is from the Catholic Encyclopedia:

> The Communion of Saints is the spiritual solidarity which binds together the faithful on earth, the souls in purgatory, and the saints in heaven in the organic unity of the same mystical body under Christ its head, and in a constant interchange of supernatural offices. (2)

Members of the church live in one of three states, earth, purgatory or heaven. We progress from one level to the next, helping each other along the way. Through prayers and intercessions, the people on earth can help those in heaven and vice versa. Sometimes we are in a position to help others and sometimes we are the ones in need of help. This ongoing process of transcommunication describes the "constant interchange of supernatural offices" and is what the communion of saints is all about.

Spiritual progression, however, is not always linear; it's more like a rollercoaster ride. We may feel we're well on the spiritual path when we suddenly experience a setback in the case of tragedy, illness or the death of a loved one. We may not only lose hope, but all psychic abilities as well. We might go from a mystic-state to a muggle-state. In the same way, a single divine encounter, such as a Marian apparition or a near-death experience, can suddenly catapult us to a higher level of spirituality and consciousness. We may become filled with immense hope, as well as increased psychic abilities. In a holy instant we can go from a muggle-state to a mystic-state. Such was the case with Saul's sudden conversion when he encountered the spirit of Jesus on the road to Damascus. The spiritual path is not a straight one; on the contrary, it is extremely crooked.

In The Transcendent Church Model, I propose that we vacillate between levels of reality and various states of the church, much like a department store elevator. We go up and down, stopping at various floors, jumping in and out of dimensions. On the first floor or physical reality, we work, learn, play and raise families. On the second floor or metaphysical reality, we pray, take shamanic journeys, astral travel and communicate with the angels, saints and dearly departed. On the third floor or mystical reality, we commune with the divine and experience magical union with the universe and God. We travel up and down the elevator of life to reach our desired level of reality.

The Transcendent Church Model also establishes that we can bi-locate or occupy two levels at one time. Our physical body may be in the physical reality of the church on earth while at the same time, our mind or spiritual body may be in the metaphysical reality of the church in heaven; that's what happens when we pray, meditate and even sleep. We are constantly going back and forth from one reality to another; from one state of consciousness to another; up and down the elevator.

Furthermore, members of the church on earth are not the only ones who vacillate between levels of reality, so do the souls in heaven. Those in the Church Triumphant make regular appearances in the Church Militant to check in on loved ones. Our deceased family and friends sometimes turn the lights or appliances on and off and make occasional appearances to let us know they're around. Sometimes they contact us indirectly through a medium. Whichever way they choose, the spirit of Grandma or Uncle Bob can pop into physical reality for a quick visit and then return "home" to carry on with their lives in mystical reality.

When we seek to be more spiritual, it means we seek to spend more time in higher levels of reality. In order to achieve this goal, we jump on the elevator of life and stop at various floors to shop for spiritual merchandise. We buy religion, meditation, yoga, spiritual books, tapes and workshops; shopping, constantly shopping for the next guru, the next secret, the next set of steps, for manifesting our destiny, for the power of intention, for enlightenment. We travel up and down the elevator shopping for alternate realities, seeking new opportunities for spiritual growth. We have a hunger and yearning to explore our true nature and connection to God.

Whether in the physical world or the spirit world we are searching, constantly searching for the next stepping stone on our path. The searching never ends because the path never ends. We continue to learn and grow throughout our lives, our many incarnations, because we are infinite, eternal beings who cannot stop creating new stones for new paths for new adventures. We create, constantly create because that's who we are and that's what we do. No matter what our state of being, we are all co-creators in the great, universal (Catholic) church of God. The Transcendent Church Model demonstrates that there is scientific support for the age-old doctrine on the communion of saints and that we are all members of this infinite and eternal community, harmoniously working for the greater good of all.

Insight

"Conversion" is another term used to describe a "brain-shift," the sudden alteration of one's perception of reality. Saul's encounter with Jesus on the road to Damascus led to a total transformation of how he perceived life, as a result, how he lived his life. Saul had a "conversion" or "brain-shift;" he went from a muggle-state to a mystical-state of awareness.

Just My Opinion

Q: *Why are mystics considered "good" while mediums are considered "bad"?*
Q: *Where do I fit in; am I mystic or a medium; holy or evil?*

As co-creators in the universe, we make an endless number of things and put a label on each item. Labeling our creations helps us to make sense of the enormous amount of material we produce; it's part of the process. Labeling helps us to categorize and organize groups of similar things: clothes, furniture, cars, homes, stores, businesses. I don't know what I would do without my Dymo label maker to organize my files, pictures and even the leftovers in my refrigerator. To put labels on the things we create helps us to identify them. We know exactly what is in the box marked "photos"; we know exactly what we are buying when we purchase "hotdogs." Labels are useful; they have a purpose. When we are dealing with inanimate objects we created, they work very well.

Labels don't work well at all when we try to place them on something we did not create. Thus, when it comes to labeling human beings, the boxes get mixed up, the labels get on the wrong box, or they fall off completely. Some people get totally mislabeled, while others don't get labeled at all. And because we identify so closely with our labels, in the physical reality, some people think they're someone they're not, while others don't even know who they are.

What we don't create we can't truly or properly identify. Therefore, when it comes to people, labels tend not to be descriptions, but judgments. When people in authoritative positions create these labels we assume they are truths. People of power often create these false truths in order to control others. They label people in groups or categories in order to include those who agree with their ideals, to ensure their continued power, and exclude those who do not.

Padre Pio is just one example of someone who was mislabeled. Church authorities called him a "charlatan," because they could not understand his psychic abilities. He did not conform to their ideals, was seen as a threat, and therefore, excluded. The physical reality people misjudged the paranormal priest; the Vatican label maker was defective. Due to their lower level of consciousness, the Papal muggles did not recognize the mystic in their midst.

The Roman Catholic Church bars people from Holy Communion based on all sorts of labels: "Protestant," "unbaptized," "remarried," "practicing gay" and "excommunicated." From the point of view of those in physical reality, the exclusion philosophy makes sense because all people are perceived as separate individuals. However, as a result of these labels, instead of uniting the children of God, the muggle leaders separate and divide them.

From the point of view of the mystical reality exclusion does not make sense because all of creation is perceived as one; there are many parts but one body. To reject one person or group is to reject God and Jesus Christ ("Whatsoever you do to the least of my brothers, that you do unto me."). For this reason, organized religion does not make sense to highly spiritual people, like Jesus. There is a saying that describes this dilemma, "Religion divides, spirituality unites."

Jesus welcomed all to his table because his mystical mind could see no divisions among the people. Therefore, he did not label or judge others; he excluded no one. Christ was the great unifier; he taught people how to be more spiritual. Teachings from the mystical reality of Jesus Christ laid the foundation for Christianity. They were carried on by the Apostles, who also operated in this level of reality through the powers passed on from their Lord.

As it evolved, the church became more and more removed from this higher plane of consciousness. Muggle-minded individuals tried to organize, teach and make rules about Christ's mystical-based thoughts. The leaders often misinterpreted these teachings because they could not fully comprehend the concepts. As a result, instead of forming an all-inclusive religion based on love, they formed an exclusive religion based on fear. And instead of embracing supernatural experiences as further testimony of God's greatness, they were banned and seen as the work of the devil. This is the reason why religion no longer makes sense to those who have had a spiritual transformation, such as enlightenment.

Many of us have been Catholic since we were born, but as we grew spiritually, we also outgrew the narrow-minded thinking and often antiquated teachings of the Church. Despite this fact, countless of us remain in our religious communities because the fellowship and tradition means more to us than the rules of the faith. We can go to church on Sundays with our family and friends, and to nourish our souls the rest of the week, we can practice yoga, Reiki, meditation, take a shamanic journey, or even attend a psychic development class. Religion is only one part of our spiritual package; limiting ourselves to one belief system only limits our spiritual growth.

As we grow, both physically and spiritually, we find sometimes we are mediums, sometimes we are mystics, and sometimes we are just hard-working muggles trying to pay the bills and survive the day. For everything there is a season, a time to go to work, a time to go to church, a time to stay home with the kids, and a time to go to the local pub to watch Monday night football. We are not one-dimensional beings, but multi-dimensional; you can't put a blanket label on anyone.

So why are mystics considered "good" while mediums are considered "bad"? The answer depends on who's doing the labeling. Our church leaders have attached the label "bad" to mediums and "good" to mystics. If you're a muggle or a mystic you are welcomed and included in Roman Catholicism. If, on the other hand, you're a medium, you are suspect and excluded because it goes against the formal teachings of the church. In my opinion, muggles, mediums and mystics are all good people; they all serve God in their own way and are all members of the transcendent church.

I started my journey by asking "Where do I fit into this picture?" Again, the answer depends on the labels and who's doing the labeling. Some people call me a medium, to most I'm more like a muggle. To some I am a servant of God, and to others I'm the work of the devil. At the same time, I label myself a writer, counselor, parapsychologist, catholic, spiritualist, wife, sister and aunt. So who am I? I have come to realize that I am all of these things and none of them at the same time. In the physical reality these labels mean something, in the mystical reality they mean nothing. According to *A Course in Miracles*, "Only that which never changes is real." Therefore, my "real" identity, the only unchanging label I wear, is "Child of God."

The church and the communion of saints is made up of many people, with many labels, living in many realities; in God's house there are many mansions. At the same time, there is only one person, one reality, one church, one God, one body - and we are it. We are the mystic, the medium, the visionary, and the psychic; we are the priest and the parishioner. We are every sinner, every saint, every man, every woman, every child and every adult. We are every color, every nationality, every religion, and we speak every language. We are the communion of saints.

In the end, it matters not what state of the church you reside in or what level of reality you've been hanging out in. It matters not whether you're a mystic, a medium, or a muggle. When you come into the presence of that magnificent, all powerful, unconditional love and light, all philosophies, all labels, all sins disappear. You will drop to your knees and bow your head in an overwhelming sense of humility and awe. In that moment you will come to know you are but a small part of the great creator and realize, "I am not God, but God is me." We are separate but inseparable, different but the same. There is only one, great "I Am."

Summary

Padre Pio was not only a mystic, he was a gifted medium. Since childhood he practiced spiritualism by communicating with the angels and saints. He also demonstrated the phenomena of clairvoyance, prophecy, healing, levitation, bilocation and stigmata. Pio's paranormal abilities were a normal part of his mystical life. His perception of the world was much different than most because he had a higher level of consciousness and spirituality. What was unreal for most people was real for Padre Pio. This common occurrence of supernatural abilities in the lives of the saints and mystics forces us to question our own perceptions of the world and ask, "Could there be more than one reality?"

The Transcendent Church Model describes three levels of reality, which correspond to the three states of the church existing within the communion of saints. The "physical," "metaphysical" and "mystical" realities represent earth, purgatory and heaven. Physical reality is the lowest level of spirituality and mystical reality is the highest. As we progress from one level to another, so does our level of consciousness, our psychic awareness, and our spiritual gifts. This Model explains the differences and similarities between muggles (non-psychics), mediums and mystics.

In each of these levels of reality, information comes to us through the use of various senses. In some levels we use our physical senses and in others we use our sixth sense. Depending on what senses we use, our perception of individuality, time, space and spiritual gifts may vary:

> *In physical reality* we use our five physical senses to receive information about our world. We see ourselves as separate individuals and time is linear. Space is a barrier to receiving distant information; some sort of intermediary device, such as a phone or computer is needed. Spiritual gifts or psychic abilities are not a conscious part of one's life in physical reality. This is the level of the Church Militant (earth) and the reality of "muggles."

> *In metaphysical reality* we use our sixth sense to receive information about our world. Although we are individuals, at the same time there is only one cosmic consciousness in which we all share. In this reality "time" is sequential but past, present and future are illusions. Space is not a barrier for communication, which occurs directly; no medium is necessary. Spiritual gifts are an important, conscious part of one's life in metaphysical reality. This is the level of the Church Suffering (purgatory) and Church Triumphant (heaven), whose members are psychically gifted. It is the reality of mediums and mystics.

In the mystical reality we perceive ourselves as part of the whole and information comes directly from a "higher power" or God. Individuality, time and space are all illusions and unimportant, as are spiritual gifts. In mystical reality supernatural abilities are extraordinarily powerful; miracles occur. This is the level of the Church Triumphant (heaven), whose members include mystics.

In the Transcendent Church Model, mystics and mediums are similar in that they share the metaphysical reality. They both have a well developed sixth sense and are able to demonstrate psychic phenomena, which include prophecy, clairaudience and visions; examples of clairvoyance were cited for both. Mystics, however, are distinctly different, not only in their higher level of consciousness and spirituality, but also in the way they live their lives. This places mystics in a whole other class by themselves.

Mystics are people who devote their lives to God and spend much time in communion with Him. They enjoy a direct, intimate relationship with the divine, which is only found in the mystical reality. Because they experience a oneness with the universe, their view of the world is vastly different from those in the physical or metaphysical reality. The mystics' personal relationship with God is evident, not only in their paranormal abilities, but more importantly in their kind, compassionate, non-judgmental attitude towards all of His creatures. The virtuous way in which they live teaches us by example and points the way to heaven. Jesus, Padre Pio, Deacon Michael Mahoney, Father Patrick Mulligan, Father Richard McAlear and Father Dan O'Rourke are six people who exemplify the concept of a true mystic.

No matter what label we wear, mystic, medium, or muggle, The Transcendent Church Model shows us that we are all one in God's mystical reality; we are many parts of the one body of Christ. No one is excluded from the transcendent, universal (Catholic) church and no one should be excluded from our churches on earth either, for we are all members of the communion of saints.

Part III
We Practice the
Communion of Saints

Chapter 9

A Circle of Saints

"For where two or three are gathered together in my name, there I am in the midst of them."
(Matthew 18:20)

As Catholics, we "believe" in the communion of saints, therefore, we "practice" communion with the saints. Although talking with the deceased, also known as "spiritualism," is an ancient tradition, it is often considered a New Age or metaphysical topic. For this reason, those who are acquainted with works by mediums such as John Edward, James Van Praagh and Sylvia Brown, will find themselves in familiar territory while reading Part III. What may be unfamiliar is that this material is being presented to a Catholic audience in the context of the communion of saints.

In this chapter we will explore the methodology of spirit communication and learn how it was practiced in pre-Biblical, as well as Biblical times. We will delve into the rituals of the mysterious "school of prophets" and compare it to the traditions practiced today by looking at the Catholic Mass. In addition, a meditation exercise is provided to assist small Christian communities in starting their own school of prophets, for the purpose of contacting non-physical beings; this is called a "Circle of Saints." Let's begin by learning how to prepare ourselves, physically, mentally and spiritually in order to commune with the saints.

Good Vibrations

You may remember the lyrics to the 1966 song by the Beach Boys, "Good, good, good, good vibrations." The phrase was as common as LSD, which was the drug that provided Brian Wilson with the inspiration to write the tune. "Dropping acid" was just one method used to raise one's vibrations for the purpose of communicating with the afterlife. In his book, *Psychedelic Experience*, a translation of the *Tibetan Book of the Dead*, Timothy Leary combined ancient spirituality with modern-day drugs. The effects could produce a mystical experience; in the same way, peyote and psilocybin were used by Native Americans and Mexicans to contact spirits. Drugs can raise a person's level of vibration, thus, opening a gateway to super-consciousness and alternate levels of reality.

This elevated state of mind often results in heightened physical, as well as psychic, senses. For example, colors may appear abnormally vivid, distant sounds are unusually clear, and telepathic abilities are increased. The drug-induced culture of the 60's brought on a euphoria that led to the "free love" movement. "Tripping" made people feel fantastic because they had an elevated level of vibration; it gave them the sensation of being "high." The experience was often described as being in a "good vibration."

But what is meant by a person's "vibration"? Basic physics tells us that everything is made up of atoms vibrating at different rates. When the vibration is at a low speed or level, objects, as well as people, appear as a solid; for example, a table or Uncle Bob can be seen with our physical eyes. When the vibration is at an extremely high speed or level, objects and people do not appear to us at all; for example, hydrogen gas or Saint Francis; they cannot be seen with our physical eyes. Psychic medium, John Edward explains this phenomenon by using a helicopter as an example. When it is on a low speed of vibration we can see the individual blades, on high speed we cannot (Edward).

Spiritual forms can, however, be seen by our spiritual eyes, which is part of our sixth sense called "clairvoyance." In fact, the center of this extra sense is called the "third eye." People who are naturally psychic (mediums and mystics) vibrate at a higher level than those who are not (muggles); Jesus is one example. Christ could not only see and hear non-physical beings, he also had mastery over matter; for example, the materialization of loaves and fishes. These are indicators that his vibration was extremely elevated; his abilities equaled those of the spirit realm. Therefore, when we seek to be like Christ, we are seeking a higher level of vibration; consequently, we will be better able to access our sixth sense.

For those of us who are not naturally gifted with psychic ability, we can learn to increase our level of vibration until we reach the same frequency as those in spirit, then we can practice transcommunication. There are a number of ways, other than with illegal drugs, by which to achieve this. Taking care of our bodies through proper diet and exercise, avoiding negative people and situations, helping others, thinking positively, counting our blessings, praying and spending time with God in nature are all methods for raising our vibration. When our vibration is high, so is our level of energy. We even have a saying that describes this spiritual state, we say that people are in "high spirits" if they are cheerful and in good health.

Insight

In his book, *Power vs. Force*, David Hawkins explains how a person's energy level can be measured through the science of kinesiology. By using these same techniques, a person's vibration level can be measured as well.

A calibration of less than 200 is in the low range and causes weakness; it includes the mind states of shame, guilt, fear, anger and pride. A calibration of 200-600 is in the high range and provides strength; it includes the mind states of courage, acceptance, love, joy and peace. From 600-1000 is the level of enlightenment, which is where the great prophets, like Jesus, rank.

Likewise, there are many factors that can lower our vibration, such as illness, depression, anger, fear, resentment and guilt. When our vibration is low, so is our level of energy. We have a saying that describes this spiritual state also, we say that people are in "low spirits" when they are depressed or sick. Having good mental and physical health is important because it affects our spiritual health, or level of vibration. At the same time, good spiritual health, or high vibration enables us to maintain good mental and physical health; this is due to the mind/body/spirit connection. So the next time you're not feeling well, try raising your vibration.

One of the simplest and most effective ways to raise our vibration is through music. Singing, playing an instrument, listening to music, dancing to music, or even writing music lifts our spirits and raises our energy levels. Music has always played an important role in communicating with God and His holy spirits. We may not know this consciously, but the use of music in church services raises our vibration so we can practice communion with the saints. We do know, however, that music makes us feel good; the reason is because it raises our spirits.

Lastly, we can raise our vibration just by being with other people who have an elevated vibratory rate. For example, imagine being in the same room as the Dali Lama. His presence can affect everyone around him in a positive way because he is a highly spiritual person; he has a high vibration. In a similar manner, when we gather to pray to God and the saints, we are exposed to their extremely high energy. Christ said, "Wherever two or more are gathered in my name, there I am in the midst of them." (Matthew 18:20). When we call on Jesus, his presence also raises our vibration and lifts our spirits.

The ancient prophets knew that in order to communicate with the spirit world they needed to raise their vibration. They may not have called it that, and they may not have known the physics behind it, but they knew the methodology. Most likely they knew how to talk to God in the same way knew how to build pyramids and Stonehenge-type constructs; they were inspired or guided by spirits. By understanding how our vibration levels affect our ability to practice transcommunication, we can better understand the methods that may have been used to teach spiritualism and prophecy in an era long before the atom was discovered.

By understanding how spirit communication took place in ancient times, we can better understand how and why we practice similar techniques in Catholicism today. There are clues found in The Bible pointing to this connection. We know from Scripture that the practice of spiritualism took place in a formal, educational setting; let's take a closer look.

Insight

Eating meat lowers a person's vibration, which is why there are so many vegetarians along the spiritual path. A low vibration makes it more difficult to communicate with the saints. This is also why fasting has always been an important ritual for cleansing the body and preparing for soul work.

The School of Prophets: Old Testament

In Biblical times groups of people were taught how to communicate with the spirit world in what was called the "school of prophets." The scholars were considered "disciples," which is the Latin word for student. In the Old Testament there are a number of references to these schools, also called "colleges." Although little is known about them, what we do know is that the Bible first mentions the schools in connection with Samuel, who was the head of the school of prophets in Ramah. It was here that he anointed Saul the commander over the people of Israel. Samuel then sent Saul to Gibeah where he was met by a band of prophets and transformed during an ecstatic state:

> When they were going from there to Gibeah, a band of prophets met him, and the spirit of God rushed upon him, so that he joined them in their prophetic state. When all who had known him previously saw him in a prophetic state among the prophets, they said to one another, "What has happened to the son of Kish? Is Saul among the prophets?" And someone from the district added, "And who is their father?" Thus the proverb arose, 'Is Saul among the prophets?' (1 Samuel 10:10-13)

In the above passage, someone questioned the identity of the "Father," which is a direct reference to the school of prophets. Each school had a master teacher called "Father"; Samuel was the Father of his school in Ramah (Wilson).

A "band of prophets" was also called a "guild of prophets," which was an association made up of seers and diviners. And depending on which version of the Bible you read, this "prophetic state" that Saul entered is also called an "ecstatic state," a "trance," or described as "speaking in tongues" or "the spirit of God was upon them." Today parapsychologists call this altered state of consciousness "channeling," which is when God, an angel or a holy spirit, such as Jesus or a saint, speaks through another person who acts as a medium. In Saul's case it was the "spirit of God" who was speaking through him (Wilson).

In his book, *Prophecy and Society in Ancient Israel*, professor of Old Testament at Yale Divinity School, Robert Wilson, Ph.D. examines the history of prophets. He explains that the word "prophet" is derived from the Greek word *prophetes*, which means to "speak forth." It was first used in connection with the oracles of Apollo and Zeus and referred to the mediums who gave divine messages from the Gods. *Prophetes* was also the translation used for the Hebrew titles of "seer" and "messenger." And because their revelations often included information about forthcoming events, the word "prophecy" eventually became synonymous with predicting the future (Wilson, 23).

Prophets played a vital role throughout history. Because God's wisdom and knowledge was made known to them through direct revelation, they were divine messengers. They acted as negotiators, mediators, teachers, guides, directors, leaders and agents of social change. They were used as consultants to warriors by providing divine strategy for holy wars. Prophets were able to protect the people by divulging warnings of impending danger. They gave guidance to rulers by conveying information received from God. They anointed leaders by bestowing them with divine blessings. Most importantly, they taught others how to become prophets by offering instruction on how to see and hear God, as well as His holy messengers, or angels (Watchman).

In another Old Testament passage, the school of prophets is mentioned in connection with David. David went to Samuel's school to escape being killed by Saul. Saul sent messengers to arrest David but when they saw Samuel and his students in the midst of a "prophetic state," they too went into trance:

> When Saul was told that David was in the sheds near Ramah, he sent messengers to arrest David. But when they saw the band of prophets, presided over by Samuel, in a prophetic frenzy, they too fell into the prophetic state. Informed of this, Saul sent other messengers, who also fell into the prophetic state. For the third time Saul sent messengers, but they too fell into the prophetic state.
> (1 Samuel 19:18-21)

When the messengers did not return, Saul went himself to kill David, only to fall into a trance state as well. Samuel was in the midst of teaching his students a lesson on "prophesying" when Saul and his messengers barged in on the class. The prophets were in a trance because they were in the process of communicating with the spirit world. When the intruders saw what was going on they must have decided to join in on the class because they too went into a "prophetic state." When people are in trance, or channeling, they are often unaware of their surroundings because God or another spirit has taken possession of their bodies. That is why David was able to escape.

Insight

Music was used in the school of prophets to induce trance states for channeling, which is why the band of prophets in 1 Samuel 10 carried musical instruments. They played a harp, a lyre, a psaltery, a tambourine and a flute. The prophets were musicians because music was an integral part of spirit communication.
(Wilson)

In a third Scripture we learn about the school of prophets in connection with Elisha. Elisha had a "house of Prophets" in which his disciples or "sons of prophets" could live. In this way the students learned how to incorporate their prophetic ministry into a lifestyle of service to God. When the number of disciples grew too large, a bigger home needed to be built.

> The guild prophets once said to Elisha: "There is not enough room for us to continue to live here with you. Let us go to the Jordon, whereby getting one beam apiece we can build ourselves a place to live." "Go," Elisha said. (2 Kings 6:1-2)

The popularity of Elisha's school was a reflection of the times. Because so many people wanted to become a seer, there was a school of prophets in every major city, Ramah, Gilgal, Bethal, Jerusalem and Jericho to name a few. There were a large number of applicants to the schools because if you had a family member who was accepted it was considered a mark of divine favor (Graves & Graves).

In addition, in Biblical times, becoming a prophet was today's equivalent of becoming a movie star. Some of the most popular celebrities of the era included such greats as Isaiah, Jeremiah and Ezekial, as well as Samuel and Elisha. As a result of their training, the graduates of the school of prophets achieved great spiritual heights and became qualified as worthy instruments of God. They also became spiritual role models as they represented a level of holiness which others could learn to reach. These prophets were God's teachers, providing guidance for others who sought to walk the red carpet that led to the kingdom of heaven (Wilson).

The purpose of the school of prophets was to teach others how to see (clairvoyance) and hear (clairaudience) God and his angels by developing their spiritual gifts (psychic ability). Much like the heavenly angels, who are God's messengers in the church in heaven, the prophets were God's "earth angels" or messengers in the church on earth. Providing this sacred service as a medium was the most important part of the curriculum. In doing so, the disciples developed an unwavering trust and faith in the Almighty Father and learned to bring their hearts and souls in close communion with Him (Greber).

The schools of prophets were schools of ministry, much like today's seminaries. Students included people from all walks of life, such as musicians, minstrels, psalmists, carpenters, fishermen and servants of prophets. However, those who were naturally gifted with the ability to see and hear spirits were given priority (Watchman). These gifts were then further developed under the leadership of a highly respected master teacher; to be a student of such a prophet was a coveted position. The chosen disciples were called "sons of prophets" or "priests." The leader, or "Father," acted as a translator when anyone spoke in trance, or in tongues. Today's priests or "fathers" perform a similar service by interpreting the word of God as written in the Bible (Wilson).

The School of Prophets: New Testament

In The New Testament we learn about another one of God's teachers, Jesus of Nazareth. Jesus was the "Father" of his own school of prophets; his first student body was made up of twelve disciples. However, instead of taking classes in a building, his students traveled with him as they learned; they were much like today's missionaries or Peace Corps volunteers, who train in the field. And instead of the students seeking out a master teacher, the master teacher sought out the students.

One of the most important lessons Jesus taught his disciples, was how to communicate with others outside of the physical realm. When talking to God, Christ provided his students with the exact words to say:

> Our Father, who art in heaven, hallowed be thy name. Thy kingdom come. Thy will be done on earth, as it is in heaven. Give us this day, our daily bread and forgive us our debts, as we forgive are debtors. And lead us not into temptation, but deliver us from evil. For thine is the kingdom, and the power, and the glory, forever. Amen. (Matthew 6:9-13)

This code of communication became known as "The Lord's Prayer." Every Christian child learns this prayer for the purpose of invoking God; it became the basic tenet of our religion. Although it was not called a school of prophets, the ministry of Christ filled the same purpose, to bring people in communion with "Our Father" (Watchman).

After the Resurrection, each of Jesus' disciples started his own school of prophets by teaching their followers what Christ had taught them. Each school formed a group, which is much like a parish community of today. One of these followers was St. Paul, who started the biggest expansion of the Christian church by teaching people throughout the Roman Empire and the Mediterranean about Jesus' ministry. Paul became one of the most important and most influential "Fathers" of the church in early Christianity. He declared:

> If anyone thinks that he is a prophet or a spiritual person, he should recognize that what I am writing to you is a commandment of the Lord. If anyone does not acknowledge this, he is not acknowledged. So, [my] brothers, strive eagerly to prophesy, and do not forbid speaking in tongues, but everything must be done properly and in order (1 Corinthians 14:37-40).

During the course of his teaching, St. Paul noticed that not all prophets had the same gifts. Some had the gift of healing, some had the gift of miracles, some had the gift of prophecy, some had the gift of discerning spirits and some had the gift of speaking in tongues, while others had the gift of interpreting tongues (1 Corinthians 9-10). Paul pointed out:

> There are different kinds of spiritual gifts but the same Spirit; there are different forms of service but the same Lord; there are different workings but the same God who produces all of them in everyone." To each individual the manifestation of the Spirit is given for some benefit. (1 Corinthians 12:4-7)

Furthermore, St. Paul felt that the gifts were supposed to be used for the whole church. He advised, "So with yourselves: since you strive eagerly for spirits, seek to have an abundance of them for building up the church." (1 Corinthians 14:12).

In early Christianity, the most gifted prophets became the first bishops of the church. The church Fathers, Ambrose, Jerome, Augustine and Gregory the Great all had psychic abilities. Qualifications for the job were partly based on academic achievement; but more importantly, they were based on the prophet's ability to see and hear the world of spirits. This was essential in order to provide the community with the guidance they sought from God, His angels, the martyrs and the saints (Kelsey).

Although God may speak directly to anyone, He often spoke through the bishops because they were better able to communicate with Him. In accordance with St. Paul's decree, the bishops used their prophetic gifts for the benefit of the whole church; they became the mediums and spokespersons for the communion of saints.

Just a Fact

"Prophesying" is the word used in some Spiritualist churches to describe the practice of giving messages to the congregation from holy spirits; it is also called "channeling."

The Modus Operandi

Nothing is mentioned in the Bible about how the students in the school of prophets were taught or what types of classes they took. What was the methodology of communicating with God and the saints? By examining the rituals and practices in past and present religions, we can deduce much information about the school of prophets. For example, we know that even the ancient Egyptians communicated with the gods through sacred rituals, prayers, songs, the use of incense and holy oils. They even built great pyramids, not only to honor their deities, but as astrological instruments to communicate with the heavens. Most importantly, some sort of sacrifice had to be offered.

In Biblical times there were many competing religions, but they all sought guidance from non-physical beings. It is most likely that the school of prophets in the Old Testament was a combination of many of the spiritualistic practices of the time. This would include both the older polytheistic (pagan) religions, as well as the newer monotheistic belief system called Judaism. We know that sacrifices remained important because the Bible provides detailed descriptions of bulls, goats, lambs and doves being used in various ritual ceremonies. We also know that music was used in the school of prophets to induce trance states.

After the first century, the teachings of spirit communication continued to be handed down from generation to generation and have been preserved in religious practices and traditions around the world. Today, Judaism, Hinduism, Islam, Spiritualism, Christianity, Paganism, Voodooism and Native American religions all teach the secrets of communing with God or gods, as well as other heavenly beings. They each have their own interpretation and system by which to do so. We can therefore assume that many of these same secrets were taught and practiced in the school of prophets.

As mentioned earlier, the Christian version of the school of prophets began with the ministry of Jesus and his disciples. It culminated with the Last Supper and the ultimate sacrifice, in which Jesus became the Lamb of God. The ministry continued, however, with Peter as the succeeding Father, or first bishop, and a new generation of schools of prophets. Eventually these schools evolved to form the basic structure and liturgy of the Roman Catholic Mass as we know it today, including the commemoration of the Last Supper.

Essentially unchanged for two-thousand years, the Catholic Mass is a virtual time-capsule of the prophetic practices taught to the original twelve students of Christ. By taking a closer look at the rituals and traditions performed in Mass, in light of today's knowledge, we can decipher the secrets of yesterday's school of prophets and see how the early disciples practiced communion with the saints.

Mass and the School of Prophets

Q: *How do we "practice" the communion of saints;*
what is the methodology?

For many of us who were born and raised Catholics, we don't spend a lot of time pondering the meaning and origin of the events which make up the Mass. Most people may be surprised to learn that the Catholic Mass is like a school of prophets. In both types of gatherings, the participants practice a set of methods that are used for the purpose of communing with God, the angels, and the saints.

One of the methods used in both the school of prophets and today's Mass, to commune with the spirits, is to raise the vibration of the congregants. This is done through a combination of prayer, song and ancient rituals, such as burning candles and incense, ringing bells, performing the sign of the Cross and even offering a sacrifice. Furthermore, like the school of prophets, during Mass, congregants receive instruction based on knowledge from spiritual leaders of the past. In addition, they are inspired by the insights and messages, which are prophesied in the weekly homilies. We even call our priests "Father" because they are the master teachers of our individual parish communities or church-schools.

Many of the prayers said during Mass not only raise the vibration, but also summon the spirit world. As discussed in Chapter Four, these prayers include the invocation of the Holy Spirit, the invocation of the angels and saints, the Penitential Rite, the Responsorial Psalm, prayers for the dead, the Eucharistic prayers, the litany of saints, the memorial acclamation and the Great Amen. We even have statues of Jesus and our canonized saints to help us visualize and invoke them. Many spiritual beings accept the invitation to come to Mass. Every week our churches are full of angels, saints, as well as many of our deceased loved ones; although muggles may not see them, many mediums and mystics can.

The level of vibration reaches its peak during Mass when all the disciples of Christ join hands to sing the Lord's Prayer in unison. This prepares us for the culmination of the sacred event, becoming one with God by partaking in the sacrificial Body and Blood of Christ.

All the rituals we perform to commune with the spirits in heaven are extremely effective. At every Mass people from both the church in heaven and the church on earth are gathered together in one great communion of saints. As a result, our vibrations and our souls have been elevated to heavenly levels; we leave Mass in "higher spirits" than beforehand. The emotional memories of our Home in heaven have been awakened and we depart with renewed hope and a great sense of peace; we have been inspired (in-spirit).

For those who are inspired to spend even more time understanding and enjoying the communion of saints, we have many other types of schools of prophets. For our children there are Catholic primary schools and for our youth we have Catholic high schools. In the summer months Bible camps are offered. For adults we have Catholic colleges, Bible studies and small Christian Communities, as well as spiritual retreats. For the ones who want to devote their lives to Christ and become master teachers, or "Fathers," seminary schools are another alternative.

In all these educational systems, we learn prayers, songs, rituals and sacraments for the purpose of communicating with God and His world of spirits. We also learn and study about the life of Jesus so that we can become more Christ-like. Through this process of spiritual development we learn how to practice communion with the saints and how to be better servants of our heavenly Father. As a result, we become closer to God and we become a better person by helping to build the kingdom of heaven. For these reasons, we can logically conclude that the Roman Catholic Mass is not far removed from the original school of prophets. In a sense, we are all like the disciples of Samuel, Elisha and Jesus; we are all sons and daughters of prophets.

Insight

The rosary is a divination tool created for the purpose of invoking the Blessed Mother to ask for her intercessions. It was inspired by St. Dominic following a vision of the Virgin.

Children of the Catholic faith are taught the *Hail Mary*, along with the *Lord's Prayer*, at an early age so they can communicate with the Saint and with God.

A Circle of Saints

The following is an exercise, which was created especially for small Christian communities or any group of like-minded people, who want to learn more about their own spiritual abilities. Although the techniques may be new to you, as we have learned, they are ancient. The prayers are familiar because they are directly from the *Sacramentary*, which is the official guidebook for Mass.

Through prayers, rituals, songs and meditation, we will hold a circle of saints in our own little school of prophets. Like the Old Testament schools, the purpose of such a gathering is to bring your heart and soul into close communion with God and with the saints in the church in heaven.

If you do not already belong to a group, these instructions will aid in starting one. All you need is a handful of people who are willing to get in touch with their spiritual side. They must also be willing to check their fear, distrust, doubts and all other negativities at the door. These thoughts create disharmony and will obstruct the flow of energy or information from God and his holy spirits.

Circle of Saints Exercise

Part I: Preparation

Music: This exercise calls for two types of music; you may use whatever you have in your collection or download songs onto your iPod or computer to play for the group. First, you will need a selection of four, good-old-fashioned Catholic hymns. My suggestions are *On Eagle's Wings, All are Welcome, Deep Within* and *Make Me a Channel of Your Peace.* Secondly, find some nice, soothing meditation music, which will be conducive to a deep state of relaxation.

Meditation: There is a guided meditation provided at the end of the exercise, which may either be read to the group or pre-recorded to play during the ceremony.

Handouts: Each person should receive a copy of the ceremonial prayers to be recited, along with the words to the songs. You may even make a small booklet or Missalette.

The Circle: Place the chairs in a circle.

The Sacred Center: Place a small table in the middle of the circle and create an altar-like setting with the following items:
- A white table cloth, doily or covering
- A statue of Jesus
- A statue of the Blessed Mother and/ or other saints
- A Holy rosary
- A large white candle
- One smaller candle for each member of the circle; tea lights and votive candle holders work well.
- Incense to purify the area.
- A small bowl of holy water: this will be used for the blessing and will also help keep the air pure.

Part II: Opening the Circle

Stand

Opening Song: Raise the vibration and energy of the circle by singing a song. Play the music for *On Eagle's Wings* or choose your own.

Join hands: Gather around the altar and join hands. This configuration of bodies will help to raise the vibration of spiritual and psychic energy needed to facilitate communication with the saints.

Opening Prayer

Start with an opening prayer that includes:

Intention:
> **Group Leader:** "Father in Heaven, we ask only for the highest and best guidance for our spiritual growth."

Protection:
> **Group Leader:** "We surround our circle with the white light of God and Jesus Christ. We call on Michael, the warrior and archangel, and all the angels and saints in heaven. May their merits and prayers protect all of us who are gathered here for communion with the saints."

Blessing of the Circle:
> The group leader will dip his or her fingers in the bowl of holy water and sprinkle it around the group while saying the Invocation of the Holy Spirit:
> **Group Leader:** "God, we ask you to bless this circle and make it holy by the power of your spirit, in the name of our Lord and your son, Jesus Christ. The holy water reminds of us our baptism in Christ and eternal life."
> **All members:** Each person will dip his or her fingers in the holy water and perform the sign of the cross.

Lighting of the Candles:

Group Leader: "The large candle on the altar represents the Holy Spirit and Jesus, which we invite to our gathering here this day with the lighting of this candle (leader lights candle).

The smaller candles represent the spirit of a person who has passed. Each member of the circle will light one candle as a reminder that the light and love of our relationships are undying and can never be extinguished, as we are all one with the eternal, divine light."

All Members: Each person will light a candle in honor of a loved one in heaven. When finished, the group may sit down.

Part III: Invocation of Saints

Prayers of Invocation
Group Leader: "We believe in the Communion of Saints. We believe that we are worthy to share in eternal life and in fellowship with Mary, the virgin Mother of God, your apostles, martyrs, and all your saints, who have done your will throughout the ages and whose constant intercession we rely for help. May we praise in union with them and give you glory through your son, Jesus Christ."

Group Recites: "From age to age you gather a people to yourself, so that from east to west a perfect communion may be made to the glory of your name. Together we come to form the Body of Christ; we are many parts, but we are all one body."

In communion with the saints
Group Leader: "You have gathered us here, in a circle of saints, in fellowship with your Son, Jesus Christ, with the Virgin Mary, Mother of God and with all the saints. In that new world, where the fullness of your peace will be revealed, gather people of every race, language, and way of life to share in the one eternal life with Jesus Christ the Lord."

Group recites the Apostles' Creed:
I believe in God, the Father almighty,
Creator of heaven and earth;
and in Jesus Christ, His only Son, our Lord;
Who was conceived by the Holy Spirit;

born of the Virgin Mary;
suffered under Pontius Pilate,
was crucified, died and was buried.
He descended into hell;
the third day he rose again from the dead.
He ascended into heaven;
is seated at the right hand of God the Father Almighty;
from thence He shall come to judge the living and the dead.
I believe in the Holy Spirit,
the Holy Catholic Church,
the communion of saints,
the forgiveness of sins,
the resurrection of the body,
and the life everlasting.
Amen.

Song of Invocation: to raise the vibration.
Play the music for *All Are Welcome* or choose your own.

Part IV: Meditation

Sit

Meditation Prayer:

Group Leader: "Jesus, you are the Father of our gathering here tonight. We ask that you bring together all souls who would like to partake in our circle of saints. We only invite those who come with permission from our Almighty Father and who bring with them His light, love and wisdom."

Group Recites: "We ask the Holy Spirit to come upon us to open our spiritual eyes, ears and senses so that we may receive the prayers and intentions of our dearly departed, our angels, guides, Jesus, and all those who have come to celebrate this communion of saints."

Guided Meditation:

- Get into a comfortable position
- The group leader will play tranquil, instrumental music and read the meditation in a calm, soothing voice, or play pre-recording.
- Focus on a question or issue needed to be answered or just be

open to guidance.

Part V: Reflecting:

Group reflects on meditation while listening to *Deep Within* or another slow, peaceful song.

Participants may use this time to write down any messages and images received.

Part VI: Sharing

Group Participation: One at a time, go around the circle and give each person the opportunity to share the information he or she received during the meditation. The messages may be extremely personal and should be treated delicately and with respect. Confidentiality should be expected by all members; what happens in circle, stays in circle.

Part VII: Closing

Prayers for the Dead:

Group Leader: "Remember Lord, our brothers and sisters who have gone to their rest before us, those marked with the sign of faith and with the hope of rising again. We ask you to bring them and all the departed in the light of your presence, especially those for whom we now pray. May these, and all who sleep in Christ, find light, happiness and peace." (Individuals may state the names of their loved ones to be prayed for).

Group Recites: "Father, when our pilgrimage on earth is complete, welcome us into your heavenly home, where we shall dwell with you forever. There, with Mary, the Virgin Mother of God, with the apostles, the martyrs, and all the saints, we shall praise you and give you glory through Jesus Christ, your Son."

Closing Prayer

Stand

Group Leader: "Father, you give us guidance from heaven. By our sharing in this mystery, teach us to judge wisely the things of earth and to love the things of heaven. May its promise and hope guide our way on earth. Our circle is closed, may you go in peace."

Group Recites: "Thanks be to God. May almighty God bless us, in the name of the Father, and the Son, and the Holy Spirit (perform sign of the cross); Amen.

Closing Song: Sing *Make Me a Channel of Your Peace* or chose your own hymn. After the song, one at a time, each person will blow out his or her candle and take it home as a keepsake in memory of a loved one in heaven.

Circle of Saints Guided Meditation

You may think of a particular loved one with whom you would like to communicate or just be open to guidance you may receive from Jesus, the angels, the saints, or God.

Close your eyes, relax your shoulders, and inhale a long, slow deep breath to the count of five. Hold that breath for a second and then slowly exhale to the count of five; one, two, three, four, five. Inhale again and repeat; focus on your breathing.

Now, visualize a ball of healing, white light on the back of your neck. Focus on relaxing all the muscles in your neck. The ball of light then moves down to your shoulders; relax these muscles and continue down to the chest, abdomen, legs and feet. Continue breathing deeply and slowly, until you release all tension and are totally and completely relaxed.

Imagine yourself walking down a spiral staircase and as you descend further and further down the stairs you will go deeper and deeper into relaxation. Continue walking slowly, down, down, down, going deeper and deeper, becoming more and more relaxed.

When you are in a deep state of relaxation you will notice a door at the bottom of the staircase. Open the door and find yourself in a beautiful field of wildflowers. Across the field, a short distance away, you see a huge, brick wall with a large, wooden door in the middle of it. Cross the field and stand before the door; there is a sign above it that says, "Welcome to my secret garden."

As you open the door you step into the most wondrous place you have ever seen. Surrounded by flowering bushes, trees and plants, you feel the warmth of the bright sun and notice an amazingly beautiful blue sky, with several puffy white clouds that look like angels. Before you is a bright yellow path made of golden bricks. As you stroll down the path, you take in the beauty and peace of all that is surrounding you.

You notice the various colors and types of flowers and smell their rich fragrance. Feel a gentle breeze blow through your hair and listen to the birds singing in the trees and to the soothing sound of crickets. As you continue on your path you also hear the sound of a running stream nearby and walk towards it. You observe a small, comfortable looking bench just a short distance away.

Go over to the bench, sit on it. Take in the beautiful sights and sounds around you and feel a sense of delight and contentment. Notice that in this place you feel safe and sound, but most of all you feel a profound sense of peace, peace, peace.

As you gaze at your surroundings, you notice someone approaching you. It may be an angel, a spirit guide, or a loved one. As the being gets closer you can clearly sense what he or she looks like. You are aware if it's male or female; notice what kind of clothes the person is wearing, if there are wings, the length of the hair and the color of the person's hair and skin. You are happy and excited as you sense a familiarity with this being; you may even recognize who it is.

As the spirit approaches you, his or her name is conveyed. You instantly feel a strong connection. Greet this person with a big hug or handshake, whatever way you normally would, and spend a moment basking in the reunion.

You are then told that there is a message especially for you. Sit quietly for several minutes while you absorb all that is being conveyed to you.

After the message is given you may try asking a question if you need guidance on a certain situation; patiently wait for a response. When your conversation is finished, thank this spirit for contacting you and express your desire for on-going communication. Make an agreement to return to this special place, this secret garden, whenever you need to talk.

When you are ready, say goodbye and walk back down the golden path in the direction from which you came. Go through the big wooden door and find yourself in the field of wildflowers. Cross the field and return to the doorway that leads to the spiral staircase.

Open the door and slowly ascend the stairs. With each step you will become more and more aware of your body, and more aware of your surroundings. Slowly walk up the stairs higher and higher; notice that you can feel your hands, your feet, and the chair you are sitting in. When you reach the top of the stairs rest a few moments and recall any messages you received.

Slowly open your eyes and take a minute to reflect on your experience. You may want to make notes in a journal while it is fresh in your mind. Afterwards, you may share it with the rest of the group.

Just My Opinion

In Biblical times the word of spirit was of major importance and the word of man was minor. Life revolved around God, the gods, the angels and saints; most people were focused on the spiritual realms. They put their trust and faith in a higher power and were directed by this Supreme Being through the prophets. When people are in close communion with the Divine, they operate on a high level of vibration; peace, love, joy and mystical consciousness develop. Spiritual riches, such as compassion, charity and relationships are most important. In the day when people's lives were entwined with the heavens, their spirits soared like an eagle and they flew with a purpose.

Today the word of man is of major importance and the word of spirit is minor. Our life revolves around technology, consumerism and entertainment; most people are focused on the physical realm. We put all of our trust and faith in science and direct our lives as spoken by the experts. When we are estranged from the Divine we operate at a low level of vibration; fear, abuse, wars, as well as physical and mental illness, develop. Worldly riches such as money, power and fame are most important. In a time when we have been banned from participating in the heavenly realms, our spirits have become flightless birds, who have lost a reason to fly.

In Biblical times and early Christianity, disciples were led by "Fathers," who were gifted mediums. Not only could they see and hear God and the saints, they taught others how to do the same. When people learned how to communicate with spirits they also learned how to take guidance from these non-physical beings. They were directly connected to the divine source and were able to think for themselves and to explore the universe and their unlimited abilities. Believers were free to search for the truth in whatever direction they wanted; those who trusted in Spirit would always find their way and always have a place in the community.

Somewhere along the line this critical teaching was abandoned. Today our churches are led by priests, who are mostly muggles. They teach people how to *talk* to God and the saints, but not how to *see* and *hear* them. As a result, most no longer take direction from the spirit world, but from church leaders who tell them what to think, say, and do, without question. Christians have gone astray from their connection with the higher powers, the universe is inaccessible, and we have become limited in our abilities. Believers today are told what the truth is and that they must all follow the same direction, if not they will become lost and excluded from the community.

By practicing a Circle of Saints we can once again learn how to soar like an eagle by reconnecting with people of the church in heaven.

These holy spirits are ready and willing to help us; all we need do is ask. If we can learn how to quiet our minds and listen, we will open a door that allows us to have conversations not only with God, but with Grandma as well; the key to this door is our sixth sense. Those who have lost their faith will find renewed hope in spiritual abilities they never knew they had. What was once thought impossible becomes probable; what was once without meaning has purpose.

Summary

Everything in the universe is made up of atoms, which vibrate at different rates. In the physical world objects and people vibrate at a low rate and therefore appear solid. In the spirit world, objects and people vibrate at a high rate and therefore are invisible to us. In order for us to communicate with non-physical beings, we need to increase our level of vibration.

We can raise our vibration through proper diet, exercise, prayer, meditation, music, and by spending time with nature and positive people. When we have a high vibration, we also have high energy, at the same time we have better physical, mental, and spiritual health.

In the Old Testament, prophets learned to raise their vibration so they could practice spiritualism by talking with God, His holy spirits and with the saints. Schools were organized for the purpose of teaching others how to communicate with, or channel, these spirits. Samuel and Elisha were just two of the many master teachers or "Fathers," who led these educational programs; they were called "schools of prophets." In the New Testament, Jesus had his own "school of prophets" in which he taught his disciples about his ministry and how to communicate with the heavens.

Prophets played a vital role in Biblical times because people lived their lives as directed by God and the spirits. For this reason, the first bishops and the Fathers of the Catholic Church were gifted with mediumistic abilities. And like the prophets before them, they used their gifts for the benefit of everyone in their community.

Although we don't know the exact methods used for spirit communication in the school of prophets, we can make reasonable assumptions by combining our current scientific knowledge with the knowledge of religious practices of the past and present. It is most likely that a mixture of prayer, meditation, rituals, music and sacrifice were used to practice spiritualism. These same practices are found in the Roman Catholic Mass for the purpose of communing with God, the angels and the saints in heaven. In addition, the tradition of passing this knowledge to others is carried on in the Catholic educational system and seminary schools.

It is my hope and prayer to start a new tradition in Catholicism called "The Circle of Saints." This is a meditation exercise designed to help introduce people to their spiritual gifts and develop them by practicing communion with the saints. When the faithful learn to listen to the holy ones, their hearts and souls will grow closer to God and help build the kingdom of heaven.

Chapter 10
Talking to God and Grandma
Maintaining Relationships
with Loved Ones in Spirit

"Don't treat your loved ones as if they were dead!"
(Grace)

The title of this chapter is from the first workshop I wrote to educate people about maintaining relationships with loved ones who have crossed over. Not only is it important to keep these bonds alive, there are also many advantages. In an era when the media is bombarding us with books and shows on ghosts, angels, mediums and the afterlife, we seek to understand how and why spirit communication fits into the daily life and practice of Catholicism.

Because I always like to begin my workshops with a story, this chapter will be no exception. The following account comes from the question I get asked most frequently, "How did you get interested in the supernatural and the field of parapsychology?" That's easy, I reply, "I grew up in a haunted house; I guess it was my destiny"; let me explain:

My Strange Story

Since childhood, non-physical beings were a part of my life. The type of spirits I grew up with, however, were not pleasant. You see, long before we lived in the four-story, Adams Family-like, Victorian house, it was a nursing home, of sorts. The former owner, my grandmother, used to take in elderly borders and care for them. But in an era before handicap accessible housing and adult protective services, 83 Big Tree Street became their prison. After death, it became their haunting grounds, and it became my personal house of horror.

Over the years, many people died in that home; the exact number is uncertain. What is certain is one of my earliest childhood memories of a box of old pictures my brothers found in the attic; pictures of dead people. The corpses were laid out on a table in their finest clothes, in what was our present-day dining room. Evidently, the abandoned seniors not only lived and died in our house, but were also put on display for a makeshift funeral, if there was anyone who cared enough to come. I learned much later in life that it was customary in the old days to take photos of the dead. In doing so, the person's spirit was captured on film, which prevented the devil from taking it.

I was terrified of being alone in our home. It was especially scary each time I had to travel down the long, creepy, unlit hallway to my bedroom on the second floor. Part of this journey included having to pass by the attic door. The attic was ground-zero for ghosts, therefore, the door was like a portal to the dark side; it was a vulnerable and frightening area. Consequently, I always sprinted to the safety of my room.

As the second to the youngest of six children, I did not know it wasn't normal to have ghosts. I did not know that it wasn't normal to hear heavy footsteps tromping up the stairs, only to stop in mid-ascent. I did not know it wasn't normal to hear water running in the bathroom late at night, when I knew everyone else was sleeping. I did not know that it was unusual to be awakened by the distinct sound of a ping-pong ball bouncing back and forth on the game table in the vacant attic.

The worst experience, however, was waking up paralyzed with an invisible entity pinning me down in my bed with such force I couldn't move and could hardly breathe. I was so gripped with shock and terror I couldn't even manage to scream. This happened on a number of occasions, not only to me, but to my siblings and friends, as well. Although all of these unexplainable occurrences were "normal," they never ceased to frighten me. To this day, I still have nightmares about the home I grew up in.

The only thing stranger than living in a haunted house, is living with seven other family members who delighted in taking advantage of the situation to play some rather incredible practical jokes. The house was rigged with many wires and extension cords for the purpose of creating the illusion of ghostly activity. It became an on-going competition as we tried to top one another in scare tactics. It seemed we took turns gaining up on each other, depending on who was the focus of being picked-on that week. Over the years, I was scared out of my wits hundreds of times. The only way I could tell for sure whether or not it was a real ghost was if the incident was followed by a cackling sound in another part of the house.

One time I walked into my bedroom and the radio, TV, and all the lights suddenly went on by themselves. Frozen in utter terror for several seconds, I then burst out of the room as fast as I could. I bolted down the hallway and two flights of stairs to the safety of the living room. That's when I heard my brother Terry laughing hysterically from a distant corner of the house; he got me.

On another occasion, we decided to get back at Terry, who not only didn't believe in ghosts, but was the number one trickster in the family. One night, my brother, Pat, along with two neighborhood friends, took Terry up to the attic to prove he was wrong about the poltergeists. At the same time, I was in one of the bedrooms below with two fishing lines that ran up through the ceiling to the floor above. One line was connected to a rocking chair and the other to a baby stroller, which were located in a darkened corner of the attic.

When the four boys reached the center of the attic, I pulled the first line on cue and the rocking chair appeared to move by itself. Before Terry had a chance to get wise to the prank, I pulled the second line with all my might, which made the baby stroller shoot across the attic floor like it was possessed. The only thing that traveled faster than the stroller was Terry, leaping down the attic stairs with such speed and panic that he smashed into the wall at the bottom. He didn't stop until he leapt down another flight of stairs in a single bound, crash landing into the kitchen.

As the boys in the attic were muffling their hysterical laughter, the rest of us managed to hide our amusement by acting scared ourselves; we wanted Terry to think it was a real ghost. We all let him squirm in petrified jumpiness for days before confessing to the trick; Catholic guilt finally won out. It wasn't until years later that I realized what a mischievously demented family I had.

Because we lived in a haunted house, Halloween was the biggest holiday in our family. We spent weeks prior to the event decorating the outside of the home and rigging up wires and props in the yard so we could frighten the neighborhood. The front lawn was converted into a grave yard, complete with a full-sized coffin. We took turns lying in the casket, pretending to be a dummy so that we could jump up at just the right moment to scare the little kids; we delighted in hearing them scream. With plenty of disembodied parts, fake blood, manmade fog and loud, scary music, each year was a scene straight out of *Night of the Living Dead*.

I'll never forget the year Mom spent hours arranging a scene on a kid-sized picnic table to add her own touch of terror. She set the table with four dinner plates, on which she placed bloody arms, legs, and a decapitated head. My devoutly Catholic, saint of a mother finished the horror scene by propping up a leaf-stuffed dummy with a fork in his hand; she was so proud of her creepy creation. Everyone in the family participated in the fun, and as a result of our hard work and deranged imaginations, the haunted house on Big Tree Street gained quite a reputation over the years; we had over a thousand trick or treaters annually.

Due to this somewhat bizarre childhood, I became quite fascinated with ghosts and anything paranormal. When I was a college student at the State University of Geneseo, I was delighted to find a class offered in parapsychology; it was another step in a seemingly natural progression. Taking a more scientific approach to the matter only increased my thirst for knowledge on the supernatural. Because a degree in parapsychology was not an option in 1980, I did the next best thing and received a BA in psychology. I was primarily self-taught in paranormal studies by devoting years of reading and research to the subject.

It wasn't until the after-death visitation from my mother in 2000 that I experienced a positive encounter with someone not of this world. Prior to this event, I felt nothing but fear towards spirits; afterwards, I knew what it was like to feel love towards them. For the first time I was deeply connected to someone who had crossed over. In the years that followed I experienced the love of many souls, who were deceased family members of clients I counseled. During my sessions, spirits often came through wanting me to convey this affection to their grieving spouses, siblings, parents and friends, and to let them know they were still a part of their lives.

After several years of counseling people who have had after-death communications from loved ones, I developed a workshop to teach interested groups more about the subject. I wanted to instruct the general public on how to maintain relationships with those who had died. Because it helped me so much, I wanted to teach others about the importance of keeping the love bonds alive and how it could aid in the grieving process.

It became my goal to teach this class throughout the country so people will not be afraid to talk about their supernatural encounters with their dearly departed. Because of the obstacles I encountered in the Roman Catholic Church, I felt it especially important to educate leaders, as well as lay people, in the Catholic community. Unfortunately, due to much ignorance and fear about the subject, I have yet to be given this opportunity. It became clear to me that much education had to be done first, which is why this book was written.

Spirit communication, in the context of the communion of saints, is a practice to be respected, not ridiculed. It is my hope that love, compassion and understanding for those who are grieving will win out in the end. When we understand how we can have a relationship with our Father in heaven, then we can understand how we can also have a relationship with Grandma in heaven.

God, the Saints and Grandma

Have you ever been so angry at God that you told him so by using every expletive you could think of? Have you ever been so grateful to God that you told him so by thanking Him profusely? If so, whether good or bad, you have developed a relationship with our heavenly Father. When we pray or yell at God, it matters not that we can't physically see or hear Him, we have faith that He is there for us. We don't question whether or not our creator is listening, we trust that He is. We trust our Father in heaven the same way that we trust a close family member.

Many of us have a personal relationship with Jesus, Mother Mary, or one of the canonized saints. We pray to them for guidance and often ask for favors. We ask St. Christopher to protect us in our travels, we ask St. Anthony to help us find our lost keys, and we ask Jesus to give us strength in difficult times. Throughout the writing of this book I kept a picture of St. John, the patron saint of writers, next to my computer; I counted on his help.

On our many family road trips when I was a youngster, whenever Dad got caught driving in hazardous weather, my mother never failed to lead us kids in praying the rosary. We trusted in the Virgin Mary to protect us countless times over the years; she always did. To this day, I break out in a Hail Mary whenever I'm driving on icy roads during a snow storm. I have faith that the Blessed Mother is there for me because of my personal relationship with her.

In the same way we talk or pray to God, Jesus and the saints, we can talk or pray to our deceased family and friends. If we can have a relationship with God and the saints, then why not have a relationship with Grandma in heaven? Don't ignore your family and friends just because they left this earth plane; they are still very much alive. This is what the communion of saints is all about, the interrelationship of church members, no matter what level in which they reside. So don't treat your loved ones as if they were dead.

In a story featured in *The Catholic Courier*, Bishop Matthew Clark of Rochester, NY discussed the relationship he has with his deceased father. The November article, *Special Ways to Pray for the Dead*, was written in honor of All Saints Day and All Souls Day.

> I do believe most deeply that those who are transformed in Christ and live fully in the communion of saints do not lose interest in those they have left behind. Rather, my conviction is that we become more deeply and ardently a focus of their attention, support, love and prayer. So today, in a special way, I ask my dad in peace and confidence to hold me close in his prayer and his affection. I even may be so bold as to ask him to help me with some of the specific concerns and questions that seem burdensome to me just now. (2)

Clark not only acknowledges his father, but also prays to him for help and guidance. The bishop's actions tell us that communication with the dead does not go against Catholic teaching. Talking with Grandma is no different than talking with God or the canonized saints; we are all members of the transcendent church.

Just a Fact

All Saints Day, which is November 1, is to honor all the saints in heaven. All Soul's Day, which is November 2, is to honor all others who have died, particularly those who passed away within the last year. The entire month of November is dedicated to all people in heaven and purgatory, especially those who have no one else to pray for them, which include the homeless, orphans and the unborn.

A Changed Relationship

Just because a friend moves away, we don't end the relationship; we keep in touch by phone or e-mail. Just because a family member loses the ability to hear or see, we don't stop associating with them; we learn to communicate by sign language or Braille. When the circumstances of our lives change, often our relationships with the people around us change as well. We may need to find alternate ways to continue giving and receiving the love and kindness which has fostered the kinships we developed. Just because a loved one has re-located or has become disabled, does not mean that they are no longer part of our lives. The ties have not been cut, they have merely changed.

In the same way, when loved ones die, the relationships do not end, they are merely different. When friends move to another dimension it does not mean that they cease to exist. Just because we may not be able to see or hear them, it does not mean they are not there; it means that we, in effect, have become the disabled ones. We may be blind and deaf to our friends in spirit; however, we can continue the relationships by exploring alternate means of communication.

Whether a loved one moves across the world or across the universe, it's up to us to keep the connection alive by staying in contact. If we stop communicating the relationship will eventually die out. If we continue to stay in touch, the bonds may remain strong, even though many years may pass without physical contact. For example, a veteran might bump into an old war buddy after twenty years without actually seeing him; as a result, the friendship may pick up again and continue with renewed interest. Likewise, when we reunite with our family and friends in heaven, our relationships will continue where we left off. We don't have to wait until we die to do so.

The Importance of After-Death Relationships

Why is maintaining a relationship with loved ones in spirit significant? In her book, *The Afterlife Connection*, psychotherapist Jane Greer, Ph.D. asserts that through continued communication we strengthen the psychological bonds; this in turn creates a strong psychic bond. Having a psychic bond with our spirit friends will help us stay connected and open the channels for further communication. Once we've established transdimensional relationships, within the communion of saints, their importance in our lives becomes clear. Consider the following results:

Provides safety and protection
Having a personal relationship with a deceased family or friend is like having an additional guardian angel. He or she can help us feel safe and protected in any situation. For example, we can call on this person to be with us when our car breaks down, when we get lost in the woods, or trapped in an airport overnight; we can be assured we are being watched over. Help from our spirit friend may come in the form of another traveler who goes out of their way to assist us. We can feel secure in the knowledge that there is always someone guarding over us.

Eases loneliness
Knowing our loved ones in spirit are around helps to lessen the feelings of loneliness or abandonment. It's especially difficult for elderly people who have lost a long-time spouse. Because their

children may have families of their own, the widowed parent may be suddenly faced with having to live all alone. When after-death relationships continue, there is a much greater chance for the survivor to receive a "sign" from the partner in spirit. Signs bring enormous comfort during times of tremendous despair and remind us that we are not alone.

Lessens fear of death

Staying connected with heavenly friends can help reduce the fear and anxiety associated with death. When we continue to make them part of our life, we get used to our deceased relatives hanging around; as a result, we no longer fear the dead. We begin to fully understand the illusion of death when we fully understand that our loved ones are still very much alive. It may actually give us a reason to look forward to death and to the time when we can re-join them.

Reminds us of reuniting

When we maintain our relationships with spiritual friends, it reminds us that we will one day be reunited. The Catholic funeral rite states, "Death does not unravel the ties that bind us in life." Remembering our eternal status as one of God's children brings comfort during a time of great sorrow. We can be confident that the relationships we sustained during life will continue after life as well.

Accelerates the grieving process

We cannot and should not avoid the grieving process. Grief is the body's physical and emotional defense mechanism; it allows us to cope with our loss. However, the length of time we grieve can be cut down considerably, when we continue relationships with those who have crossed over. It helps us change the way we look at death and moves us past the idea that that someone is "gone forever." We know our loved ones are still with us, just not physically. Once we get used to the physical loss, we can continue with spiritual and emotional connections. This active participation in relationships beyond death helps fill a void in our life; consequently, reducing the length of grieving time.

Promotes healing and gives hope

When we acknowledge the presence of loved ones in spirit, it helps us heal by making it easier to carry on with our lives. Big events, such as weddings and birthdays become more bearable when we know our friends are with us in spirit. We think of these angels during special occasions and know they are celebrating right along with us. We may even receive a "sign" from them to confirm they are watching over us. Our loved ones on the otherside give us hope for a future that can be filled with joy, despite their physical absence.

Bishop Matthew Clark has had first-hand experience with the healing powers of love bonds beyond death. In another quote from his All Saints Day article in the *Catholic Courier*, the Bishop describes how maintaining a relationship with his father has been helpful to him:

> This kind of November prayer has become more important to me as my own years grow in number. It is healing. It helps to put life's ups and downs in a broad and helpful perspective. It enhances self-understanding and understanding of others. I am glad to have caught up a lot with my dad – in part because I am now close to the age he had achieved when the Lord called him home. (2)

Clark understands the therapeutic effects of having an on-going connection with his father. Furthermore, he acknowledges that this relationship is even more significant, now that he is approaching his final years on earth.

Preserving our bonds beyond death is important, not only for us, but for our loved ones in heaven and purgatory as well. Deacon Michael Mahoney affirms this belief; he insists, "It is natural to continue important relationships so that the ties that bind us in life don't unravel in death; our sense of relatedness continues, even in heaven" (Grace, 7). Mahoney suggests that our deceased family and friends want to remain in our lives just as much as we want them to remain. This transdimensional partnership is a significant factor in the communion of saints doctrine.

The Advantages of After-Death Relationships

Besides the importance of continuing relationships beyond death, there are several benefits as well. The following are a few advantages:

Improves relationships

We can actually become closer to a particular person after they die, than we were beforehand. There are many life scenarios that put a strain on relationships, such as illness, divorce, physical or emotional distance and lack of quality time together due to a busy lifestyle. These barriers to positive and healthy relationships are no longer a problem for those on the otherside. We can now freely communicate with our loved ones and can spend all the time we want sharing our thoughts and feelings with them. The more time we make for our relationships, the stronger they will become, whether it's before or after death.

Another way in which relationships can improve after death is in cases where the rapport was not good beforehand. For those who had irreconcilable differences with a parent, spouse, or sibling who died, there is hope for reconciliation. Resolving differences is especially important because of the severe amount of guilt, which the survivor may often experience. Mental health issues, such as major depression and post-traumatic stress disorder can cause life-long trauma or psychosis. By communicating feelings, that were left unstated, healing and forgiveness can occur.

Insight

In her book, *The Afterlife Connection*, Jane Greer describes an exercise called "Eternal Dialog," which assists people with after-death reconciliation. The task involves venting negative emotions by writing down grievances and by sharing feelings of anger, resentment, and insecurity held towards the deceased. A positive change in the relationship can occur when forgiveness is extended to both parties involved.

Improves communication

Sometimes we cannot communicate with loved ones prior to death due to a disability, severe dementia or unconsciousness. Perhaps there was no communication because the loved one was missing, homeless, or had an unknown address. Maybe we just lost touch with a sibling or friend and then suddenly found out they had died. In such cases, communication can be restored after death.

Loved ones in spiritual bodies no longer have a physical disability or illness preventing them from communicating. In addition, we know their location is with God, and often with us, wherever we may be. If we want to rekindle a friendship that has waned over the years, we can do so with a simple prayer. For many, where communication before death was impossible or difficult, after death it becomes not only possible, but easy.

Increased accessibility; more convenient

We don't often spend as much time with others as we would like because of conflicting schedules, the distance between us, cell phone restrictions, or just waiting for the right mood. None of these issues comes into play when trying to spend time with someone who has crossed over. We don't need to wait until they're home (they already are), we don't need to make an appointment, and we don't have to wait until they're in a good frame of mind (living in heaven puts them there). We can talk to our spiritual friends on our schedule and can meet wherever we want. Whether we're flying in a plane or sitting around a campfire, the time and place is not a concern; whatever is convenient. Our family and friends always delight in hearing from us.

Provides a personal guardian angel

As Catholics, we were brought up with the idea that we each have a guardian angel. This ethereal being will protect us and guide us throughout our time here on earth. But what do we know about our invisible protector? Most don't even know the name of their assigned angel. How connected do we feel to someone we have never seen or met?

When a loved one dies we can take comfort in knowing that he or she will act as a guardian angel to us. We now have a divine connection to someone we know personally. We not only know their name but also their favorite things: favorite pastimes, food, sports teams, authors, movies, TV shows, actors, singers, etc. We also know what they hated, their pet peeves, and the nuances that made them unique. We have a relationship with someone in heaven we know intimately. Therefore, we feel much more protected and guided by an angel we have actually seen, talked to and shared our life with.

Improves mental health

Having a personal guardian angel is like having a psychiatrist at your disposal; it's very therapeutic. You can spend as much time as you want sharing your feelings, and there is no bill afterwards. Confessing your sins or expressing your latest joys to someone who will listen without interruption or judgment, can be extremely cathartic. If forgiveness or after-death reconciliation occurs, the survivor can be freed from feelings of guilt or sorrow; thus, allowing for emotional healing and peace of mind.

Let's Practice

When someone moves out of their body, the biggest change we have to get used to is not being able to physically see or touch the person. However, it does not mean that we will never see or touch that person again; because we are eternal, so are our relationships. During the time of separation we can find new ways to keep our relationship alive. We can learn to adjust to someone's death by adjusting the way we communicate.

The following are four suggestions for practicing communion with the saints. For the beginner, or for muggles, these methods can involve one-way communication, from physical to non-physical beings. For those who are more advanced, two-way communication can be tried through use of the sixth sense, simply quiet the mind and listen for any responses you may receive. An exercise accompanies each method so the reader may become acquainted with the techniques. Some may be very familiar while others may be new to you. At first it may seem strange or awkward to converse with your deceased loved ones, but with practice you will become more comfortable and eventually it will become second nature.

I. Prayer

The first method of communicating with spirits is very familiar to most people; it's called "prayer." Just as we trust that God can hear our prayers, we can trust that our friends, who are with God, can hear our prayers to them also. We can ask our family members for guidance or help in the same way we ask God. Similarly, we can pray to one of the canonized saints in heaven. Whether we pray to God, St. Anthony, or Grandma, it works the same way. We are using our telepathic or psychic ability to communicate with other members in the transcendent church (transcommunication). Although this practice of sharing our thoughts may be one-way, don't be surprised if you get a response; it works very well.

Prayer Exercise

Preparation:
- Think of a loved one you would like to talk to.

- Find a quiet, comfortable place or somewhere you feel connected to that person.

- Put on some soft, instrumental music to help relax you.

- Think of something in particular you would like to share with that person. It may be something you are excited about or something that is troubling you. Ask for guidance on an issue concerning you.

- Ask for protection by saying, "I am protected from negative forces by surrounding myself   with the white light of God and Jesus Christ."

Invocation:
- Silently state the person's name three times to get his or her attention. For example, "I pray to (name), I pray to (name), I pray

to (name); I value our relationship and would like to talk with you. In the name of our loving God, please heed my words."

Relaxation:
• Spend a few minutes quieting your mind. Slowly inhale a long, deep breath and then slowly exhale. Repeat this for several minutes; concentrate on breathing while relaxing your muscles.

Communication:
• Proceed to silently (telepathically) tell that person what is on your mind. You may try asking a question if you need guidance on a certain situation.

• Quiet your mind again (repeat the deep breathing steps), and wait for a response; it may take several minutes. The response might come in the form of a voice (clairaudience) or a vision (clairvoyance).

Closing:
• Thank your loved one for his or her continued presence in your life and express your desire for on-going communication.

• Take some time to reflect on your experience.

• The following three exercises will use the same format as above, but with some variations. Refer back to this section when needed.

II. Vocal Contact

Talking out loud to friends who have passed is the easiest way to contact them. This form of communication may be one-way, but is very effective. Many find it comforting to speak with a loved one while visiting their grave site. Others may like talking with their heavenly friends in the mall, when trying to decide what color outfit to purchase, or while driving in their car when trying to decide which way to turn. I don't know what I would do without Charlene, my spirit guide, who rides shot-gun in my car. When I'm lost I vocally ask her which direction to turn; kind of like a personal GPS angel. Charlene telepathically tells me which way to go.

Another example of vocal contact is given by Bishop Matthew Clark. In a final comment from his All Saints Day story, Clark describes how he has conversations with his deceased father:

> I tell him [father] about myself and entrust my concerns to his loving care. Occasionally, I go back through the stages of my life and speak with him about things I held to myself in those days and ask him now the questions I wish I had asked him then. (Clark, 2)

By asking questions, Clark suggests he has a two-way dialogue with his dad. The Bishop practices communion with the saints by confiding in his father and trusting that his dad will answer him. The following exercise will help you to have your own conversations with family and friends on the Otherside.

Vocal Contact Exercise

Preparation:
- Get comfortable, play music and pray for protection.

Invocation:
- State the person's name three times out loud to get his or her attention. For example, "Calling on (name), calling on (name), calling on (name); I value our relationship and would like to talk with you. In the name of our loving God, please heed my words."

Relaxation:
- Quite your mind and breathe slowly.

Communication:
- Proceed to vocally tell that person what is on your mind. You may try asking a question if you need guidance on a certain situation.

- Quiet your mind again (repeat the deep breathing steps), and wait for a response; it may take several minutes.

Closing:
- Give thanks and reflect

III. Writing Methods: Letter and Inspirational

Letter-writing and journaling are all easy ways to communicate to our family and friends in heaven and vice versa; it's simple and very therapeutic. Pour out your feelings, both positive and negative, and you can be sure the intended person will receive it. Trust that he or she is reading every word, the same way you trust that God hears your prayers. If a loved one died with unresolved differences then letter writing is a good way to tell that person how you really feel, thus, paving a way for after-death reconciliation. Try the following method:

Letter-Writing Exercise

Preparation:
- Get a pen and notepad, journal or laptop computer. Get comfortable, play music and pray for protection.

Invocation:
- *Write* or *type* the person's name three times to get his or her attention.

Relaxation:
- Quite your mind and breathe slowly.

Communication:
- Proceed to *write* or *type* whatever you want that person to know. You may ask a question *in writing* if you need guidance on a certain situation.

- Quiet your mind again (repeat the deep breathing steps), and wait for a response; it may take several minutes.

Closing:
- Give thanks and reflect.

Inspirational (in-spirit) writing is one way in which spirits communicate to us; poems, songs, sermons and Biblical scriptures are examples. Although we like to take credit for writing something unique, often our ideas come from our personal angels or loved ones "in-spirit"; sometimes they come from a higher source.

For example, *A Course in Miracles,* by Helen Schucman and William Thetford, and the *Reflections of the Christ Mind* series by Paul Ferrini are examples of works inspired by Jesus Christ. The *Conversations with God* books, by Neil Donald Walsh were, of course, inspired by God. Inspirational writing is also one of the easiest ways to practice two-way communication with spirits.

Simply meditate with a pad and pen in your lap, and when you get to a deep, hypnotic-like state, write down a question you would like guidance on. Hold the pen in your hand, while listening for the answer, and just start writing down whatever comes through. Don't stop to analyze or question, just write without censoring. You will be amazed at how easy it is.

The process is even easier when done on a computer. The letters "f" and "j" both have a Braille-like bump on them so it's easy to find the "home" hand position on the keyboard, therefore, making it possible to type with your eyes closed. With inspirational writing you are fully conscious and aware of what you are inscribing at the time. You may try an inspirational writing exercise by following the same procedures for letter writing.

Just a Fact

"Automatic" or "channeled" writing occurs when a medium allows a spirit to enter his or her body; thus, taking control of all thoughts and hand movements. The subject goes into a trance state and is not consciously aware of what is being written. Mediums may even compose articles well beyond their knowledge and comprehension. Sometimes the person writes in a foreign language, which is unknown to the intuitive; this is an example of "xenoglossy."

IV. Meditation

There is an old adage that asserts, "'prayer' is talking to God and 'meditation' is listening to Him." Meditation is the best way to develop our ability to communicate with spirits; it shuts down our physical senses and opens up our spiritual senses. When we quiet the chattering of our own mind, we allow the minds of others to enter. This, in turn, raises our vibration and provides non-physical beings an opportunity to communicate with us. In this altered state of consciousness we can receive information from any level within the communion of saints, from other members of the church on earth, as well as those in purgatory or heaven.

The more we meditate, the more we increase our listening skills or psychic ability. The more we practice, the easier it is to hear the voice of spirit, also known as "locutions." Spending much time in meditation is why so many priests and nuns are psychically gifted with clairvoyance (visions) and clairaudience (voices).

Meditation Exercise

Preparation:
- Get comfortable, play music and pray for protection.

Invocation:
- Silently state the person's name three times to get his or her attention.

Relaxation:
- Close your eyes, relax your shoulders, and inhale a long, slow, deep breath. Hold that breath for a second and then slowly exhale. Repeat this deep breathing while relaxing each muscle starting from the top of your head and working your way down to your neck, shoulders, chest, abdomen, legs, and feet. Continue breathing deeply and slowly, until you release all tension and are totally and completely relaxed.

- Imagine yourself walking down a spiral staircase and as you descend further and further down the stairs you will go deeper and deeper into relaxation. Continue spiraling down, down, down; going deeper and deeper into relaxation.

- When you are in a deep state of meditation, you will see a door at the bottom of the staircase. Open the door and observe before you a magnificent ocean and a white sand beach; there is no one in sight. Step onto the sand in your bare feet and feel the warmth of it on your toes. Hear the roar of the waves, feel the ocean breeze, and smell the salty air. Walk across the sand, towards the water and proceed to stroll along the beach. Feel the hot sun on your face while you delight in the myriad seashells and sea birds surrounding you.

- As you stroll along the beach, you feel safe, sound, and content, but most of all you feel a profound sense of peace, peace, peace.

Communication:
- While walking along this serene place, you notice a figure several hundred yards away; it is someone walking towards you. You recognize the person as your loved one who passed away. Greet this person with a big hug or handshake, whatever way you normally would, and spend a moment basking in the reunion.

- When you are ready, silently tell this person whatever is on your mind. You may try asking a question if you need guidance on a certain situation.

- Quiet your mind again (repeat the deep breathing steps) and listen for a response; it may come in the form of a voice, a vision or an inner knowing. Spend the next five to ten minutes enjoying this communion (this time is spent in silence as the guide refrains from speaking).

Closing:
- Thank your loved one for listening and express your desire for on-going communication. Make an agreement to return to this special place, this ocean shore, whenever you need to talk.

- When you are ready, say goodbye and walk back down the beach from the direction you came. Find the doorway leading to the spiral staircase, open the door, and slowly ascend the stairs. With each step you will become more aware of your body and more aware of your surroundings. When you reach the top of the stairs, rest a few moments and recall any messages you received.

- Slowly open your eyes and take a minute to reflect on your experience. You may want to jot it down in a journal. If you are in a group meditation, sharing your experience can be very therapeutic, as well as helpful to the other participants; it will aid in psychic development.

In Conclusion

After our loved ones die, we have to change the way we relate to them. When it comes to seeing and hearing members of the church in heaven, we have to get used to the idea that we have a disability. We can easily overcome that disability by finding alternate forms of communicating our thoughts and feeling to those on the otherside. Through the simple tasks of praying, talking (vocalizing), writing and meditating, we can let our loved ones know they are still an important part of our lives; in return, they will guide and protect us.

Wherever we go we are in constant contact with non-physical beings. Guardian angels and loved ones who have passed are always at our side. In addition, we may encounter spirits in a haunted house with ghosts, or in God's house with the saints; we are never alone. These transdimensional associations are how we participate in the greater Catholic Church and how we practice the communion of saints.

Just My Opinion

The death of a loved one can be the most traumatic experience in our life. It can also provide us with the greatest opportunity for spiritual growth. How can we say goodbye to someone who has been a partner on our earthly journey? We wonder how we will ever go on without that special person to lean on. At times like these, in the deepest, darkest pit of despair, we are forced to look to the heavens for guidance. We are forced to look at the bigger picture and to search for answers to our toughest questions, "Where did our loved ones go, why are we still here, and what is our purpose?"

By maintaining relationships with those who have passed before us, we stay connected to our spiritual home in heaven. Our transdimensional friendships remind us that we are in this world but not *of* it. It helps us understand that we are truly eternal beings. With the help and support from our family and friends in the afterlife, we are better able to take on challenges in this life. Furthermore, when two souls experience love that transcends all boundaries and conditions, they also experience their unity with each other and with God, which is the essence of our existence.

It is also the desire of those in spirit to keep our relationships alive in order to help us find our purpose in this world and to continue with our mission on earth. They are waiting and willing to lend a hand, all we need do is ask. In addition, our loved ones in heaven can comfort us when we are in the depths of depression, guide us when we feel lost, provide us with companionship when we are alone, and protect us when we are in danger. Best of all, they are there to revel in our victories and rejoice in our greatest triumphs.

Through the belief that we will eventually return to our family and friends who have gone before us, lie our hopes and dreams. When that day comes, it will be time for us to help our human companions on earth. And whenever they call on us for aid, like a shooting star across a jet black sky, we will reach across the universe to extend a helping hand of love and light. We will guide and protect our family and friends by taking every opportunity to practice the communion of saints.

Summary

If we can have a relationship with God and the saints, we can also have a relationship with Grandma in heaven; this is what the communion of saints teaches us. When a friend or family member dies it does not end the bond of love, it merely changes the way in which we express our devotion.

It is important to keep these transdimensional relationships alive in order to strengthen our psychological and psychic bonds. Having strong connections with loved ones in heaven can provide us with an extra measure of safety and protection. It can also help fill the void in our life and ease our loneliness. Maintaining relationships with friends in spirit lessens the fear of death, reminds us that we will one day be reunited, and accelerates the grieving process. Most of all, having a special someone on the otherside promotes healing and gives us hope.

There are many advantages to practicing communion with the saints. Relationships can improve, as well as the ability to communicate with loved ones who were unable to do so before death. Furthermore, our friends in spirit can aid in our mental health by acting as our personal therapist and protect us by acting as our personal guardian angel.

When someone dear to us dies, it does not mean the relationship has ended, it has merely changed. Because we can no longer see or hear them, we have to find alternate means of communication. For many, this communication may be one-way, but through practice and guided exercises we may learn how to have a two-way conversation. Transcommunication may take the form of prayer, vocalization, writing or meditation. Whatever way we choose, we can learn to practice communion with the saints. So, don't treat your loved ones as if they were dead.

Chapter 11
Spiritual Sign Language

"No you're not going crazy, and yes, I believe you."
(Gifts of Grace Motto)

In this chapter we will learn how our loved ones in heaven can communicate to us through "spiritual sign language." By being aware of these signs, we also become aware of how angelic relatives remain an active part of our lives. In addition, we will learn to set up a specific sign to let us know when our spiritual friends are present; we will be *practicing* the communion of saints.

The following account is an example of spiritual sign language. It pertains to the first "sign" I received from my deceased mother. The event occurred two months after her death and several days before my dream visit from her. This true story was originally written and accepted for *Chicken Soup for the Gardener's Soul*; however, it did not make the final cut and was never published. Little did I know, as synchronicity would have it, that eight years later I would be writing a book with a chapter on after-death communications. My story finally found a home, I hope you like it.

Secret Garden

My mother's favorite story was the children's classic, *The Secret Garden*. She not only read it to me and my sisters, but to her trio of grandchildren as well. All three generations also enjoyed watching the movie together over and over. One year I bought Mom a stepping stone that read "The secret of my garden is but one word, Love." Although she did not have her own garden, the stone reminded me of Mom's favorite story, so I presented it to her as a gift on Mother's Day. She proudly displayed the stone by the front porch step for all to see when they entered her home. That was 1996, the year Mom was diagnosed with cancer.

In February of 2000, Mom's health was failing fast, so I moved in with her to assist my brother, Dad and hospice aides in care-taking; she was able to spend her final months at home. During this time, a male cardinal started coming to the window every day. He would fly right into the glass, batting his wings and feet against the panes. He did this repeatedly, day after day. Afraid he would hurt himself, we tried everything to discourage him; we put pictures in the window and hung up signs. When that didn't work, we tried taking them down all together. This went on for weeks.

A month later, on March 12, Mom lost her four-year battle with multiple myeloma, which had progressed into leukemia; she passed away shortly after midnight. The cardinal did not come that morning and never returned. I always felt the bird had taken Mom's soul to heaven. Several weeks later, a friend told me that whenever a bird flies into the window it means someone in the house is going to die; I guess it's true.

Of course we were all devastated by Mom's death, but I don't think any of us knew to what extent she touched our lives. With each passing day I felt my mother's loss more and more; I kept finding new ways that it affected my life. There were no more five-minute messages on my answering machine (Momograms, we called them). When a show she liked came on TV, I would put a tape in to record it for her and then remember she was gone. I would think of something I needed to tell Mom and pick up the phone to call her, only to realize she was not there. Each day seemed to be more difficult than the one before; my grief was getting worse, not better. There was a great void in my life and I began to realize how traumatized I was by my mother's death; I felt lost.

In the weeks that followed, I was battling severe depression. During this time, my friend, Kim, suggested I plant a tree or garden in memory of Mom; I thought that was a great idea. There was already an ideal place in the corner of my backyard; it was the pet cemetery. The small graveyard was a triangular shaped plot, which was bordered by a creek on one side, woods on the other side, and the lawn in front. It is where we buried many of our beloved dogs and cats over the years. Since Mom loved animals, it seemed the perfect spot.

Knowing that my own mental health was becoming an issue, I felt building a memorial garden would be therapeutic. It gave me a reason to go on and kept me busy both mentally and physically. I spent the next several cold and dreary weeks planning the flowerbed. It was still too early to plant so I researched what I would need by reading gardening books, magazines and websites. The cemetery required shade loving plants that grew low so they would not obstruct the headstones and crosses marking the myriad pet graves.

In mid-April, the weather finally broke and I could actually start working in my new garden. The first thing I needed was an exceptionally nice centerpiece to serve as the focal point. In a nearby nature store I found the perfect item, a statue of St. Francis of Assisi standing in a birdbath atop an old tree trunk. Not only would it attract wildlife, it was also a natural looking addition to my woodland garden.

A spot was established for St. Francis and the flower arrangements were planned around the birdbath. I found an old bench, which was placed in front of the garden, and in a nearby tree I hung a bird feeder. All my spare time was spent working on Mom's flowerbed, fertilizing, mulching, weeding, planting, watering and reflecting. At the same time, I felt Mom was watching over me while I labored. It was a place I loved to be, as I enjoyed the birds and squirrels that had found a neat new spot to hang out. The pet cemetery became our sanctuary, it became our secret garden.

Each week I added a little more, trying to fill the area with plants that would bloom from spring to fall. As the garden started taking shape I got more and more excited and looked forward to the next day off from my job so I could work in it. I put in primrose, grape hyacinth, lilies of the valley, columbine, stonecrop, creeping phlox and lungwort. Alongside the creek, and behind the headstones, I planted daylilies, lupines and honeysuckle. I was becoming proud of my creation knowing that Mom would be pleased.

It was a sunny, spring day on May 14, 2000. Two months had passed since Mom died; it was also Mother's Day. Despite the brightness of the morning, there was darkness in my soul as I walked out to the pet cemetery to be near Mom. As I sat on the park bench, I was struck with the realization that this holiday was a cruel reminder of my loss and pain; I began to cry. It was my first Mother's Day without Mom; I never felt so alone in my life. As my tears began to subside, I managed to present Mom with the gift I had worked so hard on; I sadly proclaimed aloud "Happy Mother's Day Mom; I hope you like your secret garden."

Just at that moment, a bright red cardinal landed on a tree branch just above my head. It was the first cardinal I had seen since Mom passed away. My heart leapt as sudden elation took over; I "just knew" it was mom. The bird was quite vocal and appeared to speak directly to me, "Cheer, cheer, cheer, cheerup, cheerup, cheerup"; he seemed to be laughing. In a holy instant my grief was replaced with joy. Mom really had been watching over me and she was telling me she was delighted with my gift to her. As I listened to the comforting cardinal song, I knew that at this moment in time Mom was actually here with me, and she found a way to let me know she was alive and well! I was filled with a great sense of gratification; not only was Mom at peace, but for the first time in months, so was I.

That afternoon I took the stepping stone I had given to Mom years earlier and placed it in its new home. Mom had her own secret garden now, one she could enjoy from a bird's eye view. It's been over ten long years since that Mother's Day, and every spring I look forward to spending time with Mom in our special place. I also look forward to seeing the red velvet feathers of the cardinal and reading the words on the stone that are planted in my soul, "The secret of my garden is but one word, Love."

This account is a typical example of how we can communicate with our loved ones in heaven and vice versa. Every day I worked on the garden I not only thought of my mother, but I also spoke to her aloud; I often shared my feelings of loss and frustration. By building a memorial garden, I was conveying to my mother that I will always remember her. The garden was created out of pure love for Mom, and she knew that I put my heart and soul into making a beautiful place to honor her.

In return, my mom was able to telepathically communicate her love to me and her appreciation of the gift I made for her. In order to get my attention, she sent a cardinal, a "sign" she knew I would recognize. Through the common language of love, which has no boundaries, we were able to reconnect with each other. Despite the fact that we live on different levels within the church, Mom and I were able to communicate. In theological terms, this is how we "practice the communion of saints." Now let's take a more scientific approach.

Know the Lingo

By examining the psychological and parapsychological words which describe spirit communication, we will better understand how to practice the communion of saints. Although the following terminology sounds complicated, it is really quite simple. An example from my *Secret Garden* story will be given for each definition. The first term should be familiar by now, but let's refresh our memory:

Transcommunication

As a reminder, this term was coined by psychotherapist, Doctor Jane Greer. In her book, *The Afterlife Connection*, Greer describes this form of communication as the flow of psychic messages both ways, between the physical and non-physical world. "We not only can connect but also make a conscious and deliberate choice to initiate contact and communicate with a departed loved one" (25). This would include any contact between the various levels of the church, or within the communion of saints.

In the secret garden story, I communicated my desire to stay connected with my mother by building a memory garden in her honor. I also spoke to her while I worked in it. She was able to respond to me by sending a cardinal and telepathically impressing upon my mind that she was present and aware of my intentions. The result was a two-way communication between the physical and non-physical levels of reality; this is an example of "transcommunication."

After-death communication (ADC)

This is a term created by Bill and Judy Guggenheim, the authors of *Hello From Heaven*. They define ADC as "a spiritual experience that occurs when someone is contacted directly and spontaneously by a deceased family member or friend" (16). The contact is initiated by the spirit and no medium is used; lights flickering on and off by themselves is one example. After years of research on the subject, the Guggenheims organized ADC's into categories, such as "seeing a presence," "hearing a voice," "smelling a fragrance" and symbols in nature, like "butterflies and rainbows."

In the story about the secret garden, the cardinal represented an "after-death communication" from Mom. My mother was able to convey to me that she had indeed been watching over me while I worked in the garden. In addition, due to the timing of the event, she was able to acknowledge the Mother's Day gift to her.

Signs

Signs are a specific type of after-death communication. Although the contact is made directly by a particular spirit, often an intermediate device, such as an object, electrical appliance, or even an animal, is used or manipulated to signal the spirit's presence. Because most people are not attuned to the spiritual realm, our loved ones use "signs" to get our attention; it's like waving a red flag and saying, "I'm here, I'm here."

Signs are a way for members in the church in heaven or in purgatory to transcommunicate with members in the church on earth, without the use of a psychic medium. They are indicators that tell us that our loved ones have made it safely to the other side and are still a part of our lives.

Our friends in spirit give signs to let us know that they are with us to share in whatever life experiences we're going through. Signs often occur during significant events, such as the purchase of a new home, the birth of a child, a wedding, or an accomplishment we achieved. We may also receive a sign when we are going through a particularly difficult time, like divorce, illness, or bankruptcy.

> The cardinal, in the secret garden story, was also a "sign" from my mother. It occurred at a meaningful time; it was Mother's Day. The bird was a symbol of her on-going presence in my life.

Cathexis

This is a term used in psychotherapy that refers to a person's concentrated investment of psychic energy in a particular concept, idea, image, object or symbol. That concept or symbol is then said to be "cathectic" for that person. That same concept then becomes cathectic for you as an extension and representation of your loved one (Greer). For example: your mother's favorite movie, actor or actress, food, sports team, author, T.V. show, perfume, flower, book, or collectible objects. These are all cathectic symbols that may be used as signs.

> In the story about the garden, the male cardinal was recognized because of my mother's connection with that particular bird in the final month of her life. Seeing the cardinal reminded me of Mom and strengthened the psychological and psychic bond with her; the red-feathered friend became "cathectic" for me. Although not all cardinals are a sign from Mom, whenever I see one, I always think of her. When one appears at a significant time in my life, I will "just know" it is a sign of my mother's presence at that particular moment.

Spiritual Sign Language

Most people are familiar with American Sign Language, which is a communication system used by people who are hearing impaired or deaf. Specific hand formations and gestures are utilized to convey particular words or concepts. For example the word "love" is expressed by crossing the hands over the heart with palms facing in.

In the same way, our friends in spirit use signs or symbols to communicate with those of us who are blind or deaf to the spiritual realms (muggles). The practice of using signs for communication between physical and non-physical beings is what I call "spiritual sign language."

Collectible objects, music, electronic devices and even nature are types of signs that may be used to convey a message from a particular loved one in heaven. This symbol or "sign" then becomes that person's special calling card; in this way, his or hers presence may be recognized in future events when the sign reoccurs. In spiritual sign language, like American sign language, the feeling of "love" can be communicated, but instead of a hand signal, the sign may be expressed by a favorite flower, song or other cathectic symbol.

> Returning to the *Secret Garden*, my mother used spiritual sign language to "transcommunicate" her on-going love for me and continued presence in my life. She used the cardinal as a "cathectic" "sign" to provide an "after-death communication." As a result, her message got through.

To help further explain spiritual sign language, a classic Hollywood movie may help as an example. Many readers can recall *Close Encounters of the Third Kind*. Towards the end, when everyone was on top of Devil's Tower, the aliens communicated with the earthlings through the "signs" of lights and music. Using the same signs, the people on earth communicated back; remember the huge organ and the series of notes played (G, A, F, F, C). In a similar way, spirits can use signs to communicate with us. If we think of our loved ones as aliens, it may help us to better understand.

Just a Fact

The Fox sisters used spiritual sign language to communicate with an unknown entity haunting their house. Both the ghost and the two girls used rapping signs to converse with each other. That's how the siblings discovered that a peddler was killed in their home, and that's how modern-day spiritualism got its start.

Be Aware of Signs

Receiving a sign from our heavenly friends is an invitation to engage us in conversation. Likewise, we may use a sign to send a message back to them. Through spiritual sign language we can transcommunicate with members on other levels of the communion of saints. Those who have been given a sign understand what a great sense of peace and joy can result from such an intimate connection, which transcends all time and space. It forces us to take time out from our busy lives, if just for a moment, to remember we are spirit in essence and there are other worlds in which we are a part.

The pages that follow describe common ways in which our loved ones in heaven like to make themselves known to us. The list was compiled from the various metaphysical works cited throughout this book. For many of the after-death communications or "signs," an example is provided. The accounts are from students, clients, family, friends and personal experiences.

Mechanical or electrical failures

There is nothing more frustrating than malfunctioning appliances and electronics. However, when the cause of the problem is a recently departed friend or family member, we may view it in a new way; instead of frustration it can lead to joy.

Appliances

A spirit may try to get our attention by turning appliances on or off, often when it's most inconvenient. This is especially true for those who spend a great deal of time in the kitchen. Perhaps the electric can opener or dishwasher will come on by itself .

Radios

Radios may come on of their own accord when a spirit is trying to make contact. Often, that particular moment, or the specific song playing, has significance to either the sender or receiver of the sign.

Lights

It is not unusual for a loved one who has passed to play with lights to get our attention; lamps that flicker on and off are common signs. Sometimes a light bulb will inexplicably blow out when you walk by it. It's not unusual for a lamp to come on by itself; be sure to check the cord, it may not even be plugged in.

Unscrewed

Dave was a client with whom I had done spiritual counseling. Although he was only thirty-three when I met him, he had just been diagnosed with cancer. Ten months later he passed away. Two days after the funeral, I was thinking about Dave while I was vacuuming my living room. I couldn't help wondering if there was more I could have done for him. At that very moment, all of a sudden, the room became brighter.

I looked up at the lights in the ceiling fan and noticed that all three bulbs were lit up. This seemed impossible because I always left one of the light bulbs slightly unscrewed; it was too bright with all of them lit. Although the one bulb had been dark for years, now it was glowing. Approximately two minutes later, all the lights in the fan went out; shortly afterwards, they came back on again.

I was ecstatic; I knew immediately that this was a sign from Dave because I had been thinking about him at the time. Through spiritual sign language, Dave managed to convey to me that he was OK and this was his way of easing my feelings of guilt. The after-death communication brought me peace of mind.

Television

Spirits can make themselves known by turning the TV off or on or scrambling the picture. Sometimes their face will actually appear on the television screen.

Kenny Rogers

My sister, Eileen Moran is an Ob-Gyn nurse at Highland Hospital in Rochester, NY. One night, about three months after our mom (Millie) died, Eileen and her friend, Shirley, were having a conversation in the dining room of the family home. At the same time, they were listening to the country music station, which was on the television in the vacant living room.

Suddenly, Eileen and Shirley were startled when the TV became extremely loud. When they looked in the next room to see what was going on, they witnessed the "volume" bar appear on the television and actually saw the lines zoom across the screen as if someone had picked up the remote to adjust the sound; it was turned up to full-blast.

They were even more surprised when they realized it was Mom's favorite singer, Kenny Rogers, singing her favorite song, *The Gambler*. One of the highlights of Millie's life was seeing Kenny Rogers in concert several years earlier. After a few seconds the sound went back down by itself. The two ladies "just knew" it was Mom's way of saying "hello!"

Clocks

It is not unusual for a clock to stop at the exact time a loved one has passed. Sometimes a clock will chime at a particular time, other than on the usual hour or half-hour settings.

Dad's clock

Gary Siwicki of Greece, NY is a retired health care worker and current board member of CURE Childhood Cancer. He related this story about an ADC from his dad:

My father and I spent a lot of time in the garage working

together; it was a special place for him. It was a place where he could work his mechanical magic on the family cars and appliances. It was also a place of refuge for him after his first heart attack, when he was no longer able to work. It was a place to hide his cigarettes and liquor after the doctor told him to stop.

One day he bought a big clock especially for the garage. It was plain, non-descript. It was the type you would see in a bus or train station waiting room, or in a classroom above the blackboard. This class lesson, however, was one of inspiration and joy, a learning experience which started me on a more spiritual path in my life.

The time was 4:22 P.M.; it was January 11th, 1971. My father collapsed and died at the end of the driveway, just outside the garage. At that exact same time, the clock stopped, never to run again. The tragedy was that he was still a young man with a growing family who loved him dearly. Although I was grief-stricken, I took solace in knowing that he was OK; the clock was his signal to us.

Telephones & Answering Machines

A friend or family member who has passed may try to call you. Notice times when your phone rings and there is only static on the other end or a faint, garbled voice. If you are not home the answering machine may actually record a message from a loved one; this is known as electronic voice phenomena or EVP.

I'm Alive

Students of my workshops have had the benefit of hearing an EVP message from spirits on my answering machine. It doesn't seem to be directed to any one person and several people can be heard talking at once. The conversation is somewhat garbled and static, but certain words can be heard quite clearly. At one point an unknown voice unmistakably declares, "I'm alive, I'm alive."

Insight
Getting a sign is like a shot of Demerol in the midst of full-blown pain. The pain is still there but it becomes bearable. (Greer)

Computers

Spirits seem to be particularly attracted to computer communication. It doesn't matter if they were completely computer illiterate before they passed. If our spiritual friends think that using a PC is a good way to get our attention, then they will.

Look for out of context typed messages on a word document.

A program you are working on may suddenly change.

The image of the spirit might appear on the screen.

You may receive e-mail from a spiritual friend. Check for significance of date, time, subject and return address.

Have you ever tried automatic writing on the computer?

E-mail from Heaven
Several days after the cardinal visited me, I received an e-mail from my mother. Let me explain:

While I was checking my e-mail, I noticed that one of them did not have a return address; this alone was unusual. When I opened it, it appeared to be spam; it was regarding a place to vacation on the Gulf of Mexico. When I looked at the address, I noticed that where my e-mail address should have appeared, was my mother's name, Mildred.

How could I have possibly received an e-mail that was addressed to someone else? Furthermore, although everyone called her "Millie," mom always used "Mildred" for all her correspondence. In addition, the time the e-mail was sent was the exact time of her death, 12:28 am. The following is a reproduction of the original:

```
From:
Date:      Tue, May 23, 2000, 12:28am
To:        themildred@webtv.net
Subject:   The Perfect Vacation Spot
```

Everyone is looking for a place to relax and have a wonderful time at a reasonable cost. The beautiful Mississippi Gulf Coast is one of the most over looked vacation areas in the U.S.. You should see the golden sunsets as the soft breezes gently blow across the Gulf of Mexico.

There are perfect spots for quiet group retreats, play golf at some of the best designer golf courses, deep sea fish in the fertile waters of the Gulf of Mexico, or let us plan one of many other customized getaways for you or your group. The best part is because our wonderful area is so over looked you can vacation at prices that can fit anyone's budget.

You will never find anywhere as nice and as friendly as the Mississippi Gulf Coast. Call 1-800-974-### for more information and let us plan your trip to the most affordable and exciting new destinations in the south!

What made the e-mail even more unusual was the content of the letter. It seemed that Mom was trying to tell me she was okay and was having a wonderful time on the Otherside. The e-mail appeared to be a coded message. When I replaced the phrases "Mississippi Gulf Coast" and "Gulf of Mexico" with the word "heaven" it all became quite clear. Although she had never used a computer, Mom had managed to send me an e-mail from the otherside. Try decoding the message by re-reading it with the replacement word "heaven."

I had many computer experts look at the letter and no one could come up with another explanation. Of course I tried to respond to the letter by return e-mail but it just bounced back to me with the message, "unknown recipient." The next day, when I tried calling the phone number provided, a recording stated that the line was no longer in service.

Apports

Objects that mysteriously appear out of nowhere are called "apports"; they are usually a sign from spirit. Perhaps it's an antique brooch or a post card from another era.

Psychic Teeth

Sociologist of Gettysburg College, Charlie Emmons, has an unusual apport story, which he wrote about in his book, *Guided by Spirit*. I first met Charlie and his wife, Penelope, a medium, at Lily Dale, when I attended one of their workshops. Since then, I have had the opportunity to visit with them on several occasions. That's how I first learned about their strange experience:

I'm still looking for a normal explanation of this one. One day I found four large molars in the sink among the silverware. My mind worked overtime, accusing other people of putting them there or accidentally dropping them out of a container or something. I even hypothesized that a workman who put a filtration unit in the basement had picked up some plastic teeth down there, part of a necklace perhaps left by a former tenant. The water filtration company had to make ten trips before it could fix our drinking-water system, and Penelope thought that symbolically it was like "pulling teeth."

My plastic necklace theory was based on the fact that there were neat round holes drilled in the teeth. When I took them to my dentist, he said that they were *real* molars, perhaps from a teenage girl. The oddest thing was that they had not only holes but file marks, perhaps indicating that they had been used to demonstrate tooth structure at a dental school, the dentist thought.

It turns out that one of Penelope's grandfathers was a doctor who also worked on teeth sometimes. She often gets the sensation that he communicates with her mentally. Perhaps he left them as a joke about how the filtration repair was like "pulling teeth" (Emmons & Emmons, 129).

Gifts

Spirits like to help us out or show they still care by sending gifts. Often we do not connect the gift with the loved one because it may come indirectly, through another friend, or family member. For example:

You unexpectedly receive a dozen roses from a long lost friend.

You go to make a major purchase and the item you want, in the exact color and style you want, is on sale, and it's the only one left like it!

You're purchasing a new home and everything falls into place perfectly; the price and legal negotiations come out in your favor.

You win a trip, a 50/50 raffle, or hit it big at the casino.

The Christmas Tree

One Christmas season I decided I was finished with real Christmas trees, they were too messy, too expensive and it was too difficult for me and my husband to find time together to go shopping for one. Besides, now that Mom was gone, the tradition of a real tree no longer mattered. So I made up my mind I would purchase an artificial tree after Christmas, when they were on sale.

For several weeks prior to the holiday, I scoped out the tree I wanted. I found a nice northern pine with built in lights at Chase Pitkin; it was perfect. The original price was $325.00. When I returned the week after Christmas, the tree was still there and had been marked down to $225.00. Unfortunately, I did not have the money to buy it that day. I noticed there were about ten other trees left on display and thought it would still be there the following week, when I could afford it.

One week later, I returned to the hardware store, only to be shocked when I saw the entire Christmas display gone. Not one tree, not one sign of the holidays; a home improvement display had taken its place. When I asked a store clerk about the trees, he pointed me to the back of the store and explained that's where the leftover Christmas stuff was stored. I was crushed but went to see what remained.

I could hardly believe my eyes when I saw there was only one tree left, and it was the exact same one I had picked out weeks earlier. The price was now $80.00! I thanked my mom for putting the tree on hold for me; I "just knew" she was responsible for that magnificent holiday gift.

Odors

It is very common for spirits to make us aware of their presence through an odor that is connected with them. It could be the smell of a cigar, pipe tobacco, a favorite flower, or perfume.

Grandpa's Cigar

Rodney Himmelsbach, a machinist, lost his grandfather suddenly, due to a stroke. One morning Rod walked into the kitchen and distinctly smelled Dutch Master Cigar smoke; the specific kind his grandfather used. It was so strong he could not dismiss it. Since no one had been smoking in the house, he "just knew" it was his grandfather; the cigar was his sign.

Photographs

Many images of the deceased have shown up in pictures taken at family events. It is also not uncommon for ghostly images to appear in photos taken in areas known to be haunted, such as Alcatraz or Gettysburg.

In photographs, spirits often appear as "orbs" or small round circles of white light. Sometimes, however, actual faces can appear on the film. Both thirty-five millimeter film cameras and point and shoot digital cameras are effective for spirit photography. It's not so much the quality of the camera that matters, it's more about being in the right place at the right time.

Ghostly Grandma

Tina Vanderpool of Conesus, NY is a hairdresser at "Tangles Hair Salon" in Lakeville, NY. She called me after being referred by our mutual friend, Melissa. Tina had a spirit photo she wanted me to look at; we made arrangements to meet at her home.

The picture was taken at a restaurant while on a family vacation in Florida. I was quite surprised when I examined the most phenomenal spirit photograph I had ever seen, and I had seen hundreds. This was not a small orb, but a detailed, full-size, transparent image of an elderly woman.

Tina's father-in-law, Walt, who took the photo, swears the old woman was not there at the time, especially since he had his family pose for the shot. Furthermore, the ghostly image could not have been caused by a double exposure because it was taken with a digital camera. In addition, at least one other spirit can be seen in the picture; notice the face in the door window, below the Exit sign. Walt stated he was a non-believer in ghosts, until he saw the picture.

Posing for the picture are Tina's son, Cameron, Tina, and brother-in-law, Brian. Ghostly Grandma appears to be just passing through.

Six months later, when I was giving a workshop in Lily Dale, NY, I passed the picture around the class for all to see as an example of spirit photography. One of the students immediately recognized the ghost of the old woman as her grandmother, Lillian.

The student explained she had never been to Lily Dale prior to that evening, but for some reason was compelled to check out the web site the day before. When she saw the title of the workshop, *Talking to God and Grandma*, she was somehow compelled to come to the class. Little did she know that she would receive an after-death communication from her own "Grandma"; it came in the form of a photograph.

Animals

Spirits seem to have the ability to communicate with us through animals or birds. Pay special attention to wildlife that acts out of the norm, like a bird or deer that doesn't seem afraid and lets you get close to it. Perhaps a cat or dog that never liked you is suddenly jumping up in your lap.

The Sparrow

Tracy Cope is a hairdresser in Livonia, NY. In 1998, on the morning of her birthday, a sparrow came to her kitchen window and started pecking on the glass. When Tracy approached the window he was not scared off and persisted in pecking the glass. This activity continued for over fifteen minutes. Tracy "just knew" it was her father, who had passed away three months earlier; he managed to wish her a happy birthday.

Flowers

A favorite flower that mysteriously appears in your life is a common sign from spirits. The flower may come in any form, such as a figurine, a picture, or even a paper flower. Be open to the possibilities.

The Bouquet

Following a difficult week at my workplace, I felt it was time to leave my thirteen-year-old job as a mental health counselor. That Saturday morning, I pleaded with my mom out loud to give me a sign, and it had to be a "rose," not just one rose, but a whole bouquet. Not only that, I stated I needed the sign within three days so I could let my employer know of my decision on that Monday.

The next day I went to visit my Aunt Marie after church, as I did on most Sundays. When I pulled into the driveway I saw my cousin, Dee Dee from Colorado. Not expecting her, I jumped out of the car and ran to give her a big hug. I stopped short of my embrace, however, when I noticed the roses embroidered on her shirt. "Oh my God!" I screamed. "Your shirt, the roses, Mom came through!"

Baffled by my unusual greeting, I explained to Dee Dee my dilemma and the request I made from Mom. I then asked why she was wearing this customized shirt. She told me she had the tops made up special for the annual get-together with her three sisters that weekend. All the shirts had four roses, one for each of the siblings.

The rose was a symbol of their mother's middle name, which was "Rose"; likewise, it was my mother's middle name.

Following the conversation, I went into the house with Dee where I was greeted by the other three sisters, all wearing their rose shirts. As we sat in the living room discussing the paranormal event, I realized I was surrounded by a total of sixteen roses, a whole bouquet! Although I did not receive an actual rose flower, I most certainly got my sign. The next day I went to work and happily gave my two-week notice. Due to the sign from mom, I was confident in my decision.

Other Forms of Nature:

Rainbows and butterflies are such common ADCs that a separate chapter is devoted to them in *Hello From Heaven*. When we look to Mother Nature for guidance, we are usually not disappointed.

The Shooting Star

Patty Barber, of Wayland, NY is a nurse's aide at Conesus Lake Nursing Home. She worked with my mother, Millie, for fifteen years and was her closest friend right up until the time Mom died. Five years later, in 2005, my father, Harry became a resident of the same nursing home. We were all delighted that Patty became my Dad's aide. We "just knew" that Mom had a lot to do with how it all worked out. When I was having lunch with Dad one day, Patty shared with me a story about a sign she received from my mom:

> Every morning, before dawn, I would talk to Harry while I got him ready for the day. One day we were talking about Millie, and looking out the window at the night sky, when we saw a huge, shooting star. We both "just knew" it was her way of saying "Hi."

Patty explained that since that time, she and Harry had seen many shooting stars during their morning routine. This continued until my father's death in August of 2007.

Because of these events, whenever Patty sees a shooting star she thinks of both Harry and Millie. As a result of her sharing this ADC with me, now I do also.

Music

Many times loved ones may arrange for a favorite song to be played for our benefit and to show they are still connected. It may be heard on the radio, sung at church, or performed at a concert. It will usually occur at a special time in our life.

Karaoke Night

While my husband and I were visiting my brother in Florida, we decided to go out to a bar for dinner. For entertainment that night, Karaoke was being performed by some of the local customers. As we were enjoying our meal in one of the private booths, we reminisced about the time we played a joke on our sister, Kathy.

At a party, many years earlier, we took the recording Kathy made in Nashville and played it on the stereo to embarrass her. The song on the 45 RPM she cut was Bette Midler's *The Rose*. We all got a big laugh out of it at the time and had another good chuckle while we were talking about it at dinner that night.

During this conversation, a young woman got up from the bar for her turn at Karaoke. Upon hearing the first few notes of the song, the three of us simply froze in mid-conversation; the women proceeded to sing, "Some say love is like a river..." Out of the thousands of songs that could have been chosen, at the exact moment that we were discussing *The Rose*, someone got up to sing it; we "just knew" Mom was present.

At the same time, the hair on the back of my neck stood up and I burst into tears. I ran into the bathroom and sobbed my heart out. Although I was grateful for the sign from Mom, she had been gone less than a year and I still missed her terribly.

Any cathectic object or sign

Besides the common signs listed above, spirits may grab our attention by giving a sign that has significant meaning associated with their particular hobbies or interests when they lived in the physical world. This may include items associated with their favorite book, movie, song, sports team, collection, etc. For example, someone who was a huge Yankee baseball fan may give a sign associated with that team or a favorite player on that team.

The Doll

Julie called me for a counseling appointment following the death of her mother; we met in her home. She felt responsible for her mother's death and wanted a sign to alleviate her guilt. Since Julie's house was filled with collectible dolls, I suggested she ask her mom for a sign that has something to do with the dolls.

Several days later I received a call from Julie. That morning her bride doll, which was a favorite, was found completely turned around, facing the wall instead of forward. Julie was elated to receive a sign from her mom, as a result, the worries about her mother's death were released and she felt a great sense of peace.

Insight

People are afraid to share their after-death communications for four reasons:

- They don't think anyone will believe them.
- They don't believe it themselves.
- They think they're going crazy.
- The Roman Catholic Church's condemnation of spiritualism and the belief that it is evil.

That is why, when people are asked if they have ever received a sign from a loved one, they usually start out by saying, "Don't tell Father," or "You may think I'm crazy," but "here's what happened..."

Direct ADCs

In direct forms of after-death communications, no intermediary device or "sign" is used. For this reason, direct ADCs are not considered sign language; however, they are a form of transcommunication. The following are some examples.

Visions (Clairvoyance)

Sometimes spirits may appear to us when we are awake, but in an altered stated of consciousness, such as in meditation or just prior to falling asleep. Often the side effects of drugs, both prescription and recreational, can open a door to visionary states.

Apparitions

Occasionally our loved ones may actually appear to us when we are in the waking state. They may come to give a warning about something or just to give comfort from grief.

Voices (Clairaudience)

It is not unusual for people to receive an auditory message directly from a loved one. We may actually hear a voice we recognize as a particular friend, parent or sibling. Someone may call out our name when no one else is around; we might even be awakened out of a sound sleep.

The Whisper

Mary Beth Mangan, of Geneseo, New York is a registered nurse. She explained that she was one of nine children; therefore, eleven was the total number in their family. Her father had a favorite saying, which described the large clan, "Eleven from heaven." The number became even more significant when it came in conjunction with a sign Mary Beth received one day. She wrote the following account in her journal, which was dated February 1, 2007.

> Eleven days after Papa died, he gave me this gift. I had a feeling he would visit me on that day because "eleven" was significant for us. As I awoke early, early dawn, I was lying on my left side and my hands

were held in a prayer-like position in front of my eyes. My vision was all bright and I was surprised to see my hands immersed and surrounded by this brilliant, glittering golden light.

Everything was sparkling like diamond dust; I recognized it as God-light. As I saw this miracle, I heard my father clearly saying to me in a soft, low voice, "I'm only a whisper away; I'm only a whisper away."

Mary Beth went on to explain how happy she was to hear from her father; she felt a sense of peace knowing he was there for her. Because the number eleven was meaningful to her father, the timing of his after-death communication, eleven days after he passed, validated the event for her.

Dream visits

One of the easiest ways for spirits to communicate with us is through our dreams. When we are in this altered state of consciousness, our sixth sense is in tune with the spiritual world. But how can we tell the difference between a dream and an actual visitation from a loved one? There are several ways.

Dreams

They are usually forgotten shortly after waking up.

They are usually from the point of view of a bystander. It's similar to watching a movie; there is no interaction.

Dream visits

They are never forgotten because it was an actual experience imprinted on the person's long-term memory. Details may be recalled quite clearly, even years later.

There is usually interaction, such as hugging, touching, talking, or some other form of exchange.

The Bouffant Hair

Angela DeMaria is a legal secretary at DeMaria Law Offices in Rochester, NY. Before her grandmother, Florence died, Angie asked, "Grandma, if you ever leave will you promise to come back to visit me?" Several months after her death, Florence kept her promise; Angela explained:

> It was a dream, but it wasn't a dream. Grandma Florence appeared to me and she looked much like she did in life, with her bouffant hairdo. But she looked much younger, and healthier. And although she didn't say anything, she was so happy, which was different from how she was in real life. I felt so joyful and peaceful; I said to her, "I hope I get to see you again Grandma." She came back to visit three or four times after that.

Although years had gone by, Angela recounted the story as if it had happened recently. The event was imprinted on her long-term memory because it was a real experience, not just a dream.

Let's Practice

Spiritual sign language is another way in which we can practice communion with the saints. Although after-death communications may be spontaneous, we can help the process along by setting up a specific sign with a loved one in heaven.

In the following exercise, you will contact one person of your choosing, who has crossed over, and make an agreement on the "sign" that will be his or her signature-symbol. In addition, you may ask this individual for guidance on a particular issue or concern. This two-part method involves the simple tasks of writing and meditation or visualization. Practicing both forms will help to ensure the message gets through and that your sign will manifest.

Spiritual Sign language Exercise

Part I: Setting up a sign - writing exercise

- Get a pen and notepad, journal or laptop computer.

- Think of a loved one you would like to set up a sign with.

- Find a quiet, comfortable place or somewhere you feel connected to that person.

- Think about all the things particular to this individual, such as his or her favorite food, hobby, sports team, movie, etc. Write down these cathectic items or concepts and be specific. For example, if your grandmother loved gardening, what aspect did she like the most about it? What was her favorite flower? If it was yellow roses then write that down. Consider the following suggestions:

hobbies	collections	food	actor
cultural symbol	bird	animal	sport
TV show	drink	habits	author
pets	books	movies	college
phrases/sayings	logo	profession	religious symbol
perfume/colonge	cigar/cigarrette	nickname	favorite place

- If the person you want to contact died at a young age, or even before birth, then chose a sign that is cathectic for you. Think of your favorite things in each of the above categories and write them down. Although your loved one may have passed as an infant in this world, he or she is an old soul and will understand your list of meaningful symbols.

- Look over your list and choose one specific item that stands out as a sign you would like to use. If you can't decide on one, then have two choices, but no more.

- Below your list, write a little note to the person you want to contact explaining your desire to communicate. Request that he or she use the chosen sign(s) and confirm what it is. For example: Dear (name), I know you will always be a part of my life but I wish to receive a sign that will help me to know you are near. My sign of choice is (write in your sign) because it reminds me of you.

Part II: Meditation exercise

Preparation:
- Put on some soft instrumental music. If practicing this exercise in a group, one person may read the guided meditation provided while music is playing in the background. If doing this on your own, you may want to pre-record the meditation.

- Ask for protection by saying, "I am protected from negative forces by surrounding myself with the white light of God and of Jesus Christ."

- Think about the person you would like to contact and the sign you chose to use as a means of communication.

Invocation:
- State the person's name three times silently to get his or her attention. You may say for example, "Calling on (name), calling on (name), calling on (name); I value our relationship and would like to talk with you. In the name of our loving God, please heed my words."

Relaxation:
- Close your eyes, relax your shoulders, and inhale a long, slow, deep breath. Hold that breath for a second and then slowly exhale. Repeat this deep breathing while relaxing each muscle starting from the top of your head and working your way down to your neck, shoulders, chest, abdomen, legs and feet. Continue breathing deeply and slowly, until you release all tension and are totally and completely relaxed.

- Imagine yourself walking down a spiral staircase and as you descend further and further down the stairs you will go deeper and deeper into relaxation. Continue spiraling down, down, down; going deeper and deeper, becoming extremely relaxed.

- When you are in a deep state of meditation, you will see a door at the bottom of the staircase. Open the door and step through it. You find that you are standing in a grassy park that borders a lake; no one else is in sight. As you approach the lake, you walk barefoot on the grass and feel the coolness of the soft earth under your feet. At the edge of the water is a beach mixed with sand, pebbles and shells of all colors. The lake is surrounded by an old growth forest; there is nothing but trees on either side. You see a bench nearby; sit on it, and gaze out at the peaceful, secluded lake.

- As the sun reflects on the water, it sparkles like a million diamonds dancing on the surface. Feeling a warm, gentle breeze, you listen to the sound of the waves washing ashore and the cry of seagulls overhead. As you bask in the sun, you become mesmerized by the sparkling lake and surrounding nature. While relaxing on the lakeside bench, you notice that in this place you feel safe, sound, and content; but most of all, you feel a profound sense of peace, peace, peace.

Communication:
- You look down the beach and observe a person approaching; you recognize your loved one. Greet this person the way you normally would, with a big hug or handshake, and convey how happy you are to see him or her; spend a moment enjoying your reunion. Explain that you would like to stay connected and ask to receive a sign from time to time. State the specific sign or signs you chose.

- At this time you may try silently asking a question if you need guidance on a certain situation.

- Quiet your mind and listen for a response (repeat the deep breathing steps); it may come in the form of a voice, a vision, or an inner knowing.

- Thank your loved one for listening and express your desire for on-going communication. Make an agreement to return to this special place whenever you need to talk.

- When you are ready, say goodbye, walk back down the beach, across the grass, and return to the doorway that leads to the spiral staircase. Open the door and slowly ascend the stairs. With each step you will become more and more aware of your body and more aware of your surroundings. When you reach the top of the stairs rest a few moments and recall any messages you received.

Closing:
- Slowly open your eyes, give thanks and take a minute to reflect on your experience.

- Write down any messages you received. If you are in a group meditation, you may want to share your experience with the other participants.

Receiving a Sign

Now that you have established a sign, you must be open to all the possible ways in which it may come through. For example, if the sign was a rainbow, you may not actually see a rainbow in the sky, but you may see one on a billboard, in a book, on a TV commercial, on the side of a truck, or perhaps someone's license plate. Then again, a rainbow might just unexpectedly appear across the horizon on your way to work one morning. Once you receive a sign, ask the person to make it his or her particular signature-symbol. This way you will learn to distinguish between Grandma, your father, or your best friend in spirit.

But how do we know?
How do we know when we really receive a sign from a loved one in heaven? How do we know it's not just a coincidence or

our imagination working overtime? Several things will occur simultaneously when it's an actual sign; look for four things to happen:

You are aware of a physical sign. You experience the sign you chose in the exercise or another one that is directly connected to that individual. For example, it may be a favorite song on the radio, or the person's picture may fall off the wall. In addition, you may get other physical signs at the same time, such as rapping noises or lights flashing on and off.

You are aware of a physical change in your body. You can visibly see the hair standing up on your arm or feel a tingling sensation in the back of your neck. You feel a presence, as if someone was hovering over you. These events are caused by the spirit's electromagnetic force, much like static electricity. You may even feel the spirit touching you on the hand or face; sometimes they will play with your hair.

You experience what is called "just knowing." At the time of your physical sign, your loved one will telepathically communicate to you by impressing on your mind that it is him or her. The strength of this impression is so strong that no one can convince you that it was not a sign; you "just know" that your heavenly friend is present at that particular moment in time.

You become emotional. Your heart will be filled with a great sense of joy; at the same time you may experience a great sense of loss, depending on how long the person has been gone. Your eyes may well up with tears of joy or you may have a good cry; signs are often bittersweet. Afterwards, you will be left with a sense of peace.

At first, when you become aware of the ways in which spirits can communicate, everything will seem like a sign. To be sure that it really is, check to see if you experience at least two of the events from the above list. Maybe you didn't experience the "just knowing," but you received your chosen sign and the hair stood up on your arm. If three or four of the events occur then you can be more certain of the connection. In addition, if you are with someone who shares your experience, then you have even further validation.

Don't be surprised, however, if others don't share you enthusiasm. When you begin practicing the communion of saints, and receive a definite sign, many people will be skeptical, take offense at your actions or even condemn you. Know that this is a normal reaction based on fear and a thousand years of ignorance, religious prejudice and a society focused on science and reason, instead of faith and spirituality.

No matter what others think; if it makes you feel better to believe it was a sign, then believe it and cherish the moment. An after-death communication is a personal gift from your loved one and is something just between you and your special angel; don't let anyone take that gift away from you. On the other hand, don't be afraid to share the message with someone who might appreciate it. If, however, you are met with nothing but doubts and you begin to question your own sanity, remember the Gifts of Grace motto: *"No you're not going crazy, and yes, I believe you."*

Just a Fact

Many cultures, such as Native American and the Chinese, practice ancestor worship. These people have always carried on a relationship with family and friends on the otherside. They often seek guidance from those who have gone before them, who are thought to be wiser and more helpful in the afterlife. This practice was also a part of early Christianity and became the basis for the communion of saints.

In Conclusion

By familiarizing ourselves with the signs spirits use to communicate to us, we can recognize them when they do occur. When we are aware of signs, we become more aware of the presence of our loved ones in our life. When we know that our heavenly companions are nearby, it's an opportunity to acknowledge them and to thank them for standing by us. We may want to go further by sharing our feelings and asking for guidance on a particular concern in our lives. We may even ask a question and have them send a future sign that will give us an answer.

It is not unusual for people to receive a "sign" from a friend or family member who has passed. If someone confides this personal event to you, it's important not to discount his or her experience or try to rationalize it. Let that person have their bit of joy; it may be their only bright spot in an otherwise depressing day. Simply listen to their story with a compassionate ear and without judgment; that's all anyone wants.

So the next time you notice a flashing light bulb, instead of brushing it off as a power surge, think twice about it; perhaps it really is Grandma! And the next time you see a cardinal, think of your own loved one in heaven and think about making your own secret garden.

Just My Opinion

In each of us is buried a torch, which we carry for our departed family and friends. And each torch burns with an eternal flame; it can never be completely extinguished. The flame burns us with a homesick longing to reunite with that special angel, who touched our life so deeply. In the midst of our busy day, the flame may be small, but in the still of the lonely night, the flame burns bright; it deepens our yearning to reconnect with someone who seems just beyond our reach. In the darkest hours the pain cuts deep, as our broken heart sobs with grief-stricken tears.

But one day all that changes. It may come in the form of a stopped clock, it may come in the notes of a song, it may come in the shape of a bird, it may come in the smell of perfume, it may come as a gift, it may appear in a photo, it may come as a shooting star, or it may come in a comforting voice. It may take place in the bedroom, in the garage, or in the backyard. Everything changes when we receive an unmistakable sign that we "just know" is from our missing loved one.

When we get that sign, a connection is made that touches our soul in a way that cannot be denied. The message is clear as our spirit leaps with joy. With a sudden realization our thoughts cry out, "You're alive, you're really alive!" And at that moment, we feel a presence and know without a doubt we are not alone; we have not been abandoned. Like a bandage wrapped around our wounded heart, the sign gives us hope, and healing begins.

The signs we receive from loved ones in heaven cannot and should not be disregarded. The communion of saints is speaking and their silent voices are shouting from the rooftops, "We're here, we're here and we want to help." We can no longer ignore their presence with us here on earth. Furthermore, it's time to give credit, where credit is due. It's time to acknowledge the source of our inspiration. Whether it's from God or Grandma, our greatest creations have been guided by spirit.

Communication between various levels of the church is essential to the doctrine on the communion of saints. As a Vatican spokesman pointed out, "Where there is communion there is communication"; most would agree that we can't have one without the other (Hooper). We need to stay connected, in some fashion, to preserve the interrelationship of church members; this is how we "practice" the communion of saints.

If spirit communication continues to be banned and condemned within Catholicism, then people will become more and more disconnected, not only from their loved ones, but from the canonized saints as well. Some, however, will choose to disconnect from the church instead. When we cease to look to the heavens for help and guidance, we cease to look for spiritual solutions to our problems. If we can't take an active role in communing with our dearly departed, then the memories of our martyrs and saints will fade away like the last rays of light in a distant sunset. With each passing year, our number of heavenly role models will dwindle as fast as our number of Catholic priests, churches and schools. Indeed, this seems to be the case already.

By encouraging its members to practice communion with the saints, the church authorities can revive this great tradition of honoring all those who have gone before us. In addition, we can embrace those who are gifted with the ability to communicate with the deceased and allow them to contribute to the church treasury by teaching others. Gifts of grace are supposed to be shared with the whole church; we must first, however, give people the opportunity to do so.

We need to set aside our fears so that the love of our family and friends in spirit can flow throughout the transcendent church. Eternal beings cannot be limited to only one plane of existence. The interrelationship of church members, both within and across dimensions, is central to a holy, apostolic church. So let us celebrate our Catholic heritage by practicing communion with the saints and by talking not only to God, but to Grandma as well. Whether we are in the cemetery, our kitchen, or in our own secret garden, the key to the conversation is "love," and we are only a whisper away.

Summary

Sometimes a bird is not just a bird; sometimes it's a messenger from heaven. Our loved ones in spirit find many ways to communicate with us. They often use "signs" to show us that we are still very much a part of their lives. Signs are a type of "after-death communication," which is how our deceased family and friends are able to contact us directly; we call this "spiritual sign language."

Through the use of meaningful or "cathectic" symbols, our family and friends can make us aware of their presence. In response, we can share our feelings and ideas with them. This interchange of thoughts, between dimensions, or between different levels of the church, is called "transcommunication."

There are many signs to look for when we are waiting to hear from someone who has crossed over. Flickering light bulbs, malfunctioning electrical devices, stopped clocks, computer anomalies, mysterious phone calls, out of place odors or objects, a favorite song on the radio, or an unexpected gift, are all common events that signal a heavenly being. Mother Nature often plays a role in facilitating a conversation; look for unusual behavior by birds, animals, and butterflies; sometimes shooting stars or rainbows are a sign. It is not uncommon, however, for our special angel to contact us more directly, such as in a dream visit, by speaking to us, or by making an actual appearance.

But how do we know if a sign we receive is actually from a friend in spirit? Look for several other events to occur, such as a physical change in your body, a "just knowing," or an emotional response followed by a sense of peace. A sign is a highly personal event, which should be treasured as a gift; don't listen to skeptics, who tell you otherwise.

By practicing the communion of saints, we can maintain relationships with loved ones who have passed. This ongoing connection can help us at critical times in our life by providing us with an extra source of guidance. In addition, the more we are aware of our friends in heaven, the more we are aware of own immortality. As a result, we can fully partake in the transcendent church as an active member of the communion of saints.

Chapter 12
Just One More Opinion

Final Thoughts

"I am but a fleeting thought in the cosmic consciousness, but as integral a part of the universe, as each molecule is to a drop of water." (Grace)

This is the concluding chapter in my story about the communion of saints; the journey has been long. It's been over ten years since my mother died and since my near-death experience. Much of that time was spent researching and writing this book; it has been the most extraordinary period of my life. I have gained a lot, lost a lot, laughed a lot and cried a lot; I made a lot of friends along the way. My voyage has taken me many places; I have had many incredible experiences and I have grown a great deal in the process.

I know not what the next chapter in my life brings, but I trust that God will provide me with the perfect circumstances and events for the sometimes less-than-perfect mission that is my life. I know my Father in heaven never ceases to amaze me and always seems to have a better plan than the one I had in mind. I can only imagine what lies in store, but I'm sure there will be plenty more opportunities for spiritual growth along the way. One thing I can always be sure of, no matter where life takes me, I will always be a child of God and a member of the communion of saints. In that thought I will always feel safe, protected, loved beyond words, and eternally grateful for the sense of contentment that fills me with peace.

I want to thank you, dear reader, for walking down this road-less-traveled with me. You are a martyr for choosing this crooked, controversial, paranormal path, which was made straight by Jesus and the holy spirits. Please follow me a bit further so that I can share with you my concluding thoughts and opinions on the communication highway to the saints. When this literary journey together has ended, I look forward to the day when our paths will cross again. Although this is the final chapter on this leg of my journey, there are many more stories to write.

The Spiritual Issue

My trip into The Light freed me. I discovered that I was a spiritual being and was not limited to my physical body or the physical world. With my new-found paranormal abilities, I also discovered that there is so much more to life than what our religion teaches us. Like the title character in Richard Bach's book, *Jonathan Livingston Seagull*, I discovered new ways to fly.

Religion puts limits on us; however, there are no boundaries for spiritual beings. In the mystical reality we can communicate and interact with all members of the church, no matter in which dimension they live. Furthermore, Catholicism teaches us we are separate from each other and God, but the truth is we are all one. For these reasons, following my near-death experience, my religion no longer made sense to me; I was confused.

I was confused, I had a lot of questions, and wanted answers; no one seemed to have them. I made repeated requests to get help from my priest to understand what was happening to me. Instead of receiving the compassionate assistance I needed, however, I was banished. This devastating blow both saddened and angered me beyond words. I was hurting and when I needed my religion the most, the church door was locked. Driven from the flock, I was an outcast seagull.

I sought long and hard to find the answers as to why I was unacceptable and what I did that was so awful. I felt an injustice had been done, not only to me, but to Jesus, to God, and to countless others like me. With the help of our Father in heaven, along with a multitude of angels and much research along the way, I was better able to understand the situation. I understood that fear-based thinking and ignorance was the problem, and that love and education was the answer. In the end, I knew that I must one day return to the flock that I had been banned from, and like *Jonathan Livingston Seagull*, teach others what I had learned - new ways to fly.

I wrote this book because I wanted to right a wrong, and I had something to say; I'm not quite finished. I wanted to change the Roman Catholic Church's policies on excluding people of the faith whose beliefs are slightly different, and to enlighten its leaders about the harmful effects they are having on many of God's children. I hope that my journey will inspire some people to take positive action in making much needed amendments in our faith, so all may participate as active members of the communion of saints.

Community Worship

One way to participate in the communion of saints is by going to a place where all souls gather in fellowship. This place is called "church" and the event is called "Mass." But why do we worship God in community? What is it about getting together with like-minded people that holds such an attraction to us? Certainly we can worship God on our own; we don't need to go to church for that, yet we do. I believe that gathering together to worship is the experience of God. It connects us with our Father in Heaven, which reinforces a powerful, loving relationship our soul remembers and longs for.

We long for a connection to Home while we are struggling here on the physical plane. We find that connection in our faith community. Our parish is much more than a place to worship and means much more than any one religion. As part of our social identity, it's an integral part of our lives. Our individual faith communities are our sacred place, our refuge. It's where we go to renew ourselves by receiving the spiritual nourishment our souls hunger for. To worship God in community, with those whom we deeply care about, is our piece of heaven. It is our Home away from Home; that's why it's so important to us.

God doesn't want to be just worshiped; however, he wants to be *experienced*. We can spend our entire life worshiping God, studying Him, and learning about His son's teachings. We can quote the Bible and memorize lengthy scriptures, but until we feel God's presence, we don't know Him. God is an emotion to be experienced —He is love. We find this experience whenever we congregate as a religious community. In the words of Jesus, "Wherever two or more are gathered in my name, there I will be" (Matthew 18:20).

We experience God in many ways when we assemble for Mass. We experience Him in the music we make together and in the words of the homily that seem to speak directly to us. We experience God in the face of the child staring back at us from the pew in front, and in the cry of the baby being baptized. We experience God when we join hands to sing the Lord's Prayer and when we shake hands during the sign of peace. We experience God in the family and friends in our parish communities we have come to know and love over the course of a lifetime.

We experience God, not in our mind, but in our heart. Once we experience Him, our souls awaken to the presence of the Holy Spirit, which resides in each of us; consequently, we come to know ourselves as a part of this loving force. In our common relationship with our Father in heaven, we understand we are truly brothers and sisters and we are truly one with each other and with God; we experience unity.

When we gather for community worship, it's one hour a week when all judgments are laid down and people treat each other like the sons and daughters of God we are; we are all equal in the eyes of the Lord. At Mass, all hierarchies are dropped and everyone is on the same level playing field; we have all committed sins. It matters not whether the person you are sitting next to is a doctor or a maintenance worker. It matters not whether he or she lives in a mansion or lives on the street. It matters not whether the person is divorced, gay, or an alcoholic.

When we drop our judgments and gather for the common cause of Jesus, it makes even the most unworthy people feel worthy. It makes the sad people, happy and the lonely people, less lonely. It makes the intolerable, bearable and makes the unloved feel loved. It is the presence and experience of the Divine that brings peace and harmony to such diversity. We see the light of Christ in each other when we gather in His name. As a result, the hurting and the pain cease, if but for one hour a week, and fear is replaced with Love.

In our acceptance of each other we find acceptance of ourselves. All any of us really wants is to be loved and accepted. It is of utmost importance that our church leaders know this. It is important that they show by example that we are all lovable and acceptable just the way we are, because of who we are - a child of God. Jesus knew this and he paid with his life trying to teach us love and acceptance. Let our faith communities reflect this teaching and be a sanctuary of healing and hope.

When we gather together for community worship we become a church - an instrument of God's peace. As inspired by the prayer of Saint Francis, church becomes a place to go where our hatred is sown with love, where our injury is pardoned, and where our doubt becomes faith. When we come together for Mass, our despair becomes hope, our darkness is filled with light, and our sadness becomes joy. We gather not to be consoled, but to console; not to be understood, but to understand each other. We come to church not to be loved, but to love God and one another with all our souls. For it is in giving of ourselves that we receive and in pardoning that we are pardoned. It is when we die unto ourselves and live for each other, our community, and our shared love of God, that we are born to eternal life. Our soul yearns for Home and remembers it in our weekly mass. For one hour a week it's heaven on earth.

God is not in our religion but in our individual faith communities. However, one can find the experience of God in religion because it brings people together to worship. It matters not in which building you gather, whether it's a synagogue, a mosque, a temple, or a cathedral. The religion doesn't matter and the sermon doesn't matter. The ceremony doesn't make a difference and it doesn't matter who leads the service. The presence of God is in the people who make up the church; He is embodied in the faith community.

Organized religion, with all its rules and regulations is, in itself, silly. You don't need anyone to tell you how to be holy or divine, or whether or not you are worthy, you already are. Religion, however, serves a purpose by providing fellowship in a loving environment, and that's where God is.

We may also experience our Heavenly Father in whatever community we feel welcomed and loved. We may find God in church, but we may also find him in an AA meeting. We may find God in the homeless shelter or in a hospice home; in a program for prisoners or a mental health program. God can be found in a poker club or a health club; in a gardening group or in a group home. We may discover Him in a circle of saints or in a séance circle; on a team of writers or a sports team. Wherever you find love, acceptance and appreciation for the talents you have and the person you are, that's where Jesus is, that's where God is; that's the communion of saints.

Living in Exile

Church serves a purpose by providing fellowship in a safe, loving and sacred atmosphere. But what if that atmosphere is not so safe or loving; what if it's hurtful and unkind? What if the church atmosphere is unfriendly and less-than-holy for certain members of the parish community? What happens to those who are ostracized by their own religion?

Sadly, there are many who are not allowed to attend a Roman Catholic Mass; they have been excommunicated. They no longer qualify to play ball on the major league team because they made too many unforgivable errors. They struck out, had their final at bats, and were cut from the parish lineup. There are many who were forced to hang up their rosaries, give up their pew, and hand over their keys to the Catholic kingdom.

There are countless others who have been alienated from the church because they are allowed to attend Mass but not allowed to receive Holy Communion. "Communion" means "participation," so why would people attend a celebration of Mass if they can't participate in the Eucharistic meal. That's like telling people that they are welcome to stay for dinner, as long as they don't eat. That's like going to a baseball game and not being allowed to have a hotdog, or any food for that matter; it's just not right.

Unfortunately, there are an untold number of the faithful living in exile who don't have a welcoming Catholic community like Spiritus Christi. As a result, many are feeling lost and lonely, unloved and unaccepted, disappointed and discouraged. Many are feeling like there are two outs in the bottom of the ninth, they're down by seven runs, and their spiritual bat is broken.

If you are living in exile and in a state of despair, just remember that you are not alone. You belong to a much bigger team of believers who are cheering you on from the other side. Your family and friends in the afterlife are on hand to help you through this life. Your transdimensional friends want to remind you that you are in this world but not of it. Your heavenly guides want to remind you that in the illusion of physical reality you may feel like a loser, but in the mystical reality you are a homerun hitter, a golden glove winner, and a magnificent MVP. All you need do is to invoke those who are always ready and willing to help. Reach back to your childhood memories and call on your angels in the outfield by reciting the first prayer you ever learned:

> **Angel of God, my guardian dear,**
> **To whom God's love, commits me here.**
> **Ever this day, be at my side,**
> **To light and guard, to rule and guide.**
> **Amen**

Remember that you are never alone; you can rely on your guardian angels whenever you need help. Remember your family and friends in spirit and how much you are loved. Keep in mind that you are immortal and you have been accepted for a permanent position as a perpetual player on the timeless team roster of the communion of saints. Don't forget that no power on earth can ever excommunicate you from your sacred status, and no one can throw you out, when you're already home.

Embrace your sacred heritage and the power of divine love that resides within you and you will overcome all doubts, worries and fears. Remember that you are important and you are special, because you are the sons and daughters of God; you are worthy by birthright. So take your rightful place at the Lord's Table; Jesus is calling you up to his team. Go to your Father's house and join Him in the major league, where nobody has unforgivable errors, where nobody strikes out, where nobody is cut from the roster, and where everyone is allowed to play ball in their very own field of dreams. Grab your rosary, take back your pew, and refuse to live in exile; let no one stand in your way.

Inalienable Rights

Under the laws of our democratic government we have inalienable rights, which include life, liberty, freedom, equality and the pursuit of happiness. These basic human rights are the acknowledgement of the divinity in each and every person on this planet. This is the spiritual principle on which our country was founded, which is "One nation under God." We are inalienable or incapable of being separated from this higher power, as an attribute of our divine status and value as a child of The Almighty.

As American citizens, we are brought up with a clear understanding of our rights and we will not tolerate anyone who infringes on those rights; we sue people who do. We also know that these rights are not handed out to select individuals, such as the most wealthy, most powerful, or most popular; we have equal rights. As a country, we believe so strongly in our inalienable divinity that we are constantly striving to provide these same rights for children of God in other nations throughout the world.

Why is it, then, that we allow ourselves to give up these rights in our religion? Does our U.S. citizenship end when we walk through church doors? Why do we put up with totalitarian, discriminating laws within our faith, but would never think of doing so outside our faith? Why have large numbers of Catholics been alienated from the church? How have we become estranged from each other, and from God? Are Catholics less divine than Americans? If democracy is not practiced within our parish communities, how can we be expected to take church laws seriously? This is not what Jesus had in mind when he said, "I am the way, the truth and the life"; Jesus had democracy, love and compassion in mind.

The same democratic teachings of Christ are what the United States government is based on, which is much more spiritual than our religion. At least our government tries to unite the people of our nation and give them equal rights. Our faith divides the people of our nation and tells their members some are better than others; therefore, certain individuals have more rights than others. Why do our religious principles and practices, which should be held to a higher standard, not share this core belief in the American way? The Roman Catholic-way needs to be in sync with the rights of U.S. citizens and twenty-first century living.

We need to stop worshipping our religion and its leaders. We need to stop tolerating the holier-than-thou attitude our church leaders have adopted. We need to put an end to discrimination within the church and the erroneous belief that some Catholics are better than others. We need to stop living in fear of being exiled if we refuse to participate in church policies that abuse and humiliate us, as well as our fellow parishioners. We need to start standing up for ourselves and demand to be treated with respect and dignity as divine members of the communion of saints.

What Matters

What matters is not our differences, but our similarities. So let our human compassion and mutual love for Jesus replace our fear of each other. We are all neighbors, we are all brothers and sisters, we are all parts of the same mystical body of Christ. We are all members of the communion of saints, we are all children of God; we are all one. Therefore, what matters is that we demonstrate respect, tolerance and kindness to those who appear different from us.

What matters is not what our occupation or religion is, but how we live our life. Everything we say and do is a statement of who we are; we are guides and teachers by our actions and our lifestyle. Whether we're a sanitation worker or a CEO, we need to ask ourselves the questions that matter:

> Am I an honest worker?
> Am I kind and friendly to those I serve, as well as my coworkers?
> Am I compassionate?
> Am I here to serve or to be served?
> Am I a good parent, a good child, a good sibling?
> Am I a good neighbor, a good friend?
> Have I forgiven others, as well as myself?
> What have I done with my life?

All relationships are a relationship with God; therefore, how we treat our neighbor is a reflection of how we treat our Father in heaven. In the end, it's not between us and any other person, it's between us and God. If we can feel right with our neighbor and die tomorrow with no regrets, no anger, no irreconcilable differences; if we have forgiven, buried the hatchet, made amends, atoned for our transgressions; if we can stand in the presence of God and state, "All is right with my soul."; that's what matters. Most of all, love, "love" is all that matters because all matter, which is God, is "Love."

My Hope

I have hope; it came about as a result of my encounter and emergence into the light and love of God. To be in God's presence is to know your oneness with Him and all of creation. To be in God's light is to know that in this life we can never be separated from our Father in Heaven or from each other. As we are one with God, it is my hope that someday all people will be at one with the Church and that no child of God will be left behind or left out. We are the soul of our faith communities; we are the church. I have hope that the day will come when no one will be excluded. In the near future, I hope:

Women will be ordained and take their rightful place next to Jesus.

Divorced and remarried members of the flock will be able to partake in the healing power of Christ contained within the Eucharist.

Gay and lesbian believers will find acceptance in our Catholic churches and their unions will be recognized.

Clairvoyant believers will find open mindedness and will be able to share their gifts with other members of our parish communities.

Priests will be given the opportunity to marry, no matter what the gender of his or her spouse.

The same inalienable rights we enjoy as US citizens, under God, may one day be incorporated into our faith communities.

The muggle-minded mentality of oppression, discrimination and exclusivity will be replaced by the mystical, Christ-mind mentality of tolerance, compassion and unconditional love for all.

It is my hope that the future leaders of our church will re-think their position on separating and dividing people of our faith who do not fit into their idealisms; moreover, that they will actually practice the teachings of Christ by uniting the people of God. I hope those who have been banned from the Lord's Table, due to their marital status, sexual orientation, or spiritual gifts, will be welcomed back into the church.

I have hope that the countless sheep without a flock, will find the guidance of a good shepherd, and those who are lost will be found. Like the prodigal son, I envision all the despondent, disconnected, disheartened and downtrodden will one day be greeted with joy, open arms, and much celebration. We will bestow them with gifts of robes and sandals and prepare a great feast for them. We will set a place for them at the Lord's Table so they may share in the Eucharist with all believers in Christ Jesus and participate as active members of the communion of saints. This is my hope.

What I Learned – A Summary

During this spiritual journey, I received an extraordinary education. Through the hundreds of people I met and hundreds of books I read, I learned a vast amount of fascinating information about my faith. What surprised me the most was that I often learned more about Catholicism from people outside the faith, than I did from people within it, or even from my own upbringing as a Catholic. Looking at a subject from an opposing point of view can be very enlightening.

At the same time, I learned from many other Catholics that the experiences and beliefs with which they were raised were often much different than mine. For example, those who were taught by nuns in parochial school had a much different understanding of Catholic teachings, customs and traditions than I, who went to public school. It seems there are as many shades of Catholicism as there are members of the world-wide church.

In my research, one of the first things I discovered was that "saints" are not only the dead canonized people, but all believers in heaven, earth and purgatory, including Grandma. This group of people, which make up the transcendent church, is called the "communion of saints." The history of this church doctrine can be traced back to Judaism and the idea of a holy people sharing holy things.

I learned that the members of the tri-level church communicate with each other through a "constant interchange of supernatural offices." This exchange of thoughts and ideas, also known as "spirit communication" or "prayer," is how we maintain relationships with family and friends who have crossed over. The two-way participation in spiritual "goods and good" requires believers to utilize their sixth sense or psychic ability. For these reasons, both parapsychology and spiritualism are essential to understanding the important church doctrine on the communion of saints.

It was discovered that communication with saints in the afterlife is in direct contradiction to Roman Catholic laws, which state that the practice of spiritualism and the use of psychic gifts are forbidden. These church doctrines originated in Old Testament religious competition and have no relevant basis in today's society. Paranormal phenomena were practiced by many prophets in both the Old and New Testament, as well as by many of our Christian mystics and canonized saints; these same practices are found in today's Roman Catholic Mass. The inconsistencies in church laws, however, do not end there.

There are also contradictions when it comes to the spiritually gifted members of the church. On the one hand we revere our Christian mystics, while on the other hand we condemn psychic mediums; both use extrasensory perception. Much of the confusion stems from the language we use. Science and religion often use different words to say the same thing. For example, there is no real difference between "paranormal" and "supernatural" events; there is no real difference between a "clairvoyant" and a "visionary," and there is no real difference between "psychic ability" and "spiritual gifts of grace."

I realized that God is the creator of both science and religion; God is the creator of both mystics and mediums. The contradictions and erroneous teachings within our faith have led to much confusion and many misunderstandings about the supernatural and those who participate in it. The result has been detrimental to the emotional welfare, credibility and self-esteem of God's intuitive children.

I found that religion needs science to provide validity to its belief system. At the same time, science needs religion to give meaning to life and a reason to study it. We need both facts and faith before we can arrive at truth and conviction. Faith, without facts to back it up, leads to delusional thinking, rather than theological truth. True belief comes from within, not from without; it can only be found when our hearts and souls agree with our mind. Both religion and science are important for our spiritual growth.

It was revealed that church leaders went in search of facts to support the supernatural element in our faith; they even conducted studies on the matter. A valiant attempt was made to address paranormal issues by establishing some official procedures for analyzing apparitions, revelations and spiritualism. I also learned that the church leaders often ignored their own policies and even the results of their own investigations. They chose to suppress information that may have been beneficial to those who have had a supernatural experience. For example, the studies concluded that the practice of spiritualism does not go against the teachings of the church. On the contrary, spirit communication can help to enhance our faith, yet, it is forbidden.

I found out that religion has tried to suppress science throughout history; discoveries by Galileo, Copernicus and Darwin are examples. As a result, science has often dragged religion kicking and screaming into the present-day world. Much of that resistance has been due to ancient, fear-based beliefs, which have been dispelled with new inventions, increased technology and education; gradually our religious policies changed. When it comes to spiritualism and parapsychology, it's time for another revision in church laws to bring our faith into the twenty-first century.

My research revealed that science and religion can work together to help us strengthen our faith. Parapsychology is one science that can help us to better understand the person of Jesus. With this, comes a better understanding of the nature of man and who we are as divine children of God. As offspring of a supernatural Father, we too have supernatural abilities, which often display themselves when we are participating in alternate levels of reality. I learned that we should share our spiritual gifts and experiences as Jesus did. In so doing, we will find that paranormal abilities are to be revered, not feared, and that they "fit in" to our religion.

I studied mystics, mediums and muggles, along with the three levels of reality in which they live, mystical, metaphysical and physical. Although people can communicate across dimensions, due to the disparity in levels of consciousness, often something is lost in the interpretation. For this reason, mystical teachings are frequently misinterpreted and seldom understood by muggles. This is never more evident than when it comes to church teachings on the supernatural side of our faith, especially spirit communication. I learned it is not enough to follow the rules of the faith; we need to *experience* our faith, not only with our minds, but with our hearts and souls as well. One way in which we can have mystical experiences is by practicing communion with the saints. A "circle of saints" meditation group can open the door to spiritual experiences and provide believers with the opportunity to develop their own gifts. When the faithful learn to listen to the holy ones in spirit, their hearts and souls will grow closer to God; this in turn, helps build the kingdom of heaven. Without mystical experiences to bolster our faith, such as spirit communication, people will become more and more disconnected, not only from their loved ones, but from the canonized saints and the church as well.

I discovered that spiritualism, in the context of the communion of saints, is a practice to be respected, not ridiculed. When we understand how we can have a relationship with the saints in heaven, we can understand how we can also have a relationship with Grandma in heaven. It is important to keep these transdimensional associations alive to help ease our loneliness, help lessen our fear of death, and provide us with an extra measure of safety and protection. With the aid of spiritual sign language and after-death communications, our loved ones in spirit remind us that we will one day be reunited, which accelerates the grieving process, promotes healing and gives us hope.

Most importantly, I learned what it means to be "truly Catholic." The word "catholic" is synonymous with the "communion of saints." They both refer to an all-inclusive, universal church unbound by time and space. I learned that this church, if it practices Christ's teachings, must embrace all people, no matter what their religion, marital status, sexual orientation, or gender. Whether Jew or Greek, male or female, gay or divorced, everyone is my neighbor and, therefore, is welcome to share a meal at the Lord's Table. For all people are precious parts of the one mystical body of Christ, which constitutes the church and the communion of saints; this is what it means to be "truly Catholic."

In the end, I learned that I do not have to give up my spiritual gifts in order to remain Catholic; both are essential to full participation in the communion of saints. I discovered the importance of not trading my own truth and beliefs for a prepackaged one, and not to be mesmerized by the trappings and pretty wrappings of religion. I must take what rings true to me from the myriad spiritual teachings, and leave the rest behind; to decide for myself what to believe and to live my life in accordance with that belief. Best of all, I found there are Catholic communities that embrace a diversity of beliefs and spiritual gifts and welcome all members of the communion of saints to partake in the Eucharistic celebration.

Because I discovered what it means to be a "true Catholic," I no longer feel that I am living in exile. I am exactly where I belong, at Spiritus Christi Catholic Church. It's where I'm accepted, where I'm included, and where I'm loved, not because I fit in, but because I *don't* fit in, and that's who Jesus represented. I go to the misfit mass, the one made up of Roman Catholic rejects, in the hospital for sinners, not in the showcase for saints, because that's where Jesus is. No, I'm not in exile; I'm in my home-away-from-home at Spiritus Christi. I'm where everyone is accepted and loved for who he or she is - a child of God and a member of the communion of saints.

In conclusion, I learned that with the complete understanding of the communion of saints, the fear and stigma attached to psychic phenomena and the supernatural has been dispelled. Contacting our dearly departed and participating in the spiritual realms is no longer taboo. First-century thinking about the paranormal has been changed in light of twenty-first century knowledge. By integrating the science of parapsychology with Christian Theology, mysticism and modern-day Spiritualism, I have come to truly comprehend what it means to profess, "I believe in the communion of saints." I also discovered what it means to be a truly universal and all-inclusive church; as a result, a new age of Catholicism has dawned.

Let Me Introduce Yourself

I want to close by introducing yourself. You see, I want you to know who you are, who you really are. This is the most important part of my story because by telling you who you are, I hope to reveal to you who your neighbor is too. In the end, we will all have a better understanding of each other. When you know and understand another person you cannot judge them, you can only forgive them. This is what my story has been about, so let me introduce yourself.

You are not your name, your sex, your nationality, or cultural background; you are not your religion. You are not your sexual preference or your marital status. You are not your occupation, your educational achievement, or your level of intelligence. You are not from the country, state or town you were raised in, or where you currently live. Your earthly parents did not create you; you are an orphaned soul who was lovingly adopted.

Who you are, first and foremost, and all that matters, is a child of God. You are a holy, divine creation, and are perfect in the eyes of your Father. You are the light and the love of God. When he looked upon his creation he saw that it was good. You are worthy by birthright. You are not a sinner but a child who came to the physical world to make mistakes so you could learn and grow from them. In so doing, you will return home with a soul that is more compassionate, more tolerant, more understanding and, therefore, closer to God.

Your church is the Kingdom of Heaven and your religion is Unconditional Love. To put it in a common phrase, "You are a spiritual being having a human experience." You can't put earthly labels on a spiritual being. None of those labels matter in the presence of God. They mean nothing in the afterlife, or as I prefer to call it, the "beforelife." All aspects of your physical body are only temporal; you have had many human experiences with many labels. Your soul, on the other hand, is eternal. You have only one life, but have had many incarnations.

You can remove all your earthly labels and it will not affect who you are. Others cannot judge you, only the person they perceive you to be. Your body, with all the attached labels is all part of the role you are currently playing. They are only illusions of your real self. Any judgments that others make about you are merely judgments about the character you are playing in this charade called life. You can't even honestly judge yourself because you have forgotten a great deal about your former lives. You forgot who you are so that you can remember who you are not; you are recalling more and more each day.

It is my hope that I have reminded you of who you are and that the veil of forgetfulness has been lifted just enough so that you can see The Light in all people, but mostly in yourself. By giving you a glimpse of divinity, it is my belief that you too will see it in all of humanity. By remembering you are loved without conditions and without labels, you will love others in the same way. It is my hope that you have found your place among the communion of saints and the healing has begun - mind, body and spirit; everything is going to be all right.

The Prophet - On Religion

And an old priest said, Speak to us of Religion.
And he said:
Have I spoken this day of aught else?
Is not religion all deeds and all reflection,
And that which is neither deed nor reflection,
but a wonder and a surprise ever springing in the soul,
even while the hands hew the stone or tend the loom?
Who can separate his faith from his actions, or his belief from his
occupations?
Who can spread his hours before him, saying, "This for God and this for
myself; This for my soul, and this other for my body?"
All your hours are wings that beat through space from self to self.

He who wears his morality but as his best garment were better naked.
The wind and the sun will tear no holes in his skin.
And he who defines his conduct by ethics
imprisons his song-bird in a cage.
The freest song comes not through bars and wires.
And he to whom worshipping is a window, to open but also to shut,
has not yet visited the house of his soul
whose windows are from dawn to dawn.

Your daily life is your temple and your religion.
Whenever you enter into it take with you your all.
Take the plow and the forge and the mallet and the lute,
The things you have fashioned in necessity or for delight.
For in revery you cannot rise above your achievements
nor fall lower than your failures.
And take with you all men:
For in adoration you cannot fly higher than their hopes
nor humble yourself lower than their despair

And if you would know God not therefore a solver of riddles
Rather look about you and you shall see Him playing with your children.
And look into space; you shall see Him walking in the cloud,
outstretching His arms in the lightening and descending in rain.
You shall see Him smiling in flowers,
then rising and waving His hands in trees.

–Kahlil Gibran

Appendix A

Patron Saints and their Feast Days
Saints of Occupations, Illnesses & States of Life

Patronage	Saint	Feast Day
Actors	St. Genesius	August 25
AIDS patients	St. Peregrine Lasiosi	May 1
Alpinist	St. Bernard of Menthon	May 28
Altar Boys	St. John Berchmans	August 13
Animals	St. Francis of Assisi	October 4
Architects	St. Thomas the Apostle	December 21
Artillerymen	St. Barbara	December 4
Art	St. Catherine of Bologna	March 9
Artists	St. Luke	October 18
Astronomers	St. Dominic	August 4
Athletes	St. Sebastian	January 20
Authors	St. Francis de Sales	January 29
	St. John the Apostle	December 27
Aviators	Our Lady of Loreto	December 10
	St. Therese of Lisieux	October 3
Bakers	St. Elizabeth of Hungary	November 19
	St. Nicholas	December 6
Bankers	St. Matthew	September 21
Barbers	SS Cosmas and Damian	September 27
	St. Louis	August 25
Barren Women	St. Anthony of Padua	June 13
	St. Felicitas	November 23
Basket-makers	St. Anthony, Abbot	January 17
Beggars	St. Alexius	July 17
Bi-racial, multi-ethnic	St. Martin de Porres	November 3

Blacksmiths	St. Dunstan	May 19
	St. Brigid	February 1
Blind	St. Odilia	December 13
	St. Raphael	October 24
Bodily Ills	Our Lady of Lourdes	February 11
Bookbinders	St. Peter Celestine	May 19
Booksellers	St. John of God	March 8
Boyscouts	St. George	April 23
Brewers	St. Augustine of Hippo	August 28
	St. Luke	October 18
Bricklayers	St. Stephen	December 26
Brides	St. Nicholas of Myra	December 6
Builders	St. Vincent Ferrer	April 5
Butchers	St. Anthony, Abbot	January 17
	Peter the Apostle	June 29
Cab-drivers	St. Fiacre	August 30
Cabinet-makers	St. Anne	July 26
Cancer patients	St. Peregrine	May 2
Carpenters	St. Joseph	March 19
Catholic Action	St. Francis of Assisi	October 4
Charitable Societies	St. Vincent de Paul	July 19
Children	St. Nicholas of Myra	December 6
Choir Boys	Holy Innocents	December 28
Clerics	St. Gabriel of the Sorrowful Mother	February 27
Comedians	St. Vitus	June 15
Computer Protection	Columba	June 9
Confessors	St. Alphonsus Liguori	August 2
Convulsion in Children	St. Scholastica	February 10
Cooks	St. Lawrence	August 10
	St. Martha	July 29
Coppersmiths	St. Maurus	January 15
	St. Benedict	July 11
Craftsmen, potters	Catherine of Alexandria	November 25
Dairy Workers	St. Brigid	February 1
Deaf	St. Francis de Sales	January 29
Dentist	St. Apollonia	February 9
Desperate situations	St. Jude Thaddeus	October 28
	St. Gregory of	

	Neocaesarea	November 17
Divorced	Helena	August 18
Druggists	SS. Cosmas & Damian	September 27
	St. James the Less	May 1
Dying	St. Joseph	March 19
	St. Barbara	December 4
Ecologists	St. Francis of Assisi	October 4
Engineers	St. Ferdinand III	May 30
Epilepsy	St. Dymphna	May 15
Expectant Mothers	St. Margaret	July 20
Eye Trouble	St. Lucy	December 13
Falsely Accused	St. Raymond Nonnatus	August 31
Farmers	St. George	April 23
	St. Isidore	March 22
Firemen/women	St. Florian	May 4
Fishermen	St. Andrew	November 30
Florists	St. Dorothy	February 6
	St. Therese of Lisieux	October 1
Forest Workers	St. John Gualbert	July 12
Funeral Directors	St. Joseph of Arimathea	March 17
Gardeners	St. Fiacre	August 30
	St. Dorothy	February 6
Goldsmiths	St. Dunstan	May 19
Grocers	St. Michael	September 29
Hairdressers	SS. Cosmas & Damian	September 26
Headaches	St. Teresa of Avila	October 15
Healers	Gerard Majella	October 16
Heart Ailments	St. John of God	March 8
Hopeless Causes	St. Jude Thaddeus	October 28
Horsemen	St. Anne	July 6
Hospitals	St. Camillus	July 18
Housewives	St. Anne	July 26
Hunters	St. Hubert	November 3
Immigrants	Frances Xavier Cabrini (Mother Cabrini)	November 13
Inn Keepers	St. Amand	February 6
Invalids	St. Roch	August 16
Jewelers	St. Eligius	December 1
Journalists	St. Francis de Sales	January 29

Jurists	St. Catherine of Alexandria	November 25
Laborers	St. Isidore	May 10
	St. James	July 25
Lawyers	St. Ivo	June 17
	St. Genesius	August 25
Librarians	St. Jerome	September 30
Locksmiths	St. Dunstan	May 19
Lost Articles	St. Anthony of Padua	June 13
Love	St. Valentine	February 14
Lupus	St. Lupus	July 29
Mariners	St. Michael	September 29
Mediums	Gerard Majella	October 16
Mentally Ill	St. Dymphna	May 15
Merchants	St. Francis of Assisi	October 4
Messengers	St. Gabriel	March 24
Metalworkers	St. Eligius	December 1
Mice and Rats (Protection from)	St Gertrude of Nivelles	March 17
Miners	St. Barbara	December 4
Missions	St. Francis Xavier	December 3
	St. Therese of Lisieux	October 1
Mothers	Mary the Blessed Virgin	January 1
	St. Monica	May 4
Motorists	St. Christopher	July 25
Motorcyclists	Our Lady of Grace	May 31
Musicians	St. Cecilia	November 22
Notaries	St. Luke	October 18
	St. Mark	April 25
Nurses	St. Agatha	February 5
	St. Camillus de Lellis	July 18
Orphans	St. Jerome Aemilian	July 20
Painters	St. Luke	October 18
Philosophers	St. Justin	April 14
	St. Catherine of Alex	November 25
Physicians	St. Pantaleon	July 27
	SS. Cosmos & Damian	September 27
Pilots, Flight Attendants	Joseph of Capertino	September 18
Poets	St. David	December 29

	St. Cecilia	November 22
Poisoning	St. Benedict	March 21
Policemen/women	St. Michael	September 29
Polio	St. Margaret Mary	October 17
Poor	St. Lawrence	August 10
Possessed	St. Bruno	October 6
	St. Denise	October 9
Postal Workers	St. Gabriel	March 24
Pregnant Women	St. Margaret	July 20
Priests	St. Jean-Baptiste Vianney	August 9
Printers	St. John of God	March 8
	St. Augustine of Hippo	August 28
Prisoners	St. Dismas	March 25
	St. Barbara	December 24
Prophets	Gerard Majella	October 16
Prostitutes	St. Mary Magdalene	July 22
Protector of Crops	St. Ansovinus	March 13
Radiologists	St. Michael	September 29
Radio-workers	St. Gabriel	March 24
Rheumatism	St. James the Greater	July 25
Sailors	St. Cuthbert	March 20
	St. Brendan	May 16
	St. Christopher	July 25
Schools	St. Thomas Aquinas	March 7
Scientists	St. Albert	November 15
Servants	St. Martha	July 29
Shepards	St. Bernadette	April 16
	Simeon Stylites	January 5
Shoemakers	SS. Crispin & Crispinian	October 25
Sick	St. Michael	September 29
	St. Philomena	August 11
Silversmiths	St. Andronicus	October 11
Singers	St. Gregory	March 11
	St. Cecilia	November 22
Skaters	St. Lidwina	April 14
Skiers	St. Bernard of Menthon	May 28
Snakes (protection from)	St. Patrick	March 17
Soldiers	St. Hadrian	September 8
	St. Joan of Arc	May 30

Sore Throat	St. Blaise	February 3
Stenographers	St. Genesius	August 25
Stone Masons	St. Stephen	December 26
Students	St. Thomas Aquinas	March 7
	St. Catherine of Alexandria	November 25
Surgeons	SS. Cosmas & Damian	September 27
Tailors	St. Homobonus	November 13
Tax people	St. Matthew	September 21
Taxi-cab Drivers	St. Fiacre	September 1
Teachers	St. Gregory the Great	March 12
	St. Catherine of Alexandria	November 25
Telegraph/ Telephone Workers	St. Gabriel	March 24
Television Workers	St. Gabriel	March 24
Theologians	St. Augustine	August 28
Travelers	St. Christopher	July 25
Undertakers	St. Dismas	March 25
Vocations	St. Alphonsus	August 2
Wine growers	St. Vincent	January 22
Wine Merchants	St. Amand	February 6
Writers	St. Francis de Sales	January 29
	St. Lucy	December 13
Young Girls	St. Agnes	January 21
Youth	St. Aloysius Gonzaga	June 21
	St. John Berchmans	August 13

To find your patron saint, look for the name on the above list that matches yours. You may also adopt a saint with whose patronage you most identify with. The date provided is the anniversary of that saint's death, and is also your feast day. If your name does not appear on the list, you may use your middle name or go to www. catholic.org and search the Saints & Angels page; thousands of names are listed. In addition, on the same website you may look up the patron saint of each country.

Resources for Patron Saints (see bibliography for complete citation):

All Saints, Daily Reflections On Saints, Prophets, And Witnesses For Our Time (1998). Ellsberg, Robert

Holy Bible, The New American Bible (1990). National Conference of Catholic Bishops

Picture Book of Saints (1979). Lovasick, Rev. Lawrence G.

Saints, Who they are and how they help you (1994). Hallman, Elizabeth.

The Saint Deck Book (2000). Prioletti, Karen & Trump, Ann

Appendix B

Glossary of Terms

After-Death Communication (ADC): A spiritual experience that occurs when someone is contacted directly and spontaneously by a deceased family member or friend. The term "ADC" was created by Bill and Judy Guggenheim and written about in their book, Hello From Heaven.

All Saints Day: November 1 is the celebration of all the deceased who are in heaven.

All Souls Day: November 2 is the celebration and day of prayer for all the deceased who are in purgatory.

Apport: An object alleged to arrive by paranormal means. The materialization of matter from an unknown source. From the French word apporter, meaning "to bring."

Apparition: A visual appearance and manifestation of spirit, which suggests the presence of a deceased person or animal. Also known as a "ghost."

Astrology: A form of divination that studies the position of stars and planets to determine their influence on human affairs.

Aura: The field of multi-colored, electromagnetic energy surrounding every living being. From the Greek word aura, meaning "breeze."

Automatic writing: A form of writing that takes place during an altered state of consciousness. The written information may come from a source outside the writer or from the intuitive mind.

Beatification: "To make blessed," is a title of holiness given to those who have demonstrated an outstanding life of sanctity. It is often bestowed on individuals who are being considered for sainthood.

Bilocation: The phenomenon that occurs when a living person is witnessed to be in two different locations at the same time.

Canonize: To declare a deceased person an officially recognized saint, therefore establishing his or her role as an intercessory for prayer, which allows for public veneration.

Catholic: Relating to a universal church formed from the ancient undivided Christian church, and claiming historical continuity from its roots. A church whose principles are based on the teachings of Jesus, that "all" are to be embraced as God's people. Believers follow a set of common practices and beliefs. From the Greek word katholikos, meaning "towards the whole" and from the Latin translation meaning "universal."

Cathexis: A term used in psychotherapy referring to a person's concentrated investment of psychic energy in a particular concept, idea, image, object or symbol. That concept or symbol is then said to be "cathectic" for that person.

Channeling: A phenomenon that occurs when a medium allows a spirit to speak through, or to temporarily possess, her body for the purpose of direct communication. The medium is usually not consciously aware of what is spoken or what messages are given.

Church Militant: The portion of the church body comprised of the believers on earth.

Church Suffering: The portion of the church body comprised of the believers in purgatory.

Church Triumphant: The portion of the church body comprised of the believers in heaven.

Circle: The term given to a séance or a psychic development group, which describes the circular arrangement of chairs.

Circle of Saints: A gathering of believers whose purpose is to commune with members of the transcendent church, through song, ritual, prayer and meditation. It is one way to practice the communion of saints.

Clairaudience: The ability to hear sounds not accessible to the physical ear; French for "clear hearing."

Clairsentience: The ability to perceive information out of the range of ordinary perception, French for "clear sensing," also translated as "clear thinking" or "clear knowing." It is often associated with the ability to "sense" other people's emotions or feelings.

Clairvoyance: The ability to see things that cannot be seen with the physical eye; French for "clear seeing."

Clairvoyant: A person who is able to see or know things through the use of their sixth sense or psychic ability, often information about future events. Also known as "seer," "visionary," "intuitive" and "prophet."

Communion of Saints: A Roman Catholic doctrine which describes the church as the spiritual solidarity that binds the faithful on earth (Church Militant) with the souls in purgatory (Church Suffering) and in heaven (Church Triumphant), through a constant interchange of supernatural offices.

Day of the Dead: A Hispanic celebration of the deceased, which is marked by cemetery visits to decorate gravesites with flowers, candles and personal objects, as well as to make offerings of food and prayers. It takes place on November 1, All Saints Day.

Divination: The practice of predicting the future using supernatural means. Examples of divination tools are astrology, horoscope,

Tarot, Runes and the Ouija board.

Electronic Voice Phenomenon (EVP): A recording of a sound interpreted as a voice from a ghost or spirit; it may also be a noise, such as rapping, that originated from the spiritual realm. A technique used during psychic investigations to attempt to capture evidence of the presence of a deceased person. The sound is usually recorded on a video camera or tape recorder; EVP's are usually brief and may involve only a single word or a short phrase.

Extrasensory Perception (ESP): The ability to receive information and impressions of thoughts, sounds, smells, emotions, situations, or issues, without the use of the five physical senses; the non-physical or sixth sense is utilized. Examples are clairvoyance and telepathy.

Excommunication: A penalty church authorities impose on members whose actions jeopardize the integrity of the Church. It prohibits a person from receiving the sacraments, including Holy Communion. It is not meant as a punishment but as an opportunity for reconciliation and repentance. Officially, it does not mean expulsion from the church, but it usually has that effect.

Exorcism: A rite to expel an evil spirit, usually done by a priest.

Feast Day: The anniversary of the death of the saint for whom you were named. For example, March 17 is the "feast day" of all those named "Patrick" because that is the day St. Patrick died, which is also known as St. Patrick's Day.

Fortune-teller: A person who practices predicting the future by the use of various tools of divination, for example astrologers, palm readers, numerologist and tarot card readers.

Ghost: The spirit of a deceased person, who has left the physical body and has not yet moved on to the higher realms; an earthbound spirit.

Glossolalia: The phenomenon of speaking in an unknown or fabricated language, also known as "speaking in tongues"; it usually occurs in a religious context.

Grace (Gifts of Grace): A theological term for special talents, virtue or divine assistance given from God. May refer to supernatural or paranormal abilities. From the Latin gratia, meaning "gift" or "favor."

Horoscope: A chart of the relative positions of planets and the signs of the zodiac at a time of a person's birth date to infer the individual's character and personality traits; also used to foretell the person's future.

Indulgence: A prayer or action performed, including monetary donations, to remit the afterlife punishment for sins.

Inspiration: A supernatural influence or suggestion directly communicated to a person; a revelation. From the phrase "in-spirit."

Inspirational Writing: The process of transcribing a message which is a direct supernatural communication or suggestion from a non-physical being. The writer is consciously aware during the process, although he may not understand the meaning of what is written.

Intercession: A prayer, petition, or entreaty, which is said in favor of another.

Intercessor: A person or spiritual being, such as a saint, who says a prayer, petition, or entreaty in favor of another.

Intuition: The ability to know things not related to conscious reasoning.

Intuitive: A person who has the ability to know things through their sixth or psychic sense; also known as a medium or psychic.

Levitation: The raising of an object or person by paranormal or supernatural means.

Locutions: Supernatural words received interiorly in a clear, distinctive manner.

Lots (casting of): A form of divination involving the use of objects, such as sticks or dice, to decide something by chance or to determine one's fortune.

Magic: The use of supernatural powers over natural forces.

Martyr: From the Greek word, meaning "witness," one who willingly suffers the penalty of death for refusing to renounce his religious beliefs; the person is considered a "witness" to the faith. Martyrdom automatically results in sainthood and therefore it is believed that the martyr's soul goes directly to heaven.

Materialization: The process of a spiritual being manifesting into a visible form or material body. The act of bringing an object into material existence and making it seemingly appear from nowhere.

Meditation: The process of engaging in contemplation or reflection of thoughts. An exercise to quiet the mind to gain insight and peace or to commune with a higher source.

Medium: A "go-between" or intermediary. An individual held to be a channel of communication between the physical and non-physical worlds.

Metaphysical: Of or pertaining to the branch of philosophy that looks at the nature of reality, existence, and the structure of the universe.

Metaphysical Reality: A level of reality in which information is received through extrasensory perception or the use of the sixth sense. In this reality "time" is sequential but past, present and future are illusions. Space is not a barrier for communication, which occurs directly; no intermediary device is necessary. In the Transcendent Church Model, this is the level of the Church Suffering (purgatory) and Church Triumphant (heaven), whose members are psychically gifted. It is the reality of mediums and mystics.

Miracle: An extraordinary event that breaks the laws of nature and is believed to be an act of God or divine intervention.

Muggle: A person who does not have a well-developed sixth sense; a psychically challenged individual. A term coined by J.K. Rowling to refer to a person without powers of wizardry.

Mystic: A person whose life is centered on and around God, or a God-like concept, and through meditation engages in a direct relationship with a Supreme Being, from which he or she gains spiritual insight, as well as supernatural abilities. From the Greek word mystikos, meaning "mystery"; mystics are found in all religious traditions.

Mysticism: The practice of direct communion with God through contemplation, which can lead to the acquisition of spiritual knowledge, special graces and supernatural or paranormal abilities.

Mystical Reality: A level of reality in which information is received directly from a "higher power" or God. In this reality "individuality," "time" and "space" are all illusions and unimportant, as are "spiritual gifts." A person in this level of consciousness may possess an extraordinary degree of supernatural abilities; miracles occur. In the Transcendent Church Model this is the level of the Church Triumphant (heaven), whose membership is comprised solely of mystics.

Near-Death Experience (NDE): A spiritually transformative event which usually occurs when a person is clinically dead, facing death, or under physical or emotional trauma. An out-of-body phenomenon in which one encounters a spiritual realm and makes direct contact with an all-loving light, which is often interpreted as "God." The event creates a reality-shift for the experiencer and has a profound impact on personality, behavior, and the way he or she lives their life. Changes are usually positive in nature and spiritually-centered rather than materially-centered. (In a few cases, NDE's have been negative in nature; the person traveled to a dark spiritual realm and had a "hell-like experience").

Occult: Matters regarding secret knowledge about supernatural agencies or mysterious events. From the Latin word *occultare,* meaning "concealed" or hidden.

Oracle: A person giving wise or authoritative decisions through whom a deity is believed to speak. A shrine where one can communicate with the Gods. An answer or decision given by a deity; a revelation.

Ouija: A board inscribed with the alphabet, numbers, and other signs, which is used for the purpose of communicating with spirits. Messages are spelled out via a "planchette" or triangular device that facilitates automatic writing through light fingertip touch. Originally called a "talking board.'

Paranormal: Pertaining to phenomena outside or beyond the normal range of scientific knowledge, which includes psychic and spiritual phenomena.

Parapsychology: The branch of psychology that studies psychic phenomena or things outside the normal paradigms of science; the scientific study of spirituality and spiritualism. The prefix para is Greek for "beyond."

Physical Reality: A level of reality in which we use our five physical senses to receive information about our world. We see ourselves as separate individuals and time is linear. Space is a barrier to receiving distant information; some sort of intermediary device, such as a phone or computer is needed. Spiritual gifts or psychic abilities are not a conscious part of one's life in physical reality. In The Transcendent Church Model this is the level of the Church Militant (earth), whose members include all non-psychic people or "muggles."

Poltergeist: A form of psychokinesis involving the unexplainable movement or breaking of objects, slamming doors, etc. often generated unconsciously by an adolescent with intense emotions. From the German word meaning "noisy ghost." It may or may not involve a ghost, but is often associated with a haunting.

Possession: A state in which a person's body is taken over by, or under the control of, another entity or consciousness.

Prayer: To "entreat," "implore," "plea," or "request earnestly in a humble manner." To call on God or a god for requisition, adoration, confession, or thanksgiving. Telepathic communication with God or one of his agents, such as a saint or angel; a form of spiritualism.

Precognition: Knowledge or awareness of a future event which could not have been predicted or inferred by normal means.

Premonition: A precognitive sense of danger or knowledge of a negative future event.

Preternatural: Refers to things not "supernatural" and not "natural" in the ordinary sense. A theological term for "paranormal."

Prophecy: Knowledge about the future coming in the form of a vision or dream; the source is usually considered divine in nature. The theological term for "precognition."

Psi: In the field of parapsychology it is a simple term used to refer to "psychic phenomena," such as extrasensory perception or psychokinesis. Psi is the first letter of the Greek word *psych*, meaning "breath" or "soul" and refers to the mind and human spirit. It is the root word in "psychology," which is the science of the mind.

Psychic: Refers to knowledge, events or experiences that lie outside the sphere of physical science; phenomena that are spiritual or supernatural in origin. A person who receives information through extrasensory perception; a medium, intuitive or seer. From the Greek word psychikos, meaning "soul."

Psychokinesis (PK): The movement of external objects by the mind, without the influence of any known physical energy or force.

Psychometry: The handling of objects to obtain impressions about its history or information about the lives of people who have had contact with the object. From the Greek psych meaning "breath" or "soul," and metron, meaning "measure."

Purgatory: A state of transition after death in which the soul goes to be purified or cleansed so it can achieve the holiness necessary to enter heaven. A temporary state of misery all souls, who have not died in a "state of grace," must go through to pay for their sins; thus purgatory is referred to as the "Church Suffering." The soul's progression may be aided by prayers or indulgences.

Rapping: Loud, knocking noises made by spirits to make their presence known or to communicate with humans.

Reading: The statements made by a medium during a sitting, which can include messages from spirits or psychic information received directly from the subject; an intuitive counseling session.

Relic: Any part of the physical remains of a saint, such as a bone fragment. Any item that may have belonged to a saint or touched a part of his or her body, such as an article of clothing.

Religion: A system of attitudes, beliefs and practices pertaining to man's relationship with a supernatural or Supreme Being, which directly guides a life based on faith, rather than reason.

Retrocognition: Knowledge of a past event which could only have been learned by paranormal means.

Revelation: Knowledge gained through supernatural means; it usually refers to divine insight or a message directly from God.

Rosary: A string of beads Catholics use to count the group of prayers used to invoke Jesus and his mother, Mary. A set of prayers, which are arranged in five groups of ten Hail Marys called "decades." The act of "saying a rosary" is a meditation on the mysteries of the life and death of Jesus and Mary. The prayers, as well as the beads themselves, are considered sacred. "Rosary," means "garland of roses," a symbol of the Blessed Virgin.

Saint: To be separated from sin and therefore consecrated to God.

In the New Testament it referred to all followers of Jesus, both the living and the dead. Today it more commonly refers only to the most holy deceased, who have been canonized. From the Latin word sanctus, meaning sanctified or holy.

School of Prophets: A ritual-based system of instruction, which uses music, prayer and meditation, to train and prepare students to receive messages from the spiritual realm. A group of people who are brought together for the purpose of learning how to communicate with non-physical beings, including God.

Séance: A meeting or session for the purpose of receiving spirit communication. The participants normally sit in a "circle," which is another term for séance. From the French, meaning "to sit."

Second Sight: The ability to see remote or future events; it can refer to prophesying, clairvoyance and fortune-telling.

Sensitive: A term for someone who is psychic or has extrasensory perception. The person is said to be "sensitive" to the high frequency vibrations of spirits.

Seer: A person who is clairvoyant or possesses the gift of second sight.

Signs: A type of after-death communication from a deceased person, which usually involves the manipulation of objects, electrical devices, or even nature, for the purpose of signaling the spirit's presence.

Sixth Sense: The psychic or non-physical sense allowing one to gather information not detectable by any of the five physical senses, which are seeing, hearing, smelling, touching and tasting. Also known as "extrasensory perception" or "ESP."

Soothsayer: A person who predicts the future without necessarily using any divination tools; their knowledge is direct, for example, prophets, charmers, caster of spells, seers, visionaries and mediums. An ancient term which referred to all practitioners of the occult.

Soul: The spirit or non-physical life force that is the essence and nature of man and connects us to God and one another; it lives on after the physical body expires.

Speaking in tongues: The phenomenon of speaking in an unknown or fabricated language, also known as "glossolalia"; it usually occurs in a religious context.

Spirit: The essence or energy of a person moved on to a higher realm, after the physical body has expired; often referred to as the "soul."

Spirit Paintings: Detailed, colored portraits that materialized on canvas during séances in the 1800's. Spirit art was created without the use of human hands and without the use of brushes or paint.

Spirit Photography: Photographic images of spirits captured on film or digital cameras.

Spiritism: A popular philosophy, with the fundamental tenet being a belief in reincarnation. Founded by Allan Kardec in the 1850's in France, today it is considered one of the major religions in Brazil.

Spiritualism: The practice of communication with the heavens or people in the spirit world. A philosophy, science and an organized religion, whose basic tenet is to prove the continuity of life through the use of mediumship.

Spiritual Gifts: Supernatural or Paranormal abilities, also known as extrasensory perception or psychic ability.

Spiritual Sign Language: The use of signs, symbols, or objects for communication between physical and non-physical beings.

Supernatural: Of or relating to an order of existence beyond the physical or natural world. A theological term usually referring to something coming directly from God or one of His agents, such as an angel, saint, or other spiritual being.

Synchronicity: A term coined by Carl Jung that describes "meaningful coincidences." When seemingly random events happen simultaneously to provide meaning to one's life or circumstance.

Telekinesis: An older term for "psychokinesis"; the movement of external objects by the mind, without the influence of any known physical energy or force.

Telepathy: Extrasensory awareness of another person's thoughts and/or feelings; mind-to-mind communication.

Theology: The study of God and his relation to the world, by the analysis of the origins and teachings of an organized religion.

Third Eye: A wheel-shaped energy center, which is located in the middle of the forehead and is associated with the pituitary gland; also known as the "sixth chakra." It is responsible for psychic perception, inner vision and clairvoyance.

Trance: A dissociated or altered state of consciousness in which a medium or prophet allows a spirit to speak through him or her.

Transcendent Church Model: A concept describing three levels of reality, which correspond to the three states of the church existing within the communion of saints. The "physical," "metaphysical" and "mystical" realities represent "earth," "purgatory" and "heaven." Physical reality is the lowest level of spirituality and mystical reality is the highest. As we progress from one level to another, so does our level of consciousness, our psychic awareness and our spiritual gifts. This Model explains the differences and similarities between muggles (non-psychics), mediums and mystics.

Transcommunication: The flow of psychic messages, both ways, between the physical and non-physical world. The term was created by Jane Greer and is described in her book, *The Afterlife Connection.*

Urim and Thummim: Two stones used as divination tools by priests in the Old Testament. They operated in conjunction with the "breastplate of decision," for the purpose of consulting God in the Holy of Holies. The Urim was a black stone made of basalt and the Thummin was a white stone made of alabaster. The priest would ask a "yes" or "no" question of God and receive his answer through the stones. If the black Urim glowed the answer was "no" and if the white Thummin glowed the answer was "yes."

Vision: Something seen in a dream, trance, or clairvoyant experience. A manifestation of something immaterial; a paranormal or supernatural image.

Visionary: One who has the gift of clairvoyance or second-sight. Someone who has visions; also known as a medium, prophet, seer, or clairvoyant.

Visitation: The appearance of a spirit, either in a dream or conscious state; usually the purpose is to convey a message.

Wicca: A pagan-based spiritual practice, which is a modern form of witchcraft that venerates nature. A High Priest or Priestess leads the group of initiates or "coven" in seasonal rituals that often involve practical and positive (white) magic. Created in the 1950's by English witch, Gerald Gardner, and based on his teachings.

Xenoglossy: The act of speaking fluently in a recognized foreign language, which is unknown by the speaker; usually associated with channeling.

Resources for Glossary (see bibliography for complete citation):

Book of Spirit Communication (2004). Buckland, Raymond

Handbook of Parapsychology (1977). Wolman, Benjamin

The Complete Idiot's Guide To Understanding Catholicism (2003). O'Gorman & Faulkner

The Complete Idiot's Guide To Communicating with Spirits (2003). Berkowitz & Romaine

The Complete Idiot's Guide To Psychic Awareness (1999). Robinson & Carlson-Finnerty

The Everything Psychic Book (2003). Hathaway, Michael, D.C.H.

Voices, Visions and Apparitions (1993). Freeze, Michael

Webster's New Collegiate Dictionary (2004). G & C Merriam Company

Appendix C

Resources & Recommended Reading

Resources

Academy of Spirituality and Paranormal Studies (ASPSI): The mission of this organization is to discern, develop, and disseminate knowledge of how paranormal phenomena may relate to and enhance the development of spirit.
Bloomfield, Connecticut 06002-0614
(860) 242-4593 www.aspsi.org

After-Death.com: The website for After-Death Communication (ADC) and the ADC Project. Founded by Hello From Heaven authors, Bill and Judy Guggenheim. www.after-death.com

American Center for the Integration of Spiritually Transformative Experiences (ACISTE): Their mission is to address the integration needs and further the well-being of those who have had near-death or similar spiritually transformative experiences through research, education, and support. www.aciste.org

Aquarius Services: Website of Dennis Cole, Transpersonal Astrologer and Life Management Consultant. Dennis is a metaphysical lecturer and teacher who specializes in relationships, life focus and self-empowerment. He is co-publisher and writer for the Metaphysical Times of Central New York and is author of The Metaphysics of Love, the Journey to Meet Self. In addition, Dennis is Director of the Transpersonal Psychology Association of Syracuse, NY. Liverpool, NY www.aquariusservies.net

Association for Transpersonal Psychology (ATP): An international organization for scientific, social and clinical transpersonal work that serves the world community. Their mission is to promote eco-spiritual transformation through transpersonal inquiry and action. Palo Alto, CA 94303
(650) 424-8764 www.atpweb.org

Dharma Talks: Near-death experiencer (NDE), Dave Bennett, shares insights from spiritually transformative experiences for the benefit of all. Dave is the author of Voyage of Purpose, a fascinating book about his own NDE. He is also the leader of the Upstate New York chapter of the International Association of Near-Death Studies (IANDS). Dave is known nationally for his accomplishments in NDE work, including lectures, radio broadcasts, TV shows and his book. www.dharmatalks.com

Fr. McAlear's Ministry of Hope and Healing: Father Richard McAlear, OMI, "the healing priest" is involved in the Catholic Charismatic Renewal. His healing ministry is rooted in a scriptural understanding the human individual needs to become whole. McAlear is available for healing masses, retreats, conferences and speaking engagements. www.frmac.org

Gates Ministry: Its mission is to promote personal health and wholeness, and to improve conflicted relationships within families and faith communities. Founder Deacon Michael Mahoney, Ph.D. offers pastoral counseling, spiritual direction, conflict resolutions, retreats and workshops. New Bern, North Carolina 28562
(252) 571-1597 www.gatesministry.com

Gifts of Grace Ministry: Spiritual Counselor and Parapsychologist, Mary Grace, provides educational workshops and lectures on the paranormal, mystical, supernatural and near-death experience; a nonprofit program.
Hemlock, NY www.giftsofgraceministry.org

International Association of Near-Death Studies (IANDS): A nonprofit, educational organization that focuses much of its resources into providing the highest quality information available

about near-death experience (NDE) - related subjects. It is the only such membership group in the world. A wonderful resource with many links and books associated with the NDE.
Durham, North Carolina, USA, 27705-8878
(919) 383-7940 www.iands.org

Institute of Noetic Sciences (IONS): A nonprofit research, education, and membership organization whose mission is supporting individual and collective transformation through consciousness research, educational outreach, and engaging global learning community in the realization of our human potential.
Petaluma, CA 94952-5120
(707) 775-3500 www.noetic.org

Lily Dale Assembly Inc.: The world's largest center for spiritual development and the practice of the religion of Spiritualism. This quaint Victorian community is most noted for its "summer camp," which offers a variety of workshops, lectures, seminaries, mediumship demonstrations, healing services and development circles. In addition, it is home for over forty registered mediums. A trip to this unique and tranquil village is highly recommended.
Lily Dale, New York 14752
(716) 595-2442 www.lilydaleassembly.com

Mason Winfield: Supernatural historian and researcher, Mason has authored ten books on the paranormal and is founder of Haunted History Ghost Walks, Inc., which operates in the Buffalo, NY area. Winfield is also one of the founders of the Spirit Way Project, a society devoted to the study and preservation of the sacred/spiritual legacy of Western New York; it is co-founded by Algonquin mystic, Michael Bastine.
East Aurora, NY www.masonwinfield.com

Near Death Experience Research Foundation (NDERF): The largest NDE Website in the world with over 1800 full-text published NDE accounts. Founded by Jody A. Long, JD and Jeffrey P. Long, MD., it is devoted to the study of NDEs and provides support for experiencers. www.nderf.org

Parapsychological Association, Inc.: An international professional organization of scientists and scholars engaged in the study of "psi" (or psychic) experiences, such as telepathy, clairvoyance, psychokinesis, psychic healing and precognition. The primary objective is to achieve a scientific understanding of these experiences. Columbus, Ohio 43224 www.parapsych.org

Plymouth Spiritualist Church: The Mother Church of Modern Spiritualism serves as a spiritual home for all those seeking to come together with like-minded individuals, for building fellowship, bridges and bonds. Lead by Pastor Robin Higgins, this community offers Sunday services, as well as weekly development circles, meditation classes and many workshops.
Rochester, New York 14607
(585) 271-1470 www.plymouthspiritualistchurch.org

Rene Jorgensen: Philosopher of Religion, Near-Death Experience (NDE) Researcher, Spiritual Consultant and Author. Jorgensen explores life after death through the parallels between near-death experience and religion. He has authored three books including Awakening After Life, Behind 90 Minutes in Heaven, and The Light Behind God. He is the founder of NDE Light (www.NDElight.org), an organization dedicated to education and research on the NDE. He resides in Montreal, Canada. www.renejorgensen.com

Rhine Research Center: This Institute for parapsychology is bridging the gap between science and spirituality by exploring the consciousness, exceptional human experiences, and unexplained phenomena. The Rhine's mission is to advance the science of parapsychology to provide education and resources for the public, and to foster a community of individuals with personal and professional interests in PSI.
Durham, North Carolina 27705
(919) 309-4600 www.rhine.org

Spiritus Christi Church: A Christ-centered, all-inclusive Catholic community reaching beyond the institutional church. Led by Jesus Christ, with associates Father Jim Callan and Pastor Mary Ramerman, all are welcome.

Rochester, New York 14614
(585) 325-1180 www.spirituschristi.org

The Website of P.M.H. Atwater: P.M.H. Atwater, a three-time near-death experiencer, is one of the most noted and original researchers in the field of near-death studies. With a professional background in mediumship, astrology, numerology and sacred runes, she has authored over ten books. Her webpage is one of the internet's most comprehensive sites on the near-death phenomenon. www.pmhatwater.com

Recommended Reading:

Beyond the Light: What Isn't Being Said about Near-Death Experience
Atwater, P.M. H. (1994). Kill Devil Hills, North Carolina: Transpersonal Publishing.

Christian Mystics, Their Lives and Legacies throughout the Ages
King, Ursula (2001). New Jersey: Hidden Spring

Coming Back to Life: The After-Effects of the Near-Death Experience
Atwater, P.M. H. (1988). Kill Devil Hills, North Carolina: Transpersonal Publishing.

Communication with The Spirit World of God
Greber, Johannes (1979). Teaneck, NJ: Johannes Greber Memorial Foundation.

Conversations with God (The series)
Walsh, Neale Donald (1995). New York: G.P. Putnam's Sons.

Friends of God And Prophets, A Feminist Theological Reading of the Communion of Saints
Johnson, Elizabeth (1998). New York: The Continuum International Publishing Group, Inc.

Guided Tour of the Afterlife
Carter, Harriet (As told by the late Susan Wells) (2000). San Diego, California: Hillbrook Publishing Company, Inc.

Hello From Heaven, After-Death Communication
Guggenheim, Bill & Guggenheim, Judy (1995). New York: Bantam Books.

Life After Life
Moody, Raymond (1975). New York, New York: Bantam Books.

Love Without Conditions (The Christ Mind Series)
Ferrini, Paul (1994). Greenfield, MA: Heartways Press.

One Last Time
Edward, John (1998). New York, NY: The Berkley Publishing Group.

Parapsychology and the Christian Faith
Cluff, Charles (1976). Valley Forge, PA: Hudson Press.

Psychic Development for Beginners
Hewitt, William W. (2001). St. Paul, Minnesota: Llewellyn Publications.

Psychic Phenomena & Religion. ESP, Prayer, Healing, Survival
Neff, Richard (1971). Philadelphia: The Westminster Press.

Standing in the Light
Redonnet, Chava (2002). Lincoln, Nebraska: Writers Club Press.

Talking to Heaven
Van Praagh, James (1997). New York: Penguin Books

The Afterlife Connection
Greer, Dr. Jane (2003). New York: St. Martin's Press.

The Big Book of Near-Death Experiences
Atwater, P.M.H. (2007). Charlottesville, Virginia: Hampton Roads. This highly recommended book has an extensive list of NDE-related

resources and suggested reading, or go to www.pmhatwater.com

The Christian & The Supernatural
Kelsey, Morton (1976). Minneapolis, Minnesota: Augsburg Publishing House.

The Church and Spiritualism
Thurston, Herbert, S.J. (1933). Milwaukee: The Bruce Publishing Company.

The Complete Idiot's Guide to Being Psychic
Robinson, Lynn A., M.Ed. and Carlson-Finnerty, LaVonne (1999). Indianapolis, Indiana: Alpha Books.

The Complete Idiot's Guide to Communicating with Spirits:
Berkowitz, Rita S. and Romain, Deborah S. (2003). Indianapolis, Indiana: Alpha Books.

The Complete Idiot's Guide to Near-Death Experiences
Atwater, P.M.H., Lh.D. & Morgan, David H. (2000). Indianapolis, Indiana: Alpha Books.

The Everything Psychic Book, Tap into your inner power and discover your inherent abilities
Hathaway, Michael R. (2003). Massachusetts: Adams Media Corporation.

The Other Side, An Account of My Experiences With Psychic Phenomena
Pike, Bishop James A. (1968). New York: Doubleday & Company, Inc.

The Sacred & The Psychic, Parapsychology & Christian Theology
Heaney, John J. (1984). Ramsey, N.J.: Paulist Press.

The Saint Deck Book
Prioletti, Karen & Trump, Ann (2000). United States: The Nanta Bagg.

The Signet Handbook of Parapsychology
Ebon, Martin (1978). New York, NY: New American Library.

The Studentbaker Corporation
Callan, James Brady (2001). Rochester, New York: SPIRITUS Publications.

Try The Spirits. Christianity & Psychical Research
Moore, E. Garth (1977). New York: Oxford University Press.

Voices Visions and Apparitions
Freze, Michael, S.F.O. (1993). Huntington Indiana: Our Sunday Visitor.

Voyage of Purpose. Spiritual Wisdom from Near-Death Back to Life
Bennett, David and Cindy-Griffith (2011). Scotland, UK: Findhorn Press.

When the Lion Roars. A Primer for the Unsuspecting Mystic
Rossetti, Stephen J. (2003). Notre Dame, Indiana: Ave Maria Press.

Your Soul's Plan. Discovering the Real Meaning of the Life You Planned Before You Were Born
Schwartz, Robert (2009). Berkeley, CA: North Atlantic Books.

Bibliography

*References with an asterisk were used in research, but were not cited in the text.

Abhayananda, Swami. (1996). *History of Mysticism, Thy Unchanging Testament*. Olympia, Washington: ATMA Books.

Abbott, Walter, S.J. & Gallagher, Joseph, Very Rev. Msgr. (Eds.). (1966). *The Documents Of Vatican II*. New York: The American Press.

Alcock, James E. (1981). *Parapsychology Science or Magic*. New York: Pergamon Press.

Armstrong, Dave. *Cloud of Witness: A Biblical Primer on the Communion of Saints*. Retrieved March 8, 2004 from http://ic.net/-erasmus/RAZ94.HTM.

Armstrong, Dave. *The Communion of Saints: A Biblical Overview*. Retrieved March 8, 2004 from http://ic.net/-erasmus/RAZ530.HTM.

Atwater, P.M.H., Lh.D. & Morgan, David H. (2000). *The Complete Idiot's Guide to Near-Death Experiences*. Indianapolis, Indiana: Alpha Books.

Austen, A.W. Ed. (1960) Psychic News. "The Church of England and Spiritualism." [Electronic version]. London, Psychic Press LTD. Retrieved September 22, 2004 from http://www.cfpf.org.uk

Augustine Club. *The Communion of Saints*. Retrieved March 19, 2004 from http://www.columbia.edu/cu/augustine/a/saints.html.

Awtry, Marilyn & Vogt, Paula (1981). *The Bible: A Spiritualist's View*. Psychic Research Consultants

Balthasar, Hans Urs Von (1988, summer). *Catholicism and the Communion of Saints*. Communio, vol 15, Number 2, 161-168. (Albert K. Wimmer, Trans.)

Benko, Stephen (1964). *The Meaning of Sanctorum Communio*. Illinois: Alec R. Allenson, Inc.

Berkowitz, Rita S. and Romain, Deborah S. (2003). *The Complete Idiot's Guide to Communicating with Spirits*. Indianapolis, Indiana: Alpha Books.

Breton, O.F.M., Valentin (1934). *The Communion of Saints. History-Dogma-Devotion*. St. Louis, MO: The B. Herder Book Co.

Broad, C.D. (1969). *Religion, Philosophy And Psychical Research*. New York: Humanities Press.

Brown, Sylvia (2005). *Phenomenon* (Audio version). Minneapolis, Minnesota: HighBridge.

*Buckland, Raymond (2004). *Buckland's Book of Spirit Communications*. St. Paul, Minnesota: Llewellyn Publications.

*Callan, James Brady (2001). *The Studentbaker Corporation*. Rochester, New York: SPIRITUS Publications.

Callan, James Brady (2007). *Pioneer Priest*. Rochester, New York: SPIRITUS Publications.

Carlei, Carlo (Director). (2000). *Padre Pio, Miracle Man*. [Motion picture]. San Francisco, CA: Mediatrade S.P.A. Production, Ignatius Press.

Catechism of the Catholic Church, Second Edition. (1997). Citta del Vaticano: Libreria Editrice Vaticana.

Catholic Apologetics [1]. *A Biblical Portrait of Saint.* [Electronic version]. Retrieved March 19, 2004, from http://www.catholicapologetics.org

Catholic Apologetics [2]. *The Communion of Saints.* [Electronic version]. Retrieved March 19, 2004, from http://catholicapologetics.org

Catholic Apologetics [3]. *Praying to the Saints / Praying for the Dead.* [Electronic version]. Retrieved March 19, 2004, from http://www.catholicapologetics.org

Catholic Encyclopedia [1]. *All Souls Day.* [Electronic version]. Retrieved August 18, 2008 from http://www.newadvent.org

Catholic Encyclopedia [2]. *Beatification and Canonization.* [Electronic version]. Retrieved February 18, 2005 from http://www.newadvent.org

Catholic Encyclopedia [3]. *Indulgences.* [Electronic version]. Retrieved April 8, 2006 from http://www.newadvent.org

Catholic Encyclopedia [4]. *Prayer.* [Electronic version]. Retrieved February 2, 2005 from http://www.newadvent.org/cathen/04171a.htm.

Catholic Encyclopedia [5]. *Saints and Angels.* [Electronic version]. Retrieved May 5, 2004 from http://www.newadvent.org

Catholic Encyclopedia [6]. *St. John Bosco.* [Electronic version]. Retrieved October 2, 2006 from http://www.newadvent.org/cathen/02689d.htm

Catholic Encyclopedia [7]. *The Communion of Saints.* [Electronic version]. Retrieved March 4, 2004 from http://www.newadvent.org

CDF (Charles Darwin Foundation). About the CDF and the CDRS. Retrieved September 4, 2008 from http://www.darwinfoundation.org

Chopra, Deepak (2003). *The Spontaneous Fulfillment of Desire.* New York, NY: Harmony Books.

Christian Classics Ethereal Library at Calvin College. *The Communion of Saints.* Retrieved March 8, 2004 from http://www.ccel.org/k/kuyper/holy-spirit/htm/vii.ii.ix.htm.

Clark, Bishop Matthew H. (2004, November 20/21). *Special Ways to Pray for the Dead.* Catholic Courier Weekly. 2.

Clark, Walter Houston (1977). *Parapsychology and Religion. Handbook of Parapsychology* (1977). Wolman, Benjamin B. New York, NY: Van Nostrand Reinhold Company.

Cluff, Charles (1976). *Parapsychology and the Christian Faith.* Valley Forge, PA: Hudson Press.

Concilar, Papal and Curiel Texts (1982). *Documents on the Liturgy 1963-1979.* Minnesota: The Liturgical Press.

Cunningham, Lawrence (1996, November). *How Catholics Keep Alive Their Connection With The Dead.* U.S. Catholic, 6-12.

Daniels, Michael, PHD (2003). *Psychic Science. Introduction to Parapsychology.* Retrieved May 5, 2005, from http://www.mdani.demon.co.uk/para/parintro.htm.

Doyle, Arthur Conan (1985). *The History of Spiritualism.* New York: Arno Press. (Original work published 1926).

Dyer, Wayne (1994). *The Awakened Life* (audio version). Chicago: Nightingale-Conant Corporation.

*Dyer, Wayne (1992). *Real Magic, Creating Miracles in Everyday Life.* New York, NY: Harper Collins Publishers.

*Dyer, Wayne (2004). *The Power of Intention.* Carlsbad, California: Hay House, Inc.

Ebon, Martin (1978). *The Signet Handbook of Parapsychology.* New York, NY: New American Library.

Edward, John (1998). *One Last Time.* New York, NY: The Berkley Publishing Group.

Ellsberg, Robert (1997). *All Saints. Daily Reflections on Saints, Prophets, and Witnesses For Our Time.* New York, NY: The Crossroads Publishing Company.

Emmons, Charles F., Ph.D. & Emmons, Penelope, MSW (2003). *Guided By Spirit. A Journey into the Mind of the Medium.* Lincoln, NE: Writers Club Press.

Encyclopedia Britannica. Ockham's razor. Retrieved October 17, 2006, from http://www.britannica.com/eb/article-9373871

Evans, Hilary (1984). *Visions, Apparitions, Alien Visitors.* Northamptonshire: The Aquarian Press.

Farrington, Karen (1998). *The History of Religion.* New York: Barnes and Noble, Inc.

Ferrini, Paul (1994). *Love Without Conditons.* Greenfield, MA: Heartways Press.

Finucane, R.C. (1984). *Appearences of the Dead. A Cultural History of Ghosts.* Buffalo, NY: Prometheus Books.

Foundation for Inner Peace (1996). *A Course In Miracles. Foundations for Inner Peace.* Mill Valley, California.

Freze, Michael, S.F.O. (1993). *Voices, Visions and Apparitions.* Huntington Indiana: Our Sunday Visitor.

Gallagher, Sean (2005, September/October). *Who Was St. Benedict? The Catholic Answer,* Volume 19, No. 4., 10-12.

Gibran, Kahlil (1997/Reprint). *The Prophet.* (A. Knopf, Trans.). New York: Alfred A. Knopf, Inc. (Original work published 1923).

Grace, Mary (2004). *Mystics, Mediums, and Priests: Interviews for Communion of Saints Research.* Hemlock, NY: unpublished.

Graves, David & Graves, Jane (1995). *The Prophets, Origin of Prophecy.* Retrieved June 12, 2008 from http://www.abu.nb.ca/ecm/topics/books5.htm

Greer, Dr. Jane (2003). *The Afterlife Connection.* New York: St. Martin's Press.

*Greber, Johannes (1979). *Communication with The Spirit World of God.* Teaneck, NJ: Johannes Greber Memorial Foundation.

Guggenheim, Bill & Guggenheim, Judy (1995). *Hello From Heaven. After-Death Communication.* New York: Bantam Books.

Hallam, Elizabeth (1994). *Saints, Who they are and how they help you.* New York: Simon & Schuster.

Hathaway, Michael R. (2003). *The Everything Psychic Book, Tap into your inner power and discover your inherent abilities.* Massachusetts: Adams Media Corporation.

Haugen, Mary (1950). *We Are Many Parts.* cited in Gather (1994). Chicago, Illinois: GIA Publication, Inc.

Hawkins, David (1995). *Power vs. Force.* California: Hay House, Inc.
Health & Yoga (2006). *Meditation...Its Benefits.* Retrieved September 4, 2008 from http://www.healthandyoga.com

Heaney, John J. (1984). *The Sacred & The Psychic. Parapsychology & Christian Theology.* Ramsey, N.J.: Paulist Press.

Heredia S.J, Carlos (1924). *True Spiritualism.* New York: P.J. Kennedy & Sons.

Heron, Lawrence Tunstall (1974). *ESP In The Bible.* New York: Doubleday & Company.

Himes, Michael & Himes, Kenneth, O.F.M. (1993, Sept/Oct.). *The Unity of Human Kind.* Catholic Megatrends, 205.

Hooper, John (January, 1997). *Dialogue with the Dead is Feasible, Vatican Spokesman Says.* The London Observer Service. Retrieved on October 10, 2004 from http://www.after-death.com

Hull, Moses (1895). *Encyclopedia of Biblical Spiritualism.* Wisconsin: Amherst Press.

Jacobs, Claude F. & Kaslow, Andrew J. (1991). *The Spiritual Churches of New Orleans, Origins, Beliefs, and Rituals of an African-American Religion.* Knoxville: The University of Tennessee Press.

Jaffe, Aniela (1963). *Apparitions and Precognition.* New York: University Books.

Johnson, Elizabeth (1998). *Friends of God And Prophets.* New York: The Continuum International Publishing Group Inc.

Johnson, Elizabeth (2003). *Truly Our Sister, A Theology of Mary in the Communion of Saints.* New York: The Continuum International Publishing Group Inc.

Johnson, Paul (1976). *A History of Christianity.* New York: Simon & Schuster.

*Miller, John Franklin (1993, October) In *Defense of Religion. The Journal of Religion and Psychical Research,*Volume 16, Number 4, 182.

Kegan, Paul (1978). A Catholic Dictionary. *Prayer.* London: Kegan Paul, Trench, Truben & Co. Ltd.

Kelsey, Morton (1976). *The Christian & The Supernatural.* Minneapolis, Minnesota: Augsburg Publishing House.

Kramer, Heinrich & Sprenger, James (1486). *The Malleus Maleficarum.* [Electronic version]. The Windhaven Network. Retrieved September 21, 2006 from: http://www.malleusmaleficarum.org

Lamirande, Emilien, O.M.I. (1963). *The Communion of Saints.* New York: Hawthorn Books.

*Lauderback, Delany (2001). *Two Great Spiritual Awakenings: The Apostles and Modern Spiritualism.* Retrieved November 8, 2005 from http://www.ggsc.org

Lee, Carroll & Tober, Jan (1999). *The Indigo Children.* California: Hay House, Inc.

Lovasick, Rev. Lawrence G. (1979). *Picture Book of Saints.* New York: Catholic Book Publishing Company.

Lovelace, Wicasta (1998). *An Introduction to: The Malleus Maleficarum, of Heinrich Kramer and James Sprenger.* (Electronic version). The Windhaven Network. Retrieved September 21, 2006 from: http://www.malleusmaleficarum.org

Mackenzie, Andrew (1983). *Hauntings and Apparitions.* Great Britain: Granada Publishing Limited.

Majority Report of the Church of England (1939). *The Church of England and Spiritualism.* [Electronic version]. Reprinted c1960 by London, Psychic Press LTD (A.W. Austen, Ed.). Retrieved September 22, 2004 from http://www.cfpf.org.uk

Malinowski, Bronislaw (1954). *Magic, Science and Religion.* New York: Doubleday & Company, Inc.

Martin, Ebon (1968). *Prophecy in Our Time.* New York, New York: The New American Library, Inc.

Martin, Ted (1997). *Psychic and Paranormal Phenomena in The Bible.* Nashville, TN: Psychicspace.company.

Marthaler, Berard L. (1985, Fall). *Interpreting the Communion of Saints.* Liturgy, Volume 5, Number 2.

Maynard, Nettie Colburn (1891). *Was Abraham Lincoln a Spiritualist?* [Electronic version]. Philadelphia: Rufus. C. Hartranft Publisher. Retrieved August 27, 2008 from: http://books.google.com

Merton, Thomas (1966). *Conjectures of a Guilty Bystander.* New York: Doubleday.

Moore, E. Garth (1977). *Try The Spirits. Christianity & Psychical Research.* New York: Oxford University Press.

Murphy, Gardner and Ballou, Robert O. (Eds.). (1960). *William James On Psychical Research.* New York: Viking Press Inc.

National Spiritualist Association of Churches (2002). *Declaration of Principles and Definitions.* Lily Dale, NY: NSAC

National Conference of Catholic Bishops (1990). *Holy Bible, The New American Bible,* Fireside Family Edition, Kansas: Catholic Bible Publishers.

National Conference of Catholic Bishops (1989). *Order of Christian Funerals.* New York: Catholic Book Publishing Company.

National Conference of Catholic Bishops (1974). *Roman-Franciscan Sacramentary.* New York: Catholic Book Publishing Company.

National Liturgical Office (2003-2004). *The Living With Christ Sunday Missal.* Toronto, Ontario: Novalis.

Neff, Richard (1971). *Psychic Phenomena & Religion. ESP, Prayer, Healing, Survival.* Philadelphia: The Westminster Press.

New Catholic Dictionary. *Prayer* [Electronic version]. Retrieved January 26, 2006 from http://www.catholic-forum.com/saints/ncd02215.htm.

O'Gorman, Bob, Ph.D. & Faulkner, Mary, M.A. (2003). *The Complete Idiot's Guide to Understanding Catholicism.* Indianapolis, IN: Alpha Books.

Old Catholic Roots (1941). (Author unknown). Woodstock, NY: The Catskill Mountain Star. Saint Matthew Ecumenical Old Catholic Church website, Retrieved March 1, 2003, from http://www.saint-matthew.org

Paul VI, Pope (1965). *Gaudium Et Spes, Pastoral Constitution On The Modern*

World. *Promulgated By His Holiness, Pope Paul VI On December 7, 1965.* [Electronic version]. Retrieved on August 18, 2008, from http://www.vaticancouncil.org

Paul VI, Pope (1964). *Lumen Gentium, Dogmatic Constitution On The Church. Solemnly Promulgated By His Holiness Pope Paul VI On November 21, 1964.* [Electronic version]. Retrieved August 18, 2008 from http://wwwvaticancouncil.org

Philipps, James (2000). *Communion of Saints. Top Team of All Time.* Youth Update. Retrieved September 6, 2004 from http://americancatholic.org

Pike, Bishop James A. (1968). *The Other Side. An Account of My Experiences With Psychic Phenomena.* New York: Doubleday & Company, Inc.

Pius XII, Pope (1943). *Encyclical Letter of His Holiness. On The Mystical Body of Christ And Our Union In It With Christ.* Washington, D.C.: National Catholic Welfare Conference.

*Pontifical Council For Interreligious Dialogue (2003). *Jesus Christ The Bearer of the Water of Life.* A Christian Reflection on the "New Age." Retrieved on September 6, 2004 from, http://www.vatican.va

Prioletti, Karen & Trump, Ann (2000). *The Saint Deck Book.* United States: The Nanta Bagg.

Redonnet, Chava (2002). *Standing in the Light.* Lincoln, Nebraska: Writers Club Press.

Rice, Chris (2004). *Go Light Your World. Short Term Memories* (CD). Franklin, TN: Rocketown Records.

Robinson, Lynn A., M.Ed. and Carlson-Finnerty, LaVonne (1999). *The Complete Idiot's Guide to Being Psychic.* Indianapolis, Indiana: Alpha Books.

Rossetti, Stephen J. (2003). *When the Lion Roars. A Primer for the Unsuspecting Mystic.* Notre Dame, Indiana: Ave Maria Press.

Sacred Congregation for the Doctrine of Faith (1978). *Norms for the Sacred Congregation for the Doctrine of the Faith about How to Proceed in Judging Alleged Apparitions and Revelations.* [Elecronic Version] (J. Bouflet & P. Boutry, Trans.) Retrieved May 11, 2006 from http://.theotokos.org.uk

Schonborn, Christopher (1988, Fall). *The "Communion of Saints" as three states of the Church: pilgrimage, purification, and glory.* Communio, 15, number 2. 169-181.

Schwartz, Gary (2001). *The Afterlife Experiments.* New York, NY: Atria Books.

Sharp, Lynn L. (1999, October). *Fighting for the Afterlife: Spiritists, Catholics, and Popular Religion in Nineteenth-Century France, Journal of Religious History,* Volume 23 Issue 3, 282-295.

Sexton, Rev. George (1877). *True Spiritual Magazine,* Vol. XVII , 97-99 (as cited in Thurston, Herbert).

Society For Psychical Research (1990, October). *Proceedings of the Society for Psychical Research.* List of Members. Volume 57, Part 216, 227.

Spaeth, Paul (2005). *The Thomas Merton Archives at St. Bonaventure University.* [Electronic version]. Retrieved September 4, 2008 from: http://web.sbu.edu

*Spong, Bishop John Shelby (1998). *Why Christianity Must Change or Die. A Bishop Speaks To Believers In Exile.* San Francisco: HarperCollins.

St. Albans, The Duchess of (1983). *Magic of a Mystic.* New York: Clarkson N. Potter, Inc. Publishers.

St. Clair, David (1976). *Pagans, Priests, and Prophets.* New Jersey: Prentice-Hall, Inc.

Sugrue, Thomas (1942). *The Story of Edgar Cayce, There is a River.* New York: Dell Publishing Co., Inc.

Tallant, Robert (1974). *Voodoo in New Orleans. Louisiana.* Pelican Publishing Company.

The Essential Catholic Handbook. "Spiritism" (1997). U.S.A.: Liguori Publications, 246.

The Zondervan Corporation (1994). *Holy Bible,* King James Version. Grand Rapids, Michigan: Zondervan.

Thigpen, Paul (2005, September/October). *What About Ghosts? The Catholic*

Answer, Volume 19, No. 4, 18-20.

Thurston, Herbert, S.J. (1933). *The Church and Spiritualism*. Milwaukee: The Bruce Publishing Company.

Trabold, Alphonsus (1979). *Psychical Research and the Nature of Man*. Theology 364, Course syllabus at St. Bonaventure University, Olean, NY.

Trabold, Alphonsus (1979). *Cult and Occult*. Address at the Convention of the National Catholic Education Association, Philadelphia, PA.

True Catholic.org. *Interrelationship of Church Members*. Retrieved September 6, 2004 from http://www.truecatholic.org/grmembers.htm.

United States Conference of Catholic Bishops (2002). *New American Bible*. Wichita, Kansas: Catholic Bible Publishers.

Unkelbach, Mary A. (1983, October). *Intercessions, the Communion of Saints and Supernaturalistic Metaphysics*. Journal of Religion and Psychical Research, volume 6, number 4, 261-267.

Van Praagh, James (1997). *Talking to Heaven*. New York: Penguin Books.

Walsh, Neale Donald (1995). *Conversations with God*. New York: G.P. Putnam's Sons

Watchman, The Ministry of. *The School of the Prophets*. Retrieved May 13, 2008 from http://www.ministryofthewatchman.com/school.html

Webster's New Collegiate Dictionary (2004). Springfield, Massachusetts: G. & C. Merriam Company.

Whelen, Michael D. (1991, May). *The Litany of Saints*. Worship, volume 6, number 3, 216-223.

Wikipedia. *Ouija*. Retrieved December 6, 2006 from http://wikipedia.og/wiki/ouija

Wilson, Robert R. (1984). *Prophecy And Society In Ancient Israel*. USA: Fortress Press.

Wolman, Benjamin B. (1977). *Handbook of Parapsychology*. New York, NY:

Van Nostrand Reinhold Company.

Zimmerman, Odo John, O.S. B. (1959). *Saint Gregory the Great. Dialogues* (Translation). New York, NY: Fathers of The Church, Inc.

Acknowledgements

Thank you God: for giving me a second chance and for this opportunity to serve you.

Thank you Jesus: for showing me the way, the truth, and the life.

Thanks Communion of Saints: for your constant guidance and helping to manifest my dream.

To the Saints in the Church in Heaven:
I thank those on the otherside who have been my faithful companions and guides:

My mom and dad, Millie and Harry Moran: for giving me my faith foundation.

My Grandma, Rose Eberhard: for your dream visitations and reassurance.

My Godmother and Godfather, Joan and John O'Neill: for your inspiration.

My best friends, Mikey and Lucey: for being my writing companions.

My angels and guides, Nephy, Bill, Zebedee & Charlene: for your constant guidance.

Anne Hayes: for being my guide and friend, before and after death.

Father Thomas Hoctor, my dial-a-priest: for the years of friendship and support, for being my theological consultant, and for keeping me laughing.

Reverend Jerome Schifferli: for being such a good friend to my dad.

Bob Krest Sr. (Ogre): for taking in all the strays from the neighborhood, including me.

Kelli McMahon: for being my companion and entertainer in Chiapas, Mexico.

Especially Father Alphonsus Trabold: for being my friend, my mentor, my guide, and my intercessor; you are a true angel.

Thanks to the many authors who laid the foundation for this work, especially: Bishop James Pike, Rev. Johannes Greber, John Heaney, Herbert Thurston and William James.

To the Saints in the Church on Earth:

Thanks to those who shared in my vision for the book and helped make it a reality:

Dr. Michael Mahoney, Ph.D.: for all the editing, spiritual counseling, support, encouragement, and for inspiring me to write this book.

Father Jim Lagona: for editing and for keeping me in touch with Father Al.

Harold Schmidt, Literary Agent: for believing in me and for sticking with me throughout the writing process.

Naomi Orwin: for all the editing, writing tips, and for being my fashion consultant.

Mike Costanza: for editing and for all the support and encouragement over the years.

Ron Nagy, Lily Dale Historian: for helping me with research on Spiritualism.

Freidsman Memorial Librarians at St. Bonaventure University: for assisting me in research; you were invaluable to this work, especially Paul Spaeth, Dennis O'Brien, Dennis Frank, Michael Spencer, Theresa Schaffer, Taresa Carro, Nancy Schultz.

St. Bonaventure University (SBU) professors: Terrence Moran Ph.D., Father Peter Schneible, O.F.M., Father Alphonsus Trabold, O.F.M.

Jim Knapp of Franciscan Institute Publications at SBU: for connecting me to my publisher.

Dr. Erlender Haroldsson: for your encouragement and feedback on the book.

Dr. Harold Koenig: for your feedback and encouragement.

P.M.H. Atwater: for your encouragement and for all your NDE research and books.

Don Fox: for your thorough editing and thoughtful feedback.

Jeffrey Campbell and the staff of Tau Publishing, LLC: Thanks a million for taking a chance on this work and for trusting in the communion of saints.

Beverly Carr: for your meticulous editing and encouraging feedback.

Lorien Sheppard: for your kind, patient editing and creative book work.

Thanks to those who participated in my research by granting interviews:
Father Dan O'Rourke, Lynn Forget, Mary Oakley, Father Jerome Schifferli, Father Richard McAlear, Father Alphonsus Trabold, Deacon Michael Mahoney, Father Sebastian Falcone, Father Thomas Hoctor, Ginger Smith, Kitty Rugani, Ron Skowronski, Shirley Smith, Albert Batten, Margaret Mary (Marge) Hefner and Father Patrick Mulligan.

Thanks to everyone who shared their stories of after-death communications:
Tracy Cope, Gary Siwicki, Mary Beth Mangan, Angela DeMaria, Eileen

Moran, Shirley Briggs, Rodney Himmelsbach, Charlie Emmons, Tina Vanderpool, Melissa Simandl, Bishop Matthew Clark, Deacon Michael Mahoney, Ph.D.

Thanks to Spiritus Christi Catholic Church of Rochester, NY:
Senior Pastor, Jesus Christ, Pastor Mary Ramerman, and Associate Pastor, Father Jim Callan: for your spiritual leadership and for being the pillars of an awesome, all-inclusive church. Former Pastor, Rev. Denise Donato (current Priest of Mary Magdalene Church in East Rochester, NY): For leading the inspirational retreats at Silver Lake.
Jeff Wilson, musician: for his original song, *Lament for Lost Souls*, and for being the beautiful voice behind the book.
The Slinky Chiapas Group, led by Ritaclare Streb: for the spiritual journey in Mexico.
Chava Redonnet: for documenting our church's story in *Standing in the Light*.

To my rocks, on which I built this book:
I thank those who have supported me throughout the trials and tribulations of my life, regardless of the many mistakes I made along the way:
My Husband, Bob Krest: for all your support and faith in me and for keeping me grounded; you are a true Christian to all who know you.
Aunt Marie Hochreiter: for being my adopted mom and for Sunday afternoon visits.
My brother and sister in-law, Michael and Toni Moran: my cross-country cheerleaders.
My sister, Kathy Moran: for helping to manifest my dream by helping to shop for book-signing outfits and for showing me what it means to have hope; you are my inspiration.
My sister, Eileen Moran: for being the family nurse and for all your wonderful baking and entertaining; you keep our family connected.
Paul Meyer: for all the car repairs so my sister could come visit.
My brother, Pat the Rat Moran: for being my soul mate and for proofreading and editing.
My brother, Terry Moran: for getting me away on day trips to wine country and for connecting me with many angels at St. Bonaventure University.
My nieces: Andrea, Hanna, and Mackenzie; for keeping me fashionable, helping me to shop, and for joining me in fright-night.
Doug, Kyle, and Chad Ricketts: for helping Bob around the house, which gave me more time to write.
Mary Krest: for being the best mother-in-law and for taking care of all my tailoring needs.

David Carey: for the tech support; I couldn't have done it without you.

John and Tracy Cope: for their generous donation of a new office/camper, to replace the one that was totally destroyed in a fire.

Bob Finster: for being my friend since kindergarten; you will always be my first love.

Angela DeMaria for being a good friend, taking me out when times were tough, and for always providing comic relief.

Kim McCaw: for being a good friend, inspiring Mom's memorial garden (pet cemetery), and for our vacations together.

To our Texas Hold 'Em gang: for all the laughs and for getting me out of the office; you are a great bunch of friends.

To Stinky and Mercy, my cats: for being my constant writing companions.

In addition, thanks to:

Mike and Valerie Allen: for believing me and for convincing me that I'm not crazy.

Kathy Mrzywka of the Assisi Institute: for your spiritual guidance and great book recommendations.

Mason Winfield: for your connection with Father Al and for Elegy for an Exorcist.

Dave and Cindy Bennet of Upstate NY IANDS: for all your support and guidance.

Melissa Simandl, my paranormal friend: for making me look good and sharing your ghostly encounters. Also, Lynn Simandl for all your encouragement.

Friends at the Livonia Fitness Center: for your encouragement and for keeping me in shape.

Friends at The Livonia Inn: especially Ralph Parker for putting up with our card parties.

Father John Hayes: for being my greatest teacher.

Kim Scheurer: for the spiritual guidance and workshops in your basement.

Pat Barone: for helping me through the first few post-NDE years.

Sherry Gendreau and Mary Ann Thompson: for your great, spiritual friendship and for being my co-directors of the Holistic Resource Network of Livingston County.

I thank those who went before me and wrote about their own paranormal experiences and spiritual gifts; without them I would not have had the courage to tell my story.

All authors and publishers listed in the bibliography and appendixes: you were the foundation for my work.

Wayne Dyer and Deepak Chopra: for your spiritual insight and guidance.

Thanks for the picture:
Tina Vanderpool: for the Ghostly Grandma photo.

Thanks to the following Organizations:
Community Resource Network of Livingston County.
Holistic Resource Network of Livingston County.
The Lily Dale Assembly and the wonderful residents of Lily Dale.
Plymouth Spiritualist Church of Rochester, NY.
St. Matthew Church Community of Livonia, NY.
The International Association of Near-Death Studies (IANDS), especially Diane Corcoran, Chuck Swedrock, Joan Donavan, and Bruce Greyson.
The American Center for the Integration of Spiritually Transformative Experiences (ACISTE), especially Director Yolaine Stout.
The Abbey of the Genesee, especially Brother Christian and Brother Louis.
Family Life Radio Network in Bath, NY: for your inspiring words and songs.
K-LOVE Christian Radio Network of CA: for keeping me connected to God via music.

To those who endorsed my work:
I am truly grateful and it means so much more than you know: Father Jim Callan, Rene Jorgensen, Bill Guggenheim, David Bennett, Mason Winfield and Dennis Cole.

Index